Existential Anecdotes for the Meditative Mind

A Collection of Stories by

John C. Mason

Essential Anecdotes for the Meditative Mind

tellwell

Tellwell Talent
www.tellwell.ca

ISBN
978-1-77302-507-0 (Paperback)

'One of the penalties of an ecological education is that one lives alone in a world of wounds.

'An ecologist must either harden his shell and make believe that the consequences of science are none of his business, or he must be the doctor who sees the marks of death in a community that believes itself well and doesn't want to be told otherwise.'

Aldo Leopold

Table of Contents

Preface

The reader will notice that I have drawn my creativity from a number of societal areas of concern. Most of the stimuli have come from my intellectual exposure and reactions to social change, or lack of it, secondarily personal, and from situations told to me by friends and relatives. The themes reflect my existential outlook on life, and as in my poetry efforts, urge heightened public concern for the socio-economic milieu that swirls around us and holds us back from aspiring to the stars. My aspirations are primarily for spirituality, intellectual progress, and more effective control of the ego. Not efforts guised primarily as such but in actuality, not appearing as thinly disguised continued personal and nationalistic efforts struggling for ego-driven power, its dogmatic desires reflecting pseudo-tribal ignorance at both the personal and collective level.

I hope that my literary work, as in my ecological scientific work, is stimulating and adds support to the general desire of so many throughout the world for a more peaceful and socially productive world in the future of this small but beautiful planet.

War of the Roses

After the month of February spent relaxing and sunning in Acapulco, the Saunders fly home to Victoria, Canada. The weather is cool in contrast to their beach condo and Margaret shivers as they wait at the rack for their bags. "That was a long flight scenario, three stops, Los Angeles, San Francisco, and Seattle before Victoria. I'm exhausted!" she says. "We're nearly home, love" says Lionel. "I'll get the bags then we can pick up the car and be on our way."

The bags arrive a few minutes later and Lionel grabs them both then they make their way to the parking lot, load up and leave after paying their parking fee at the exit gate. Lionel tucking away his wallet, "that was a hefty fee but what choice does one have. It's either that or pay duplicate fares by cab to and from the airport. As they say in the army, airport management has you by the short hairs." They both laugh. Lionel is a retired colonel from the Canadian army and his wife, Margaret is a retired nurse.

By mid-afternoon, the traffic on the Pay Bay highway to Victoria is light although the traffic speeding towards Sydney is picking up. Turning off onto Mackenzie Avenue, they proceed towards Oak Bay on Shelbourne Avenue, then turning on Landsdowne Road towards their beach house off Gonzales Bay. Foul Bay Road is a twisting, narrow and winding road with many blind corners that ends on Gonzales Bay. The Volvo engine splutters and dies. Lionel manages to steer the slowing car over to the side of the road. “Dammit, I’m out of fuel…. that’s not possible but the gauge shows empty. I filled the tank before going to the airport on our trip.” He puts on the emergency flashers. “What a place to have car problems …..on this road. My cell phone is dead, blast! There’s a driveway a few yards ahead, I’ll stay in the car if you will ask to use their phone, okay, my sweet?” Call our gas station perhaps Cliff can bring out a can of fuel. Be sure to tell him where we are.”

Hopefully the residents are at home, says Margaret over her shoulder as she leaves the car and proceeds down the long driveway towards the house looking for assistance. A huge laurel hedge nearly obscures the house from the street and Lionel quickly loses sight of her. Large rhododendrons initially line the driveway then are replaced by lower plantings of deciduous azaleas, revealing a large English-style house set back behind the circular driveway. Within the driveway loop is an imposing rose garden in the center of which a statue of a nymph holding a shallow basin filled with water.

Margaret is intrigued by this residence which lies on her grocery shopping route and she has often wondered who lives there. Climbing the three steps on to the entry way, she rings the ornate brass bell and waits. Pressing the bell several more times fails to elicit a response so she raps on the brass-studded oak door. Still no response and rapping again much harder, she discovers that the door in slightly ajar. Pushing the door open, she steps inside, assuming that the residents are in. “Hello, hello” she calls loudly as she walks into the hallway, then into the drawing room. She calls again, “is anyone at home, could I use your telephone? It’s a bit of an emergency.” Looking about her, Margaret notes that the paneled walls are covered with framed pictures. She calls again and begins to examine photographs on the adjacent butlers table. Unbeknownst to her, she is being watched by a shadowy figure that has appeared from the adjoining room.

The female figure comes forward saying in a rather imperious voice, "who are you and what are you doing in my residence?" Her voice projects a commanding presence supplemented by considerable irritation but without fear. Margaret is startled and embarrassed by her snooping behavior and launches into a long, defensive reply in a quavering voice. "We.....I mean my husband and I have run out of fuel just in front of your driveway. I knocked several times after ringing your bell several times. We are returning home from a holiday and our cell phone is dead, could I use your telephone to call for assistance? I apologize for this intrusion but my husband is waiting in the car and the winding road is dangerous for parking. He will be wondering what is keeping me so long."

The owner is a tall, striking women of aristocratic bearing, dressed in gardening clothes and carrying a trowel in her right hand. She approaches Margaret smiling, "these mishaps can happen. I heard you knocking, the bell doesn't work of late and I've been working on the rear flower beds." She smiles once more, "seeing that the evening is approaching and the light is falling fast, I can best assist you by offering the can of fuel that I keep in the garage. Why don't you return to your car and ask your husband to come down and collect the fuel? I'll wait for him by the garage door. By the way, I'm Hilda Tischler."

Nodding in obedience to her Teutonic air of command, Margaret introduces herself likewise then walks rapidly up the driveway to the car where Lionel is patiently waiting. "What took you so long, Marge? It's getting dark." She explains her delay somewhat. "She's waiting for you at her garage doors with a can of gas." Lionel bails out of the car and hurries down the driveway, meeting Hilda. "I must apologize for disturbing you. I assume that my wife explained our predicament." Lionel is unaware that Margaret entered the house without permission.......and also snooped about. "No problem, I am Hilda Tischler and I'll open the garage door for you." She keys the lock on the automatic door and points to the fuel can which is located near the right door of her BMW sedan. "That should be enough fuel, some ten liters, to get you safely home or to a garage. I understand that existence can provide situations beyond our immediate control or anticipation, yes?" Would you return it tomorrow morning …..say at ten o'clock, as I would like to discuss this encounter with you. Your wife need not accompany you." Lionel is somewhat puzzled but intrigued by her commanding presence. "I shall return the re-filled can as you ask at ten o'clock in the morning." He smiles, stifles a rising salute and beats a hasty retreat up the driveway. Hilda watches his departure with interest then turns, closing the garage door. With a thin smile she disappears into the house. Lionel empties the fuel into his tank and starts the car after pumping the gas pedal several times. He then drives off to their home.

Lionel unloads their luggage and hauls it into the house as Margaret unlocks the front door. Dropping the bags in the hallway, Lionel exclaims, thank God we've made it home without further mishap. Margaret pats his arm reassuringly and says that she'll make some tea. "Let's not unpack now, we can do that in the morning." Margaret has been ruminating on the way home about the requested meeting tomorrow. "What does that women have in mind that needs discussion without me being present", she asks Lionel as she pours their tea. "Did I detect a Germanic accent in her voice. She seemed somewhat officious and commanding?" This conversation occurs while drinking their tea and eating some digestive biscuits from the kitchen cupboard. Lionel, sipping his tea, "yes, her accent seemed rather clipped, definitely European. Actually, she reminds me of my commanding officer, Colonel Hanson, during the war and during my captaincy for some reason that I have yet to explain to myself. I don't think that she is the Valkerie type though ….too feminine. I wonder what she has in mind?" He is intrigued but tries not to show it.

Margaret is feeling in a confessional mood. "I failed to mention that I pushed open her front door. It was barely ajar….but I did ring the bell several times and knocked loudly without apparent success. Do you think that she is going to lecture you over my illegal entry? I hope I've not put you in any trouble." Lionel raise his eyebrows, "a lecture? Perhaps? I'm not overly concerned. I'll take care of it in a diplomatic fashion….in my diffident manner. Perhaps a little self-effacing persona will do the trick!" He chuckles, "now let's finish our tea and get some shut-eye. This has been enough excitement for our first day back in Oak Bay. I fully intend to lodge a complaint at the airport concerning their parking security. The parking fees are outrageous enough, one has to endure fuel thieves, too! Where is their security?"

Margaret nodding in agreement, "it's been a very long day, a tedious flight and incompetent parking security at the airport. Why is it that security personnel here in Canada make me feel like a terrorist from their manner?" Lionel smiles, the answer, my dear, is poor training and feelings of self-importance. It's best to appear somewhat dense and obedient…..that makes their day….adds to self-importance and imaginary power. Perhaps calm and self-confident passengers stimulate their low self-esteem and encourages their Dick Tracy act. Border personnel seem to be getting worse since the Yanks have been pushing the terrorism button. Perhaps putting the pressure on us? A strong streak of paranoia in media and government propaganda usually has ulterior motives. The Bush gang seemed to have used that strategy to push through the Patriot Act with minimum objection in Congress". The Saunders climb wearily up their stairs to the second floor after dimming the lights.

After a fitful sleep and a hearty breakfast, Lionel prepares to return the fuel can. He drives to the gas station, fills up the tank and re-fills the fuel can. The station owner comes out to greet him and they have a short chat. Lionel regales him with the fuel theft at the airport parking lot. Cliff checks under the Volvo for possible leaks and assures Lionel that his tank is sound, so fuel loss must have been due to thievery.

At precisely ten o'clock, Lionel drives into Tischler's place, parks near the garage and retrieves the filled fuel can from his trunk. As he does so Hilda appears at the front door and opens the garage door to allow Lionel to deposit the fuel can inside, where he found it. "Do come in, I've made some coffee", she says. "Wouldn't you like a cup? We can enjoy it on the patio, it's such a lovely morning". Lionel follows her into the house, noting that she has a coffee service ready on the patio table. He also notices her lithe physique and graceful movements emphasized by her silk summer dress, a pale floral print that accents her ash blonde, up-swept hairdo.

Lionel takes a chair while Hilda pours the coffee. "Do you take cream and sugar? I prefer my coffee Viennese style, black and demi-tasse." Lionel agrees, black for me, too, why spoil good coffee…… such a great aroma, too! Hilda smiles, "it's Italian coffee and I am so glad that it is available here in Victoria." She eyes him intently as he sips his coffee. "Perhaps you are wondering why I requested this meeting?" I was somewhat apprehensive, replies Lionel but to be honest, also curious. Hilda confesses that she might be a bit opportunistic, "I did find your wife in my house, unannounced and surveying my drawing room paraphernalia, so many photographs collected over the years." She reassures him that the snooping did not perturb her and launches into a history of her interest in human behavior.

"Both my husband and I graduated in medicine at Heidelberg. We married during our internships in psychiatry in Zurich, hence, behavior we find most fascinating, providing a rich source for interpretation and analysis. Once a psychiatrist always one, my husband used to say." "That's quite interesting", says Lionel but you must be retired now. Your husband is not at home?" Hilda ignores his possibly probing question,and continues. "We started our practices in 1930 in Berlin but after the war ended we moved south to Munich and practiced there for some fifteen years before emigrating to Canada. It was so painful for us to see Germany split in to two political camps, East and West, although the outcome provided substantial opportunities for us in Munich as a consequence of the social and economic disruption in the country."

Lionel, eager to connect with her geography, "I was a captain in the Canadian Army stationed in Europe and spent time in West Germany, primarily in the British Zone. Berlin must have been a beautiful city before the war. I was taken aback by the destruction meted out to both Berlin and Hamburg by allied bombers, much more intensive bombardment than that dealt on English cities." Hilda nods her head in agreement. "Living in Berlin was a terrible nightmare for most people. Ernst and I lived some 20 km southwest of the city proper near Potsdam. Ernst inherited a country house there. We moved south to Munich shortly after cessation of hostilities, then on to Canada in 1960. In some respects we were fortunate, having no children but we both lost most of our relatives, either in military action or through bombing raids."

Lionel then nods in compassion, "we are childless too. I assume that in your case, being childless refers to the potential obligations put on German parents by the National Socialists through the well-organized Hitler Youth system?" Hilda sighs, "yes, parental obligation, we had much distress in some of our patients over that situation. The youth of both sexes were highly motivated and the opportunities for city kids for outdoor sports, camping and hiking etc. were almost limitless. Children joined eagerly, got uniforms, flags, badges and absorbed the associated propaganda like sponges. The entire educational system was locked in, including the majority of educational staff." She stops to take takes several sips of her coffee, then continues, "Ernst and I were too swamped with our psychiatric practices to find time for procreation. Having children in that expanding national fervor that emphasized loyalty and service to the State gave us serious concerns about parental authority, family security, and their potential erosion by the State."

Lionel, biting his lip several times," yes, I remember that children turned against their parents, reporting them to the authorities for even mild criticism of the cultural milieu."

Hilda, pouring more coffee for both of them, "I doubt if anyone outside of Germany during that pre-war decade could appreciate the well-executed pressures to conform. Eventually, we found it necessary to join the Party so as to maintain our patient obligations. This led to working for the Reich part-time in state institutes and serving high-echelon party members and their families on demand." Lionel's eyes

plug, and fuses fail? Ernst dispatched such difficulties with ease. They make me panicky and feeling helpless and technical people, like plumbers and electricians, seem to act with the self-importance and time constraints of neuro-surgeons. Lionel claps his hands, no problem, call me any time when things go awry. I am Mr. Fixit at our place." Hilda walks him to the front door.

Lionel, turning and smiling as he opens his car door, "again, many thanks for the coffee and stimulating conversation." Hilda agrees…"it has been most enjoyable. We must do this again. Next time bring your wife and do tell her that our confrontation in the house is already forgotten and that I look forward to meeting her again." She stands at the front entrance and watches Lionel drive out through the circular driveway.

It has been nearly ninety minutes since he drove to the gas station to fill both his car tank and Hilda's gas can. Returning home he finds Margaret cutting a bouquet of flowers. Margaret looking up…"finally the prodigal returns! What took you so long and what happened? I have been conjuring up a slew of possible scenarios....some of them dark and dangerous. Maybe we've been watching too much TV." Lionel laughing, "calm down dear, everything went smoothly. Hilda is a most interesting and worldly woman. We had coffee on her patio."

"What did you two talk about? The weather and her rose garden?" "Marg, do I detect a hint of jealousy? It was all very innocent. We talked about Germany and the war years. You remember that I was stationed in West Germany as a captain. Hilda and her husband who died early were psychiatrists who moved their practices from Berlin to Munich, avoiding the Russian occupation tactics that led to the Airlift and the Berlin Wall, then decided to come to Canada. They came here in 1960, first to Toronto, then to Victoria." Margaret is still showing some concern. "She didn't mention my burglary attempt?" Lionel laughs, "calm down, Marg! She made particular mention of your incident as I was leaving, saying that she looks forward to meeting you again under more relaxed conditions. Hilda is really a nice person, well-educated and civilized. I'm sure that you two would find much in common. After all, you were a military nurse for several years during and after the war before you went back to school to get your license in pediatrics. I'm sure that you would find much of common interest."

Margaret, reflectively looking back, "I think her manner and accent put me off. Besides, I have been feeling guilty. Did she do that to me, or am I an amateur burglar and a snoop by inclination?" Lionel, laughing, "Marg, you are such a nice person and it really bothers you when you think that someone dislikes you. I think that your prairie farm background and your Sunday school training combine sometimes to bring out the urge to scourge yourself! How about some lunch but first get those flowers in water before they wilt!" Rolling her eyes skyward and shrugging her shoulders, Margaret gets a little defensive. "Just remember that those prairie farmers...most of my relatives for several generations have worked hard to provide your anticipated lunch, and this prairie gal will put your lunch on the table!" Lionel laughs gently, and putting his arm around her waist, he leads her into the house.

At lunch, Margaret returns to the subject of Hilda Tischler. "Is that all you talked about....Germany and the war? Surely, living in Oak Bay, Victoria, B.C. in such an attractive house with lovely gardens allowed them to heal whatever psychological wounds they had collected during the war?" "Well, Hilda did mention that her husband suffered from cardiac problems which were common in his family. Perhaps she lived under the apprehension of cardiac arrest due to overwork and politico-economic tensions due to the early years of the new Reich. Ernst died in 1968, two years ago at age 58."

Margaret is feeling compassionate, "I am beginning to step into her shoes. Should we invite her to lunch next week? How about mid-week? Let's see, what for lunch, Kaiser rolls, assorted cold cuts from Freybe, a German white wine...say a Mai wine and for dessert, strudel and coffee, yah?" Why don't you invite her yourself, says Lionel. "That lunch sounds delicious!" Margaret is phasing into the hostess mood, "first I want to scout out the menu for availability".

The telephone rings and Margaret answers. That was Hilda. "She seems to be a little rattled. Something about fuses as she can't get the oven to work. Would you go over and fix it for her, Lionel?" Lionel is finishing his sandwich and the last of his tea. "Tell her I will be over there in about 20 minutes." Margaret relays his message, then hangs up and turns towards Lionel, "she seems quite flustered. Well, you have volunteered your services as Mr. Fixit. As I am going shopping shortly, I'll drop you off there and pick you up when you ring the house."

Getting ready to go, Lionel says, "I had better take some tools in case the problem is more than a fuse, and an assortment of fuses. Meet you at the car in 10 minutes?" He leaves for the tool room and gathers his gear while Margaret quickly makes her shopping list and readies herself for town. After dropping off Lionel at Hilda's driveway, she proceeds into downtown Oak Bay. Waving goodbye, Lionel and walks down the driveway to find Hilda waiting at the front door. She is wearing an apron. "You are so soon", she says! I had a premonition yesterday that something in the house would fail. The stove is electric and fairly new but electric stoves I don't like. Unfortunately, natural gas isn't available in this neighborhood." Lionel retrieves his tool box, saying that it is probably just a fuse. "I'll look at the fuse panel and you should watch so you can check yourself next time." They walk into the kitchen and he inspects the fuse box. Hilda, watching him, "the top burners all work...I tried them all but the oven doesn't heat and I have made a cake batter."

Lionel looks at her…."it must be the 30 amp fuse for the oven then". He removes the fuse panel and finds the oven fuse is separated. "Look Hilda, see that the wire strap is broken? She looks over his shoulder, breathing lightly on his neck as he replaces the fuse. "Now if you turn on the oven it should heat up." She leans over his shoulder again and turns on the oven dials to bake at 400 degrees. Lionel stepping back, "there, the lights are on." He opens the oven door and thrusts in his hand in momentarily. "Yes, it is working, presto! You can now bake something." Hilda then turns off the oven. "Oh, could you take peek at the doorbell for me? It stopped ringing last week, not that I have many visitors."

Lionel hums, "it's probably just a contact loss at the switch. I'll check it". He takes off the brass plate to find a loose wire that when re-attached sounded the chimes." Hilda laughs lightly, "ah!, the chimes are working once again! You are so clever! Now I have one more task for you. The outside faucet for the front garden is leaking badly and I must use that hose to wash off the greenflies on the rose buds. I found a hose washer in a kitchen drawer but I can't undo the hose at the faucet." That should be no problem, says Lionel. "The female connector has probably rusted on the threads. I'll get it off with my adjustable pliers. Bring that washer with you."

Hilda laughing again, "I have it here on my finger." She waves it at him and laughs lightly as they proceed outside onto the patio. Lionel replaces the washer and turns on the faucet. "See! No leaks now." "That's great, Lionel, now I can wash off those sap-sucking aphids off my rose buds. Watch me!" She proceeds into the rose bed and asks him for the hose. Lionel follows her into the bed and hands her the hose. Hilda picks an opening bud and smells its aroma. "This is a beautiful yellow bloom, take a sniff!" Lionel leans over to her and the rose bud is sampled simultaneously, eye-to-eye.

Suddenly Margaret appears on the patio. Margaret has driven into the driveway simultaneously and stops by the rose bed. Bounding out of the car she screams: "Lionel! Returning from town, I had the sudden urge to pick you up after shopping. So, what do I discover! A little fusion going on, I see! Fuses, my grandmother!"

Stomping on to the lawn, she picks up the garden hose, snatching the hose end out of Hilda's hand. Like a busy fireman at a conflagration she aims the full pressure nozzle directly at them both. Lionel and Hilda are aghast at Margaret's sudden and aggressive action. Stumbling around while trying to avoid the blast of cold water, their visibility severely compromised by the powerful spray, they try to leave the rose bed despite thorns tearing at their limbs. Margaret, enjoying her self-righteous opportunity reduces them both to half-drowned rats. "This is a second War of the Roses, eh! I like the sound of it..... sounds quite historical....or should I say, hysterical." She is giggling and sobbing at the same time, then dropping the hose, she turns and begins to storm back towards their car.

Quickly regaining the safety of the lawn and looking woefully bedraggled, Hilda and Lionel seem rather unprepared for any foreseeable events. Hilda, shaking her dripping dress vigorously, "how unfortunate! Quite a Shakespearian reaction, I'd say! I could apply some of my clinical tactics to reassure her feelings of domestic security?"

Lionel, shaking his head vigorously, "no, no, that won't be necessary, thank you very much! It's my concern." He hurries off in pursuit of Margaret before she leaves him stranded ......with Hilda.

A Wartime Military Heist

Routine road security is considered boring by the Alpi Graie as all the remaining five Divisions are actively serving on the Russian Front or in Jugoslavia, Greece, and Albania, receiving significant losses. Alpi Graie soldiers on both sides of the French/Italian border areas receive much harassment from the German forces whose arrogance is much resented, seeing as both Axis powers are committed to fighting the Allied forces of Britain, France, America and the volunteer forces of Poland, and Czechoslavakia who escaped from German forces in Europe. Particularly galling of German troops are the raucous comments about the feathers in the Italian Mountaineer uniform caps and reticence to eat with them.

Highway security stations are operated, one at the French Border at Modane, west of Torino cooperatively run by Vichy and Italian forces, and the second station at Susa some two hours driving from Torino. Three security teams of nine men each, on 24 hr. duty, had been assigned to the second station at Susa who replace each other on a weekly basis from regimental quarters near Castello di Revoli. One of the three teams assigned to Susa are twenty-five year-old mountaineering and skiing enthusiasts, Cpl. Victorio Palermo, and

Pvts. Renaldo Glaritan and Marti Mogli. Routine passage of German trucks and their drive teams coming from Lyon carrying miscellaneous cargoes have to submit to routine inspection of transport papers and truck contents, reflecting the authority of the Italian forces.

Persistent difficulties with the truck teams become a major sore point with all three Italian security teams, compounded by the refusal of the German troops to eat or socialize with the Italians during their driving breaks which reflect the tortuous alpine road conditions between Lyon and Italy. Upon receiving a dispatch from HQ alerting them to a shipment of gold bullion by armored car on a specific date which coincides with the Palermo duty schedule, the three Italians, at the instigation of Cpl. Palermo, entertain the idea of confiscating the bullion and escaping the rest of the war by high-tailing it to Switzerland and a plan is made to accomplish this feat which would surely enrage the Germans. The bullion is intended to finance German occupation wages after being converted to lira at appropriate Italian banks distributed south to Genoa. The heist escapade is carefully planned to include the escape route north and potential final routes to arrive in Switzerland by mountainous terrain not patrolled by either Italian or German authorities.

DETAILS OF THE PLAN

Seizing the German truck team must be a surprise action hopefully regarded by the Germans as a routine inspection and care must be taken to disarm them, inspect the contents to insure that the bullion is stowed, otherwise the heist is of no useful consequence, and decide what to do with the Germans. Marti knows of an abandoned sheep farm a few kilometers down the way so they decide to esconce them there, bound-up to insure time delay necessary to gain the Swiss frontier. The escape route north from Susa, apart from the short-term delay at the abandoned sheep farm just south of the main road at Avigliani, about one hours drive away, is another hours drive over 60 km to Torino.

At the outskirts of Torino they decide to take the flat country road to Varese on SS233, then on to Olona, then turn north up through the mountain pass to Ganna, on through the Parco delle Cinq Vette and Largo de Ghirla to Ghirla. The heist proceeds smoothly despite the loud protestations of the German guards now disarmed and manacled, enraged but impotent and told to shut up, or else! At the abandoned sheep farm they are gagged, securely bound hand and foot, and left in an animal stall of a small shed. Laughing uproariously and making quips about Switzerland and Swiss misses, the three Italians drive back to the main road and continue towards Torino.

"I'm wondering", says Victorio, "can we carry all that bullion in our army knapsacks"? Renaldo replies, "we are strong and fit for the mountains but, if necessary, we can stashed any extra weight in a hiding place and come back for it in the future. Let's concentrate on the route and side-step before the city and make for Varese." Their adventure is steadily becoming routine driving as no complications occur on the road, probably due to the nature of their conveyance, a heavily armored German truck festooned with large black swastikas. At Ghirla their confidence is steadily mounting as the Swiss Alps loom ahead. All three of them are very familiar with the terrain as they pass through the flatland beyond Ghirla, then on towards Gugliate-Fabiasco.

Unknown to them is the unlucky discovery of the three bound and gagged prisoners by a couple of German troopers hiking in the area and who entered the sheep farm remains in search of a well or spring water. The alarm is quickly raised in both Italian and German military establishments in Italy and in Vichy France at the headquarters of General Heinrich von Spech in Vichy and that of Colonel Guiseppi Estesa in Castello di Rivoli near Torino.

It is now mid-afternoon and two Heinkel fighters are despatched to search of the armored truck on all roads leading north to Switzerland. One pilot locates the truck some 90 kilometers south of the frontier, avoids alerting them with low level passes, and radios in his position overflying highway SS233 north of Parco delle Cinq Vette and Lago de Ghirla in an open area. Both pilots are then instructed to return to their base near Milan. A SS detachment based near Ponte Tresa on the Italian side is at alerted and sent to intercept them. The SS detachment sets up a roadblock outside Categliano-Viconago with machinegun nests on either side of the winding road with steep lateral slopes.

The miscreants are planning to take a familiar backroad north of Categliano-Viconago, clearing the mountain chain that is projecting to the south and staying in the foothills west of Ponte Tresa . This would allow them to ditch the truck in the forest, load-up the bullion after secreting the excess in a selected place in the forest and be some two kilometers from the frontier and adjoining river on the Swiss side. They are beginning to ready themselves, stopping for a few minutes to load up their backpacks and preparing to look for a suitable location in the approaching forested areas to ditch the truck and bury the surplus gold.

Coming around a sharp curve in the fading light as dusk approached, they are met by a roadblock with no possibility of turning about in an attempted escape. Blinding search lights from a large German truck catch them by complete surprise and they realise quickly that the game was up. An SS captain with a megaphone demands that they stop, throw any weapons out onto the road, get out of their truck and stand with their hands behind their heads, or be shot immediately. There is a machinegun team on either side of the road, he says. So, if you wish to live, follow my orders now!

They comply quickly by standing in front of their headlights, casting their rifles aside. The SS captain and five rifle-bearers advance slowly with weapons ready to fire. "Get down on your knees" shouts the captain waving his drawn pistol. They comply and are then manacled with hands behind their backs as the SS captain, red-faced, stands glaring at them. "I should shoot you all right now, but my hands have been tied by General von Spech. I am to deliver you to your commanding officer, Colonel Estasi at Castello di Rivoli. Have you broken into the bullion stores?"

The boys meekly nod their heads and point to the truck where their backpacks are found and emptied back into the bullion stores remaining in the back of the truck. They are then thrown into the SS truck and, guarded by two riflemen, begin the uncomfortable ride south, accompanied by their confiscated armored car in which the SS captain is riding. The remaining Germans are sent back to their frontier base near Ponte Tresa.

JUDGEMENT AND OUTCOME

After a tortuous and cold four hours on the road, bouncing on the truck bed and being kicked by the two guards for entertainment, they arrive at Castello di Rivoli after midnight. Colonel Estasi has given orders to put them in the guardhouse, part of the original dungeon and to show the SS captain to his quarters on the third floor. He greets him warmly at the door and offers him a hot meal and a glass of brandy. He thanks the captain profusely and congratulates him on his well-executed military capture of the three prisoners.

"Would you give me an account of the procedure you employed and the reactions of the prisoners upon their arrest?' The captain is eager to illustrate his performance and is pleased to see Estasi nodding his head in agreement. "I shall be sure to relate this account to General von Spech as he plans in flying here shortly to discuss the matter. We Axis officers must remain concerned that our cooperative actions reflect our individual professional military procedures".

The adjutant steps forward to re-fill the captains brandy glass on the eye of his commander who then informs the captain that suitable overnight quarters have been arranged for him and three men and signifies that the meeting is over. The captain salutes smartly with an audible click of his heels and leaves with the adjutant. Colonel Estasi sighs in relief and prepares to turn in himself.

After breakfast in the Officers Club, Estasi repairs to the guardhouse and regards the three prisoners through the bars, noting their pale faces and haggard looks. He waves to the jailor to open the cell and escort them to the adjoining interrogation room and to arrange for regular prison uniforms for them. He waves them to sit down, instructs the jailor to remove their wrist manacles and regards them carefully as he lights a cigarette, noting that they all follow his actions. He gives his silver cigarette case and lighter to the apparent leader of the group and watches them light up appreciatively. Victorio hands the case and lighter back to Estasi, voicing his thanks.

Following several inhalations, Estasi holds up his right forefinger, "I'm curious, what were your motivations for committing this outrageous act in time of war?" The three look at each other and Victorio volunteers a response, relating that they were fed up with German arrogance, particularly their reticence to eat communally with us Italians and their obvious sneering at the feathers in our caps. Also, the military situation in North Africa resulted in some 160 thousand Italian troops being taken prisoner there, that the Italian offensive in Greece was routed, and that other units of the Alpi in Jugoslavia were severely mauled, leading to major mortality. That General Badaglio resigned from the army in disgust over the lack of required military support in Greece has badly shaken our morale. The Germans take every chance they can to deride our army and we take that personally. So, I guess that this plan to swipe their earnings came from feelings of resentment and revenge.

Colonel Estasi nods, as if in agreement, and secretly admires their audacity and planning which would have probably exceeded had the trussed up German truck guards not been found so soon at the abandoned sheep farm. He decides to learn more about their backgrounds as they are all volunteers and asks them of their pre-military backgrounds. As they all worked at Alpha Romeo motor works in Milan and volunteered together when the company abruptly changed to producing engines for fighters, he understands their comraderie. That Claritan and Mogli were precision machinists and Palermo is an expert watchmaker gives him some defensive ammunition against any demands by General von Spech to have them court martialed and summarily shot.

Colonel Estasi decides to discover more about them. "Corporal Palermo, I have checked your official record, and see that you were born a Sicilian, is that right." Yes sir, but I left Sicily at age twenty and came to Florence where I worked for a wealthy owner of a prestigious company specializing in antiques. He drove an Alpha Romeo sedan, a very fancy model but sold out and put his money in Alpha Romeo and recommended that I join them to design instrumentation. With his assistance and his stature at Alpha Romeo I landed a good position with them and got to know these two (he points to the others listening) and worked with them in fabricating my designs. The colonel persists, "so you weren`t just a watchmaker were you."

Palermo shrugs, well I have a knack for fine mechanics and timing devices, in fact that got me in great trouble in Sicily. Oh, says Estasi, explain that comment. The local Mafia Don`s fancy watch I repaired and he asked me if I could fix an antique clock to explode after several weeks of winding, he wanted to snuff out the Chief of Police with about three sticks of dynamite secreted in the clock, the time interval long enough from the gift date to snuffing that would disconnect him from any connection. I told him that I could do it and a significant reward was offered but I decided to leave Sicily as I was sure that other similar jobs would be expected of me.

Edstasi looks intently at the floor for several minutes then thanks them for their frankness, saying that their fates were be decided within a short time. He leaves the guardhouse and instructs the jailor to provide them with beds and three meals daily of significant nourishment until commanded otherwise. The three jailbirds are somewhat confused despite the frank chatting between them and the colonel and the dire threat of execution remains fresh in their minds.

Going over the more recent occupational plans in Italy of the German High Command, Estasi reviews the recent suggestion that a fuse manufacturing and assembly plant be organized in Milan where such facilities were available. Apparently, the main manufacturing plant in West Germany had been badly damaged recently and more raids were expected if the Allies suspected recovery which would have taken much time, anyway. Milan was scheduled for the new plant and the SS would be involved in managing the slave labor necessary to combine with skilled workers from both Germany and Italy.

General von Spech arrives the next day in late afternoon and is brought to Castello di Rivoli in Colonel Estasi`s staff car along with his pilot. Estasi meets him at the main entrance and invites him to his quarters for a relaxing drink. They avoid confronting the embarrassing incident as neither man wishes to show a hand that might be antagonizing to the other. Estasi has arranged for a superb dinner in his quarters which is well-received by the General who mentions that he has had much difficulty with the French cuisine, laden with overly-rich sauces resulting in stomach objections.

After the main course, coffee and cigars follow and Estasi puts on his gramophone and begins to sing an aria from Figaro. The General claps, "Verdi, and you have a fine tenor voice!"

General von Spech mentions that he was in a chorus at Heidelberg and that his favorite music was German operetta and the works of Franz Lehar. Estasi realises that they have common interests and points out that the finest German lyrical tenor is Richard Tauber for whom Lehar has composed several scores. Also, Tauber was known for his renditions of Italian opera roles, like Don Itavio in Don Giovanni.

General von Spech laments that Tauber left Germany and Austria at the start of hostilities to live in London. Estasi reminds him that Tauber`s encounters with anti-Jewish German thugs in Vienna after the Anschluss in 1938 were involved, even though his mother was a Viennese Aryan actress and his father only half-Jewish.

The General is becoming expansive from the good brandy and comments that many such thugs seem to have found positions in the SS. He then mentioned that he had to threaten the SS captain following his demand to execute the Italian prisoners from the gold escapade. "We Wehrmacht professionals have a low regard for SS staff although they are Hitler`s favorites for political and security reasons."

He then changes the subject by asking Estasi about his musical talent. Colonel Estasi admitted that he attended the Conservatori Musica in Milan in 1920 and became a secondary understudy for

Enrico Caruso at La Scala although Caruso died the following year at the age of 48 years. After two years of bit roles he had a serious hunting accident at Lugano, shot by a nephew of King Emmanuel, collapsing his left lung and was advised to quit singing as a career.

"If I`m going to be shot at, I might as well join the army" he says and they both laugh. "When Mussolini took control of the country I was sent to Military College, followed by duty in Libya then Ethiopia, returning to Italy as a major. Mussolini promoted me to colonel rank in 1932 as he was busy building up the army.

Enough about me, perhaps you wish to discuss my intentions regarding the prosecution of the three enlisted men under my command?" General von Spech nodded affirmatively, saying that prosecution, judgement, and punishment should be in strict accordance with Italian military traditions, reflecting our national relationships and common ambitions.

Estasi realises his cue, "yes, our common ambitions…..I understand that the German High Command wishes to convert some existing manufacturing capacity in Milano to manufacture weaponry fusing systems to offset the recent destruction of the main industrial complex in Germany by Allied bombers. I suggest that rather than executing these men by firing squad their most potential use would be in the proposed Milano plant, under strict supervision, of course, possibly by the local SS commandant who will be involved due to slave labor needs?"

The General slaps his thighs and agrees enthusiastically. "This plan thus would side-step our common reluctance on capital punishment for this unmilitary activity and allow the SS commander in Milano to assume authority and responsibility. More importantly, such a decision would enhance the potential success of the fusing project in anticipation of the vigorous defence against the anticipated invasion of Italy!" They both drink to this solution and retire to bed.

The three enlisted men are left stewing in their cell for over a week then receive special orders signed by the colonel to proceed to Milano to be assigned to special manufacturing duties under the auspices of the local SS commandant. Their army identities are erased and they are now civilians working under German authority. They are thankful for escaping the firing squad and successfully integrate themselves with the incoming German civilian staff for setting up the facility.

Their abilities and experience with mechanical control systems relating to timing requirements are well recognized by Captain Wolfgang Rhinehart, the SS commander who rewards them with equal status to the German workers, above the slave labor gangs, including meals and housing. Within a year of full operation, with production peaking, the Allies begin the invasion of Sicily in July, 1943.

Fusing systems are sabotaged without detection by German overlords by making minute and intricate alterations in movement action resulting in nearly 35% of production, particularly in cannon shells and grenades, is rendered ineffectual. Quality control efforts by German supervisors are confounded by such alterations which remain undetected by bench-testing procedures.

In early August, Estasi`s regiment is sent south to the port of Spezia to defend against possible Allied raids. The invasion of Mainland Italy in September, 1943 coincided with the ejection of Mussolini by the Grand Council of Fascism and control of the army is returned to Italian King Immanuel who signed an armistice with the Allies on September 3, 1943. The Italian forces in Vichy France were then disarmed and sent to slave labor camps in Germany, courtesy of General Erwin Rommel.

Estasi`s regiment in Italy was disbanded and many joined the Co-Belligerent Army involving General Badaglio. Mussolini and his Blackshirts moved to control Northern Italy along with the retreating Germans, under a new Fascist State. Although the Germans surrendered in Italy on May 2, 1945 the Fascists did not surrender until later, although Mussolini was caught by partisans and executed on April 28. The fusing manufacture continued until the Germans left along with the SS.

Watching the news, the three miscreant Italians managed to return south to join Badaglio`s forces against the Northern Fascists and eventually returned to true civilian life. Victorio married in his hill-top village and his family, now three with a young son also named Victorio, emigrated to Canada and settled in Toronto`s lively Italian Quarter. His two cohorts disappeared into their own private lives and their sympathetic former colonel, Guiseppe Estasi, became Director of the Military Music Academy in Rome.

Psychic Events and a Directive Dream

Others may have had similar experiences but without this particular outcome. My wife died rather suddenly of lymphoma. She had the non-lethal form, called Hodgkin's Disease for many years but this condition can transition to the lethal form without notice. Naturally, I was completely devastated. We had enjoyed a fifteen year, intensive relationship that was terminated within two years of her retirement from teaching. I remained in the family house for a year before moving to a condominium.

Within that year I experienced several events which are usually considered unreal.

Several weeks of her passing, she woke me out of a sound sleep in our bedroom. The first time, I awoke hearing her loud voice saying "wake up, John.......wake up!" Thoroughly startled, I sat up in bed but as no further took place I broke down in tears. I assumed that she needed to give me a message but nothing else happened. A second event also occurred in bed within two weeks. This time I was woken by a persistent and rhythmic pressure on my right forearm which was outside the covers. Again, upon wakening, I realized that she must have returned once again.

I remained in the house for almost a year, along with the family cat, Pushkin, following the advice of several mutual friends not to make any serious decisions until then. Pushkin was a long-haired Persian who normally slept downstairs but came upstairs in the mornings and jumped onto our bed. Following my wife's passing, Pushkin refrained from her morning habit and would not go upstairs. Putting her on the stairs resulted in her fleeing downstairs quickly. She also took to sitting on the sidewalk in front of the house, next to my wife's car. If I deigned to use that car, she would be found walking up and down the sidewalk as I returned from my chores.

Several weeks later, as I was mowing the back garden lawn, Pushkin was laying on the cedar sun deck sunning herself. I sensed a presence nearby so stopped the electric mower and looked at the cedar fence at a location where a large clump of magnificent white dahlias were in full bloom. I had turned the back garden into a white floral development as white flowers were Dalia's favorite flowers.

We had often sat in that garden under bright moonlight and I intuitively knew that she had selected that clump of dahlias to communicate with me once more. Looking at the dahlias, I quietly said, "I know you are there and that this is the last time here that you will visit. Go peacefully to your next sojourn, Dalia. Hopefully, we shall meet again when I pass over and search for you." I was surprised to see that the cat, Pushkin, was sitting bolt upright now, her ears pricked forward as she looked intently at the dahlias.

When I returned to my mowing chore several minutes later, Pushkin had regained her original sprawled out posture on the cedar deck.

In the following days, I noticed that Pushkin came much closer to me in the house. She would jump up into my lap in the TV room and gaze intently into my eyes. Clearly, this was a significant change in her behavior but she never ventured upstairs again.

On the first anniversary of my wife's passing, a close friend of hers, also a teacher, telephoned me, asking if I would like to attend a church that they had both visited twice during the previous year. She explained that the two ministers at that church held an annual flowers tribute in memory of the deceased. They were both psychic mentors with an international reputation with considerable travel schedules.

I had declined to accompany them on a previous occasion, my reluctance reflecting my scientific background and some pressing maintenance jobs. I accepted her invitation and promised to bring white flowers from the garden. Before attending the church, I cut two large bouquets of white flowers and we took them to the service. As an agnostic, I have never been a churchgoer, and remain so. We two sat in the second row and I noticed that both bouquets were prominently placed on the stage with several others. A routine program unfolded with several hymns (songs), prayers, then a short a sermon, and passing around of the tithe baskets.

Both ministers stood quietly on stage, hands clasped, and heads down for several minutes. One of them then strode to the microphone and looked out over the congregation. I am getting a strong connection with these white flowers, he said. They are from a white garden and I believe the garden of a lady who died last year from cancer. Who brought them here? He looked out across the room and I raised my hand to acknowledge their origin. I was totally surprised by the accuracy of his statements and wondered how he knew such personal facts. Later, when questioned by me, my associate was adamant that she had not ever talked to either minister and didn't attend their services but rarely.

At that moment, the other minister also became active. "Your wife is here, standing by me and expresses that she is glad at your coming. She has been wishing this for several months." Both men were very stirred by this apparent connection. They made some fourteen comments reflecting our personal lives. These were followed by a vision describing a cattle ranch, then an elderly rancher who was now standing next to my wife. "Do you know such a man?" I shook my head, saying I had no connections with ranchers. They suggested that I think about such a connection after returning home, then….."your wife is chuckling, apparently after finishing breakfast you would start on a crossword puzzle and that would make it difficult for her to discuss something she needed to talk about."

The other minister then commented, "you were looking at some jewelry a few days ago, weren't you?" That comment really floored me……why? I had taken a friend for a day-sail locally a week before and he had invited me to join him and his wife for dinner at the local country club. On the day of the dinner, I had just finished showering and shaving, then I looked up at a silver necklace hanging on the mirror and tried it on.

The pendant was an engraved amber sun icon which I had purchased for Dalia during our holiday to Cancun, Mexico several years before. It was the only piece of her jewelry that I kept, having given most of her jewelry to her daughter. Only one spirit, Dalia, would have known of my donning of that necklace.

On returning home after this initial church experience, I began thinking…….where did these men get all this personal information? The crossword and necklace incidents were totally personal. Through these two mediums she also apparently thanked me for our last holiday in Southern California several months before she died.

Thinking about the rancher, I finally realized that fellow perhaps was the father of Dalia's first husband who had a cattle ranch in the Okanagan Valley. He was the father who had disowned his second son as he deserted my wife during her pregnancy after she had refused to obtain an abortion. The father had died years ago but he had kept a relationship with Dalia until he passed on.

Due to my scientific curiosity, I returned to that church a few months later, to see if I could recognize any techniques that they might be using in their factual comments or vision descriptions.

During that meeting, one of the ministers on stage looked over the congregation. "Someone in the congregation is wearing a hand-knitted garment with embroidery on it. I can see the garment. Where are you sitting?" A lady in the very back row raised her hand in acknowledgement. "You are from the Prairies, are you not," he continued. She answered, yes, from Saskachewan. Here for a few days but I'm not a member of this church. "You are a widow and your husband died last year?" She nodded. "He died of cancer?" She nodded, once more.

This is where it got quite interesting. "Did he have an old green pickup truck, a Ford?" Again, she nodded. "I'm beginning to visualize your home now, he said. There is a big garage full of tools where he used to spend much time. I also see a nearby apple tree and a wooden chair where he used to sit and smoke. I see in the garage a long line of tobacco cans nailed to an overhead shelf. Did he roll his own cigarettes? She answers again,"oh no, he bought store ones but a close friend of his did that and gave him the empty tins for his nuts and bolts." "Thank you for your cooperation, these visions have been very clear to me and I hope that this experience has been useful to you."

I left that church very perplexed and have never returned. How could these mystics operate without collusion, gaining specific facts as though reading the memory of another person?

These two experiences stimulated in me to continue my own investigations. More importantly, they precipitated some earlier memories which I now realize were psychic in origin. I can describe four experiences that could fall into that category. The first one happened when I was ten years old. My family lived in London, England throughout WWII.

As we lived adjacent to a large RAF camp at Uxbridge, we were nearly bombed in 1942. Two of our Sunday school friends whom my older sister, Belinda and I accompanied to Sunday school lived nearby were killed in a bombing raid a few minutes before we reached their house on a dire Sunday.

Our parents decided that my older sister and I should stay upcountry with relatives. We stayed with our great aunt Mary in Lincolnshire, close to the Sandringham estate of the Royal Family for over six months. One Sunday after church, she took us to Sandringham, to Saint Mary Magdalene church there. I rushed in ahead and stood at the altar and started feeling rather odd. As my sister and aunt approached me, walking up the aisle, I said, "I feel funny, like there are strong vibrations coming up from my feet.......up to my head." My great aunt looked down then and said, "if you step off that commemorative brass plate for Prince John you might feel better." Prince John had recently died and was buried in the cemetery. I stepped off the plate and the vibrations ceased immediately. I never thought about that experience again for many years but since have recognized it as a psychic event.

The next two events relate to Coastal Indians in British Columbia. The first one occurred about 1970 while on a road trip west of Campbell River to the West Coast of Vancouver Island. I had stopped my car by the roadside to relieve myself and while doing so looked down across a meadow surrounded by fir trees on three sides. There was a large gathering of people there, some were whites and many were native Indians, some wearing fancy clothes and headdresses. The vision disappeared after a few minutes and I returned to the car.

The second event concerning coastal Indians occurred in 1990 when I was engaged in biological research on Haida Gwai in the Louise Island and Cumshewa Inlet area. I knew there was an abandoned village on Skedans Point and wanted to visit there. I arranged for a native Haida to accompany me by boat. As we pulled in to the beach in front of the village site, I stepped out of the boat to haul it up on to the beach.

As I let go of the tender I could hear loud laughing and joyful screaming of playing children surrounding me on the beach. When the native stepped out of the boat, after shutting off the engine, I asked him if he could hear anything unusual. I don't hear nuttin, he said. Walking up the beach to the village remains, I saw several skulls half-buried in the ground moss and remained somewhat shaken by my auditory experience which ceased with the Haida's reply.

My last historic psychic event occurred in 1993, involving a near-fatal collision with a fierce storm while sailing southward from Haida Gwai along the West Coast of Vancouver Island.

Two of us were upside-down in a capsized multi-hull sailboat for eighteen days. Luckily we had some provisions and adequate fresh water. The second night of this fierce storm with winds blowing over seventy knots, I left the boat, looking down on it receding as I ascended into the night. Looking up I realized that we were in the eye of the storm and stars were moving to the left. I was unafraid and curious as to what was happening.

Suddenly the darkness was replaced by a blinding white light and I found myself laying on a white bench. Unable to look directly at the light, I could see in a large arc in front of me, defined by a surrounding wall of energy almost waist-high. The floor was a complicated geometric pattern in black and white. I remained not the least bit afraid, in fact curious as to my surroundings.

Was my cranial nervous system being recorded? The light ceased after an unknown period of time and I found myself again looking up at the stars which were now moving to my right, suggesting that I was returning to the capsized boat. My situation seemed to be quite logical. I became aware of the panicky atmosphere, the hull heaving in the gigantic swells and half-full of seawater sloshing from one end of the boat to the other, resulting in horrific air pressure changes that induced repetitive dense fog. I had been sent back ….. not ready yet and more things to accomplish were thoughts on my mind…..perhaps a suggested message?

On the fourteenth night of that sojourn at sea I had a dream that we would be rescued by a freighter proceeding to the Orient. I had tried to reassure my companion for many days earlier that there was a likelihood of being discovered by a commercial fisherman highballing further out to sea, looking for albacore tuna. We were some 75 miles west of the Brooks Peninsular.

On the next Sunday, we were rescued by a freighter heading for Japan from Vancouver with a cargo of barley. We two and a Cairn terrier, Caesar, had a survival party several weeks later in Victoria. That is when I met my second wife and enjoyed fifteen years of connubial bliss until she passed away.

I have spent many hours reviewing that out-of-body experience (OBE), researching the psychiatric and related literature with little success. Finally, I dove into the psychic literature, including near-death events involving accounts by medical doctors and nurses. My experience at sea differs from many OBE accounts but was similar to medical accounts which noted that fear was absent. In my experience, lack of fear was accompanied by curiosity aroused in a logical atmosphere, and the experience was indelibly marked on my memory.

Several years later while clearing out bookshelves at the house by request, I was removing National Geographic magazines that my wife had collected for many years. I spotted on one cover a photograph of the Taj Mahal and was intrigued. Looking through the article and several photographic plates, I became suddenly shocked by the geometrically patterned floor in one of the interior rooms. The black and white wood patterning was identical to that which I had seen during my OBE from the capsized yacht. I called my wife and showed it to her. She mentioned that a long-term friend was going to India, including the Taj Mahal……she should look for that room. Although that particular-floored room was photographed by National Geographic staff, she was unable to find it during her tour of the Taj Mahal, suggesting that it was not included in the routine tour itinerary.

In a more recent dream, my deceased wife telephoned me from Seattle, saying that she was living happily with a young couple in a modest but neat house. I asked her for the address. She said it was in Faremont. I asked her for the address: Osborne Avenue, number …….12. Her voice became bedraggled and I could only catch the last two numbers. I searched the Seattle maps for Faremont but failed to find it. Talking to a Seattle tourist some weeks later, he told me that Faremont used to be a separate entity but is now a suburb of the city and has undergone some major changes to allow freeway access.

In talking to close friends of both Dalia and I and describing the dream, they urged me to go to Seattle and try to find the house. This couple are both Buddhists but I initially found their urging to be too difficult but finally decided to investigate. Upon reaching Seattle which, other than the main freeway through to Vancouver, was unknown territory for me, I found Osborne Avenue by laborious searching. It was only two blocks in length now, due to highway changes. I drove up and down the two blocks, looking for house numbers that ended in 12 and found one house located next to the freeway wall and the hurrying traffic below.

It was a modest, neat house and I finally decided to go up and ring the bell. After a couple of minutes, a young colored girl opened the door, holding a very young baby. It was too difficult for me to explain my mission, so I made the excuse that I had the wrong number but complimented her on her baby……a girl named Delilah. At the sound of my voice pronouncing her name, she gurgled, looked at me and raised her right arm in my direction. Her mother laughed, saying that this is the first instance that her baby had reacted to her name and was so aware of her surroundings. Regaining my composure, I apologized for bothering her, giving her an excuse that my address was faulty. She accepted my apology graciously as I turned quickly, retracing my steps to the car.

I then drove off to find a coffee shop to settle my thoughts and prepare to drive back to Vancouver, Canada. Thoughts of soul migration were buzzing through my head and I decided to look further into Tibetan Buddhism. If Dalia had returned into a colored baby ……that would not suprise me. As a primary school teacher all her professional life, she was also anti-sectarian, lit candles in many religious sites, was a God-botherer, concerned for social justice, equality, with a heightened concern for the welfare of children.

I have since discovered a number of well-documented incidents of children between the ages of two and nine that have expressed specific and verifiable information describing previous lives. This discovery quietened my mind. The advent of soul migration in many cultures particularly in Southeast Asia and is well-accepted in the selection of Tibetan Buddhist leadership.

(For reasons of privacy the Seattle address in this incident has been fictionalized)

Hallelujah, I'm A Bump

PREFACE

Age seems to be catching up with me. Perhaps my accumulated life experiences have resulted in crotchiness and impatience with the social games we play with each other. Displays of ego and narrow-mindedness lubricated with hypocrisy and selfish desire are well-illuminated across the public screen. Western culture suffused with materialism is surely a major vehicle for such displays at both national and international arenas of discourse.

A thought struck me.......what could be the outcome of an inspection visit to Vancouver by Christian messiah, Jesus. A short tour here in preparation of a major assessment report requested by MOTU, the Master of the Universe. Let's see!

ARRIVAL IN VANCOUVER

It is a typical late winter day in Vancouver, drizzling rain and dreary streets although Christmas lights have sprung up in preparation for the Yuletide season and the related shopping habits orchestrated for coordinated gift-giving and Santa Claus epiphanies.

Jesus finds himself walking down a back alley in East Vancouver strewn with garbage and water puddles. Overhead, the power lines on either side, held aloft by telephone poles contrast against the grey overcast. The constant drip, drip, drip is occasionally relieved by the screaming of gulls or crows fighting over alley tidbits. He walks carefully, in sandals, oblivious to the wetness around him despite his white gown and rope sash. He approaches a jumble of commercial cardboard and spies an interior space occupied by a vagrant.

"Hello there! Why are you covered in newspapers and cardboard?" The derelict looks up saying "man, it is cold and I have no other place to go. Don't you feel the cold yourself? Just wearing sandals and a flimsy robe! This is December in Vancouver and it's also raining……. as usual! You must be crazy! Did you get away from them?" Jesus smiles, "I don't feel the cold or the rain but I see that you are shivering. When was the last time that you ate?" He fails to respond to the query as to possible escape from an institution.

The vagrant continues, "I ate yesterday. I lined up at the Gospel Mission and got a bowl of soup. That's all I could eat without throwing up. I've had a fever for three days now and someone in there stole my raincoat. You can't trust anyone these days, it's a dog-eat-dog world even when you are a downed dog!" Surely there is a place where you can warm up, get some dry clothes, and some medical attention?, says Jesus. "Look, your dirty, torn tennis shoes have holes in them so your feet must be wet, too!"

About this time, a police patrol car swings into the alley and stops near them. Two burly policemen get out and approach. One cop: "What's going on here! Are you two doing drugs…..you Jesus-looking creep! What's your story? Haven't seen you around here before…..I'd remember you. And in a white robe and sandals…..and long hair and a beard! Where did you spring from?" The second cop comments, "guess we should take him in and check the loony register for AWOLS."

Other cop, "first, let's try to get some information out of him. What's your name and where did you come from?"

Jesus is showing signs of concern. This encounter with the law reminds him of his Garden of Gesthsemane experience. "I really can't tell you that as it's not in my travel instructions. I'm on an inspection tour, a local tour to observe the present state of things here." Cop two is getting irked, "come on! That's enough of your bull shit, you freak! Where's your ID?" Jesus looks mystifies, "ID? What do you mean?"

Cop one raises his right hand with a pointed finger, "come on, joker! Start cooperating! You gotta medical card? Anything with your name on it? We need some identification, like a health card. I'm sure that you don't have a driving license. God forbid! Seeing you behind the wheel! There's enough nut cases wearing regular clothes……and driving!" Jesus raises both hands in an outward, apologetic gesture. "I'm sorry to cause problems but I have nothing like that but I'm very well known. My transportation here, well, you would consider it most irregular and no doubt illegal. But I assure you that I have been in your bodily form intermittently for over two thousand years by your calendar."

The second cop, "cut the crap! You must have a name! You do have one, don't you?" Jesus sighs, "yes, I do, well, actually several names: Son of God, Redeemer, Jesus, Savior, Messiah, although there is considerable objection to the last name in my original location in Palestine by those in power there even presently."

"That does it" says the first cop. "This character looks and acts like a schizophrenic to me and hence potentially violent. Best take him in, check him out before his medication runs out. Put the cuffs on him." "OK Redeemer," says the second cop, "hold out your hands, you are coming with us." Jesus obeys quietly while the manacles are secured to his wrists and he is steered into the patrol car. The first cop looks back at the bearded and ragged form sheltered under his cardboard and gestures towards the other cop. "What about the other one?" The second cop replies, "he's a local. I've seen him before panhandling on Main and Pandora, he's harmless so let's go and unload this joker."

The derelict peers out of his cocoon shelter, "catch you later, man! Don't let them kick you around! Stand up for your rights! It's a free country, isn't it? I feel free in my lifestyle but freedom is a slippery noun……and this is a slippery world!" The squad car drives off to book Jesus at the station.

At the station, Precinct No. 2, Jesus stands in front of the massive desk while looking at the man sitting behind it. The desk sergeant, Tim O'Reilly, looking up from his paperwork, "where did you fellows drag him from? He's a possible mental escapee? …….Maybe a schizophrenic? You both did well hauling him in even in the absence of any criminal behavior. Okay, put him in the General Tank with all the others. The shrink can look him over tomorrow and decide what to do with him, looney bin or whatever."

Walking down the corridor, the senior cop stops in front of the General Tank, unlocks the manacles and shoves Jesus inside. Jesus finds a vacant seat and looks around smiling at the sea of pallid, questioning faces around him. After a few minutes, one prisoner gets up and stands before Jesus. "What the hell are you grinning at, nut case! You another Jesus freak! This is the second one I've seen in here!" His eyes widening, Jesus appears interested. "Pardon me, you've seen others like me?" The prisoner smirks and, looking around at his peers, feels important. "Not here in the Tank but every now and then a long-haired freak shows up in town raving about the End of Times and Armageddon."

Jesus nods sympathetically, "that's interesting! The End of Times? Armageddon? Sounds familiar but there have been so many confusing and contradictory claims. Take the accounts of my short life Palestine, making miracles and so on!" A second prisoner steps up, "hey, lay off you phony! If you are going to come on like Jesus Christ you should bone up on all the necessary details. They are all in the Book…..the Book has all the answers. Anyway, that's' what they tell us at the local eateries."

Jesus raises his right hand with index finger pointed. "I sympathize with you. After I left Palestine there was much effort by script writers for several centuries, especially the first three, to create an account of my short life that borders on the magical, as if the writers recorded what they wanted to believe themselves and expected everyone else to believe their stories, too! I did come out of their stories looking really good although fatefully unfortunate.

The first prisoner, whistling through his teeth, "shit, this guy actually believes that he is Jesus, not just a wannabee! He is livening things up in here!" A third prisoner, obviously drunk, pushes the other two aside and faces Jesus squarely. "Let's have some fun! Some questions for him! How did you turn water into wine, eh? I'd really like to know! Come on, give us the dope! Sure would save most of us from a lot of begging and cajoling on the streets!"

Jesus, looking rather regretful, "actually I never did it. The wedding party was in full swing and the wine flowed like water. Everyone was feeling no pain but the jugs eventually ran dry. I happened to find some more in a back room, stored in a water tank and someone yelled, it's a miracle so I became the toast of the party. The story spread like wildfire, like most wishful thinking. So much wishful thinking may have accounted for the rapid spread that added to my fame."

The swaying drunk roared , "damn! I should have known it! Nothing could be that easy and convenient, anyway. Scraping the coins together for a cheap liquor store buy is hard and tedious work! You have to lie to passersby when they ask you if you intend to spend their miserable coinage on booze! I get really irked at their self-righteous attitudes especially as I suspect that most of them have well-stocked liquor cabinets at home and resent the act of charity which their assumed faith expects of them." Another prisoner pipes up from his bench, " bet this guy has an answer to any question about miracles! How about walking on water, eh? You gonna tell us you can do that?"

Jesus sighs and chews his bottom lip, "again, this was also a bit of exaggeration but not by me. When it happened I should have corrected that idea promptly but that episode had such a powerful effect on everyone at the beach. Here goes, I was in a fishing boat on the Sea of Galilee with several followers when a strong wind blew up suddenly, pushing the boat towards some large rocks. Not being swimmers, they got hysterical, so I stepped out of the boat onto some near-surface flat rocks that I spied. Leaping with agility from rock to rock shoreward with the boat tender in hand, I managed to slew the boat around to avoid collision with the large rocks and leaped up onto the beach. My actions resulted in safely grounding the boat on the sandy beach. My cohorts were so relieved that this had happened that one of them screamed hysterically that I was walking on water. From their narrow escape from possible drowning, they were willing to give me that power! I let it go as this incident profoundly enhanced their motivation. Hiking about the Palestinian countryside in the hot sun and not eating regularly as my followers were exposed to wasn't that easy."

Another prisoner eagerly supported his explanation as logical and possible but said he had other concerns. "What about raising people from the dead…..like that guy Lazarus? I think that is far more significant. How did you accomplish that feat? Sounds absolutely impossible to me!" There was a general roar of agreement to his words. By this time, Jesus had become quite interested in their questions and attention to him and continued his explanations……this time about the Lazarus episode. "That fellow Lazarus apparently had been in a deep coma for several days after falling off his donkey and hitting his head on a nearby rock.

I just happened to be passing by his tent and leaned over him to check his pulse and breathing. Putting two wetted fingers on his lips I realized that he was breathing faintly so I wet his lips from my canteen. At that stimulus, his lips quivered and his eyelids flickered, so I sat him up and gave him more water which he drank greedily, then moaned aloud. At the sounds of him moaning his mother appeared, realizing that the burial preparations were unnecessary. That he was returned to life at my command she announced in a very loud voice that I had raised her son from the dead. Many others gathered quickly and my actions were termed a miracle, especially by my followers. I used that situation opportunistically to stress that there is a life beyond the grave if you are willing to believe it.

By this time, the first prisoner who had called Jesus a nutcase wanted to reaffirm his status in the group. He stood squarely in front of Jesus, jabbing his finger in his face, saying "that's just about enough bullshit out of this character, entertaining or not! I feel like beating him up!" He grabs Jesus by the throat and pins him against the cell bars while drawing back his right fist in preparation to strike him in the face. Jesus throws both arms up, palms outward, saying, "hold on now, there's no need to get violent! Have I hurt you in the past? Back in my earlier days I was concerned to convince people to look after one another, especially children, and to think outside themselves, their personal greed and comfort. That there should be more to life than fighting and arguing, cheating each other, hoarding gold, whining about the Roman Governor and his taxes. Doesn't that sound okay to you?"

Lowering his fist and chortling loudly, this prisoner releases his grip. "Doesn't look like you succeeded, did it! You pissed off all the priests, the money lenders, and the sellers of sacrificial animals. Telling everyone to love each other.....then going on a rampage in the Temple, scaring the hell out of them! Lost your temper, didn't you! You cannot be as perfect as the script writers who wrote up This is Your Life would have us believe!"

Jesus is quick to counter him. "We must all remember that only MOTU is perfect. I had a short fuse on that day in the Temple. It was the Sabbath, the day of prayer and meditation, and no labor. The priests were in cahoots with the moneylenders, charging them rent for space in the Temple......money, money, money!" Most of the prisoners are now looking bewildered and one ventures to ask, "who is this MOTU. Never heard of that one. Sounds like the name of a kids robotic toy! What does it stand for?" Jesus replies, " it means Master of the Universe, another name for God, Allah, Yahwe, Atman, Brahma etc. MOTU prefers this label as it overrides all the sundry names drummed up by priests of every persuasion on this planet."

Another prisoner jumps up, “I’ve been listening to all your crap and excuses. Sure, you are quick with words but I think you are just another religious phony acting like a holy man and competing with us genuine beggars on the street! Someone should crack your head and knock those lies out of you!” He jumps up, grabs Jesus’s robe and raises a clenched fist to strike him. Jesus begins to glow like a light bulb and his latest assailant falls back, his mouth agape, in fear and amazement. Jesus casts his eyes heavenward as his glow subsides, quietly muttering “thank you, father, time to leave this place.”

Turning to face all these quaking winos, petty thieves, and street fighters, he says, “nice chatting with you all. You have my sympathy and concern but you must learn that although others may have treated you badly, you must try to improve your lives yourselves.” With that said, he turns and glides through the bars, disappearing slowly as he makes his way out of the precinct to the street.

The cell population, stunned and quiet, look at each other in disbelief and wonder. One prisoner comments, “now that shows he’s not one of us! Genuinely scary and our aggression directed at him merely reflects our own fears and weaknesses. We are afraid of ourselves, so afraid that we have assisted our detractors in building our personal prisons, padlocking the doors and throwing away the keys. I read a lot of philosophy in the public library.” Looking resentful, another prisoner says, “are you saying that we are partly responsible for our situations? If so, we should do something about it! Anyone got any ideas?” The badly alcoholic prisoner, his daze wearing off and his headache accelerating, staggers to his feet, raising his shaking arms, “arise, derelicts, alcoholics, druggies, and beggars! We have nothing to lose but our chains! My God, I wish I had the keys!”

MALL ENTRY

Walking up Howe Street, Jesus is thinking to himself. Perhaps I should change my costume, this one is getting me into much trouble. Glancing up he is attracted to a large, imposing building complete with flashing neon lighting. Christmas carols are emanating through the revolving doors, inducing him to enter. Inside, sitting on a throne-like chair and surrounded by stuffed reindeer, one with a red, blinking snout, is an obese-looking, white-bearded individual dressed in a flaming red suit with shiny black boots. A long line of waiting parents with young children are gathering in line before him.

Jesus walks up to him and stands next to a reindeer. "Hello, you in the red suit! Are you a prophet?.....long beard and all but you are too well-fed to be a prophet! Perhaps your prophesies are a source of great wealth. Do you accept coins for your prophesies?"

The waiting mother in a near front position with her young boy gives Jesus a dirty look. Santa plays along but is unsure how to respond as a long line awaits his attention. No one has told him to expect competition, especially from someone dresses like an Arab, perhaps like Jesus? "What's your game?" says Santa. "These kids are supposed to be hypnotized by me, my jolly laugh, my long, white and curly beard, and of course, my assumed power to get them whatever they want."

Jesus answers him, smiling, "actually, nobody knew I was coming here. I was attracted by the bright lights and music. I assume that you are acting out the part of Saint Nicholas, bringing gifts to children? Do you really think you are doing them any favor? More importantly, I see that some of these youngsters are visibly scared to death, being shoved onto your lap by grinning parents clutching flash cameras. What are you promising them? Toys and other playthings? Childish things which they can turn into more expensive material things when they mature, like automobiles, TV's, CD players, cell phones etc.? All the possible goods apart from decent housing for all, productive work, nourishing food, a well-rounded education and the ability to care for each other in sickness and health? Not to mention caring for and loving all children, not just your own!"

"This is one of my pet peeves about you so-called modern humans, concern only for your personal reproductive success. Very primitive! Only excusable in tribal groups constantly on the brink of starvation.

Even in those tribes, there seems to be more sharing than in wealthy Western societies enjoying abundant food, clothing and shelter." Santa is intrigued somewhat with these comments. "You identify me with Saint Nicholas, you must be a European! I remember that name from stories my grandmother told me as a child. Anyway, you are disrupting my work. The Manager expects me to process a minimum of two hundred children across my lap today. There's only two more Saturdays before Christmas Eve and I want to collect my bonus. Should he arrive here and sees all these children milling around while we're chatting……all hell will break loose! I've had this contract for eight years now and this job helps tied me over the winter months until the extras jobs in TV, movies and advertising pick up in the Spring!"

The mother first in line is getting more irked and a number of children are now standing close to Jesus and looking up at him. Jesus apologizes to Santa for delaying him, "children seem to be drawn to me. I do remember making statements some two millennia ago indicating my concern for children. Look at this little boy in front of you….he looks petrified and is clinging to my robe."

He reaches down to hug the boy who is on the verge of tears. The mother lets out a loud shriek, "leave my child alone…..you, you pervert!" She looks around screaming, pointing at Jesus. "This man in the robe is obviously a pedophile"! Her screaming sets off more screaming coming from adjacent mothers. A security guard comes rushing up, calling 911 on his cell phone. Jesus apologizes to the boy's mother "I was just trying to reassure your boy…..he seems so scared of Santa yet isn't scared of me."

The security guard, with his right hand on the butt of his revolver, "come away from here, you are causing a disturbance." He grabs Jesus by the arm and propels him towards the Security Office down the hallway. In the office he begins questioning Jesus, "who are you dressed like that. Just asking for trouble? Are you in a biblical show here in town? If so, why are you here in the mall dressed like that?" Jesus realizes that he is in trouble again, thinking, I knew that I should have changed my clothes. This is the second predicament I've put myself in today.

Several minutes later two policemen enter the office. "This looks like the character who escaped somehow from Precinct No. 2 this morning and they are still trying to figure out how he got away! Has he got ID?" Jesus sighs, not again, "I have no ID and I have several names: Jeshua, Redeemer, ….." He is interrupted by the second cop, "I think this is the same nut case from Precinct No. 2. Cuff him and let's take him in." The security guard leads them out through the Service Corridor, rather than through the open mall…..bad for business, watching them climb into the black Mariah parked in the service lot. Jesus, ensconced in the locked rear drifts out through the side of the van as they pass a small park off Main Street and watches as the van disappears further downtown.

ON THE UBC CAMPUS

Jesus has had enough of the street scene for a while so he appears on the UBC campus still in his robe and sandals. Luckily he escapes the eyes of the campus police as he surveys several buildings, selecting an impressive edifice having a large brass sign: SCIENCE. He mounts the steps, noticing that the vertically-fluted concrete walls have been brutalized, a lovely descriptive term coined by engineers. He enters a biology lecture room filled with students and takes a seat in the back. Students fail to notice him as they are busy scribbling down notes.

The professor on the stage, leaning on his podium, is explaining the extinction of the dinosaurs due to the impact of a large meteorite near the northeastern coast of Mexico. A huge crater several miles in diameter now underwater is estimated to have produced a complete blanket of suspended material in the upper atmosphere for some time, possibly years. The total darkness caused a complete collapse of the major biota which, in turn, caused mass starvation of the vegetarian dinosaur species, hence starvation of their predatory cousins. Those animal groups living underground or underwater were less affected, thus accounting for the survival of such ancient forms as the crocodilians, sharks and rays, and lower reptiles.

With some degree of satisfaction he stresses that the earliest forms of the mammalian line were rat-like species and probably survived by living underground, consuming the prodigious carcasses of dinosaurs. They survived to evolve into the complex series making up the present-day mammals. Although this general explanation remains a theory, the massive meteoritic crater off Mexico remains discernable today. A student in the second row raises his hand, "if birds descended from the dinosaur lines, some of these lines, perhaps small species, must have survived this mass extinction, no?" The professor acknowledges his statement, suggesting that we have not yet derived a satisfactory explanation for selected survival of dinosaur lines that led to the birds.

Jesus stands up at the back of the lecture hall. "I would like to add that the cataclysmic event that you have so admirably described is more than a theory. Actually, MOTU had become totally dissatisfied with the outcome of his evolutionary plans." The lecturer looked up at the back of the hall, "excuse me but you do not appear to be one of my students. However, being open-minded I welcome your comments despite your odd costume. The label MOTU escapes me, please explain." At this remark a large number of students turned in their seats and craned towards the rear of the hall. Jesus, still standing, answers in a clear, oratorical voice "that's the preferred title of the ultimate power authority, MOTU, Master of the Universe."

The professor smiles and points out that this is a science lecture and must follow established scientific procedures. He takes this opportunity to illustrate his pedantic prowess. "Science is based on the collection of verifiable evidence (data) with the interlocking of various sources of data allowing the development of conceptual models we call paradigms when direct evidence is yet unattainable. Hence, we advanced mammals are not in a position to directly attest on events that occurred prior to mammalian development except through interpretation of fossils."

Some snickering is heard from his students. Jesus continues, "that is precisely my point for MOTU was in that position. Let me explain." The professor smiles sardonically, saying that we are all ears.

Jesus again, "as I mentioned, MOTU was unsatisfied with the progress of his evolutionary plans. Why? Because MOTU had aspirations for this planet that included being able to communicate with advanced forms wherever life has emerged. Intelligible life forms had not yet reached a stage of development that would allow fruitful communication. The evolutionary patterns in the dinosaur lines resulted in either massive plant-munching creatures, or worse, massive and brutish predatory creatures short on brains but long on blood thirst destruction. Hence, MOTU threw a large fireball at this planet with the intent of starting anew.

The rat-like primitive mammals, beady-eyed and considerably more intelligent than their prolonged meals of dinosaur carcasses seemed like a reasonable alternative. Ergo, here you are.....but with a long way to go. That's where I came into the picture, to endeavor to speed up that possibility. Not that I have been very successful." The professor frowns, "you are losing me again.....just where did you come into the picture?"

Jesus continues, "as we already know, bipedal mammals, or mankind, in its various forms, mostly now extinct, having developed increasing brain power, more than any potential rivals, were able to modify and stabilize their environments, develop and control food production, also increase spare time and develop a thirst for travel. Travel allowed for new challenges, the experience of new environments etc. which rewarded those groups capable of recognizing and utilizing new opportunities. These changes continued mental, physical, psychological, and spiritual evolution. Unfortunately, the relative rate of progress in the last category has lagged dangerously behind and that's where I was scheduled to enter the scene."

The professor chuckles....."do I detect a significant degree of megalomania here? Haven't many deep thinkers in ethics and philosophy graced this planet, particularly in the past thousand years?" Jesus responds, "surely, but the cumulative effects of their often painful contributions have failed to ignite detectable progress even in their particular cultures. Collectively, their impacts have been on a minor scale, hardly detectable as the history of Homo sapiens emphatically illustrates! Constant wars, genocides, massive slavery etc. Do you need more proof? What is needed is a new relationship with MOTU, a new covenant, if you like. MOTU has grown tired of broken covenants and all the hubris and tribal arrogance that has accompanied them. Still, MOTU is an optimist so that is where I was to enter the scene."

Realizing that his control of the conversation is eroding, the professor endeavors to steer the topic, "this discussion is moving dangerously close to theology and I remain apprehensive of your stated role in providing solutions to human weakness. However, this verbal interplay has been interesting for me and hopefully to most of my students."

Jesus interrupts him, "I was granted unusual abilities in order to bring about accelerated change in human spirituality, his acknowledged place in Nature, and his appreciation of Nature's bounties. In my own earthly cultural experience I was up against story lines extolling aggression, dominion over the natural world, in fact, dominion by Man over everything, including peoples of other cultures, and a self-proclaiming fancy that my people were chosen by MOTU! The hubris is staggering, and still exists, although MOTU has excused their persistent disobedience too many times and his Universal patience is not an inexhaustible well!"

The professor holds up his hand, "for a fellow who just wandered in here and has consumed much of my lecture period but not without my intellectual tolerance, you have run a good mile. But now you are wasting our time……these students have spent a great deal of money on tuition fees and expect to pass my course, move on to graduation and prospects of employment. Therefore I must ask you to vacate the hall before I call Security.

Jesus steps into the aisle and thanks him for his time and patience. "Perhaps I should have appeared in a psychology, philosophy, or theology lecture. I apologize if I have accelerated your lecture schedule."

He quickly moves to the doors and disappears. On the steps outside, he is relieved that the campus police are nowhere in sight and finally decides to change his costume to a shiny black suit and reversed collar by blinking his eyes. He now looks like a respectable man of the cloth.

Walking across the campus he sights an impressive older building, almost gothic, and contrasting to the neo-Soviet building with the vertically-fluted walls of brutalized concrete. This older building contains the College of Theology, dominated , of course, by the Anglican Church of Canada. He mounts the steps and glides in through the massive wooden doors. A notice indicating a seminar on the New Testament catches his eye so he proceeds to the lecture hall, enters quietly and takes a seat in an empty back row. The professor is addressing the class which has just commenced. "You are all familiar with the Petrine Theory so we can move on to the concept of the Trinity, can't we?" A student holds up her hand, "before we go on, why is it called the Petrine Theory? I understand that Peter clearly stated that Jesus gave him authority to organize the Christian church with him as the Rock."

The lecturer clears his throat, "academically it is safer to call it a theory as belief without proof is frowned on……especially in Science. At this point, Jesus stands up saying "I agree with you. Anyway, I don't recall telling Peter to call himself the Rock or to proceed to organize a church that has no essential difference from the Temple in Jerusalem! My brothers and I, especially James, were dead set against the continuation of over-organized and bureaucratic religious organizations dedicated to concentrating power and authority in their hands, also with the monetary opportunities! How many hours did my twin brother Thomas, my elder brother James, and I spend harassing in the Temple, rejecting the "business as usual" attitudes among the Sanhedrin…..and their materialistic obsessions? That's why we organized the Essenes and moved to the mountains!"

The professor waves his hand, inviting Jesus to come forward to the stage. "I appreciate your style of speech, speaking allegorically as the Messiah himselfl! Very effective and attcntion-getting! I see that you are a minister. Welcome to the seminar group and please come forward and take a chair adjacent to mine. You are certainly not the first one to question the Petrine Theory. It has a long and arduous history involving much genocidal activity promoted by the Roman and Avignon Popes who diligently defended established dogma. That is, dogma developed at various international meetings……we call them "statements of faith" don't we, a rather unholy alliance between faith and dogma, in my mind. He is obviously trying to impress his students with his liberalism.

Taking the proffered chair, Jesus smiles at the professor of theology. "I see that you are a progressive theologian…..at least in your mind, if not your actions. You were about to discuss the concept of the Trinity……another enormous leap into dogma, to be sure! I have heard many leaps! No wonder the Jews and the Moslems find that concept troubling……actually, illogical! I believe it is tommy rot myself! I do admit making a number of outlandish claims during my preaching days…..perhaps some bordering on arrogance, but claiming to be both God and his Son isn't one of them! It's such an insult to MOTU, isn't it?"

The prof raises his hand, "excuse me! MOTU? What or who is MOTU?" Jesus apologizes for moving so fast, "It's an acronym for Master of the Universe, Master not having identity awarded normally to personalities. The term is more acceptable to those who have passed over and realize the dogmatic shortcomings in all major religions, particularly those reflecting Western culture." The professor endeavors to hide his uncertainty by returning to Trinity concepts. "You are talking like an adherent of Socianism, is that true? I had planned to cover that subject in a subsequent seminar."

He writes SOCIANISM on the blackboard. Perhaps our visiting minister would care to define the term?" Jesus rises and goes to the board, "I prefer to simply identify its meaning in terms of what it fails to support in Christian dogma." He writes down ten identities:

1. The concept of the Trinity is rejected.

2. Jesus Christ was a man, not divine, and the begotten son of Joseph.

3. His mother, Mary, wasn't virginal prior to his birth. (An aside, after all, he had several brothers, a twin brother Thomas, and an older brother, James who became head of the Essenes.)

4. Mary cannot be called the Mother of God, from 2. above.

5. The concept of Original Sin is debasing and obscene. (it's difficult to make babies feel guilty)

6. There is no place as Hell. (another aside, there's plenty of hell here on this planet)

7. Christ's death and passion cannot insure redemption from personal sins. (Aside, I love that poem by Omar….the moving finger writes and having writ moves on…….he was a Moslem)

8. Free Will in mankind is self-evident from our transgressions.

9. From 8, pre-destination or fate is rejected out of logic.

10. Similarly, Gods (MOTU) may be omnipotent but only in the sense of knowing what will happen, not what MIGHT happen. (Aside, this allows the advent of free will in human affairs…… perhaps merely a philosophical nit-picking statement).

He regains his chair and watches the students furiously note-taking from the board. The professor, clapping his hands in admiration, "thank you sir! That is a coherent list that soucians have held for some 600 years. On the subject of free will…….and many philosophers have made their bread and butter here……if one considers the range of Christian interpretations over the past two thousand years, free will seems hardly debating. Then, if one adds all the theological interpretations since the time of Nebachednezzar……" (he looks at the clock). "I must bring this seminar to a close. I would like to thank you, minister, for your inciteful remarks, and for the allegorical role of Jesus that you have played with such feeling, indeed passion!" Jesus replies, "having enjoyed this experience, I leave here hoping that your students, with your assistance, will come to better appreciate the historical role of dogma in theology. The various strains of much I find worrisome, such as the pseudo-academic attempts to debate the number of angels capable of depositing their posteriors on the head of a pin! Too many words and not enough action! A Chinese poet remarked that the more talking and thinking, the further from the truth! The wizardry and showmanship in Christian churches is quite ludicrous! Just how many jaws had the donkey on my fateful journey into Jerusalem……and all the bones and fingernails of so-called saints, that's surely most bizarre! On arrogance, the declaration of the Pope's infallibility was decided at the First Vatican Council in 1870. Control, control, control, nearly two thousand years after my earthly demise! Goodbye to you all." He stands, and evaporates, leaving everyone rubbing their eyes.

ENCOUNTERS AT A BANK

Returning to downtown Vancouver from the park-like headlands and the UBC campus,he finds himself walking past an imposing neo-Hellenic and massive concrete bank building. A pair of policemen are accosting a street person sitting on the steps near the revolving brass doors. He steps into the fray, "excuse me! What has this fellow done wrong?"

One cop looks up and recognizes Jesus as a minister, "this is a respectable area, reverend, and his presence here ……begging……. is embarrassing clientele, so we are asking him to move along." Jesus comments, "I don't find his presence here unwarranted, and I'm sure that he would agree. I note that he is obviously in need of some assistance, being badly dressed, in rags, unwashed, and somewhat wild-eyed."

The second cop opines, "I see that you are a liberal man of the cloth, perhaps you could persuade him to move along peacefully? If he takes much more of our time we will take him in and book him on a charge of vagrancy. The bank manager is quite piqued at his continued presence here, right next to his revolving doors."

Jesus chuckles, "ah! more revolving doors! How interesting! They accelerate the comings and goings of people spending, borrowing, and lending money! I think that this poor vagrant has chosen wisely in his selection of location…..lots of exposure could lead to the occasional coin being dropped into his ragged cap!" The first cop, in a terse tone, "come on, Reverend, don't make our job any harder than it is already! People are busy breaking laws all around us……..running red lights, speeding, knocking down pedestrians in crosswalks, shop-lifting, purse-snatching, selling themselves. The list of crimes is endless! Give us a break!"

With his right foot now resting on the first step, Jesus adopts a philosophical air, "the last two crimes are noteworthy……a needy person snatches a purse out of desperation and this is considered criminal behavior but the banker who snatches from private accounts, think more than nearly 20 per cent interest on credit cards, is lauded as an upstanding, honest citizen …….as is the hidden moneylender who fails to actively contribute to productive work! Also, prostitution is narrowly-defined…..I wonder how many people going through these revolving doors are prostituting themselves in one way or another, selling their souls, so to speak, to obtain money?" Both cops look at each other in exasperation. "Come on, Reverend, we have a job to do!" "So do I, says Jesus…..we all do"!

One of the cops has a suggestion: "I have a suggestion, why don't you act like the Good Samaritan and invite this beggar somewhere for a cup of coffee? How's that for a solution?" Jesus says that the bank may have coffee for its clientele, "I don't carry money and have little use for it, literally or figuratively." The second cop interjects, "don't get any absurd ideas about inviting this bum into the bank, in search of a cup of coffee! We could have you up on a charge of obstruction! We have our duty to perform!" The other cop slaps his side, "what the heck, it's Christmas!" Removing his wallet from his back pocket he offers a bill to Jesus. "Take this five dollar bill and take yourself and this bum off the street to a coffee bar." He hands Jesus the note.

The beggar eyes the bill, gets up off the steps and nods to Jesus. "Cuppa coffee sounds good to me.....kind of cold and windy here and pickins are slim anyway. Lotsa moolah here coming and going but out of my reach!" Jesus looks at him...."you're on for coffee, then! Thank you officers, have a good day, you have been most helpful." He and the beggar move off down the street as the cops return to their squad car and depart.

Looking at Jesus beside him, the beggar points out a coffee bar halfway-down on the next block. Jesus stops. "Actually, I don't drink coffee, tea, or coca cola.....sometimes a little wine......but we don't have enough money for wine. Here, take this paper and do what you like with it. I'm going back to have a word with the bank manager." They part company and Jesus returns to the bank.

As he enters the revolving doors he is greeted by a beaming, young receptionist who takes him to the manager's office. She knocks on the door, opens it on hearing his command to enter, and leaves to her position. The manager is sitting behind a large desk sipping a coffee, a pile of applications in front of him. Jesus smiles, "I was right, this bank does have coffee!" The bank manager looks up startled, "pardon me, reverend?" Jesus replies, "there was a confrontation a few minutes ago outside your premises involving a street person but I helped relieve that." The manager nods and smiles, "oh yes, Security had informed me that a beggar had deposited himself on the steps below the revolving doors and I instructed them to call the police. We can't have such sights right in front of the bank! It's bad for business and may affect customer relations. We are here to assist clients with their financial problems.....mortgages, tax accounts, investment portfolios, and the like. Beggars at the entrance don't exactly contribute to our up-scale image. Prosperity and financial growth hardly relate to beggars or other itinerants, do they?"

With a frown-knitted face, Jesus begs to differ. "Isn't prosperity intrinsically-linked with economic unfortunates? Someone has to gain at someone-else's expense, no? Isn't that recognition reflected in charitable works like subsidized housing, meals for the hungry, food stamps, clothing for the ragged, and free medical attention for the sick? Isn't it socially acceptable that there exists a low level of "give" for a very high level of "take"?"

The manager takes a swig of his coffee before replying, "reverend, you are misinterpreting my comments! This bank gives significant assistance to the needy, our employees contribute the all the annual charity drives, Red Feather Day, the Red Cross etc." Jesus remains dissatisfied with his answer, "these activities that you mention, they smack of a corporate nature, no? The organizers and chief officers are salaried from the donations? My idea of charity is quite personal,….. in the Now….as in a few kind words as the coin is dropped into the beggar's cup or shriveled hand…..from one fortunate human to a less-fortunate one…..accompanied with feelings from the heart. Giving to a large corporation-style organization seems to be more obligatory than personal charity…..and possibly also serving as a tax write-off!

At this last remark, the bank manager is getting peeved, "where have you been, for heavens sake! This is the twenty-first century! Everyone is busy getting things done, earning money to pay bills, meeting all the various expenses of modern living, automobiles, (perhaps several of them), house mortgages, insurance premiums, (in case the earner(s) die or become incapable of earning money, otherwise all the material gains could be clawed back), new furnishings, and clothing, vacations, etc."

Jesus nods sympathetically, "I appreciate all that but what does it have to do with personal charity……the simple act of uttering a kind word while giving a coin to a beggar on the wet street? I have observed that in Islamic cultures the faithful are expected to give ten per cent of their annual material wealth to charity. This tithing originates in the Old Testament but the gifting is done on a personal and private level…..not through tax write-offs or well-publicized donations, decals on one's front door stating the "WE Gave" sort of message."

The bank manager gulps down the remainder of his coffee, “this conversation is going nowhere….is there any way that I can help you with your personal or organizational finances? If not, I must insist that I return to my work. This pile of mortgage applications must be processed today! The real estate market is humming these days. Clients are fully aware that costs are steadily increasing and expect prompt assurance that their dream house is affordable before lending rates start to climb once more. I do thank you for dropping in, discussion has been interesting ….if a little off the beaten path.

By the way, on the subject of theology, I understand that Orthodox Jews are forbidden to charge interest when lending money to others of their kind. Interest is only acceptable (according to the Talmud), on loans made to non-Jews. Similarly, in Orthodox Islam, as in Iran, profits generated from accounts in the State Bank are disallowed, and they are transferred to State accounts and used in the public interest. How can such banks operate! Sharia Law has some 73 restrictions against usury!”

“If my memory serves me correctly”, says Jesus, ”in my religious training, the profit motive was associated with taking advantage of the unfortunate, an Old Testament concept, now completely out of fashion in capitalistic systems which operate on the assumption that maximizing profit is good business sense…..and totally necessary in the commercial world of competition rather than cooperation.” At this comment, the Bank manager says “enough, you are moving into political values so I must ask you to leave!” “Of course, says Jesus. We obviously have insufficient moral grounds in common. In parting, I would like to remind you of a certain parable concerning a rich man, the eye of a needle, and access into heaven. Good day!” He rises, shakes the manager’s hand and departs, leaving him somewhat pale and agitated.

AT ST. JOHN THE DIVINE CHURCH

Walking down Burrard Street, Jesus nears a church, wedged in between high rise office buildings. He reads the sign outside: Saint John the Divine, walks through the open door, takes a seat in the first pew and regards the altar and his icon pegged to the cross. Arching across the stage front he reads an intimidating message in large gold capital letters: SILENCE! GOD IS HERE! To himself, Jesus muses, "why silence? Why not HALLELUJAH! or WE ARE OVERJOYED AT YOUR PRESENCE!......or, WE RAISE OUR VOICES TO SING OF YOUR MIGHTY WORKS!

A man approaches, vacuuming the plush, red aisle carpet. As he nears the figure sitting in the first pew, this janitor begins to apologize for disturbing him. "Excuse me. Reverend, I will be quick about this.....but the Bishop has the eyes of a magpie, capable of spotting even a shred of lint on this aisle carpet. He is merciless in his lectures to me and reminds me of a sergeant I had in the army. I still shudder remembering his white glove inspections of my barracks. Scrubbing the latrine floors with toothbrushes was a living hell for us poor recruits.....and hard on the knees, too!"

"Please, take your time and do a good job, says Jesus. I'm reminded of a saying that I heard in a London Sunday School: cleanliness is next to Godliness. I wonder if churchmen so obsessed ever thought about ancient times in Christianity when the singular act of submergence during baptism was the only complete lavable event in the lives of so many? Other than in the River Jordan, water was scarce in those desert regions." The janitor chuckles, "guess things have changed! I remember the reluctant Saturday night baths in front of the fire. Even weekly baths were the source of audible groans from me and my brothers, especially from the last one in the tub!" Jesus smiles broadly, "I wonder when frequent baths, bodily scrubbing, the obsession with cleanliness replaced concern for clean thoughts and the seeking of a pure heart and mind?"

The janitor is enjoying this conversation, "it probably started with the advent of modern plumbing, I guess. Hot water heaters, daily showers, thick bath towels, and lotsa mirrors! Soap on a rope, hair shampoos, body washes…..the works! Yet, despite all this washing activity, there is voluminous dirty talk, off-color jokes, …..often pornographic in detail….and much swearing! Taking the Lord's name in vain is common practice!" Jesus, sucking his teeth, "hmmm! You had better finish your carpet-cleaning, I don't want to hold you up." The janitor nods and moves off to the rear. The sound of his vacuum cleaner grows faint as a door opens off to the side of the apse and a clergyman steps out wearing a purple vest. Seeing a fellow minister sitting in the first pew, he steps down and approaches him. The Bishop is a middle-aged, rotund individual who stands beside the first pew, "I hope that I'm not disturbing your thoughts. It's rare to see another churchman in the pews.

We are usually upstage, aren't we! I was intent on inspecting the aisle carpet for errant shreds. I've found the occasional earing, missed during the vacuuming rite! Once I found a handwritten note on the flyleaf torn from a prayer book suggesting a post-service tryst! That was probably directed at some young lady dressed to the nines in a new Spring outfit! That reminds me of that song from Camelot…..The Merry Month of May!" He proceeds to sing the first verse: "It's May, it's May, the lusty month of May, that lovely month when everyone goes blissfully astray. It's here, it's here, that certain time of year when tons of little wicked thoughts merrily appear. It's May, it's May, that gorgeous holiday, when every maiden itches for fun, wholesome or un, It's mad, depraved in every way, those dreary vows that everyone takes, everyone breaks, everyone makes divine mistakes, the lusty month of May! Do you like musicals? I thoroughly enjoy them, especially Gilbert and Sullivan operettas. A distinct change from our usual repertoire of hymns. Confidentially, I find Onward Christian Soldiers, Onward as to War, a bit much! The world news is sufficient reminder of Man's favorite pastime without pasting it onto a hymn!"

Jesus is regarding the Bishop rather quizzically, "yes, music soothes the savage beast in all of us, except martial music which stimulates the hearing and eyesight with waving pennants and thumping drums! All designed to raise the bold pressure, stamp the feet in cadence, and march away to some distant battlefield with the anticipation of spilling the blood of antagonists. Wasn't it Adolph Hitler in his book Mein Kampf who recommended keeping people marching as they are not then thinking! He had a good grasp of the human mind....at least the Teutonic one."

The Bishop, still emotionally riding his ditty, "you are an interesting fellow! I must admit, most of my cohorts are rather staid, bland personalities, seldom expressing more than a modicum of enthusiasm....... well, with the exception of the fire and brimstone types. Intuitively, I feel that you can be highly aroused on the right occasion. Am I right?" Jesus nods positively,"yes, I'm known to rouse a congregation to near-fever-pitch emotions.....sometimes to my disadvantage. I have also expressed considerable umbrage at situations encouraged by Temple officials that transgress the sanctity of that place." The Bishop, with a confused look, "the mention of Temple officials confuses me, what denomination are you associated with?"

Jesus replies, "my inclinations, based on considerable experience, are to avoid sectarianism. The proliferation of biblical interpretations has resulted in long-standing antagonisms, turf wars, verbal and written nit-picking. I fail to understand how and why we humans are so inclined to ignore or overlook the fundamental messages in favor of persistent argumentation. Look at the Disputations during the Middle Ages! How could serious and intelligent men argue so......in front of large audiences too, playing up minor points of interpretation that serve only to separate, to alienate, one group from another? The growth of sectarianism alarmed me in the past but one must resign oneself to the inevitable. Many developments were quite farcical, weren't they? Like the Nestorians who climbed up trees to pray..... to be closer to God! These tree-climbers were present in the court of Genghis Khan! The Mongols much have been much amused!

Another interesting group were the Collyridiamists in Arabia, about 300 years after my earthly demise. Mostly women, with priestesses who offered bread to my mother who they worshipped as a Mother Goddess. The list goes on……as for angels, they weren't officially recognized by the Catholic Church until the 1400's and what a flurry of veneration painting followed that decree, particularly in conjunction with the dogmas of perpetual virginity, my virgin birth, and my mother's bodily ascension to heaven as decreed in 1950 by Pope Pius XII. One artist even depicted my mother throwing down her girdle from heaven, I guess that she had no need for it there! The flabbergasting arrogance of naming all those hierarchical cohorts as saints……what next!"

The Bishop nods in apparent agreement, "we love to argue, find differences, amplify them, and use them as instruments of diversification, serving only to divide and conquer. This devilish propensity often led to wholesale slaughter, even the immolation of one's friends in the church! John Calvin burnt his friend, Servetus, over minor points…..since Servetus criticized his book! The thirst for power, ultimate authority and control has over-balanced interest in simple, fundamental truths? I think we have much in common, you and I, we realize that this historical process is still ongoing…..much like the Tower of Babel? Much to our discredit as church leaders, our ecumenical attempts are half-hearted, effectively serving in the media, that despite our underlying antagonisms, we are searching for common grounds, ego-fogged by distrust and orthodoxy."

"Appreciation of history, its lost opportunities, should serve to change human ways", says Jesus. "Even the threat of the Mongol invasions failed to prompt several Popes to do more than appeal to them to stop killing Christians. Two Mongol envoys met with Innocent IV in 1248. William of Rubruck , a Flemish Franciscan monk met Mangu Khan in Karakorum in 1254, noted that Nestorians were present in his court and participated in theological discussions there with Buddhists, Moslems, and other Christians. Mongols were tolerant of foreign religions, starting with Genghis Khan. Kublai Khan sent back the Polo brothers to Venice, requesting 100 ecclesiastics to his court to instruct in Christian theology. He also asks for a bottle of holy oil from the Sepulchre in Jerusalem.

This opportunity was wasted due to in-house wrangling and politics in appointing a new Pope. The oil reached Kublai Khan by way of Marco Polo on his extended return trip and two decades of service to Kublai Khan. Unfortunately, before Kublai could re-unite all the Mongol tribes, he died, and his relative, Haluga, surged West again and burnt the library at Baghdad, decimated Delhi in India and killed hundreds of thousands in the process." The Bishop laments, "opportunities lost. Our past is replete with them!"

Shall I go on, then, says Jesus. "Temur, a later Khan sent an embassy to the French Pope, Benedict XII in 1336. This Pope sent fifty representatives in 1338 but the Mongolian Empire dissolved shortly thereafter......bad timing. By then Islam had taken root, leading to the Moghul Empire in India and the Tumarid Empire in Central Asia under Tamerlane. Most of Asia could have been Christianized under the right conditions, perhaps staving off the collapse of the Byzantine Empire centered in Constantinople. Modern times may have been quite different had higher spiritual values been paramount." The Bishop comments, "historical analysis always contains much speculation but I wonder if Pope Gregory X regretted his dismissed opportunities.... or remembered the ignominious entreaties displayed by Pope Leo I when faced with Attila in 452 AD? With all the theological wrangling going on in the Catholic Church during those centuries, I wonder if mass conversion of the Asiatics could have been accomplished? All the necessary soul-searching!

Jesus raises his right fore-finger, "the common ground requires little soul-searching. In my preaching, I made a determined effort to set my message in simple terms. Not because I considered my congregations as dense but because the truths surrounding human behavior and related needs are universal. If people would just concentrate on the parables which defy being twisted and distorted, or otherwise manipulated, they would show the way to the good life. The proliferation of creeds would be avoided.

Now, the urge to proselytize, I have a soft spot for my twin brother, Thomas, who's discovered Acts circulated widely in the fourth century. He threw a wrench into the dogma machinations that ultimately spread. Many of my parables are recorded there and there was a wide-spread tradition in early church documents acknowledging that Thomas and I were twins. His writings, discovered in the Egyptian desert in the 1960's failed to mention crucifixion, resurrection, final judgment, and a messianic role for me. His works weren't declared heretical until the Council of Trent in 1545-63. But Saint Jerome declared about 400 AD that all my brothers were just cousins!

Thomas's guidance on the need to overcome ego-related lusts and attachments might have served well had his writings been recognized more than 1900 years ago. He was a fearless preacher in India, China and Persia, founded more than a dozen churches in Southern India, forbade adherence to casteism in those that he baptized, but was speared by an outraged Brahmin in Madras."

The Bishop is now becoming alarmed at the conversation of Jesus referring to parables and to Saint Thomas as his brother. "You have been speaking in terms of past pastoral work and in terms of the parables. I take it that you are no longer an active man-of-the-cloth? Your reference to Thomas as your brother……please elucidate for me." Jesus touches his arm, "I have not spread the word for many centuries and my identification with my brother, Thomas, and the parables, no doubt confuse you. Confidentially, I am wearing this garb to avoid further interactions with the police in public where my traditional clothes generated considerable concern, even hostility and accusation. Isn't my present costume reassuring to you and conducive to our discussion?" The Bishop replies, "I admit that the cloth stimulates comraderie and I appreciate that you are retired at such a young age but my curiosity remains aroused. What is your usual garb and why do you speak as though your usual clothes are accepted elsewhere?"

Jesus realizes that the time has come for him to depart. "I must leave you now with your curiosity and some possible forthcoming realizations. We have had an enjoyable hour together and other locations require my attention." He smiles, offers his right hand in friendship. Then standing, he physically backs out through his pew and the five rows of pews behind him, turns in the aisle, appears in his white robe, sandals, long hair and beard, then disappears in a flash of intense light.

The Bishop is left gripping the back of the first pew to steady himself, with transfixed face. An overpowering realization brings amazement to his expression......how to deal with this experience? Announce it to the world? Risk being classified as a nut case..... submit to a sanity hearing? Lose his Bishopric at the insistence of the Archbishop and his congregation? Renounce his position and quietly fade away.....perhaps to India to follow in the footsteps of Thomas? Oh, such agony and potential embarrassment .....after singing joyful, hedonistic ditties to the Redeemer himself! Inspections of the red aisle carpet have faded in his feelings of reduced self-importance.

IN THE CENTRAL LIBRARY

Jesus switches back to his street clothes, reversed collar and all, and wanders up West Georgia Street, enters the Main library, finds a chair in the Reference Section, and begins to read the Vancouver Sun. Shortly, a middle-aged, slim,and bearded man sits down at the adjacent table, sets down a pile of books, and starts scanning one of them. Jesus notices that all the titles of this fellow's books involve psychic phenomena and is intrigued. He looks up from his newspaper and announces loudly that someone has won forty million dollars in a lottery and the winner maintains that he got the numbers in a dream. His comment does the trick and the adjacent literature searcher looks up saying, "that's quite interesting. Maybe the winner is a psychic but doesn't realize it."

Jesus moves to an adjoining seat at the table. "Why should number combinations have any other-worldly significance. Perhaps it was just chance! Will other lottery enthusiasts now get busy, dreaming up number sequences in their sleep!" The searcher shows signs of defensive message in his facial expression, "I take it that you are a skeptic when it comes to paranormal events or experiences?" Jesus parries his comment, by events, do you mean situations that cannot be explained by evidence, that is, by facts?"

The searcher slowly closes his book and takes that comment as needing some elucidation from him, "considerable literature exists on unexplained experiences, for example, on near death experiences. Many patient experiences have been documented by medical doctors and nurses, such as out of body experiences where the patient dies, floats up from their bed and watches the medical staff frantically deal with cardiac arrest, giving injections, applying defibrillators, thumping the patient's chest etc. Revived patients have described such activities in detail, even knowing which thigh the injection was applied to…… or that several ribs were fractured during resuscitation attempts.

The example that really astounded me was the case of the female patient in the Toronto General Hospital. She left her bed, floated up through three floors and out of the concrete building. Looking down on the building, she saw a tennis shoe lying on a third floor window sill. The following day, during medical inspection, she described her experience to both MD and nurse. Leaving her to attend to other patients, the nurse eventually went up to the third floor and found a tennis shoe on a window ledge!"

Jesus nods as if in agreement, "that could be a coincidence but I do agree that many such phenomena have been recorded and attested by reliable witnesses, events unexplainable by what is called reality. I've had such experiences myself. May be all of you have the ability to "see" beyond accepted reality but most people lose this ability as they grow up, become conditioned by parental discipline and a formal education lock-stepped into rational interpretations for all events in our experiences."

The searcher is now getting quite enthusiastic, "I've had several psychic experiences during my lifetime but I failed to recognize them until I had an out-of-body experience, an OBE, a few years ago." "OBE's you call them, I've had several of those myself, says Jesus. "Would you care to describe yours?" The searcher takes a deep breath, "I've only confided to a few close friends but now realize that psychiatric literature fails to account for my OBE which is quite different from the OBE's of others, some involving aliens, for several reasons. I was sailing down the West Coast of this Province with a friend when we were capsized during a sudden and vicious storm with winds exceeding seventy knots. We spent eighteen days in that overturned yacht before being rescued some seventy miles west of the Brooks Peninsular by a freighter returning to Japan."

Jesus leans forward with great interest, "that must have been a frightening experience, tell me about the OBE." The searcher continues, "the first two days were terrifying, with huge waves sweeping over the boat which was half full of water rushing from one end to the other as the surging waves passed over us. I had the OBE during the second night……I left the boat, looking down as I ascended. Looking up at the night sky which was clearing, I observed that the stars were passing to my left, that I was travelling to my right. I was not a bit afraid but curious……where was I going? The stars then disappeared and were replaced by a blinding, white light coming from behind me. I was laying on a white couch, like marble, but comfortable, knowing that I couldn't look directly into the light but could look sideways across the floor towards a perimeter of arcing, blue-white energy that rose about five feet from the floor.

Occasionally, I could see shapes moving behind this curtain of energy. The floor was patterned in a black and white geometric configuration, …..I can still see that pattern clearly in my mind. I felt that everything was being taken out of my head……recorded, perhaps….. then the brilliant overhead light stopped and I found myself again in the night sky. But the stars were moving to my right and I concluded that I was returning to the boat where I did wake up, back in that terrible predicament, with the message……you have been sent back, you are not ready and there are more things to accomplish."

Jesus comments, "that experience…..so detailed in specific yet not unusual observations. You were not afraid, at all?" "That's what is so incredible, I was totally relaxed and observant……finding the event both lucid and interesting..….thinking logically with interest throughout my time away from the boat. Four days before we were rescued, I had a dream that we would be picked up by a freighter going to the Orient. I had several surprises after our rescue which led to my meeting someone who became my second wife. I will tell you of one. I was packing up my wife's collection of old National Geographic magazines and leafing through them found an article on the Taj Mahal with beautiful photographs, one of which showed the geometric floor in a particular room. I was instantly shocked as I recognized the patterning as identical to the one in my OBE!"

How did you react to that vision? "Being a well-trained research scientist, I had considerable difficulty dealing with the OBE and the flooring patterns. Naturally, I wanted to interpret these experiences and undertook an exhaustive search of the psychiatric and related literature on dream states, visions, OBE accounts and any related medical histories. I found no parallels to my experience, other than the bright light. In many near-death accounts, patients reported bright lights, looking down tunnels, seeing dead relatives etc."

"My experiences (OBE's), says Jesus, were different in one major respect, they are described by relatives and companions who saw me after my death in several locations……and spoke to me." The searcher comments, "you mean that you didn't share those experiences with them?" "Well, it was rather like a play…..I was seeing them onstage…..myself with them yet not actually with them…..as though a cloned image of myself did the interacting. May be we can be in more than one place at particular times. That ability has been described by several mystics throughout human history."

The searcher nods in emphatic agreement, "there does seem to be a dimensional screen within which most of us are confined but extraordinary individuals can peek through. Some psychics can tune in to messages from the deceased, describe physical situations involving them prior to their demise, even to acknowledge their presence while doing so." "You must be familiar, says Jesus, that many people, both in and outside church hierarchies have claimed to converse with angels conveying instructions from God. One ethnic group to whom I was connected, claim to be chosen by God, or Yahveh, as they call him, and have amassed a written record documenting their privileged position with the Almighty, despite his several condemnations of them and their broken Covenants!"

The searcher chuckles, "the range of wishful thinking is enormous but the ultimate results have been bitter argumentation, genocide, and all forms of cruelty. But we are straying from our personal psychic experiences and I cannot escape from my intellectual conditioning in Science. In our modern times, our expanded abilities now allow us to determine how electrons dance about their nuclei yet psychic experiences persist and often involve intelligent, logically-trained individuals. The psychic experiences of Bishop Pike, Episcopalian Bishop of California come to mind. Trained as a lawyer, author of legal manuals, a captain in Naval Intelligence during WWII, he serves as a good example. He kept diaries with scrupulous care, probably reflecting his training in military intelligence. Do you know of him?"

"Yes, I do. I was particularly interested in his life-time search for the historical Jesus, also his off-the-cuff remark while being photographed in his official robe and paraphernalia at his swearing-in as Bishop: just to let you fellows (photographers) know, the crook is the one on the right!" The searcher laughs at that remark and adds, "the more we talk, the closer we seem to be, I've had a number of psychic experiences but would like to share my first one with you. I was almost ten years old and was staying with my 84 year-old great aunt in Norfolk, in the English countryside. My older sister and I were sent to live with her during the massive bombing of London where we lived. After church on Sundays, she would take us on long hikes, once to a local chapel on the Sandringham Estate owned by the Royal family.

I ran ahead into Saint Mary Magdalene Chapel and stood in front of the altar. Standing there I felt very light-headed and felt waves of strong vibration emanating from my feet, rising up through my body. As my great aunt and sister approached me I said that I felt really funny. My great aunt looked down at the red carpet and noted that I was standing on a brass plate commemorating Prince John who died at my age and was buried in the graveyard. Perhaps if you step off that plate you may feel better, she said. I promptly did just that and the vibrations ceased. Many years later I recalled that experience and realized that it was a psychic event.

In my later years as a biological researcher, working in the Queen Charlotte Islands, I visited an abandoned village called Skedans, located on the outer edge of Cumshewa Inlet. I took a Haida native with me by boat. Coming ashore I stepped out of the boat with the tender rope and pulled the boat up on the sandy beach. Standing there as the Haida climbed from the boat I was struck by the loud laughter and shouting of playing children all around me on the beach. Do you hear anything, I asked my companion. He answered, I hear nuttin'. Most of that village had died of small pox many decades ago and the few survivors vacated the village and went to the Skidegate native community. There were several skulls half-buried in the ground moss in the area. I realized the enormity of their cultural tragedy and the vulgarity of colonialism."

That colonial powers acted as they did should not surprise you, said Jesus. "Usurping land, stealing their artwork, denying them the potlatch ceremony, and shipping off their children to church schools where they were punished for speaking their own language? Look what Moses did to the Midianites, killing all the males, men and boys, all married females, and keeping the young virgin females for tribal reproduction (Numbers 31). Moses claimed that God had given him instructions!" The searcher says that he is familiar with the Old Testament, "surely, Moses was the first recorded genocidal maniac, plundering, murdering, and stealing lands of others. Isn't that what the Jews in Palestine have been doing since the middle 1800's there, accelerating since the end of WWI?"

Jesus nods sadly, "they are certainly persistent in their arrogance and willful denial of their wisest religious leaders since the Exodus. It has not gone unnoticed and their redemption will require much soul searching and repentance. There remains a significant difference between philosophy and religions as the former relies on reasoning and logical thinking, most usefully disciplined with moral concepts. Some of the ancient Greeks had valuable ideas. It has been fruitful chatting to you about psychic phenomena. Is there value in including them in modern concepts of reality? I must leave you now." He rises and disappears down the adjacent staircase.

That evening, under a clear and star-lit sky, a flood of telephone calls inundate the local radio stations and police departments. A large UFO, outlined as triangular by bright lights is seen hovering momentarily over the city, and suddenly disappears into the night sky.

The Fireman's Lift

(On the outcome of winning the lottery)

PREFACE

Lotteries have always lurked in my mind as strategies to surreptitiously avoid increasing taxes through government pandering of the subconscious desires of people to solve their economic problems. Personal dreams that winning large amounts of cash would elevate one to the class of capitalists in modern society, the dream of being relieved of debt worries or simply an expressed desire of material greediness. The only major lottery that I remember from childhood was the Irish Sweepstakes for which one could buy tickets with the profits going to children's hospitals in Ireland.

I notice that in Britain, following the end of World War Two, when rationing and related restrictions continued for some time, reflecting the dire economic straits of a people that had endured materiel and food suffering for over six years, that the penny football pools sprang to life with great success and public enthusiasm, the minor investment in ventured pennies reflecting the economic state of the common people.

Question popped into my mind concerning the burgeoning development of governmental and private lotteries all over the world, for the most part in nations suffering from several economic ills and low standards of living. The questions popped: how were these fortunate winners affected and what did they do with their winnings? Did they all become happier and more relaxed, were they generous with their winnings, did others find themselves embroiled in family disruption, did their children ultimately benefit from parental winnings, how did the unmarried winners react to their fortune?

These questions cannot be answered easily since they involve private lives, potential violation of privacy by snooping individuals perhaps primarily independent of government. An academic case could be made by sociologists but that would suffer from massive reaction of those with neo-liberal mindsets, all defenders of capitalism as we endure it in modern times, and bureaucratic managers of lottery corporations who are reaping salaries comparable to their ilk in alternate corporations. To answer this intriguing set of questions in my own mind, I began writing of a theoretical individual who won twenty-eight million dollars in Lotto Canada, a retired fireman living in Calgary, Alberta. Not surprisingly, his life changes and economic decisions reflect my own tendencies.

A HABIT PAYS OFF

Fred Stuart is a retired Calgary fireman. Fred is 67 years old, a widower, having lost his wife to cancer four years ago. His primary companion is his Dalmatian dog who keeps him company in his utilitarian house located on a hilly two acres located on the outskirts of Calgary. Following his wife's sudden death some four years ago, his family doctor, Dr. Brightsen, concerned about Fred's health and sustained depression following his wife's death, recommended geriatric service last year. A geriatric nurse, Lila Nunez, takes up the task of Fred's dietary needs. She prepares dinner for him on Mondays and Fridays. Fred has three children, two girls, Silvia and Melody, and a boy, Toby. They all live in Calgary but lead relatively different lives and are occupied with their own realities.

Lila arrives in her rattletrap car on a Friday ready to prepare his dinner. Fred and Lila have developed a friendly relationship that concentrates on her motherly concern for his diet. Fred meets her at the door, hello, Lila! I get a decent dinner tonight!"

Lila, climbing out of her car with a bag of groceries, "you know this is Friday so you shouldn't be surprised. How long have I been doing this? Nearly a year! You retired people! Not busy enough to remember what day it is. Anyway, how are you feeling?" Fred is still grinning at the door, "you are something! You come breezing in here all cheery and sprite! I look forward to your visits even if I don't always remember what day it is. You brighten up my life, Lila, and Carlo (Dalmatian) always welcomes you at the door! I'm feeling fine, really fine!"

Entering the house, Lila sets the grocery bag down on the kitchen table, "I've brought some groceries...hamburger and such...and am going to make you Swedish meatballs with egg noodles. Does it sound weird that a Mexican RN would cook Swedish meatballs!" They both laugh and Fred says, "as you know, Doc Brightsen suggested that I should quit trying to survive on TV dinners and popcorn.....and sent you over. What a lecture you gave me on dietary needs for old fogies like me, so I caved in. Thank God, he sent me a senorita yet.....to cook me Swedish meatballs! Carlo hears that rattling Honda of yours way before you turn in to the driveway and starts his serenade!" Carlo is wagging his tail and looking up at Lila who gives him a pat.

Lila responds, "Fred, you are my most cooperative client. You eat what I fix and you follow my diet instructions like a boyscout working on a merit badge! I've brought a three-bean salad, too, that should last you a couple of days. Out of some twenty patients that Doc Brightsen has saddled me with.....and some of them are inclined to be cantankerous, you are the model one! You get the prize!" Fred, reaching down to give Carlo a pat, "you're just saying that because the Easter dance is coming up at the Masonic Lodge and we had such a good time there last year!" Lila grins, "quit teasing me! We did have fun there, didn't we? I think it was the first time in many a year that you kicked up your heels, no?" Fred nods his head slowly, "yes, I had been quite the hermit since Rosalie passed away. God, how time flies! That was nearly four years ago! What made you get involved with geriatrics anyway?"

Lila sitting down at the kitchen table, "it's a long story...do you really want to hear it?" "As a curious old fireman, yes. How did you ended up in Canada, having been born and raised in Mexico?" Their relationship is based on informality and honesty and Fred takes her admonitions about his health with appreciation. This allows him to ask Lila some personal questions. He also sits down at the kitchen table and Lila begins to answer Fred's questions. "I got married after graduating from Nursing School in Mexico City but that turned out to be a catastrophe. After my divorce, I looked after my mother in her last years. That opened my eyes to old age difficulties. A nurse doesn't usually see geriatric patients until they are quite advanced and in hospital or a long-term nursing home. I got to know the onset of physical and mental disabilities from my mother's case. Knowing how energetic, alert, and optimistic she was before she fell and broke her hip and became forgetful. As she grew steadily worse and Alzheimer's set in, I decided to look after her full-time, rather than put her in an institution. In Mexico, the desirable facilities are privately run and very expensive, hence, out of the question in our case".

Fred, breaking in, "you were a loving and dutiful daughter, your mother was very fortunate, in that way. So, after she died what made you decide to come to Canada?" He gets up and puts the kettle on for some tea and Lila continues, "frankly, I wanted to make a fresh start. A divorcee in the Mexican culture is put in a difficult position socially and psychologically. Mexico is a very Catholic country! I was in my middle thirties, had no other family ties. Besides, Mexico City is so crowded, noisy, smoggy .....I wanted to quiet time but not in any rural areas of Mexico. So, Canada beckoned and as an experienced nurse I was warmly welcomed. Also, I had heard of Calgary...the

Stampede...the wild and open West. Everyone was so friendly and down-to-earth here."

The kettle whistles and Fred prepares the tea. From the stove he grins mischieviously, "with those flashing black eyes and infectious smile, I'm surprised that you haven't been roped and branded by now.....by some ambitious cowboy!" Ha!, answers Lila, "Fred! I'm not a spring heifer! Anyway, next time, if there ever is a next time, I don't want to be roped and branded! I've had my fill of macho types..... the Latino male! Ego, bravado, and narcissism! Guess I'm showing my cultural shift, aren't I? Cultural freedoms change ones outlook on life." Bringing the tea paraphernalia to the table, Fred regains his seat, "I think I know what you mean, even though I haven't travelled myself. Well, Saskachewan to Alberta, that's hardly a broad cultural experience! We've known each other for nearly a year now and I feel that I can talk to you confidentially...is that ok?" Lila laughs, "oh, you have secrets you'd like to tell me?" "It's nothing very personal says Fred.....or may be it is! You know that I have been buying lottery tickets for several months at the gas station when I fill up?" Lila nods affirmatively, "yes, I took it as a good sign that you were coming out of your shell and getting out of the house more often!"

Fred, "that's true! Anyway, I always check the winning numbers... for something to do, I guess....for the hell of it!" Fred pauses, pours their tea and takes a deep breath. "From the newspaper, the winning number for Lotto Canada is the same one as on my last ticket.... it's the same number combination! I've checked it five times..... no mistake.....I have the winning number! The prize is 28 million dollars!" Lila stirs her tea and looks at Fred steadily, "you are sure of it? Perhaps we should check it again together......I woudn't want to see you disappointed, particularly when you are alone."

Fred gets up and walks over to the fireplace, "I'll get the ticket, it's behind the clock on the mantelpiece. The Calgary Herald is on the kitchen table next to you". They both sit down at the table and Fred places the paper page results next to the ticket]. "Ok, Lila, I'll read off the numbers on the ticket and you check them against the newspaper. Then we'll reverse the procedure, you read them off the ticket, ok?" Lila, shifting in her chair, "this is getting exciting. I've never bought lottery tickets either in Mexico or here. In Mexico, it seems that only the desperately poor buy them…..it's their only possible way out of grinding poverty."

Fred, grasping the ticket after putting on his reading glasses, "here goes: 543 219 805 7791". Lila, somewhat startled, "that's what I get here! My God! Change places! They do that and Lila reads off the numbers on the ticket. 543 219 805 7791."

Fred shouts, "that's it, then! I've won 28 million dollars! Lucky that I checked the numbers. Sometimes I forget! I've found tickets weeks later and checked them as losers at the gas station. Guess I should call in to the telephone number and let them know". Lila raises her right palm, "I suggest that you wait a few days…..to collect your thoughts. It is remotely possible that the newspaper has misprinted the results. Anyway, get prepared for an avalanche of publicity and phone calls. Does that sound reasonable?" Fred nods appreciatively and Lila continues, "another suggestion, don't let your kids know before the official results are made public. That will give you a chance to think what you want to do with all that money!" Scratching his scalp, Fred comments, "those are wise suggestions…..I need some breathing space. After all, how often does a retired working stiff stumble on a gold mine? Thanks for verifying the numbers with me and let's be quiet about it for a few days...at least for the weekend."

Taking a sip of her tea, Lila replies, "don't worry about me! You tell the world when you are ready...it's your show! Right now I'm going to start dinner. This might be the last meal we have together... who knows what you will decide to do with your new life?" Fred, laughing, "come on, Lila! You know me better than that! I'm a retired Calgary fireman, not very sophisticated or cultured...but sensible and conservative. Don't think that all this potential money is going to change me into some hedonistic playboy of the Western World! Right now I'm looking forward to a plate of your Swedish meatballs!

We should make this a celebratory dinner, just in case. I'll crack that bottle of red wine someone gave me last Christmas while you are slaving at the stove! You will stay and eat with me? I'll take Carlo out meanwhile for a breath of fresh air and some exercise. Carlo and I are both getting a bit chubby in our sedentary ways." Fred leaves the kitchen whistling for Carlo to fetch the leash while Lila turns to the refrigerator.

An hour later Fred and Carlo return, both panting from the exertion of climbing up the hill in back of the house. Their return is announced by Carlo bounding in the door. Both Fred and Carlo are savoring the kitchen odors emanating from the stove. Lila suggests that he feed the dog before they sit down to eat and to open the bottle of red wine. She is stirring the meatballs in gravy and waiting for the egg noodles to finish cooking. Fred uncorks the wine bottle and sets out the dishes, cutlery, and wine glasses on the kitchen table then feeds Carlo a pan full of biscuits. Carlo sets in with gusto, making a racket pushing the pan over the kitchen floor, coming to rest under the table. As Lila prepares the dinner plates, Fred pours the wine, then they sit down to eat.

Fred raises his glass and toasts their dinner, diving in and exclaiming his appreciation for the food between mouthfuls. Lila smiles and watches him eat with such joy, and joins in. After dinner, Lila prepares to leave for town and hints that he should do the dishes before she returns on Monday evening. Waving, she roars off into the night, the sounds of her rattling car becoming faint as she enters the highway.

Saturday and Sunday, Fred spends most of the time gardening in his vegetable plot but he calls Lila Sunday evening, "hello Lila! Yes, I'm fine. Spend most of the weekend pulling weeds and thinking. I find that gardening is close to meditation and pulling weeds, clears the brain. I hope you are coming tomorrow?

There's no reason why our schedule should change, is there, she replies. "I'm calling the lottery people first thing in the morning, to confirm my win" says Fred. Lila replies, "I'll be there in the afternoon, Fred. Should I go shopping for New York steaks or a plump roasting chicken with mashed potatoes, gravy and peas?" Whatever you like, says Fred. Just put it on the bill…..both sound delicious. See you tonight, then?" They both hang up their phones, wondering about tomorrow and the Lotto ticket. Fred goes out to his chicken house, collects a few eggs from his five hens, and checks their food and water. Carlo accompanies him and sniffs the pen periphery for signs of raccoons or other marauding animals.

VERIFYING THE TICKET NUMBER

Fred calls the Lotto number in Toronto on Monday morning after breakfast. "Hello, I need to confirm my lottery ticket number....I think its the winner". A secretary answers……"just a minute, I'll put you through to Mr. Williams". (Fred hears the extension phone ringing). "Hello, this is Mike Williams. To whom am I speaking?" "This is Fred Stuart here in Calgary and I think I have the winning ticket for the last draw". "You think you have the winner for the latest draw, says Williams. "Yes, I've checked it upteen times with the Calgary Herald paper and a friend checked the numbers with me". "You could check your ticket at an outlet in Calgary". "Frankly I don't trust them.... heard too many stories about winners being cheated."

"I understand, says Williams. I am flying into Calgary Wednesday morning to our local office. We could meet there sometime after lunch." "I'd rather not go into downtown. I'll give you my address and phone number and we can meet here at the house. Is that alright with you?" "Sure, why not. You sound very certain and I would like to be there when we confirm you as the winner." Fred gives him his address and phone number: 311 Pine Canyon Road, RR1. Tele 487-8935. Fred, "See you here then on Wednesday afternoon. Be sure to bang on the door, I may be taking a nap. My dog will hear you anyway and will wake me." He then hangs up the phone. Fred debates calling his kids then decides to follow Lila's advice and wait until after the official confirmation.

Lila arrives at 5pm, armed with groceries and Fred helps carry them in to the kitchen. Fred, "I called Toronto about the ticket and some big mucky-muck by the name of Williams is flying out Wednesday to check the numbers and will be here at the house after lunch. He wanted to know why I haven't checked them with a local outlet and I told him straight out that there have been too many stories about people being cheated out of their winnings. He didn't quibble about that". Lila replies, "you are going to be on tender-hooks until Wednesday, aren't you? Drumming his fingers on the kitchen table, Fred replies, actually, I am feeling a bit paranoid....this ticket is worth a pile of money and Carlo and I are going to guard it with the double-barreled shotgun. Who can say how many peoplewill know this winning ticket's location in the meanwhile? Patting his arm, Lila replies, "calm down, now. Just put it in a secret place if it will make you more comfortable .....and don't tell me, either, I don't want to know. I've put a bottle of Chardonnay in the fridge to cool. If you would like to help, peel the spuds! Rosalie must have been a good cook, I see lots of spices in the cupboard and I forgot to buy some seasonings for the stuffing. "She was a good cook.....but no better than you.

Guess I'm just a lucky man! I'm getting out of the kitchen as soon as I've done the spuds. The chicken house needs a clean out after the long winter and the proceeds are bound for the vegetable garden for mulch and fertilizer. Fred and Carlo slip out the side door. Later that evening they sit down to dinner. Fred pours more wine, "drink up, Lila! Let's finish this bottle of wine with dinner. The chicken is delicious, the gravy and mashed potatoes fantastic!" After dinner Lila prepares to depart, leaving Fred with the kitchen chores, "see you on Friday, Fred! take care!"

It is now Wednesday noon and Fred had retrieved the ticket from his right hiking boot and put it in Carlo's bag of giant dog biscuits. At one-thirty a car pulls up into the driveway and Carlo issues his warning bark at the front door. Fred jumps up from reading his newspaper and opens the door, "come in gentlemen! Williams and his assistant smile and enter. "Please sit down at the kitchen table and I'll get the ticket."

Fred returns, giving Carlo a large biscuit from the bag. "Here is the ticket!" Williams puts on his reading glasses and pulls a paper from his pocket, scans the numbers and hands the ticket to his assistant.

Turning to Fred with a wide grin, "congratulations, Fred, you are definitely the grand winner this time, to the tune of 28 million dollars! We have brought along all the necessary paraphernalia for a media event, including the usual gigantic copy of your winning check..... just in case. I would like to call the event for 4PM downtown. I like to see the media people scramble for their copy and pics! Can you be there by four? The formalities wont take long and we need to make the necessary arrangements with your bank for transfer of funds. My assistant and I have time for a quick meal then hop a plane back to Toronto. Time and the lottery business wait for no man! If you give me a blank bank check I can take care of the funds transfer to your bank."

Fred "Phew! I'm sweating as at a three-alarm fire! Sure, I'll be there! Thanks for coming by, that was very considerate of you. I admit to being a little paranoid for the past two days." Williams nods in sympathy, "winning a lot of money seems to affect people differently at the time of realization. I can only wish them the best of luck in dealing with it and, of course, feeling a bit envious! See you at 4pm." The public announcement takes place in the local TV station where some twenty people adjusting video cameras etc. are waiting. Williams identifies Fred as the winner and hands him the huge check with his name on it. Fred is grinning like the Cheshire cat while holding the enormous check. He quickly thinks of something to say, "guess that I'll be on the local evening news tonight. I feel like a bank robber who has pulled off a successful heist and never got caught!" Everyone laughs and Fred escapes from the stage through a side door and drives home.

At home, Fred's phone rings and he answers. It's Lila calling. How did it go? Fred answers with a panting reply, "the money is mine...and will be my bank account soon through the miracles of electronic banking! I hope I didn't make a fool of myself. I made a quip and everyone laughed. Is that because they feel obligated to humor a rich man?" Lila chuckles, "whatever! I'll look for you on the TV this evening and congratulations!" Fred suggests that he should take an axe to the telephone line but Lila cautions him otherwise, no, that will just result in people dropping in unexpected. "I may need crowd control and I can see my life and Carlo's undergoing unwanted changes and interference, Lila! How will the kids react? Why don't you come over?"

Calm down says Lila, you'll get over it. Look on the positive side. It's still your life and your decisions on what to do with it. OK, I'll be there shortly. Lila arrives about 45 minutes later. Fred meets her at the door, "I guess the kids will see it on the local TV news sometime this evening. I should call for a family meeting this coming weekend.....on Sunday afternoon. That shouldn't inconvenience the bible bunch. I'm going to ask you for a favor....would you be able to prepare dinner for six adults (that includes you and me) and four kids? A Sunday night dinner....something simple...I don't want to get into a lot of talk about the money. I'll just tell them all that I need time to think. Naturally, they will be thinking about it...probably making plans about some of it coming their way."

Lila shakes a finger at him, "forget the winnings for a minute. Imagine that it is but a dream of yours. Imagine that your health is failing and you need 24-hr care in a geriatrics facility. Perhaps Alzheimer's is setting in. How do you see them reacting? Would they band together and, if necessary, help financially? I know the range of care conditions available in Alberta, much depends on one's ability to pay. You get what you pay for. If you can't pay much there can be much misery at the end of life. Would they take care of you...to the best of their ability?"

I've never thought about that possibility, says Fred, but I know that the Masonic Lodge would be right there, doing what they can. My son, Toby, likes flashy cars, expensive cloths, and nightclubbing. He is probably careful with his money...RRSP and so on...but he has a mortgage on his condo and how far does a bank teller's salary go, anyway? My oldest daughter, Phyllis, she and her husband, Robert have three kids...they are expensive these days.....they support their church and its programs, and there is a large mortgage on the house. Phyllis isn't working since the kids arrived but Robert seems to do ok. He made agent-of-the-year for the highest sales record last year.

Now, Melody, she has lots on her plate.....disengaging from her husband and taking care of Timmy, her four-year old That marriage has been a losing proposition from the start and I have never liked him for his coldness and selfish nature. Kids have to make their own decisions and learn to live with them. Right now she is having a rough time but…..of the three kids…..she would do her best to care for me."

Lila breaks his line of thought, "I make that suggestion so that you would be better prepared for your decisions regarding money. Whatever you decide to do with that money, there surely will be some pressure exerted on you, pressure from various sources, including family and family can involve much emotionality." Fred nods emphatically, "I see what you mean and I appreciate your wisdom. Taking care of geriatric patients has given you much experience in dealing with family relations. Let's look at the eight o'clock news. There it is! I'm on TV and....along with my quip about bank robbers. Look at that grinning ape accepting that giant check. My bank manager will be happy...he'll be calling me by my first name next time I enter the bank!"

The phone rings several seconds later and its Phyllis on the phone, "hello, Dad it's Phyllis. What a big surprise!" Fred, "for me, too! An awful lot of money?...Yes, it is. How are the kids? I haven't seen any of you since Christmas. Could you all come over for dinner on Sunday, about 3 PM? We can chat more then. Good, see you on Sunday, 'bye". Fred can hear Robert was whispering about potential real estate investments. He turns around to face Lila, "I could hear him! He was whispering something about real estate." He turns to sit down when the phone rings again. "Hello, Toby? How are you? Yes, it's 28 million. Do with it? Your friend Keith can help with investments? That's down the road, Toby. Would you come for a rare family dinner on Sunday...about 3 pm? Good, see you then".

Fred hangs up the kitchen phone and pours himself a glass of water at the sink. The phone rings again. It's Melody calling. "You've been trying to get through to me for ages....a busy signal? Yes, it's true, 28 million dollars. Gold seekers! Yes, I'll watch out for them! Come to an early family dinner on Sunday, ok?"

(Fred hangs up the phone for the third time....then it rings again, several minutes later. "Yep, it's you, Cameron. I recognized that Gaelic tongue of yours. Yes, you are right, the Gods are smiling on me! Yes, 28 million! You have some suggestions for it? No, I don't intend to trip over my sporran! I'll be at the Hall soon and we can have a chat, goodbye!" Lila has been putting away kitchen items and she turns around and says, "you see, the avalanche is beginning!" The phone rings once more and Fred answers it then hangs up.

Fred is standing there shaking both fists, "I don't believe it! Damned cheek! That was the dog-catcher reminding me that when he picked up Carlo two years ago on the road that he brought him back to the house instead of taking him to the Pound. Seems the SPCA wants to expand the kennel facilities and is organizing a funds drive!" Lila laughs, "Fred, get used to it!"

FAMILY GET-TOGETHER ON SUNDAY

Lila has arrived on Sunday at noon to help prepare the family meal, "I thought we could make hamburgers....and hotdogs for the kids. I've made a pot of chili to go with it...hope it's not too spicy! And there is a three-bean salad, as well." "Hey! that sounds great! I'll do the meat on the BBQ and we can eat outside on the picnic table." Lila organizes the paper plates and plastic cutlery. "There's frozen lemonade in the fridge and beer for those who don't think drinking is a sin", says Fred as the phone rings. It's Toby on the phone asking if he can bring Keith with him. "Yes, do, there's plenty of grub!"

"Someone is coming up the path, says Lila. It's a girl with a little boy. It must be Melody and Timmy!" At the front door, Fred lets them in and picks up Timmy and swings him around. Rather apologetically,

Melody says, "we're a bit early, dad! Can I have a chat with you before the others arrive?" In the living room, "You are looking thin, girl!" Melody tosses her head, "I've lost some weight...too much on my mind lately, at least since Christmas."

Fred realizes that she has been under much tension, "has Steve moved out yet, and how is Timmy taking it?" "The answer is yes, thank God, and Timmy is taking it fine. Steve is staying at the oilpatch now.....even on weekends. We haven't seen him for nearly a month but he did mail a check for the rent last week. Timmy and I are getting by. He is in day care and I am working part-time with an interior decorator. I've been keeping things to myself, not wanting to bother anybody. I did call Phyllis about a month ago as Steve was bullying me and getting aggressive. She suggested that we join her church and get counselling from the pastor. Steve just laughed.....and then left. He seems to be unhappy with his job and coming home on the weekends has turned into a chore for him. He has no patience with Timmy, either. Coming from a broken home himself you'd think that would motivate him to provide a better home for his own child. Anyway, enough! It's not the end of the world!"

Fred takes on a more serious expression, "I never liked Steve.....he always has a wall up between us and I never liked his attitude towards the family, either.....although he was welcomed with open arms. Don't worry, things will improve for you! Don't worry about money...it's there for you...to get on your feet. You mentioned at Xmas about going back to school and getting your M.A. Let's sit out on the porch where we can keep an eye on Timmy...he is playing with Carlo." They move to the porch swing.Melody says "I remember sitting here with you when I was in high school, Dad!" Fred remembers too, "yes, we had some long chats out here, didn't we? The boys were buzzing about you like bees around honey!" They both laugh and Melody continues, "yes, Dad...those were happy days and Mum was still with us. Sweet sixteen and life seemed so joyous and predictable. Do you remember that boy, Larry Summers? He asked me to marry him at the high school prom but we both went off in different ways...different universities.

He is now a big-time lawyer in Edmonton. Perhaps I should have said yes! My life would be quite different now."

Fred waves his hand, "don't fall into that common mental trap... should have stuff...the past is just the past. The future is more important than arranged memories, arrangements we are all inclined to make to please ourselves, our conscience...or to take the sting out of bad decisions." Melody, setting her jaw, "I am determined to file for divorce and to keep Timmy." Has it crossed your mind that Steve may have found someone else, suggests her Dad. "That thought has crossed my mind but he sure has emotional problems that I didn't recognize earlier. He is so withdrawn from both me and Timmy .....as though he is in a trance. Furthermore, I'm now afraid of his temper tantrums over insignificant incidents. It can't be a money problem as he makes good money and we have not had serious bills. He hasn't hit me but the look in his eyes scares me."

Fred turns quickly towards his daughter, "I had no idea that things were so bad between you two. You are right in deciding to seek a solution. If he has refused to seek professional counselling together what recourse is left to you? May be he has a drinking problem?" Melody, "when I suggested counselling he just left and I haven't seen him since. Maybe a secret problem."

"Honey, I am not going to standby and see you and Timmy treated that way. If Steve is mentally-ill, he could be dangerous. If you have decided that you are at a dead end. .....bite the bullet and get out. Don't worry about bills...I'll take care of them." "I've already decided on a divorce, go back to school and get my M.A. in Design. Then I can eventually start my own business and be financially independent. The last time Steve was at the house he mentioned the possibility of returning to Halifax. His older brother has a successful plumbing business there and that's Steve's training, too". Fred urges, "if you know what you want...go for it! The financial support is there for you. You are talented and hard-working gal and I'm behind you all the way!" "Thanks, Dad! That really takes a weight off my shoulders. I want a happy and secure life for Timmy and I. He deserves it and I am determined to see that he gets it." Fred gives her a hug, "we'll see this through together. That's what families are for. Now I'm going to show Timmy the chickens. He can look for eggs. Want to go with us?" "Yes, let's do it! Then I will help Lila with the preparations. She is quite the lady and has a warm and understanding heart." "That's for sure. I intend to see much more of her if she is willing!" They move off, calling Timmy and proceed to the chicken house.

As they return from the chickens, Timmy is throwing a ball for Carlo. A large SUV pulls up in the driveway accompanied by three blasts on the horn. Melody looking up, "that must be Phyllis and the Tribe in a new vehicle and Robert's red jacket matches the car, too!" Fred glances that way, "must have just bought it." Phyllis climbs out of the suburban waving, " Hi everyone! We have arrived! In case you haven't noticed, we have a new, red SUV. It came with all the perks, heated seats, a console DVD player and a stack of kiddy movies. The girls love it! Oh, and the throne seats in front, make you feel like royalty!" Robert interjects a word, "lotsa storage space, too!"

Fred and Melody meet them as the girls pile out of the car and they all walk towards the house. "A fancy wagon, that's for sure! Come into the kitchen, I want you to meet a friend." They all enter the kitchen where Lila is busy preparing food. Fred stands beside her, "this is Lila, my accomplice in a balanced diet. Lila was recommended to me by Doc Brightsen and she has been my health guru for some time. She is originally from Mexico and is a specialist in geriatic care."

Lila is smiling and wearing a posy of artificial flowers in her hair and a necklace of brightly-colored, hand-painted wooden beads. "Nice to see you", she says, wiping her hands on a tea towel. "We should have met before this." Phyllis assumes the social lead, "these are my three girls, Susie, Brenda and Carrie. Susie is going into Grade 4 this fall, Brenda into Grade 2, and Carrie will be starting Grade 1. The two older girls are eyeing Lila's necklace and artificial flowers in her hair. We have a wonderful pre-school at the church for Carrie as the congregation is now large enough ....and mostly of young families. Robert and I are very active in the church programs and it's so nice to have all the children in Sunday Schoo.l. Robert steps forward, "yes, and Susie is older enough to attend church camp this summer on Lake Apiata. Many of the church families live in our residential area, so we are a close-knit congregation!"

"In the service of the Lord, says Phyllis. Robert has helped many incoming families to locate in our area through his real estate business. The influx of families is related to the oil developments, I guess". Robert again, "I have been so thankful to be of service to house-hunting families and to welcome them to our church, if they show any spiritual interests..

Fred gets a word in, "the girls look so cute...all wearing the same outfits"! Melody pipes up, "yes, like Siamese triplets!" Phyllis ignores or doesn't catch the quip and continues, "I make most of their clothes. The new sewing machines are a real whiz to use. Besides, kids clothes are so expensive these days. It sure helps having three girls for hand-me-downs despite the modern fashion of discarding clothes." Robert, hastening to avoid any possible interpretation as self-righteousness on Phyllis's part, "of course we give any unneeded clothes and shoes to a church committee concerned with needy families." Turning to Melody, Phyllis remarks, "I see that Steve isn't attending this get-together!" Her sister is not phased. "No, he is hard at work keeping the oil flowing that is making our province so wealthy, providing jobs, and stimulating the real estate marke.t. Phyllis, looking at Robert, "oh, I see." Melody goes on, "I've been very busy working part-time with an interior decorator. Some of the new houses in town being built for oil tycoons and their managers are huge! Five-to-six thousand square feet, triple garages, and swimming pools! The demands for showplace designs are high!"

Robert, trying to change the emphasis from materialism. "oh, we haven't even congratulated your father on his good fortune, yet! I was quite surprised to see him on the evening news and the spread in the newspaper this morning. We are so happy for you, Fred ,and what a lot of money! 28 million! It leaves me quite breathless, just thinking about it! How are you bearing up under all the publicity? Have you been deluged with telephone calls?" Fred …."actually, not too many calls outside of the family. I suspect that people are waiting to hear of my plans for all this sudden wealth. I have been thinking about it... nothing certain yet. Melody changes the subject, "when do you all want to eat? Lila and I can set out the food whenever. Or shall we wait for Toby to arrive?" Fred brings the Toby topic up to date, "Toby called earlier and is bringing a fellow-worker from the bank. Meanwhile I'll light the BBQ. The kids know where the swings and see-saw are. Robert, would you keep an eye on them. I see that Carlo is waiting on the lawn, his ball between his teeth!" Melody asks her older sister if she would mind giving Lila and her a hand with the table?

A car approaches with an audible roar and parks next to the red SUV. It's a two-door racy hot-rod. Two men step out to greet everyone. Toby says, "Hi everyone! I'm late, as usual but I see you aren't eating yet! I'd like you all to meet Keith…..a good friend of mine at the bank. He is our investment specialist." Toby and Keith are both wearing white Bermuda shorts, knee-high white socks, sandals and colorful Hawaiin shirts in large floral prints. Melody runs up to Toby, "Hi, Bro! I love the color of your Camaro. It's obviously a cross between violet and lavender...so the blues change the shade according to the light level! That's incredible! We need more color in our cars, bridges, and houses in Alberta! Brighter colors would get us through the long, dreary winters and the drab summer landscapes. Look at the beautiful and bright houses in Europe, especially in Denmark and Holland!" Toby gives her a hug, "thanks, sis, for the compliment! I have no trouble finding my car in a crowded Mall parking lot and I doubt that anyone would try to steal it!"

Robert cannot resist chiming in, "that's for sure! Most males prefer more traditional colors!" (Toby ignores the jab and smiles infectiously at Keith who grins back. Lila has been listening to the family repartee and detects undercurrents of sibling rivalry and possible homophobia in Robert, the born-again real estate salesman). She says, ces, "if everyone is ready to eat, I see Fred is busy flipping the hamburgers and hotdogs. The condiments, including chili, are on the picnic table along with the plates and cutlery. I see that Fred has set up some folding tables and chairs in the shade of the apple trees. Please make yourselves comfortable and...bon appetit!

Robert, Phyllis and the three girls arrange to sit together. Carrie is on her mother's lap clutching a hotdog). "What is that scent that Toby is wearing, asks Phyllis quietly. My God, it smells like Chanel No. 5!", Robert says. Phyllis (chuckling], "I think it's one of those new products for men. Keith seems to be wearing it, too! Sure brands them, eh?" Robert with his chili spoon brandished in his hand, "can't see any real men running around reeking like that!" Phyllis, snickering, "I bet it isn't called "Roundup Time in the Rockies" or "Evening Campfire"...or "Branding Time at the Ranch"! Did you notice the blonde streaks in Keith's hair?"

Fred comes over to check on them, "I see the girls are chowing-down on the hamburgers! That's what I like to see...kids with hearty appetites!" Phyllis...."we didn't each lunch after the Service and Sunday School this morning, so they are probably famished and are surely growing like weeds." "I am really enjoying this hamburger and the chili is superb, says Robert. Eating outside is so much more enjoyable than in the house or in the church basement."

Keith, Toby, Melody, Timmy and Lila are eating together a short distance away. "Lila your chili is fantastic", says Keith! "Can I have the recipe? Is it a secret that you brought from Mexico?" Lila responds, "actually, I have a little recipe book just for chili. This one is called "Dallas Jailhouse chili". The secret to good chili con carne is not to use hamburger but a good beef roast as the base, diced up and cooked first with lots of onions. Then add it to the over-night soaked beans and diced tomatoes. I prefer to use black beans and little red beans rather than kidney beans due to gas and I often make it for some of my elderly patients." Toby joins in, "I agree with Keith.....it's delicious and fit for all ages!"

It's so nice to have someone else cook for a change", says Melody. We don't eat out much...too expensive. I find myself making alphabet soup or opening cans of animal pasta. Timmy loves french fries and root beer, so I take him to MacDonalds once a week for a trea.t. Lila responds, "I hope he is getting his fruit and vegetables, too? I can give you some good recipes for children to start them off on a well-balanced diet." "That would be great! I'll give you my telephone number and we can get together sometime. Look at Timmy on his second hotdog and Carlo is patiently sitting next to him, hoping for a bite!" By this time everyone is stuffed and Melody rises to gather the used plates and plastic cutlery.

Fred approaches, "pitch all that stuff in the garbage pail and I'll deal with it later. If we are all through eating I have some paper kites and bubble pipes for the kids. There are prizes for the biggest bubble and highest kite! While the kids are occupied I would like to say a few words to my kids, so please gather your chairs around and I'll begin." Expectant looks are cast about. Phyllis, whispering to Robert, "bet this is about the lottery money!" Robert agreeing, "he's got to say something sooner or later...why not now?" Fred, raising his arms in a gather together motion, everyone, Lila and Keith too, please join us! May be some of you have guessed ....it's about the lottery money and what I plan to do with it.

Firstly, I am inviting all of you to a ten day holiday at Maui...on me. Everyone can have their own cabana on the beach for privacy and we can all eat at the hotel restaurant. I'll arrange for five cabanas ...a super-sized one for Phyllis's family. It just remains to arrange your schedules so we can be there all at the same time. The basic schedule is up to you. Phyllis is a good organizer so she can work with all of you. How does that sound? "Let's do it! When do you want to go, Dad, says Phyllis? He replies, "I would say before July...before it gets too hot at the beach." Phyllis, looking about, "if everyone would give me their first, second, and third choice of dates, I can narrow down the time slot."

Toby hugs his father, "Dad! This is really generous of you! What a great family trip that will be! Thanks!" Melody….."I second that!" Lila raises her hand, "I'm willing to come along as the sunburn RN…..to keep you all in good health! We'll need sunglasses, big hats, and lots of sunscreen." Fred and Lila had talked about such a trip previously. Fred…"the only disappointed one will be Carlo! He'll have to go to the dog-sitting kennel while we frolic on the beach and take in all the tourist sights. Phyllis, let me know the final schedule as soon as you can and I'll make the reservations, including airline tickets for eleven people. That includes you, too, Keith!"

Everyone is excited about the forthcoming trip and Phyllis does a superb job of organizing the schedule for the middle of June. The idea for separate beach cabanas avoided potential difficulties and much time was spent on the beach with the grandchildren and eating together in the hotel restaurant. Fred had to speak to Phyllis once about needling Melody about her failing marriage. Fred and Lila were able to get away for some private time. Fred has realized that Toby and Keith have a strong emotional relationship but enjoyed playing with the kids and teaching them how to swim. Interestingly enough, there was no attempts by anyone to bring up the subject of money, partly because Fred had taken care of all the expenses. One outcome of this trip was a softening of sibling rivalry aggravated by Phyllis at Robert's insistence. The flight home went smoothly and plans were made to socialize together as a family more often.

INEVITABLE FUTURE PLANS

Lila is preparing dinner one Monday evening several weeks after their return. There have been no substantial changes in either Fred's or Lila's schedules. As usual, Lila comes on Mondays and Fridays to prepare dinner but she now stays to eat with Fred. At dinner, Fred asks Lila could she arrange to eat together every day instead of seeing her rush off home after eating. "Eating with company is so much more civilized that eating alone," says Fred.

At Fred's insistence, Lila has found an assistant, telling Fred "it's only been in the last two weeks that I have had an assistant. She is a recently-graduated nurse who wants to specialize in geriatric care, including nutrition. "I must be getting a reputation, she remarks, since the business is steadily expanding."

Fred shows his concern for her, "I appreciate the time you have given me for the past year but now I would like to see you slow down....spend more time with me. I'm going to need more of your advice and assistance from now on. Can't you coordinate with the Meals on Wheels program for new cases and spend more time with me?" Lila admits that it has been rather taxing, spending time with needy patients living at home and insuring that their nutrition is appropriate. "Your suggestion about Meals on Wheels is appropriate as I can exert my influence on such an arrangementment some time ago and it is now coming on line".

Fred continues, "another concern...I worry about you driving after dark, especially during the winter months. That ramshackle Toyota of yours doesn't have four wheel drive, either!" "Well, Fred, that's my job...something that I have selected. I could be working in a hospital environment or in an MD's office instead. I admit that staying and eating with you after a long day has improved my diet too. Too much snacking and quick meals....and I do enjoy your company! My assistant is working out well, taking any night calls, and coordinating with Meals on Wheels for those clients in need of nutritional assistance"

Fred becomes more insistent. "Is there any reason why we can't spend even more time together? Have you ever thought about marrying again? Frankly, the subject has been on my mind since the Maui holiday. You fitted in so well there and I suspect that the grandkids would like to call you Grandma." Lila laughs, perhaps a little nervously. "Your grandchildren are wonderful kids and, yes, we became quite close on Maui. Phyllis's two older girls were quite shy at first but we "clicked" in no time. Now Susie wants to be a nurse! But, seriously, Fred, although kids are important, it's our personal relationship that should be our primary concern. We've known each other for over a year now, in a nurse-client relationship. I've always been upfront with you ...say what I think in reference to your health.

If we were to change that relationship it should be more emotionally intense and personal. If you are hinting, beating about the bush about marriage, quit hinting and say it! Remember, I'm a Latina!" Fred puts down his water glass, "I know that! Marry me, Lila! I want to spend the rest of my life with you. We are meant to be together." [He gets up from the table and wraps his arms around her waist, kissing her on the neck while she is stirring a stew pot. Lila puts down the wooden spoon and turns to face Fred with a joyous chuckle, "I must admit that I have had several dreams recently where you proposed to me... and I accepted every time!

You are a taciturn Scot and I (well, at least used to be) a devoted and red-blooded senorita! My marriage didn't last long....it takes two to tango, not a string of others. The macho obsession has ruined so many Latino marriages or seen them become total hypocrises. One of the main reasons that saw me come to Canada at the age of 33 was to escape that unfair and hypocritical culture, dominated by males. Living in Canada these past 15 years, making my own way, have been satisfying and happy years for me. I didn't think that I could be happier but you have re-awakened yearnings in me that I thought I'd buried forever.

Fred, looking into her eyes, "well? Don't keep me hanging, Lila! Is it a yes?" "Of course I'll marry you, Fred! Why has it taken so long for you to ask me? I'd have married you nearly a year ago! Kiss me again! On the lips, this time! Basto me mucho, mi cabellaro! Then, let's sample the stew....there's dumplings too!" Fred yells "great balls of fire, I'm breaking out a bottle of red wine...a Chilean Merlot. This is our first dinner as more than just friends! Let the vino flow!" I've another surprise, says Lila. I have made a typical Spanish desert for us...it's cooling in the fridge...the national desert of Spain and popular throughout Latin cultures. It's called crema Catalana...or rather, flan, because the caramellized sugar is on the bottom rather than on the top.

Fred is deliriously happy now, "bottom, top...who cares!" They enjoy the meal and discuss wedding plans in Calgary so that all the family can attend. "Its getting late and I think you had better stay the night!" They move to the bedroom after coffee and Carlo follows them. "Carlo is probably wondering why you aren't leaving for home as you usually do following dinner, and leaving me with the dishes!" Lila chuckles, "Fred, you are so romantic…..wondering what the dog is thinking! From now on, you have to wonder what I'm thinking ....can you read minds?" "No but if you could read mine I bet you would get red in the face!" Lila smiles coquettishly, "I do feel a little flushed...may be it's the wine!" Fred leads Carlo to his sleeping mat in the living room and returns, closing the bedroom door.

Breakfast is late...and it's Saturday so no appointments for Lila. Fred with a mouthful of French Toast, "you know, we could have been married in Maui last month with all the family there...on the beach in our bathing suits! Now, Calgary will do but we could go back to Maui for our honeymoon! How does that sound?" Lila pouring the coffee, "who cares where we go as long as we are together! Maui sounds great! There are still places there that we haven't seen. We can go horseback riding and sail on that big catamaran that we saw in the bay. How long do you want to stay over there?"

Fred "At least two weeks, maybe three. What do you think?" Lila…."perhaps we should start thinking more long-range…..I don't mind continuing my practice...I was planning on at least another ten years." "Oh no! Ten years waiting for you to come home from the office! That's not my idea of an ideal marriage! You wont have to work any more so why not turn your responsibilities over to your assistant.....perhaps keep an eye on her for a while...if she feels she needs it." Lila nods, "she is very competent, well-trained and was head of her class in school. Also, she is level-headed, takes pressure well when clients act up. Doc Brightsen has a connection in the School of Nursing and recommended her to me."

"Okay, here's my suggestion, Lila, broach the subject with her on Monday and give her a few days to think about it. I want to make some plans for us to do some real travelling. After the honeymoon, how would you like to spend a couple of months travelling throughout South America? Perhaps go all the way to the south end…..may be to Antarctica? See Argentina, Brazil, Peru, Chile? Go up the Amazon River?" Heh, slow down, conquistador! My head is already spinning!

A trip like that would be really exciting...but you have to start learning Spanish, at least enough to communicate. You can do that on the internet as there are several good courses for travellers, and I'll coach you on your accent! I can take care of more complicated communication but you should be able to say simple sentences, ask questions and the like. Latin people appreciate Norte Americanos making an effort to speak their language. I guess its their experience with American tourists who expect everyone else on the planet to speak to them in English, or their version of it, anyway!"

Fred agrees. "Yes, I want to start as soon as possible. Let's go into town this afternoon and pick up a Spanish course. When do you think we should spring the news on the kids? I suggest that we ask Phyllis to organize the wedding plans.....she did such a good job on the family Maui trip. I'll phone Cameron at the Lodge...I'm sure he would like to be the best man and Phyllis's girls could be the bridesmaids!" "I know that you belong to the Masonic Lodge but I would prefer a civil ceremony, or at least in a non-denominational church, Christian, of course! I left the Catholic Church when I left Mexico, unimpressed with the priesthoods attitude on poverty and abortion. I saw so many poor families in Mexico City struggling to make ends meet yet being threatened and admonished by priests to keep on reproducing...at the expense of their children's opportunities and futures. I avoided pregnancy while working as a nurse and, thank God, there were no children to suffer from the the break-up."

"I see that you had wisdom even in your earlier years and you were right in taking the route that led you here, says Fred. "Guess I was lucky, too, comments Lila. It took more than two years of married life before I caught on to his philandering .....while I was working hard as a young nurse! Another year before I realized that the situation wasn't improving, that the macho culture supported his behavior and I couldn't accept that. Being a nurse and dealing with seriously ill patients of all ages, including young children and babies, made me ethically very strong, with little patience for weak, self-gratifying personalities."

Fred is open to whatever kind of ceremony that would make Lila happy. "Mi amiga! My love....it's been so long since I've spoken those words and I love the feeling it gives me! If it's ok with you, I'll call Phyllis and ask her to assist with the planning." "Sure, go ahead! My head is going to be so filled with my withdrawal from practice." Fred goes to the kitchen phone and calls Phyllis then returns to the kitchen. "She was surprised but willing to take it on and will call back tomorrow with some ideas. None of the kids expect me to re-marry. Not after nearly 40 years with their mother! Dad is supposed to potter around in his garden and see them on occasion! May be forever!"

Lila......"nobody lasts forever. We must all meet our Maker but all in good time.....his time...not ours! He (She) has given us the brains to live sensible, productive lives...and, most importantly, to care for others. I never did like the notion that if one doesn't get a fair shake in this life, that you'll get one in the next! Not when so many people are busy shaking you down in this life to their own selfish and materialistic advantage! You have raised three good kids, Fred, who have done well, or are trying to, staying out of trouble. You have four beautiful grandchildren and that's not to be sneezed at....not when the media coverage is full of kids on drugs, hanging about in malls, and bullying others. Maybe malls are replacing churches and schools for much of our youth, and their parents, wandering about the merchandising outlets, dazzled, perhaps hypnotized by all the available goodies!"

Fred, knocking on wood, "I've been lucky with the kids...I know some parents, good ones at that, who have been nearly destroyed by wacko kids. Drugs, sex, and rock'n roll have destroyed many a family...even in rural Alberta!" Lila....."so many parents have the pseudo-genetic idea that their offspring will be faithful images of themselves ...or should be. Nothing could be farther from the truth.... kids like that are a rarity. Similarities often skip generations within families, even identical twins are not totally identical...there are always some detectable differences between them." Fred shakes his head, "you constantly amaze me with your observations...of course, working for more than two decades with patients stressed with ill-health and their family reactions to sickness and death have given you much perception on the human condition. Now, let's go out for a walk and some fresh air. Carlo, fetch your leash, boy, the hillside out back awaits us!"

On Sunday afternoon the red SUV arrives. Phyllis is driving and alone. The rest of her family is involved in activities at the church. Fred lets her in ......anything wrong, Phyllis?" "No problems, Dad, I came alone so we wouldn't be disturbed. I am so happy for you both! I talked to the pastor....how about having the ceremony in our church?" Fred looks at Lila for her reaction...."Why not! It's a Christian church and marriages are basically non-denominational in that tradition... except for the Catholic Church which has some restrictive provisos." Fred is enthused, "that sounds great!" Please let your siblings know the plan and give us a firm date...in August? My long-term friend at my Lodge will be my best man, says Fred.

Lila...."should this be a formal affair...you know, monkey suits and long silk gowns?" That's not necessary in our church, just Sunday suits. I want to make brides-maid dresses for the girls, though! Lila and I can figure out the announcement cards and you two can mail them out!" "Things are coming together...it never crossed my mind that we could have this celebration at your church, Phyllis! What a good idea! Keep us informed with the details...Lila is withdrawing from her practice meanwhile and we are planning on returning to Maui afterwards for a honeymoon."

Phyllis....."that's settled then. Now I must be off...we have a do this evening at the church". "Thanks for coming over, my dear!" Fred and Lila walks Phyllis to her car and Phyllis drives off smiling.

Fred turns to Lila, "now I must sit down and draft a common letter to the kids. Just to make sure that they know they are being treated the same in sharing in my winnings. My plan is to give each one 1 million dollars for now and perhaps more next year after I see how they have reacted to their good fortune! Also, I want to donate five million to the Shriners Hospital for Children, through the Lodge. That way, all the members get some credit for the donation." Lila whistles through her teeth. "that sounds very generous. That's a substantial gift and the kids will have no financial worries after that, providing that they are sensible about using it. The hospital donation is really impressive...and a very worthwhile cause. After all, happy, healthy children, even those with disabilities, have a future. You are a good man, Fred!"

Fred, pouring himself a cup of coffee, "I've been thinking. After spending most of my life fighting fires, fires can have both positive and negative outcomes. On the plus side, saving lives is so satisfying even at the risk of your own. But fires caused by smoking in bed, faulty or overloaded electrical outlets, malfunctioning heaters, and so on....often signs of careless and irresponsible behavior, they are irksome! Fires that destroy due to substandard, greedy landlords collecting tenement rents……. get the people out and let it burn, baby! Everyone needs a safe place to call home, even if they don't own it." Lila puts her hand on his shoulder, "now Fred, you can't take on all the world's problems".

I know that and society has the prime responsibility. In the case of cities, they are prone to major fire hazards, industrial areas with flammable chemicals, fuel depots and our rail systems that transport such materials, the safety regulations need to be upgraded, organizations held more accountable. Dangerous derailing of railcars containing toxic chemicals is far too frequent in Canada". "Don't you think, says Lila, that others have made the same observations, and have made them many times? There must be reasons why such changes and improvements don't occur as speedily as they should? Consider corporate greed, bureaucratic apathy, old-fashioned corruption in high places, for example. As individually-concerned citizens, we can only push so hard on the many needful fronts. There is our developing life together, our plans, they should be our main concern...they may be challenging enough!"

Sipping his coffee. Fred shrugs, "yes, I'm just a retired fireman. Time is needed to do other things...things with you, my love! Nevertheless, those 9-11 firemen who lost their lives...343 of them... their families...I want to donate 3 million to their families. That should amount to about 100,000 apiece, enough to take the edge off any financial burdens that they have inherited from that disaster beyond that they have received from insurance pay-outs. What do you think?" "It's your money, Fred, and you are a very generous man. How many other lottery winners have shown such concern for others?" "I have no idea about other lottery winners but we don't need it so why not spread it around. That's what I believe. I doubt that most people who play the various lotteries are very secure financially. Do wealthy people play the lottery! Most of that lottery money comes from people who have little...many of them buy tickets knowing that, although very remote, their chance of winning big is the only way they see to solving their basic economic problems". I bought tickets just to have something to do."

"I understand how you feel, Fred, and don't forget that governments rake in much of the revenue from ticket sales. In my mind, that is merely a backdoor strategy to avoid raising taxes. At the same time, they are inclined to lower corporate taxes under the guise of stimulating employment! Let's face it, Fred, we live in Alberta, Western home for neo-liberal economic dogma that was hatched on Bay Street, Toronto!" "I shall no doubt be more prone to make outrageous statements now that I am no longer a poor, working stiff (retired, yet). I must secure the services of a good lawyer to do the legal footwork for all my planned donations and fund transfers within the family. I also want to set up a trust account for each grandchild, accessible when they reach 21. That will insure there will be money for continued education after high school. They should be able to borrow on that collateral until they come into their majority.

We should be left with about 15 million to do what we like with perhaps more donations as the need arises. Do you think we can get by on 15 million?" Lila chuckles loudly, "I haven't the faintest idea what 15 million dollars looks like means but I am sure that we can find many worthy causes to unload it on...if it becomes a burden! My head is still spinning from the idea of marriage again and a long trip to South America! I must decide how to quit this nursing vocation and am concerned how to fill the gap!"

Fred walks over to the front door to let Carlo out, "I want you to quit so we can be free of obligations, free like migrating birds. After being retired for some five years, my greatest task has been to not listen for that fire bell at the station that can go off at any time, day or night. Not that I don't think of the crew down there every time the siren goes off. Force of habit is hard to break! Now I must draft that letter for the kids but I'm not setting a specific date for transfer of funds to them. That date will be determined by the date of melody's divorce decree. That way, with the Newfie out of the family picture, he will be unable to cause any problems." Fred goes to his computer corner in the living room.

MARRIAGE, TRAVEL AND A NEW HOME

The marriage ceremony goes off smoothly, Fred and Lila leave for a two week honeymoon back on Maui. On their return, they call the kids and invite them over for a photo show at noon on Sunday. Melody pulls into the driveway. "Hello baby! How is the divorce coming along? The sooner that is out of the way, the sooner we can transfer funds. Then you can decide on going back for your M.A." Melody gets out of her car, "I wanted to get you up to date on things but not on the telephone. I've been pushing the lawyer for an early court date. Steve dropped by unannounced last week and mentioned going back to Halifax. The case could be settled by mid-October. I think Steve just wants out of the marriage. The offer we made him of no binding support obligations, me footing the legal bills, and me financing a weeks trip for him to see Timmy once a year did the trick. We just have to sign off the agreement. As he has never mentioned

Timmy since he stopped coming down weekends, I doubt if he will even bother with visitation rights".

That's good progress, Honey, just keep up the pressure and let me know the final date." "I sure will, Dad! You and Lila were the perfect couple at the wedding and that photographer took zillions of pictures! I hope I can have some copies?" "Come over next Sunday for lunch, the others will be here too. I've arranged for each of you to get a complete album, the same ones Lila and I will have.

The family gathers at 2 pm on Sunday to view all the pics taken on Maui. Lila insists on a mid-break for tea and sandwiches. After lunch Fred has some announcements. "This house is too small to continue having you all here at one time. Something has to be done about it. I have a surprise for you all! Lila and I looked around in Maui for a condo on the beach...one that everyone can use. We were offered a fantastic deal on a four-bedroom place, ground floor, three bathrooms, complete with a jacuzzi, tiled floors, and air conditioning! It was fully-furnished by the previous owners from San Francisco and meant to be a family condo. We bought it for family use. The management company looking after it has all your identities so all you will have to do is phone and make your arrangements. They will be maintaining it, providing security, and renting it outside our scheduled occupation periods. Do you all like that idea?

They all agree that it will be a wonderful holiday place to be shared by all. Fred claps his hands for more attention, saying "Lila and I are planning a two-month trip to South America, leaving in three weeks. I'm learning Spanish...at least enough to pay the bills and ask where the local bank is located! You all got my letter regarding the fund transfers to you. The date of transfer is determined by Melody's date of divorce, for obvious reasons. We will probably still be away but all the necessary documents have been signed and witnessed. Our law firm will contact you when that date arrives. Lastly, I would like to thank you all for being so kind to Lila and accepting her into the family. One more comment and I will shut up! Lila and I fervently hope that the sudden and drastic changes in all our lives, I'm referring to the winnings, not our marriage, (everyone laughs) will not jeopardize the family relationships. If I can weather these changes at my age, you should have no difficulty either. As you can see from that letter, the grandchildren will be well-supported in their later years, at least to be able to take advantage of their trusts to further their educations in whatever areas they chose to follow. I've been talking so much that I need another cup of tea!" More tea is poured...everyone goes outside and the kids are playing tag and fetch with Carlo and some of the adults join in.

Lila taking Fred aside in the kitchen, "what was that comment about the house being too small for family events? I thought that family reunions world-wide involve crowding and elbow-to-elbow communication, kids sleeping on beds, on the floor, and tumbling all over the furniture? Also, there should be pinatas at birthdays and at Christmas. We should hang some pinatas so that these kids can experience what Mexican kids do! Smash at the pinatas with sticks to break them open so the candies fall out!" Good idea, Lila, you arrange to get them. If they aren't available in Canada, we'll make our own, paper mache and paint them! I like that idea! It's better than trick-or-treating, ghost and ghoul costumes, skeletons and vampires. Kids will get their portion of being scared and frightened as adults in this so-called modern world!"

Phyllis comes up to them with Robert in tow. "We should leave now as there is school tomorrow and Carrie is falling asleep. We've had a great time". Robert seconds her remarks. "Yes, thank you again! You two are a source of pride for us. People at church are still talking about the ceremony...and Phyllis took the opportunity to invite the entire congregation to the event! You must have noticed all the people there in the church! Your generosity and concern for all of us is much appreciated and we can't thank you enough! You two are real Christians!" Toby approaches, "must be going too, Dad. I would have brought Keith with me but he arranged to drive up to Edmonton to visit his parents this weekend. You will meet them before too long as the family grows. I hope that Melody gets sorted out without too much difficulty, she deserves the break more than any of us. She should get her M.A. as she is the talented one in the family. I just dabble in painting but Melody has real artistic talent. If I don't see you before you leave on your South America trip, take lots of photos! By the way, there's a rumor floating about at the bank that I am getting promoted to Head Teller. The present one is transferring to Toronto as a bank manager. Wish me luck!"

Fred, hugging him, "Toby, you don't need luck. You have given the Royal Bank some fifteen years of diligent service. I bet that promotion is yours already!" Fred and Lila both hug him and walk him to his car where Phyllis and family are being loaded into their SUV. Walking back to the house, Fred asks Lila, "where's Melody, Lila?" She's out with Timmy walking Carlo. I gave him the leash and he was so proud, taking command of Carlo! I see them coming in now". "We must be off now, too", says Melody! Thanks for a wonderful afternoon. I don't know quite what to say about the money. I feel as though a great weight has been lifted from my shoulders. That lawyer you recommended is very considerate and understands the time frame we are working under. I'm not planning any moves until the fateful day has arrived, then I'll decide where to do my M.A., hopefully here in Alberta. We should be going now, I have an early appointment with an oilman's wife who has very definite opinions about décorating! Timmy is doing well in play-school. His teacher says that he is a natural leader but not bossy, and plays well with the others. I'm thankful for that, since he has had little attention from his fathe.r. Lila makes a comment, "it's a very good sign in so young a child. You are his rock, Melody!"

"Keep in touch Honey, says Fred. "In two weeks we are leaving for Rio and Lila has promised to teach me the cha-cha! What next? The tango!" Fred and Lila walk them to the car and watch the little Toyota rattle off down the road. "I'll stick my neck out! Of the three kids, Fred, I like Melody the best! She is a real prize and that oaf of a husband deserves a swift kick in the pants for not appreciating her!" Fred grunts his approval, have patience! He will get his before too long! Let's you and I go to a movie tonight! I have one picked out. It's called Broke Mountain. People are talking about it. It's about two cowboys who seem to be a couple. It might help me to better appreciate a side of Toby that I have been unaware of...at least before the Maui trip. They prepare to leave for town shortly thereafter, leaving Carlo to look after the house.

Ten weeks later Fred and Lila have returned from their South American trip, having seen much of Brazil, Argentina, Chile and Peru. Fred calls Melody and she comes over after lunch while Timmy is in pre-school. Melody arrives in her second-hand Toyoto early in the afternoon. "You gypsies are back after such a long trip". "We had a fantastic time, Honey, wait until you see all the photos! The prints should be ready by the weekend. How are you"? "I am so happy! Things are going so smoothly! Steve has agreed to all my suggestions and is keeping his new 4X4 diesel truck. The agreement papers have been signed and the divorce papers just need to be registered, perhaps within two weeks. As Steve hasn't even asked about Timmy lately, I doubt that he will claim his visitation rights in actuality but that's his decision. I have given him that opportunity and have total custody".

Lila was in the back bedroom and now appeared with an armful of laundry. "I have been eavesdropping! I'm so happy for you, Melody! I remember when I broke free. The energy surge was like a rocket ride! Can you stay for a while"? "Must run now. Have to pick up Timmy. I just wanted to tell Dad that my troubles are nearly over. See you later! I must pick up Timmy soon and do some errands". She waves hastily , jumps into her little car and disappears down the driveway.

Fred, turning to Lila, now to pursue our plans. As your assistant has things totally under control, are you ready to quit work?" Lila has been anticipating his plan. "I'm going into the office in the morning. If everything has been going smoothly and Janet (her assistant RN) is ready, I plan on transferring the practice into her name and be available as an advisor, if she needs me." "That's my gal! See our lawyer if you need legal stuff done. He does business contracts. Perhaps you and Janet should see him together. It might speed up things. Now, on another subject, I've been thinking". "Oh, oh! What about? We've hardly had time to take off our coats...and we have to collect Carlo! He will be jumping for joy, to see us after nearly three months! What's on that busy mind of yours?" "Carlo will be even more excited if my new plan materiallizes! I was thinking that we should get out of this place and find something bigger, with more acreage." "Well, out with the details." "Once a fireman, always a fireman. How about us raising pedigreed Dalmatian pups? We could give free pups to every fire station in Alberta that wants one! When we have run out of takers here we could expand our efforts to include British Columbia....then points east! I would have a proper kennel designed and built at the new place, hire expert help and secure good bloodlines through the Canadian Kennel Club. A dalmatian in every fire house! That would be my motto! What do you think?"

"Hah, I think you want to take advantage of my clinical and practical experience once you have levered me out of my office! However, I always wanted a puppy when I was a child. Never had the opportunity as we lived in Mexico City...in a small apartment. I could keep the books and breeding records, and do the nutritional monitoring. Let's do it together, and I promise not to keep too many pups for ourselves!" "It could be great fun...work, too! But we are both used to that. With a paid assistant, we wouldn't be tied down completely. While I have you on track, Lila, there's more! After seeing all those alpacas and llamas in Chile and Peru, I'd like to raise some here. They are very efficient feeders, intelligent, and can be trained as security guards! They also provide a beautiful fleece without lanolin for spinners. I think the grandchildren would like to have a dogcart pulled around the ranch by a llama! What do you think of my idea?" Lila thinks for a minute, " well, you would have to do most of the work! I could help with birthing and feeding of the young. You mentioned a ranch? Just what do you have in mind?"

Fred's plans are too much for the small acreage that they have. "I would like to find a place about 200 acres, or more! Good pasture, a permanent creek, a nice view from a hilltop where we can build our dream house. That would be a big enough spread to guarantee us privacy and peaceful surroundings. Because both alpacas and llamas have similar pasture and diet requirements, we should be looking for a sheep ranch! They are both much more efficient feeding on pasture than are other animals. Let's start looking in the foothills west of town. You know, we could have some Chilean and Peruvian kids here during the summer months. What do you think of that possibility?" Lila brightens up, "you are a crafty one, aren't you! There are lots of under-privileged kids there. We saw enough of them. They could learn English, too! I have had thoughts of contacting some of the native communities here, seeing that I am quitting nursing full-time, get involved with them. After all, going back far enough, we share some common ancestry!"

Fred raises both arms as though seeing a heavenly sight. "I can see it now! Peruvian and Chilean kids showing our native kids how to work with llamas! I'll have to build some sturdy dogcarts for races around the paddock! There's so much to be done! Finding the right ranch property, setting-up for Dalmatian breeding, and locating some yearling llamas!" "A word of caution, Fred, remember, when we find the right place, if there's no suitable residence we'll have to build one...one with plenty of bedrooms, or better still, build an annex dormitory. I will need an extra-large kitchen and dining area in the main house, to plan nutritious meals with an international menu.... lots of maize, beans, chicken, and fish! We'll need a big vegetable garden, also. Are we going to have fun!" Fred gives her a hug. "I'm looking forward to all the fun but you know, Lila, we would have fun regardless of the lottery winnings, wouldn't we?" Lila begins to cha-cha, "that's for sure, mi cabellaro! So let's get to it!"

END

The Priest and His Incubus

A Semi-historical and Semi-fictionalized Account Involving the Anglican Church and the Ministry of Children and Family

PREFACE AND ACKNOWLEDGEMENTS

This story is based on people and the events in which they played their roles in this semi-fictional account of affairs conducted in relation to the Anglican Church in Canada and the British Columbia Ministry of Children and Family. The primary roles and the description of influencing and exploitive behaviors of persons encountered here are only partly fictionalized in order to minimize potential embarrassment of those readers who might imagine themselves mirror-imaged in this story. I apologize expectantly to any individuals whose personal pains and memory may be so stimulated.....unless their roles and behavior have been duly recorded.

1. Graduation and Becoming a Rector
2. Saint Hillary School for Girls
3. Prayer and Escape to India
4. Return to Church Practice
5. Practice, Preaching and Sexual Abuse
6. Judgment and Imprisonment

CHARACTERS:

1.	Wiley Benton Chase	Anglican priest
2.	Ian Roman Journeyman	Bishop
3.	Charles Enright Gatewell	Principal
4.	Jillian Macintosh	School Nurse
5.	Preston Roundbottom	Entrepreneur
6.	Chandra Ely Norton	Asst. Dir. Orphanage
7.	Setton Major Gile	Anglican deacon
8.	Carolyn Flynn	School Therapist
9.	Catherine Scrubbe	Synod Comm. Sexual Abuse
10.	Ruby Roe Donne	Victim of Abuse
11.	Ophelia Legett	Victim of Abuse
12.	Nancy Nobadi	Victim of Abuse, R.N.

1. GRADUATION AND BECOMING A RECTOR

Wiley Benton Chase graduated in languages (BA) from the University of New Brunswick in 1965. The elation and satisfaction of companion students on the campus escaped him due to the sudden, week-before announcement by a girl friend whom he imagined would marry him that she was engaged to marry one of his class-mates.

Wiley returned to the family home in Kedgwick and fell into a general depression brought on by his jilting. He was the object of much motherly concern and her attention was to urge him to concentrate on his Anglican upbringing as she was a devout churchgoer in Kedgwick. His father had a Catholic upbringing but has not attended church for many years. Wiley's faithful attendance at the local Anglican church included participation in bible study groups, and active volunteerism over the course of more than a year. His dedication earns him the respect of his priest who recommends him for church work to the bishop. Meanwhile he is leaning on a meagre living teaching French language at a small private school, a job secured for him by his priest.

Wiley is parsimonious with his meager savings but saves enough money to take a holiday to Paris. His priest encourages him to take this trip in order to regain his social confidence. On the 747 flight he meets a steward who invites him to his apartment in St. Denis. This Montrealer shows him Paris, including the gay nightlife and Wiley enjoys himself immensely and is quite infatuated by his new-found friend who wearies of his constant attention and advises Wiley to return home . Wiley returns to Kedgwick with considerale guilt and throws himself back into his church work. His two younger brothers being gay is not removing his doubts about his own sexual identity, and the youngest brother had committed suicide during Wiley's last year at university and Wiley had refused to attend his funeral.

Wiley is eventually elevated to a Rector's position at a small Anglican parish church, Saint Stephens at St. John's, on the Bay of Fundy. He begins a bible study group, mainly of local women, who rotate the study sessions through their residences. A particular parishioner, Ruby Roe Donne, catches his eye. During a study session held in her residence. Wiley ventures to risk starting a personal relationship with her. As the study session ends, Wiley says…."ladies, I hope that this meeting has been instructive and uplifting to you all. I'm most pleased with your responses. The parables of Our Redeemer, Jesus, are replete with both obvious and hidden meanings. We have explored some of them here this evening with both reverence and awe at his wisdom and righteously-applied power of persuasion. See you all at Ophelia's home in two weeks. Now, a short blessing before you depart. Dear Lord, we pray that our efforts here yield fruit...that we all will benefit by incorporating your thoughts and actions into our daily lives, Amen". The ladies smile at each other, some hugs are exchanged, and there is a group-inspired common thanks given at the door as Wiley and Ruby see them out. Ruby gently closes the door behind them.

Wiley…" I should be on my way, too". Ruby desired to chat with him and possible make some tea, "no, please stay a while, I have something to get off my chest. Ruby is a healthy, younger woman, amply endowed. Wiley's eyes widen, "of course. My ministration work has no timetable. It's part of expressing my parish duties. What's on your mind?" Ruby…. "first I'll put the kettle on and make some fresh tea and there's a plate of cookies left uneaten". She turns and proceeds into the kitchen, his eyes following her graceful walk. Filling the kettle and putting it on the stove, she returns to the living room where Wiley is making some notes in his parish diary. Wiley…."please refresh my memory, Ruby. The lady in the green dress, do you know her?"

Ruby…."yes, her name is Ophelia Legett. She's married to Tom Legett, a grocer where I shop regularly. They have two children, a young baby and a seven-year-old girl named Rosemary. As the new grade-school teacher in town, I know that much". Wiley…."as with you, I must get to know all my parishioners so as to maximize my effectiveness. The congregational response to my Sunday sermons for the past several months has been gratifying. As the new rector, I want to further that response, perhaps to reassure myself that I'm developing as a good shepherd to my flock". Ruby sitting down beside him on the chesterfield, …. don't be a doubting Thomas, Wiley. May I call you Wiley?" "Call me Reverend....or Wiley...whatever apellation makes you feel most comfortable". Ruby continues …."from what I have gathered in the community, they are rightfully impressed with your spiritual ardor and candid expressions of joy in pursuing your work here". A feeling of concern and undenied ardor are simultaneously welling up in her breast. "These past several weeks of bible study have re-awakened me. I haven't yet had the opportunity of developing any personal relationships here in St. John's. Perhaps I am still recovering from the break-up that impelled me to transfer here from my grade-school in Bathhurst". Wiley is warming to the occasion and smelling opportunity in the air.....and her body scent. "Ruby, we are all children of God and subject to earthly disappointments in pursuing our needs for emotional security. I've had my own disappointments, recently during a holiday in Paris, and previously. After graduation from U. New Brunswick, I returned to the family home and fell into a prolonged period of depression. My love at university decided to marry another classmate, leaving me in a descending vortex of emotional agony". He mentally congratulates himself on his choice of words …….. descending into a vortex of mental agony....and sits silent for a moment, waiting to see its effect. Ruby, bouncing in her seat, "there! I knew it! We are birds of a feather, you and I! Squirming slightly on the couch, she lifts her head and gazes at the ceiling, as though expecting a sign of affirmation from heaven.

Wiley…."birds of a feather!" He moves closer to her. "Perhaps lovebirds?" He throws his right arm across her shoulders and squeezes her gently, drawing her even closer to him. "Life can be so lonely.... we all need some one close and supportive in our personal lives". He squeezes her again on the shoulder.

Ruby gives an audible sigh ...almost a yelp. She suddenly turns and plants a kiss on his nearing cheek, then draws back. "Oh Dear! What am I doing! I apologize for being so forward. I just couldn't help myself. It's been so long!" Wiley…."no apology is needed. I am flattered". Putting his left hand on her left knee while turning more towards her, he returns the kiss...not just a peck...but a prolonged, ardent kiss. Ruby emits an audible moan. In response, he strokes her neck, then her heaving breasts. The kettle whistles its command and Ruby rises automatically, as in a trance, and goes to the kitchen and turns off the gas burner. The whistle subsides slowly as she turns, appears from the kitchen and smiles at Wiley. " Let's have tea later, I'm getting the giggles". She beckons Wiley and walks into her bedroom. Wiley is quick to follow while tugging furiously at his ecclesiastic collar.

A few weeks later as Wiley is working in the evening in his rectory office...the sermon for next Sunday is his chore. A knock brings him out of his reverie. His encounter with Ruby has been repeated on several occasions, also late in the evening. The secrecy of it excites him. "Come in, the door is unlocked". Ophelia Legett appears, rather dishevled and obviously agitated…." I am sorry to interrupt your work but I have no-one else to turn to at this late hour. I must talk to some one and you came first to mind". Wiley puts down his pen…." I was just working on my sermon for next Sunday....."Who is a true Christian?" …." I am here for you.....what can I help you with?" Wiley is secretly pleased that she has come to his office.

Ophelia is much agitated and embarrassed, "my husband, Tom, He has never hit me before! I've never seen him so angry. It was so frightening. Luckily both children were in bed asleep. I just rushed out of the house and drove down to the park. I just sat there for a while. Finally, after calming down I began to get angry and resentful. What gives any man the right to hit a woman, not alone his wife and mother of his two children?" Wiley…."so, you and your husband had an argument that led to him hitting you. Are you injured....I mean, physically?" Ophelia replies, …."he cuffed me on the left ear...very hard. I just threw on my coat, left the house and drove around. Finally, I ended up in the park, my ear still ringing, and took a few minutes to calm down. Tom was so angry. I've never seen him so angry! His face was so red!" Wiley…."do you want to tell me what brought this anger on? There must be a reason for him to lose his self-control"

Ophelia…".well, I found out, through a neighbor, that he has been seeing another woman in town. You know how rumors get around in small towns. I confronted him with it....not as an accusation but as a rumor.....and asked him if there was any truth to it. I thought I'd asked a rather mild question. His response indicated to me that something was going on between them. Why would one react that way unless something was actually going on?" Wiley, thinking of the possible explanations, "perhaps he is innocent .....perhaps he was upset that you were losing your trust in him. People, seemingly quite stable, can fly off the handle when the wrong button is pushed. Maybe his business is not going well? Has he been sleeping soundly and eating well?" "his business is flourishing....we have no money problems. He has been working late in recent weeks but there have been renovations in the building. He eats like a Viking and sleeps like a top". "There!", says Wiley. "the stress of work....decisions about plans and associated expenses...has his talk at home given you any clues?" Ophelia shaking her head,…."nothing seems amiss. If anything, he has been unduly high-spirited since the renovations started and that is finished now, anyway. No, there is something else going on...I's sure of it. Call it a women's intuition, if you like. Something undue, sneaky perhaps ......like an affair outside of our marriage. Do you think that I'm speculating and imagining things?"

Wiley…."I suggest that you go home, I will follow you in my car....just to make sure that you are going to be safe. Knock on the front door...I will be able to observe you from my car...if things are safe give me a wave. Tell your husband that I am willing to assist you both. Marriage is a sacred state and I know that you two were married in Saint Stephens. I have been examining the parish registry". Ophelia…."I must take that chance, I guess, perhaps he is sorry and wants to apologize. The longer I wait, the more awkward the situation might get, don't you agree?". Wiley, standing up, ….."that's the plan then! Let's go...there is no time to lose. Strike at disharmony with a righteous sword! I hope your family life is not at risk". They get into their cars and proceed to Ophelia's home. Ophelia drives into her driveway while Wiley parks across the street where he has a clear view of the front door. Ophelia rings the bell and Tom opens the door and folds her into his arms. They enter the house after kissing on the front step. Satisfied that nothing serious is imminent, Wiley leaves and drives to see Ruby.

In the next few weeks, Ophelia appears at bible study and Wiley observes her closely. She is a strikingly-attractive women, long and lustrous red hair, and a pleasing figure. She reminds Wiley of his university girl....both must be kelts....with dark, red hair and pale blue eyes. At the last study meeting, Ophelia indicates in a note surreptitiously slipped into his jacket pocket that she has things to tell him. They meet the following afternoon at the rectory. Wiley has been much intrigued that she has slipped the note into his pocket. "Sit down Ophelia, and tell me what's on your mind. Hopefully, you two have resolved apparent differences, it certainly looked that way on the doorstep?" Ophelia appears somewhat resigned…"well, as I suspected, there are differences in our understanding of integrity, loyalty, and fidelity. He finally confessed one evening about two weeks ago. Guess he had to get it off his chest and apologize for hitting me. Tom was remorseful but now expects "for the sake of the children.....and his local business" that I accept his philandering with the Mayor's wife. The mayor and his wife have an open marriage no children....Tom wants me carry on as his wife. Maybe he will get over this .....and return to normalcy but what about me? I have my standards, derived from the bible and my common sense". Wiley….."hmmmm, a honest apology ...straight from the heart...deserves, or earns an apology, doesn't it? Perhaps you should be the righteous and forgiving wife? Play the role...like that successful American female politician who recently has eclipsed her presidential husband in public reputation and power".

Ophelia…."I am just a simple country girl. I have no desire for national fame or power. My kids are now my life and, if the marriage is going to be steady, if off-course, then so be it. Anyway, apologies should be accompanied by promises to refrain from whatever behavior caused the problem in the first place! I have the right to be happy as a woman, as happy as Tom is with his affaire du coeur!" Wiley…."two wrongs don't make a right, do they? But if you are willing to stay the course in your new relationship with Tom, you are playing the high road as long as the children remain unaffected. I will endeavor to assist you in that regard but the secret must remain ours. Do you agree?"

Ophelia studies the floor for a moment, "luckily the children are still too young to be psychologically harmed. Tom is a doting parent and the baby boy is his hearts delight. I visualize it to be a balancing act lasting for some time, I guess. But I am hoping that he will see the light in the future and return to me.....I remain hopeful". Wiley is becoming insistent, "yes, but do you agree that the secret must remain ours..."for our eyes only" as they say in the Secret Service. Otherwise it might get a bit sticky....I mean, if Tom found another man in his garden....he would consider it revenge on your part, wouldn't he…. and feel like the cuckolded husband?" Nodding in agreement, Ophelia says, "yes, I agree but I don't really care! This is as good a time as any to make a confession to you". Wiley's eyes widen indicating his excitement, " what another secret! Two secrets in the same day! What is it now?" "I have been coming to the bible study sessions for many months now and must admit that I see you in a much higher light now relative to my husband. You seem so open and pure of spirit.... unlike any other man I have known. You have become my ideal male and I have had erotic dreams lately of us together in a physical yet spiritual way. There! I have said it. Confession is good for the soul, they say, and I do feel much better having said it". She looks at Wiley straight in the eye, waiting for his response. Wiley…."love, love. The Redeemer wanted everyone to love one another although he seemed to be still tied to the Jewish faith in many respects. Who was it who said "Love is the only gold"......yes, Alfred, Lord Tennyson. A liberal arts degree can be useful on occasion....and this appears to be such an occasion! This is the sort of unusual challenge that can be thrown at churchmen who then must rely on their ethical training, intuition, and desire to fulfill their obligations as a good shepherd to the flock. I feel bound to help you and your family. We must figure out a strategy to accomplish your desires but I would be a little uncomfortable if I thought that you were secretly harboring thoughts of revenge. Are you acting in revenge against Tom? That would be sinful!"

Ophelia is quick to respond,…."revenge! Not at all! My heart is too open for that sort of thing". "Then let us proceed. He draws the office curtains, puts out his "not in" sign and locks the door. I have a bed in the back room...I sleep here sometimes when I am too tired to go home....wrapped in the throes of writing a sermon or wrestling with the latest problems identified in the diocese or the Church at large. The possibility of female Reverends and Priests is a weighty subject..... and the idea of gay marriages in the church is hideous to contemplate! Also, there are personal experiences in Paris to overcome". Ophelia dutifully follows him into the back room. Thus begins a long series of therapeutic sessions between churchman and parishioner. But where will it end and who really is the patient?

The bible study sessions are ongoing, attended by the usual group of female parishioners. Wiley maintains his usual aplomb when discussion centers around the role of Mary Magdalene in the life of Jesus especially when male dominance reveals the jealousy of several apostles who resenther presence in discussions. Wiley…."we must acknowledge that Mary Magdalene was an accomplished and forthright woman, fiercely loyal to Jesus. Some biblical comments appear to reduce her role amongst the intimate followers of Jesus. I suspect that such efforts merely reflect the male-dominated culture of the time". Ruby pipes up, …."circumstances haven't changed much in 2000 years, have they? As a school teacher I am saddled with a male principal who lords it over the female teachers despite that some of us are better trained in the modern aspects of teaching than is he. It's about time things changed! And why, seven, not one, evil spirits cast out by Jesus?"

Ophelia…."I agree. Where do males get the notion that females are emotionally questionable .....seven evil spirits cast out? Any emotional fragility in women is due to our cultural upbringing....what is expected of us by men! Sure, we remain the subservient sex but remember, the mother has far more potential influence over the development of children than do teachers of either sex. With that realisation, the differences between male and female teachers is of minor importance. Remember, ego trips are common in all organizations, among and between both sexes".

Ruby senses a degree of antagonism in Ophelia's reply but she supports her…."males still seem to assume that they are the rightful inheritors of power in most cultures, including those representing Christianity. Surely, the developing fracas over the desirability of female priests in our Anglican church is symptomatic of a power struggle. I see it as dominant males fending off attempts by females to usurp male authority and privilege.

Wiley senses that these two women are dueling. "Are we drifting off the subject of Mary Magdalene here? Ruby is giving Ophelia a cold stare and Wiley, glancing at both of them, has an uncomfortable feeling in the pit of his stomach. "I suggest that we go on.....remember that there was jealousy among the disciples not related to Mary Magdalene. Jesus seems to have had a more intense relationship with Thomas than with the others, one centered no doubt on philosophical questions, particularly those involving mystical considerations and our obligations to each other in this world". Ruby is persisting…."I would like remind Ophelia that many female teachers are mothers, too, hence in the position of viewing the upbringing of children from a more complicated and professional point of view. Again, she is giving Ophelia another cold stare.

Wiley…." Let us return to Mary Magdalene. Whether or not she was married or had children remains unknown but some would picture her as a prostitute. There is reason to believe that she was an independent business woman, an unusual role in that culture dominated by males. Her inclusion in the immediate followers of Jesus was probably at the invitation of Jesus who may have recognized her unusual capacities. Also, Jesus was way ahead of his Jewish time in recognizing the female attributes of gentleness, mothering nature, non-aggression, and source of new life recognized in previous religions". He hopes that his words will defuse the antagonism that he suspects is arising between Ruby and Ophelia and wonders about its source.

Ruby…."Could we move on….I suggest that we turn to the subject of Judas Iscariot? As in the case of Mary Magdalene, serious maligning efforts in the New Testament brand him as a turncoat and hypocrite who finally hung himself in remorse for his role in the crucifixion of Jesus. Some authorities believe that his role was predestined and recognized by Jesus as necessary to allow his death and resurrection. What should we believe? If he hung himself after his betrayal, who wrote the Gospel of Judas? Again, according to theological scholars, the gospel of Thomas preceded some of the gospels in the New Testament and includes half of the material found in the New Testament".

Wiley, returning to Judas, "the account in the New Testament uses the unfortunate word "betray" as used by Jesus. Regardless, the important outcome of the crucifixion was his death and resurrection by which he has saved us all. Keep that in mind. He also is thought to have uttered "my God, why have you forsaken me""? This remains another enigmatic comment attributed to him. Make of it what you will. Does it suggest that his faith was wavering in light of his pain and suffering? Remember that he was born of both forms....human and God. Again, the main drama remains his crucifixion, resurrection, and return to heaven". Most of the women have remained silent during these sallies, and the atmosphere has become decidely uncomfortable at such displays of intense analysis of dogma they had simply accepted as unquestionable and written in stone. Far beyond them are the theological discussions and arguments raging for many years, including those put forth by non-Christian theologians perhaps antagonistic to accepted Christian dogma. Wiley continues, "let me suggest that we turn to another subject, namely the upcoming celebrations of Easter.

I note that this church has never conducted an Easter Sunrise service. Can anyone familiar with the local geography suggest a suitable mount that faces the East and would not be too challenging to our older parishioners? I would like to see a large number there, including the choir, to sing as the sun is rising. We will need to light the way also, so a safe path is required. We don't want any twisted ankles or broken bones, do we?" One of the women identifies herself as a hiker and accepts the challenge of locating a suitable route and hilltop.

Wiley remains concerned about Ophelia and Ruby and decides to end the session…."on that note I would like to bring this study session to a close. Please rise for a short prayer. They all obey in subdued fashion. "Oh Lord, we thank thee for all thy blessings. That you have given us the capacity to think and to understand the holy writings brings us closer to you in our continued search for wisdom. Amen". They all file out of the room and depart for their homes except for Ruby who is hosting this study session once more. After the group has left her house, Ruby has something to say…."I suppose that you think me irksome considering my replies to Ophelia this evening?"

Wiley…."I was a little startled at your tone of voice. Have you two had some kind of falling-out?" "I've heard rumors, says Ruby… ."Ophelia has been seen coming to your rectory office frequently in the late afternoons. Am I right?" " Who has had the time to spy on my office? On comings and goings? Ophelia has some personal difficulties which I am sworn to assist her with. Who dares to do that and rumor-monger about it? This is an outrage! An attack on my integrity, my pastoral duties, and my spiritual honesty! Name this person!" Ruby remains unaffected by his outburst…."her name is unimportant, however, she is not a member of our congregtion but a teacher at my school who lives close-by". Determined to retain his authority, Wiley continues,…."Ophelia has a difficult marriage and I am helping her find some solutions. Solutions that might save her marriage....in the long run....and help keep the family together". Ruby's voice rises…."help! help? With all the blinds promptly drawn as soon as she enters, and your "BUSY" sign hung outside! Are you meditating in the dark! Wiley, bristling….are you accusing me of something, Ruby? "Yes, actually. I have corroborated her sightings on several occasions and the meetings" or dare I say "matings" have lasted for approximately thirty-five minutes, each time. Interestingly enough, that is about the same length of time that you take when you see me in the evenings. What a timely coincidence!" Wiley's face is now suffused and red with anger. "We are finished! He shouts in a rising voice. I don't want to see your face again, and if you continue these false accusations, may God strike you down! Don't you understand that I am doing the work of God? Can't you see that!"

Ruby now realises that she has struck home with her comments and is gaining strength. "Furthermore, I fully intend to see the Bishop about this and I don't think that he will take it lightly. I'll give you two weeks to mull over this discussion. Then, unless you have realised your error and returned to your senses (and to me), the Bishop will be informed. We all have a responsibility to safeguard the sanctity of the Church, including those in this parish. As a responsible parishioner, I am determined, otherwise, to see you removed, hopefully de-frocked and drummed out of the Anglican church. A woman so basely used, scorned, is a wrathful sight to see and I intend that you see it. You have over-stepped your spiritual authority and the clear definitions of pastoral duties as outlined in the Diocese Guidelines". Wiley whirls and bounds out the door, screaming invectives and again, threatening the wrath of God on her.

2. SAINT HILLARY SCHOOL FOR GIRLS

Wiley has departed from Saint Stephens church and St. John's after tending his resignation to the Bishop on the grounds of ill health. He returns to the family home in Kedgwick where his mother is living alone, since the death of his father. His other two younger siblings are living independent lives, one brother in Toronto and the other, the youngest in Fredericton. His departure from St. John's was facilitated by the bishop who gave him a letter of recommendation exhorting Wiley's record as rector of St. Stephens. Wiley is waiting for a reply from Saint Hilary's School for Girls in Toronto, a school soliciting for a French teacher in the Anglican Press. The reply came shortly.....we would be pleased to appoint you as a Senior teacher in Languages, specifically French Language and Culture. Wiley telegrams back accepting the position and sets off for Toronto. He meets the school principal three days later, after securing temporary lodgings at Saint Crispins.

Principal Gatewell "Well, you arrived in good time. The Fall Term starts in several weeks so you have some time to get settled in and go over the curriculum and course work that you will be responsible for. I am very pleased to have you here. Your bishop gave you a glowing recommendation and we are indeed fortunate to have a reverend here on staff with parish experience and an Honors degree from UNB as well!" Wiley is still congratulating himself for a clean getaway from Ruby and St. Stephen's, "I am looking forward to teaching full-time. From my resume you already know I was tutoring private students in French for two years after graduating from UNB". "Yes, that caught my eye immediately. I'm sure that you will find this school a rewarding experience. Most of our girls have families in Toronto and are in residence here during the week, going home for the weekends. That gives them a certain amount of independence while retaining strong family ties. Many of our graduates go on to university and we are well-known for bagging more than three times as many scholarships as other similar schools". Wiley...."that reflects a strong academic system here and I hope to add to it. Gatewell smiles, "have you found suitable accommodations here in Toronto? The north end of the city is preferable if you plan on commuting. Some of the single staff live in residence here which is convenient, as some of our students come from foreign families hence are here throughout the school year, going home to far-flung places during our summer. Where are you staying presently?" "I am at Saint Crispins temporarily at the invitation of the Rector but must find more permanent accomodations shortly. Gatewell again, "we turned one end of the dormitories into suites for single staff. That gives us a week-end staff supervisory potential on campus. The rental costs are nominal in return. We may have a suite coming up as one of the female staff is getting married this weekend. If you are interested I can make arrangements for you to move in next week.....after any re-decorating needs are taken care of".

Wiley, relieved…."that sounds marvelous! What a relief that would be to me as I am not familiar with Toronto.....I'm just a small-town fellow ,frankly, the size and traffic here is personally quite overwhelming". "No problem here, give me your phone number at Saint Crispins and I should have good news for you by late Monday". Wiley is elated and excited, …."what have I done to deserve all this good news.....new position and probable housing, too! How can I express my gratitude to you?" Looking pleased with himself, Gatewell smiles, …."be the best darn French teacher in the Province of Ontario!" Wiley…." I don't intend to disappoint you, sir". They both rise, shake hands and Wiley leaves the Office of the Principal.

Several weeks later, Wiley has moved on campus and has familiarized himself with the facilities and the grounds at large. What teaching staff have stayed over the summer have extended a warm welcome. Everyone is preparing for the return of students in early September. Wiley has spent some time with the school nurse since she invited him to a summer play in town. Jill is single and also lives in residence. She meets him walking across the quad one morning.

Jill…."good morning Wiley....what perfect day! Do you play tennis by any chance? The tennis courts need some play!" "Yes, I do....I played singles at University but never had time for the team....too much studying to do. I'm a bit rusty but willing to give you a run for your money! How about after lunch? I see that the residential staff are making use of the common kitchen facilities but I now have my kitchen in order. I've made some clam chowder...good, down-east clam chowder. Jill grins…."Ok, I'll come up at noon. They part company and Wiley checks his mail then goes to his suite to prepare lunch. At the stroke of twelve, Jill raps on his door and he lets her in. "Welcome to my lair! Things aren't yet as I would like to have them". Books are piled on the living room floor and several framed pictures need to be hung on the walls. Looking around her, Jill exclaims…." I've seen untidier bachelor pads in the past. It looks like you are going to have a cozy place here".

Wiley…."My previous rectory digs were rather sparse. I need to get some bookcase material. Perhaps some pine planks and bricks for the time being". "That's easy but you don't have a car, do you? We could take mine to the lumber yard and get whatever you need. Best to get everything shipshape before the return of the multitude. You won't have much free time later". Wiley smiles, …."I'll take you up on that offer. Do I have to let you win on the court first?" "Win or lose...who cares. Just enjoy the game, I say. We can sally into town later. The chowder smells great.... let's eat! I have brought a loaf of French bread...seeing that you are the new French teacher!" Wiley is tuning up to the repartee…"I wonder what I would have to bring to your place to reciprocate? Iodine and bandages don't sound too appetizing, do they? Jill laughs. "Some time you can bring some succulent steaks and I will make a salad that will knock your socks off!" " Wow! A salad that could be dangerous to other pieces of clothing?"

Jill is quick to recognize the banter…." I can see that you need to be taken down a few points on the tennis court!" They finish eating and leave the table as Wiley looks at her white shorts and tennis shoes...and her shapely legs. "I see that you are ready for action. Give me a minute to prepare myself and we can get to it". He goes into his bedroom and reappears a few minutes later in his court gear and clutching two rackets. Jill…." a two racket man, are you? Sounds a bit professional to me...one racket is all I have ever owned but I do have new balls.... an unopened can ready for sacrifice!" They leave for the courts across the quad and next to the oval track. After a set which he loses 6-4, he calls for a time out…. "not playing for some time is death in singles play. I've been spending too much time balancing teacups on my knee and listening to middle-aged ladies chatter. I intend to get back into shape and give you a better game next time". Jill laughing, "I forgot to tell you that I was County champ back home in Waterloo. We girls have to create an edge somehow.....to challenge the male ego. You will find that a noted characteristic of our Toronto girls is equality consciousness. Many of them come from wealthy families who expect them to do well in the modern, competitive world as professional equals. That's why we have such great facilities here ....generous alumnae with high standards of performance". Oh my, "not content to drub me on the court, you find it necessary to deflate my ego! But seriously, I feel no threat and have had a great time playing with you. We must do this again before I get even further out of shape. As for the students, I intend to find as many Mary Magdalene's as possible and imbue them with a sense of purpose, dedication to culture, and self-confidence. That is, if they don't have those attributes already". Jill…."well said. You take care of their minds and I'll see to their cuts, bruises and hygiene. Now, let's go downtown and find your pine boards and bricks". They return from the courts and proceed downtown in Jill's car.

Several weeks into the new term, Wiley has developed a lusty and satisfying relationship with Jill, the school nurse. The Fall term has gone well, his students like him and some of the older girls are romantically-inclined, his poetry readings in French have a powerful effect on them. Following the end of the winter term, class is in session and Wiley reminds the classes of their term paper. "For the senior class….the deadline for term papers in French on whoever poet you have chosen is due at the end of this month. Several studious girls have already turned in their papers. I see that several girls are working industriously in the library, class is dismissed". Two senior girls stay in the classroom. Wiley looks at the quizzically…"what can I do for you two?"

Sandra Fellon…." May we talk to you? It's about the term paper". Wiley…."I was just about to start grading some papers that have come in. I am very pleased with them, too! My efforts this year are beginning to pay off. What can I do for you?" Both girls sit down on adjacent desk tops by his desk. Brenda Lathrope is the leader….."we are finding this assignment very challenging, both of us. We want to graduate but are anxious about this assignment. We don't want to fail the course. That would be a black mark, wouldn't it?" Both girls look expectantly at Wiley, hoping for some sort of reprieve from what they have agreed amounts to execution, as far as their parents are concerned. "Just what is the difficulty? Do your best and things may turn out to be for the good". Sandra remains concerned, "What If we turn something in that is unsatisfactory, what then?" She looks at her companion, squirms and pulls her already short skirt higher on her thighs. From behind his desk Wiley notes her pink panties showing seductively and reacts by swallowing hard. His reaction, flushed countenance and rapid eye movements encourage Brenda to imitate her friend's actions.

Wiley is getting somewhat nervous at their behavior. "Just what are you inferring, girls? Without another word, both girls slide their panties down to their ankles and stand beside him at his desk, gradually hoisting their skirts to their waists to reveal their upper thighs and beyond. Sandra looks coolly at him as he leans forward as if mesmerized. Endeavoring to recover his composure, Wiley shows anxiety…."I am at a loss to react to your behavior, girls. You must desperately need to pass this course. Am I right?" Brenda, ….you said it, Reverend.....we are desperate. So why don't you make a reassuring move. My thighs are aching for a caress or two". Sandra joins in, …."mine too. Even more than that if you are up to it and it is necessary".

Wiley suddenly leans forward, moaning. He grabs both sets of buttocks and buries his head successively in their crotches, his tongue searching for the hidden openings. Reappearing several minutes later he is panting hard but trying to regain his self-control. "There are some attractions that can drive a man wild and you two girls surely have them. I must contain myself....this has gone too far already. Please pull up your panties while I recover myself". Smiling at each other in triumph, both girls adjust their underwear and sit back down on their desks tops. Wiley resumes his teacher role, …."you girls really surprise me! I would never have guessed that girls at this uppity school could have the nerve to do such a thing!" Sandra explains, …."

We do go home on the weekends, you know. So do boys from other like schools. We girls have learned here that getting what you want is of paramount importance in life, so why the big surprise?" Benda joins in to justify their actions, …."don't forget that we have been going to the country club for years and have seen much worse than this in responsible parents. Now, where to we stand ...so to speak.... regarding the term papers?" Wiley looks like a cornered rat,…."you girls have put me in a potentially dangerous situation....my job could be at stake here! This incident could become deadly serious for me, and you girls, as attractive as you are, would be defended to the teeth both by your righteous parents, the Principal, and even the Board of Governors! You have me over a barrel!"

Sandra giggles, …."at least you didn't have to put us over that barrel!" Both girls laugh uproariously and the potential significance of Wiley's predicament continues to sink in to his head. "Ok, ok....here is what I propose to do...If you turn in papers in French, no matter what the quality, you will get at least passing grades. I am unwilling to do more than that. Would that be satisfactory to you?" The girls look at each other, shrug, and agree to his proposal. "Now, leave my classroom and remember, there is to be no further mention of this to anyone.....agreed?" The girls agree and leave after looking down the corridor to see if the coast was clear. Senior term papers are all turned in and the senior class await their grades. A few days go by and Wiley has surmised that he has escaped the potential crisis. Jill meets him in the main hall and signals she needs to talk, suggesting the staff coffee room after classes. Wiley appeared in the empty coffee room, waiting for Jill who joins him shortly. "Hello, super-woman! What's up!"

Jill is wearing a serious look,…."believe it or not but rumors are circulating that you have been entertaining girls in your digs at night. Is this true? Surely not since we have developed an ongoing sexual relationship since the beginning of the school year?" Wiley is somewhat confused, …."I did have an incident after class recently. Two senior girls wanted some help with their term papers. That is all. I now realize that was an irresponsible decision but nothing happened and they left after a few minutes. See if you can find out who is in back of these rumors, will you? Now I'm beginning to worry". Jill feels rather motherly and concerned, "don't panic. I'll fish around. Girls can be spiteful and perhaps some girl is busy getting her own back with others". She leaves to return to the infirmary. Checking his mail the following morning, Wiley finds a scrawled note signed by Sandra and Brenda. They are unhappy at receiving passing grades in his course and are demanding at least B grades.....or else. His promise of B grades should be in writing, and given to them after class the next day. The ultimatum is clear. Wiley cannot refuse and writes a note on school paper, making that promise, giving it to Sandra after class. Sandra slips the note into a text book but in the process of walking to another class, the note drops out on the hall floor. It is retrieved by the Principal who just happened to be walking by.

Charles Gatewell calls Wiley into his office. Gatewell, coughing… .."I picked up this note from the floor of the main hall a few minutes ago. It is written on school stationary and suggests that you are promising B grades to both Sandra Fellon and Brenda Lathrope. They are in your Senior class, no? Is this a forgery....the school stationary is not available to students under any circumstances?" Wiley turns several shades of gray…."I confess...I am the author...I signed it. Let me explain. Both girls engineered me into a compromised position after class several days ago". Gatewell's eyes are bugging out and he licks his mouth nervously,…."a compromised position? Just what are you saying? Was this a sexual position.....with both girls! I am aghast! How could you? And Sandra's father is on the Board of Governors! Say no more!" He is shaking in his chair….you are finished here at the end of this term. Wiley tries to redeem himself…."Sir, I would like to explain the circumstances!"

Gatewell, shouting in a quavering voice, …."I don't want to hear all the sordid details...you have shamed the school, created what could become a major scandal...with my neck in the noose! A Reverend of the Anglican Church...my church and that of the predominate members of the Governing Board, in fact, all of the Directors! I want to keep this under the rug....at least until after school closes for the summer. Meanwhile I shall find out how many persons know about this and will take all the necessary precautions. As far as you are concerned, you will never teach in Ontario again". Wiley begins to sob and whine, what about my career? Gatewell studies his face with utter disgust…"my part is this unholy bargain to write a recommendation to your next potential employer on your behalf.....hopefully your next assignment will be in Katmandu! Now get out of my office and be gone within days of term end". Wiley beats a hasty retreat from the school after telling the teaching staff, including Jillian Murdoch, that the Almighty has instructed him to search for another position.

3. PRAYERFUL ESCAPE TO INDIA

Having resigned from his teaching position at Saint Hilary Girls School, in Toronto, Wiley returns to St. Crispins and the sympathy of its rector. Over the next few days he spends many hours praying and in meditation. While searching through recent editions of the Anglican News, Wiley spots an intriguing advertisement. He applies for the position which is located in India not in Katmandu as Director of an Orphanage financed by the Anglican Church. After a successful interview with the Governing Board in Victoria, British Columbia, armed with a glowing recommendation reluctantly delivered by Principal Gatewell, Wiley prepares to leave Canada for the Indian continent.

He arrives in Mumbai at the end of the monsoon season, staying at the Royal Bombay Hotel for three days. There he meets Preston Roundbottom, a wealthy Canadian with vast business interests in India. They meet during his first evening in Mumbai in the hotel bar. Preston sidles up to him and recognizes Wiley as a tourist. "You look like a recent visitor to India, am I right?" Wiley replies, "I just got in from Frankfurt last evening. A gruelling journey starting in Victoria, then to Toronto, then on to Frankfurt and here. I slept for twelve hours and have not ventured out of my air-conditioned room until now".

Preston pats him on the arm, "so you are fellow Canadian having had a grueling trip. You need a stiff drink, poor fellow! I insist on you having one, or two, and joining me for dinner here at the hotel. On me. of course. I've been here in India for several years, off and on, and would like to hear from the old country".

Wiley hastens to tell Preston why he is in India, " I am an Anglican Reverend posted out here to run an orphanage. What do you do here? They are both sipping gin and tonics at the bar. Preston replies., "I'm here in Mumbai completing some contracts, mainly with the State government. I am a computer engineer by trade and have started several companies here to do with media transmission systems, microwave stuff. You know, business success is mostly about being in the right place at the right time. I got here just at the right time having sold my Canadian company to Telus and brought that capital here just as the economy was heating up. In ten years I have become the dominant mover in media transmission and information processing in India. That has left me a very wealthy man. I keep a suite here at the RBH for my business arrangements. Drink up chum, I don't like to imbibe alone". Wiley gulps down his drink while Roundbottom motions to the hovering waiter for another round.

The order for another round of drinks prompts Wiley, "frankly, I'm starving. Can we take our drinks into the restaurant and order some food?" Preston, smiling, "of course! He snaps his fingers and instructs the Head waiter to have the second round brought to the dining room. There, at an ornate table they recommence their conversation. While examining the menu, Preston mentions that the Bombay Duck is exceptionally good here...even if it isn't duck!" He laughs at his own joke as Wiley had no idea of what constitutes Bombay Duck and looks confused. "Have you eaten much Asian food", asks Preston? Wiley shakes his head, no, other than curried chicken I am a complete neophyte. I must adjust my system to spicy foods as I may be here for several years". While waiting for their meals, Preston becomes curious, "where is your orphanage, I assume that its location isn't too far from Mumbai?" Wiley pulls out a piece of paper from his pocket, "it's at a town named Igaputi, some 110 miles northeast of Mumbai, on the edge of the Chandor Hills. I believe the orphanage is about fifty miles from the coast on a main road and railway from Mumbai. That information I was given by the Governing Board in Victoria.

Preston…."that's quite close to my mountain refuge, what a coincidence! I bought a small palace, what they call a palace in India. It was terribly run-down and reasonably-priced but I liked the location, high in the hills and much cooler than down below. By the way there is another orphanage further northeast, about 80 miles, from your place run by the State government here in Maharashtra Province". Their dinner arrives and they begin eating. Preston…."would you like some wine with your dinner and please call me Preston". Wiley replies. "no thanks on the wine, Preston, perhaps some ice water, though". Preston laughs and signals the Head waiter who is standing nearby in his exotic costume, "some ice water for the sahib!" He gestured, pointing at Wiley. Preston continues on the subject of the State orphanage, "I became good friends with the Director there for several years until he was relieved of his position for some obscure reason. Positions in government here are rife with political favoritism and nepotism. I was there frequently, a familiar sight, I'd say. I gave substantial contributions to the operation and to new facilities but now am forbidden to set foot in the place". He defers from further elaboration on the subject.

Wiley is gaining strength as he tucks into his dinner, "you know, Preston, the first odors that hit me after getting off the plane.... and driving through the city....a heady mixture of marigolds and human faeces! Roundbottom laughing, "you will get used to that. The Occidental nose cannot object to the powerful odors of India for too long. In no time you will be able to detect a wide range of Asian odors. The cuisine here is marvelous, they use many herbs and fresh spices...fascinating combinations that feature in both meat and vegetarian diets". They finish their dinners and Roundbottom calls for brandies. Almost apologetically he says, "I am steadily more wealthy by the day and my task now is where to put it all. I shall visit your orphanage soon and see what I can do for you". Wiley is elated at that prospect, "Preston, you are most kind. I have no idea what I'm in for at Igaputi but I hope for the best. Tomorrow I must start up there. I see there is a railway connection from Mumbai. Can I arrange reservations from the hotel?"

Roundbottom...."certainly, that's part of the attraction of living here in India as an Occidental. They will wait on you hand and foot and enjoy doing it. Something leftover from the British Raj days, I suspect. I will arrange for your taxi and your first class tickets .....on me, reverend. We should stay close while you are here, at least until you learn the local ways. We will be neighbors, you and I". They make plans to meet again in Igaputi after Roundbottom has finalized his business contracts and Wiley begs off further drinks and retires for the night.

The following morning, Wiley proceeds to Igaputi by train. On instruction from Roundbottom, a hotel security guard escorts him to the railway station and ensures that he is directed into a first class carriage and his luggage is duly marked. The security man hands him a small leather purse before leaving, for the tips, sahib! He smiles, waves and disappears into the milling crowds. Wiley is met at the Igaputi train station by his Indian assistant, also arranged by Preston, and drives to the orphanage in the dilapidated van whose markings in Hindi he assumes mean Anglican Orphanage at Igaputi. After a bumpy drive on dirt roads, they arrive at the orphanage where the entire staff awaits them in front of the main building. Stepping out of the van. "Good day to you all! I am Reverend Chase, here as the newly-appointed Director of the orphanage. I will meet you all individually in the next few days. Meanwhile, please go about your routine duties. His assistant introduces himself in cultivated English, " I am Chandra Seti" "Do they all understand English?" asks Wiley? Seti smiles, saying in perfect English, most of them do. And so begins Wiley's first day on the job.

Wiley, taking a deep breath, "the air here is bracing and clean.... unlike Mumbai". Seti...." yes, we are in the Chandor Hills, almost

1000 meters above sea-level and the stifling heat of the plain is below us. Permit me to show you our facilities, then we can have a light meal. You will find the rhythms of life and eating a little strange, at first but we have perfected them over many thousands of years, here in India. Our main meal is eaten in the late evening, a light breakfast at 7 am, a light lunch at noon, followed by a two hour rest during the hottest part of the day. Even at our altitude, the sun can be very intense. I must warn you to wear a sun helmet....I have one here, hoping that it is the right size". Wiley puts it on, "well bless my soul! It fits perfectly!" Seti ...."I take it as a good omen for your work here. I have been "holding down the fort" as the English like to say, and hope that you will find the management here satisfactory.

Wiley continues," before arriving here from the railway station, the potential language difficulties lay heavily on my mind. Your English is almost perfect, hardly any accent at all! If any, a trace of British. Explain that to me". Seti smiles, "I was an orphan adopted by an English couple in New Delhi at the age of five. When they returned to England and another posting in His Majesty's Government to Northern Ireland they took me with them. I was ten at the time. My formal education has been in Anglican schools in many locales, ending at Cambridge where I took a degree in Asian philosophy, then returned to India. There are so many towns and cities scattered all over the Western World with the name Cambridge.....Oxford, too. If only the academic search for truth and wisdom associated with those institutions had accompanied the names". Wiley is relieved, "ah, yes! I can see that we will get on well together...two dedicated Anglicans with shoulders to the wheel! I am anxious to see the facilities and to meet the staff, both academic and menial. Where can we start?" Looking at his watch, Seti says, "at the present time, the boys are all in class. Perhaps you can meet them in the main dining room at noon. Meanwhile, I'll show you the dormitories, the health clinic, and the general grounds". They set off briskly for the dormitories, then, crossing the football field in the direction of the gymnasium, Seti stops to talk with two men marking out the pitch. The conversation was accompanied by much waving of hands and voluble speech. Wiley is standing by observing them. When the conversation is over, " I assume that was the Hindi language? How did you become fluent in that language?" Seti chuckles, "my foster parents insisted that I speak the language while we lived in India, and I had an Indian governess until the age of ten. Their decision proved most provident as I studied the Indian classics in Hindi at Cambridge, a personal facility that was most appreciated when obtuse translation into English was encountered either by me or by fellow researchers in my department".

Wiley…."surely, with your academic background you could be on a university faculty here in India?" Seti sighs, "undoubtedly, but I view my good fortune as a child and student as a sign from God that my work is with the poor, specifically orphans....as I was. There was nothing keeping me in England after my parents died in a horrendous car accident on the M-1 one foggy evening". They enter the gymnasium and Wiley is surprised at the equipment and the facility, " quite impressive! You have all the bells and whistles!" Seti nods in agreement but with caution, "the equipment is well-maintained, however, we are short of gym clothes and sandals which wear out rapidly. Also the mats are beginning to shred". Wiley agrees and comments that perhaps some purchasing can follow a look at the accounting books,…."I need to appreciate the financials as maintenance funds come in from Victoria and the possibility of asking for more funds, and the long-term balance, of course". Seti suggests that they do that the next day. "Meanwhile, I suggest that you become familiar with the teaching staff first, and the general curriculum. We keep boys here until the age of sixteen, then they are transferred to government trade schools. In the case of exceptional students, we try to find them scholarships to regional colleges. Some of them have technical courses. It is most difficult for me to be unable to find further academic opportunities for really bright boys. But this is India, where the state financing is pulled and stretched in so many ways due to the socio-economic conditions. Let's go for lunch now...the noon bell has rung". The main dining hall is filling with students who sit quietly at the long, wooden tables arranged with utensils and bowls. An impressive male cook starts doling out the lentil soup while his helper hands each boy a small loaf of bread. The hall is quiet and when all are served, the cook nods up at the stage. Seti gets up from his chair and strikes a small brass gong and commences to speak In Hindi, then in English, "the Lord is generous in all his bounties. Let us thank him with all our hearts and strive to become his good servants in all our ways, Amen". A chorus of blended voices fills the air.....Amen.

Wiley is sitting at the head of the table on stage with Seti at his right side, "I am glad to see that we are all partaking of the same food and I think the soup is delicious!" I shall convey your sentiments to the cook, said Seti. "You may have noticed his magnificent moustache, he is a retired sergeant-major from the Indian Army. He also coaches both soccer and wrestling......a busy man here". Everyone gets busy on their soup and bread.

Seti....turning to Wiley, "before the Lunch End bell rings and the students retire to the dorms for study and rest, I shall introduce you to the academic staff here at our table". He says a few words in both Hindi and English and the staff members rise and form a line, each one shaking hands with Wiley as they pass from the stage. The hall becomes silent once more as Seti and Wiley are left at the table. Wiley...."I was presently surprised to see that all the academic staff have a grasp of English, so they are all bilingual?" Seti...."certainly bilingual in the routine use of the English language, some better than others. The course work is all in Hindi, of course. These boys are, for the most part are taken off the streets of Mumbai where many of them have been surviving like wild dogs, scavenging for their meagre food and sleeping wherever. When I first accepted this position under the previous Director, God rest his soul, I was amazed at the lack of discipline problems and social equality of these orphans. They seemed to appreciate immediately that we were offering them a real chance to be secure and happy".

Wiley...."in my short time here I have already learned a great deal and need to integrate these realizations with my own experience.

Now I, too, must rest". He returns to his accommodations and slumps onto his bed.

Several weeks later, Preston Roundbottom calls, wishing to visit. Wiley is looking forward to seeing him again and advances an invitation to come on following Friday. Roundbottom arrives that morning, chauffeured in his Mercedes sedan and parks next to the ramshackle van. Wiley greets him, "hello, Preston...it seems like yesterday that we were dining at the Royal Bombay Hotel. I forgot to get your telephone number or address or I would have communicated before. Time flies here and I find settling in and running this place, even with the excellent assistance of my Assistant a great challenge. I'm afraid that my Hindi lessons are few and far between and I thank God for Seti! Let me introduce you to him....Chandra this is Preston Roundbottom, a fellow Canadian who lives down the road...so to speak". Chandra and Preston shake hands. Chandra starts to leave to get about his business. Wiley says, " I am going to show Preston the facilities. We can meet again at lunch. Preston, let's walk-about, as they say in Australia. I'll take you first to the gymnasium"

Preston…."that sounds great!" He tells his chauffeur to occupy himself while he inspects the orphanage. The chaffeur smiles....almost knowingly and bows in respect. At the gym, exercises are ongoing... the main coach explains the routines. Many of the boys are shoddily dressed for gym work. Preston comments, "one can hardly expect boys to train properly without adequate equipment. I see that the floormats are badly torn and grubby". He walks around, coming to a halt where boys are using the climbing ropes and looks up at them as they take turns pulling themselves up to the ceiling. Surely this exercise is restricted to older boys, isn't it? I remember in my school that gym classes for kids under twelve were restricted to less arduous exercises". Wiley…."you are right. As you can see, these boys are in a senior class, 14 to 16 years of age. Their physical condition is adequate, considering that when they arrive here at a much younger age they are half-starved, under-weight, and many suffering from dietary deficiencies". Preston, looking closely at some of the boys, "the older boys do look quite healthy, some even robust, and with a sparkle in their eyes that tells me that you are doing well with them. Do they ever get the opportunity to go on outings....visit parks, museums, swimming pools etc.?" Shaking his head, Wiley, "unfortunately not recently. The old van is reserved for emergencies and bringing in supplies. We are having constant difficulties keeping it going. Luckily, one of our staff is mechanically-minded but getting spare parts is difficult". Preston reminds Wiley of their conversation at the hotel…."I mentioned that I had given considerable support to that government-run orphanage some distance from here? Wiley…."yes, I remember and understand that you were generous but it wasn't appreciated due to staff changes and politics". Preston expresses his disappointment again, …..sighing….." I was so disappointed at that turn of events. But now we have another opportunity....non-government run ..... and I would like to help. We have seen the Gym.....I would like you to purchase the required number of gym items that need replacing, clothing and mats, for a start and send me the bills". The lunch bell rings and they proceed to the main dining hall where the usual soup and bread is eaten. Wiley makes room at the staff table for Preston amid many bows from the staff....he is treated like a local rajah. Rumors have already flown that he is going to help financially. After lunch they repair to Wiley's office where the audit books are shown to Preston.

After a few minutes Preston comments that they are operating apparently on a shoe-string, "I suppose that your occasional plea for more funds is granted?" Wiley shakes his head and mutters "seldom, very seldom. They can come back with a litany of excuses....budgets are tight everywhere and I sympathize with the Board of Governors, there is only so much money to go around". Preston, sympathetically, "ok, and your vehicle is a wreck....without it you cannot expect to keep the operation running smoothly. I am going to send you a new van...one that has several rows of passenger seats in it....like a mini-bus with adequate stowage for your trips to town. I'll arrange it on Monday...delivery should be by mid-week. How does that sound?"

Wiley claps his hands together, "I am so grateful! I think that God had a hand in us meeting in Mumbai. I shall include you in my daily prayers. What a relief that is to me! Relief from imminent breakdowns!" Preston goes on smoothly, "the next time I visit I would like to go over the academic expenses with you....like textbooks and supplies...do you have a library?" Wiley describes the library as a small collection of books, mostly out-of-date material, technically, that we keep in a small room. No, we have no library by Western standards.

That brings me to another concern, says Preston, the older boys, those about to leave the orphanage must have such limited experiences with the outside world. Now that they can see it in a more productive light reflecting your good work here, I suggest that seeing the weekend starts tomorrow, that I take a couple of senior boys to my residence for the weekend. I could have them back first thing Monday morning. I have a swimming pool and a games room that they would enjoy, and several ponies in the stable that they could ride. I think it would be an illuminating experience for them....widen their experiences. What do you say to my suggestion? They would be perfectly safe, my servants would look after them and they would get an appreciation of the advantages of the commercial life and the hard work invested in it ..... and its potential rewards". How could I refuse, says Wiley, your generosity has been overwhelming. "Good", says Preston, "you pick two boys who you think would best appreciate the experience and I will do the rest. They can ride back with me today when classes are over. I promise that they will be returned promptly Monday morning. Perhaps two boys with a smattering, at least, of English?"

Wiley selects them shortly. He has two in mind who are intelligent and good students, "perhaps this arrangement could lead to them getting employment , with all your connections?" Preston is on a roll, "the sky is the limit! I would like them to appreciate that notion. This enterprise and experience could lead to their material salvation in their immediate future. Having no sons of my own, perhaps I am searching for father-son connections in my personal life, for family, I guess". Wiley chimes in, "family, we are all God's family, the human family....all his children! God bless you for your good works". Later that afternoon, Wiley waves goodbye as the Mercedes disappears down the driveway with two excited teenage boys sitting in the spacious back seat, on either side of Preston, who is smiling contentedly.

The following Monday morning Preston's Mercedes has brought back the two boys in time for classes. Later in the day, a teacher points out to Wiley that one of the two boys is sporting a nice wristwatch and his class-mates are envious. Four days later a new School bus arrives at the Orphanage, complete with flashing lights and enough seating for forty students. Wiley and the staff are goggle-eyed at the sight. The sales representative had his car in tow behind the bus. The school bus driver, too, is beside himself, swelling with pride and pointing out the sides of the bus.....Igaputi Anglican School No. 1. Roundbottom calls later that afternoon, "hello there, Wiley! I decided to opt for a real school bus. I'm a man of big ideas. The cost was not much more than a large van with multiple seats.....so, what the heck! I would advise you to go out with your driver to make sure that he uses the rear-view mirrors and avoids backing up unless it is absolutely necessary. Wiley is ecstatic, "thank you so much! Our driver was a tank man in the army and has never as much put a scratch in the old van. Thank you again!"

Preston enquires about orders for the new clothes, shoes, and gym mats? Wiley explains that they are assembling the orders presently.... sizes and all, and will let him know. "Do you want a copy of the orders?" "Heavens no! Just send me the bill and I'll take care of it. By the way, the two boys had a great time here and I gave one of them a Timex wristwatch. I only had one on hand but will get more if more boys are allowed to spend weekends here. It was so heartwarming to see his reaction...it seemed to lift his spirits and give him more self-confidence. Must go now, business calls. I will telephone you in a couple of weeks....perhaps more boys can visit me. If so, I will send the car for them. Goodbye for now!". Wiley thanks him again for the bus. Preston has hung up. Weekend trips for the boys continue....into the early summer, and many senior boys seem to be wearing Timex watches. Gym supplies are delivered making the Head coach proud of his spruced up facilities and smartly-dressed boys.

The local newpaper in Igaputi has wind of a story on the orphanage as the new school bus has been well-advertised by its shiny newness, kept up by daily washings by the driver who now sports a leather cap. Wiley's phone rings two weeks later. It's the editor of the Igaputi Weekly, who would like to do a story on the orphanage. Also, to send out his senior reporter and a photographer? Wiley thinks fast….."as final exams are fast approaching, I would prefer if you could wait, perhaps for our graduation exercises? We should have twenty-two senior boys graduating, some are going on to local colleges and the rest to work in various enterprises throughout Maharashtra State. The editor is delighted to hear of the success and promises to call later at graduation time. Wiley Chase has been sending monthly reports to Victoria, touting his successful upgrading of the facilities, including a new library building. The Anglican church congregations in Victoria have banded together in a book drive and several hundred pounds of donated books have been shipped at a special educational rate. A teacher of English has been hired who also serves as the new librarian.

The Director of the government orphanage some eighty miles away has been apprised of Chase's success, particularly of the intended placement of ten senior boys from Igaputi with scholarships in the local colleges. Applications from his establishment this year have all been denied, and he is ready to cry foul. He has also discovered that Roundbottom visits the Igaputi orphanage regularly and donates large sums of money. Suspicious and knowing of his connection with the previous government agent at his orphanage, he contacts the Maharashtra Ministry of Social Welfare and exhumes the sordid case. A Ministry representative, a Dr.Kilah Rafani is assigned to look into his allegations and phones for an appointment. Rafani…."this is Dr. Kilah Rafani representing the Ministry of Social Welfare. I would like to inspect your orphanage and to talk to students, especially the Senior boys. Would next Wednesday be convenient?" "Just a minute, let me check my schedule...one minute, please. What does she want flits through Wiley's mind.....is it about Preston Roundbottom? So many boys with wristwatches! So many boys weekending with him. So many senior boys displaying their watches to younger boys and giggling. All these thoughts flash through his mind at lightning speed. "Yes, I can be available next Wednesday. Please come directly to my office, I shall be waiting for you there". Rafani replies "I should arrive in the morning, say about nine am? And would you make a list of the Senior boys as it may be necessary to interview them. Just a routine matter, Reverend. You seem to have garnered a large number of scholarships this year. We have received an official complaint. You must have some exceptional academic students in your care and I think you should be congratulated on this accomplishment. I'll look forward to meeting with you next Wednesday morning".

Wiley Chase is torn between fear and anger. Anger he directs mentally at Roundbottom. What has he been up to that is bringing the Ministry down on his head? He calls Roundbottom, "hello Preston. Sorry to bother you at this hour but I just had a call from a Dr. Rafani, Ministry of Social Welfare. She wants to interview the Senior boys.... it's about their scholarships. Do you know anything about this?" Roundbottom replies, " I have made some good connections with the State scholarship committee. In fact, I'm setting up an endowment fund to expand their available funds starting next year.....calling in ten marks on this year's funds". Wiley groans aloud, "for God's sake! I think that we were awarded the entire lot....and that has started some loud screaming from somewhere. Round- bottom says that he has heard that the government orphanage was denied any scholarships this year, that's probably where the whining is coming from. So what"! Wiley remains in borderline hysterics…."she intends to interview the Senior boys! The watches you gave them were rewards, weren't they? Rewards for what? I had an unsigned letter several months ago suggesting that you were a dangerous pedophile with a lengthy record from that state orphanage. From the new Director there.....may be he has heard of the new bus as well!". "That's not good, says Preston! Christ! Maybe I've been too careless. If the boys keep their mouths shut we are safe. Nothing can be made out of gifts to poor children, can it?" Wiley asks him a straight question…."have you been ...... messing...playing around...with my boys? Are you a sodomite? And I have visited your estate with them on several occasions! Good Lord! The weekend activities seem to be quite natural, but what about those at night?" Preston admonishes him for being so puritanical. "Boys have been buggered in India for centuries. Young lads going into domestic service in the wealthy houses, particularly Brahmin houses, are expected to "give in" so to speak, to the head of the house and they left at the marrying age with a nice pot of money to establish themselves in business. It's a cultural given, with parental assent. I suspect that it is still going on. Cultural traditions here are hard to break and often very convenient". Wiley persists, "you still haven't answered my question, cultural traditions aside!" Roundbottom getting exasperated, "after all I have done for you! The snake that bites the helping hand! I take that back.....the snake in Original Sin mythology is enough. Call me as soon as she leaves next Wednesday....we must find a solution that protects us both. Stay calm and call me".

Wiley is on tenterhooks waiting for Wednesday.....the Day of Possible Doom. Seti senses that something is in the wind a few days later, "what's bothering you Wiley? Are you feeling the heat? The dry season affects some people unduly, those not yet fully acclimated to our climate". Wiley is feeling in a confessional mood, "I must tell you, the impending visit of that Ministry woman has me on edge. Why is she coming here...poking around .....and so many Senior boys sporting watches. What do you think?" Seti begins to calm him down beginning with his suggestion that Wiley may be reflecting a cultural dilemma that's causing his worries. Seti volunteers to talk to the Senior boys.....in Hindhi of course, reminding them of their good fortune and in light of our cultural values here in India. He refuses to believe that the scholarship Board is going to backtrack on their decision. It's just not the Indian way. "Of course there is the possibility of some back-room skulduggery but that appears to be offset by anticipated fresh infusion of scholarship funds starting next year courtesy of our Mr. Roundbottom". Seti`s training in ethics of the Indian mind suggests that long-term outcomes in effect are of most importance as Roundbottom is providing a large endowment invaluable in future years. Wiley is reestablishing his unagitated state of mind…."you seem to know more about these things than do I! Yes, talk to the boys, they should be grateful for their own opportunities and support those for students following in their footsteps. I leave it to you, then".

Fateful Wednesday arrives and so does Dr. Rafani.....punctually at nine am. Wiley hastens to meet her as she leaves her car, "hello Dr. Rafani! Are you a medic? Rafani explains that she earned her doctorate in Sociology from Birmingham. "Have you arranged with the Senior boys, and where can I interview them?" Wiley…."you may use our new library. It is large enough. Come with me there and while you are settling down, I will fetch the boys. They are presently with my Assistant, Chandra Seti. Make yourself comfortable, there are plenty of chairs and desks there. Wiley Chase goes to a spare classroom where Seti is talking to the Senior boys for the second time in two days, reminding them of their obligations to the orphanage that has succored them for so long. "The doctor is in the library waiting for the boys. See if you can stay for the interview, Seti. Remind her that you are a Cambridge graduate in Asian Culture. I will be waiting in my office".

One hour later a boy knocks on his office door, saying that all is finished. Wiley walks quickly over to the library where Seti and Rafani are having an animated conversation about ethics in the modern world. Set turns to greet him. "we've had a nice chat and Dr. Rafani is pleased and impressed with the responses of the boys to her questions". Dr. Rafani begins to gush her response…."it has been an enjoyable experience. To see waifs formerly living on the streets of Mumbai preparing for higher education. You should all be proud of your accomplishments. That is the message I shall take back to the Ministry. Your work here is indicative of the potential for social change in the lower classes. I intend to visit the government-run orphanage northeast of here and am eager to compare your respective results with

Senior boys. Cumulative conditioning over several years, especially those of the early teen years is surely a reliable indicator of success. I must be going now, thank you for a most inspiring visit". She climbs into her little car and disappears in a whirl of dust. Seti turns to Wiley, "the dry season...so dusty. Do you think that Mr. Roundbottom could be convinced to pave the road. At least down to the main gate?" Wiley, exhaling a huge sigh of relief, "I will get it paved from my own salary, if necessary! What a release! I need a drink!" They both heave sighs of relief and return to the main building for a cool lemonade.

This experience has severely shattered Wiley's confidence in Preston Roundbottom, especially in his apparent motivations. The visage of Charles Enright Gatewell's facial paroxysms comes as a mental flashback. The guilt he generated at St. Hillary's has now been compounded by his recent experience at the orphanage, including his apparent failure to recognize Roundbottom's pederastic inclinations. Did he have a mental bloc due to his own two brother's sexual inclinations? He begins the onset of extended prayers in the evenings, for several days, pleading for advice from the Lord Above to assist him in his decisions. Wiley tends his resignation as Director of the Igaputi orphanage to the Board of Governors by telegram and recommends that Seti be promoted to that position, citing his steadfastness, integrity, and ability to compromise effectively with State government officials. Seti`s Anglican background is hardly ignored by the Board, also him being a dark-skinned Cambridge man. His resignation is accepted and Wiley packs up with relief and returns to Victoria. There, over the period of two years, and financed by an admiring, middle-aged Anglican female, he earns his doctorate in Philosophy with a thesis on Ethics in the Modern World.

4. RETURN TO CHURCH PRACTICE

Dr. Wiley Benton Chase desires to obtain an appointment in Victoria as an Anglican priest. To that end we find him being interviewed by the Bishop of Southern British Columbia, C. Roman Journeyman. The

Bishops Office is located in Saint Albans church. Dr. Chase knocks confidently on the large oak door precisely at his appointment time.

Bishop…."enter, this is the House of God.....everyone is welcome!" The slight, dapper man sporting a short and grizzled full beard enters the room. "Take a seat Reverend Chase, while I finish signing this document". Chase obliges, sitting in the leather chair in front of the bishop's desk. He glances around the wood-paneled walls which are covered with photographs, many showing the bishop in groups of parishioners and sundry other churchmen. One large, colored photo in a rich ebony frame is placed strategically on his desk. Looking closer, Reverend Chase identifies the white bishop standing out centrally wearing the scant costume of a Zulu chieftain, among brown-skinned Zulus festooned with ostrich feathered capes and head-dresses. He is leaning on a large ebony rendition of the Cross. "There, that's finished!" Looking up over his bifocals, the Bishop he sees that Chase is seemingly mesmerized by the prominently placed photo. "That was quite a trip and a great coup for the Church, getting an agreement to allow church schools throughout the Zulu homeland. That the king and I were at Cambridge together as under-graduates probably helped".

"Now to present business! I have looked over your records, reminded that you have trod on a Dark Continent, too......hmmm.... Director of the Anglican orphanage at Igaputi". I vaguely remember some difficulty there in India involving a wealthy Canadian patron overly fond of young boys. Temptation abounds, doesn't it and comes in so many forms. Now, to move on, sadly, the rector at Saint Thomas's has succumbed to the pressures developing world-wide for female emancipation, specifically for female priests and homosexuals in general. He has bolted into retirement. Saint Thomas's is one of our oldest parishes here in Victoria and well- funded, shall we say by a well-heeled clientele, to use the modern vernacular! The majority of parishioners are steadfast traditionalists and they resent that trouble-making minority who have been working like beavers to turn the tide. That is to say, turn Saint Thomas's into a forward-looking and modern establishment. As the newly-appointed Rector, how would you handle the situation. Many of the traditionalists are retirees, squeak ing by, so to speak, poor as church mice. Significantly, a considerable number of the thoroughly-modern Milly's are very well-to-do. Do you see my point?"

Taking a deep breath and determined to show his potential as a problem-solver, Dr. Chase begins a seemingly appropriate dream, "I visualize a clear and straight path before us. Like modern Essenes, the ethical arena must be entered with stout hearts and firm commitment. As you know, my doctoral thesis here was centered on ethics in the modern world". The Bishop seems to be impressed, "yes, I get your intent but how, specifically, would you move on the matter?" He raises his eyebrows in anticipation.

Taking a deep breath and with fervor, Dr. Chase continues "I would wield the broom of righteousness with vigor and sweep out the opposition. A clean slate is easier to write on, no?" Bishop...."truly! but you have yet to identify the sweepees! Unfortunately, they include the majority of the congregation " Wiley...."I have been given to understand that a minority of parishioners have been financing the operations and are determined to accept the New Order. That is, ordination of females and toleration of homosexuals in general. The mission of the church must be defended financially or steeples will collapse, organs sound turn sour, and homes for the aged and poor will suffer. There will be paltry funds for our overseas work. Need I go on?" The Bishop becomes analytical, "so, as I hear you, let the hide-bound go elsewhere and let us rebuild the congregation on the theme of Christian tolerance and love...... to overwhelm the dogmatic aspects of role and function in the church. Couldn't that be a bit risky? Where could it end! We remain saddled with a definition of toleration and love!".

Wiley falls back on his recent academic studies, "I have never wavered from the concept that the Redeemer expects us to redeem ourselves. We must have faith that change in the world can be redeeming and uplifting to the human spirit! We need change and coming together". The Bishop, leaning back in his armchair, "I am known for my ecumenical leanings. Churchmen the world-over are facing common dilemmas...a fast-changing world, population explosion, rapidly-reducing finite natural assets, pollution, and the expanding pox of excessive materialism. The population question raises more than eyebrows in the Vatican and I fear that ecumenical concerns will turn to dust before ultimate disaster strikes. God help us all! Meanwhile we must soldier on. You have my blessing for your new appointment. It will be promptly processed. Keep me informed through my aide-de-camp. I am presently organizing a church foray into the Pacific Islands, starting in Samoa where the king has indicated a warm reception. I may be absent for more than three months, starting in November, back in the Spring. Go about your business now. You have much to do in anticipation of your new role as Rector of Saint Thomas". He extends his right hand across his desk. Wiley kisses his ring, bows obediently and shuffles backwards out the door.

Wiley introduces himself to the congregation on the next Sunday, having met again with the Board of Governors for the Orphanage at Igaputi shortly after receiving the bishop's blessing. He had no doubt that their enthusiastic reception of him upon his return had percolated upward to the Office of the Bishop. Apparently, the orphanage has thrived under the caring hand of Chandra Seti. At St. Thomas's the choir stands and sings "Onward Christian Soldiers, Onward as to War" and Wiley wonders who selected that hymn. It does not integrate well with the theme of his upcoming sermon. The common sing is "Oh, Jerusalem!" which doesn't improve his spirit, either. The congregation then sits and expectantly awaits his sermon.

Wiley surveys the size of the congregation and sets his jaw. "Welcome to you all! Although I have met the laity leaders here in the parish, the general congregation and I are personal strangers despite being Anglican brothers and sisters in spirit. My theme for the sermon this bright, sunny morning is tolerance and acceptance of change. Just as Jesus and his Essene brethren, including James his brother, thought hard and prayed for strength of purpose in dealing with the Temple in Jerusalem and its materialistic and wayward priests, so must we carry on their work started so long ago in Palestine. Nowhere on this glorious planet, our gift from God, have we, the inheritors, escaped the pain and doubt that all mankind has faced in times of change? Thoughtful change since historic times can lead us forward and closer to God and our obligations to understand the true meaning of life in our search to peace and happiness. Jesus stressed in his teachings that no man or woman should stand alone, apart from their fellow human beings. Such loneliness whether by personal decision or through circumstances beyond personal control, such as leprosy, a crippled body or mind, genetic factors, also leads potentially to enforced separation from the Almighty, as we are a profoundly social species. Yet the history of Man tells us that we have actively and with malice, expressed through tribal, cultural, or religious affiliation expressed deadly intent on the unfortunate or strangers among us.

To accomplish these ends, identifying and separating persons" "different from us"" has been, and still is, a significant interest and intent in all societies today. One could almost call it a social game, an evil game that can suddenly turn deadly, even be formalized into political doctrine and organized with technical procedures to rid us of such undesirable people. I remind you of the ovens at Buchenwald and Auschwitz, and the state of those fortunate enough to survive. Yet, such activities continue into the present time, and surprisingly enough, pursued by ethnic groups previously exposed to that treatment themselves". He takes a drink of water, then continues.

"Oh yes, we are a cunning and devious species, justifications and rationalizations abound...""".tit for tat, " "they did it first"".....behavior that rightfully belongs to the childish and brutal ages of Man's earlier history. What have we learned? That ethics and politics don't mix well, that greed and brutality can get you what you want, Might against Right, that it's" "US"" against" "THEM"" for whatever reasons appeal to your personal bias and prejudices, or can be propagandized to appeal to the majority, even in a so-called democracy? Witness the recent identification of ethnic groups as" "terrorists"", the Evil Empire, and calls for a modern crusade. Surely attempts no more

Christian than the original Crusades to take back Jerusalem, or the present attempts to keep that holy city for one's own kind". Another drink of water follows. One's own kind! How tribal can one get! If we are going to support the concept of Original Sin, and insist on turning it into granitic dogma, let's be more honest about it. We are our brother's keeper, as recognized and written down probably more than three thousand ago by the few wise men of that time. All else in human behavior in all its perturbations fall within this domain which defines us as civilized human beings. To use ancient dogma to pursue separation, insure isolation, identification as" "less than us"" is unchristian at the least, and essentially evil at its worst. This brings us to the ongoing question of allowing female priests in the clergy and the acceptance of homosexuals in the church at large. Is this really a difficult conundrum? Wasn't Mary Magdalene accepted by Jesus as an equal among the apostles? Didn't Jesus emphasize the importance, the necessity, of recognizing the female traits of gentleness, reverence for life, life-giving itself, as attributes necessary in the search for a spiritual life, traits present in older religions at the time but absent in Judaism? The priest is not your "father", your Father is in Heaven, probably watching for your essential righteousness to prevail on this subject. I am closing this sermon on that note. Beware of outmoded dogma, react to suggestions for elevating change in a tolerant and truly Christian manner. You will sleep better and expand your understanding of Christ's fundamental message: LOVE ONE ANOTHER and so trace your steps further into the light. Amen".

A silence descends on the worshipers. Many are uncomfortable and dismay abounds throughout the pews. Many have never experienced such an all-embracing summary of man's evil to his fellows. His allusions to Mary Magdalene and female emancipation in the church are accepted primarily by the younger women less steeped in the dominant history of their elders. His suggestions that we have not come far from the entrance to the primordial cave are disquieting to many, both male and female, wrapped as they are in the security blanket of routine Sunday rituals and the associated social rites of post-service tea and chit-chat. Others are confident that he has spoken wisely and to the point. They are the minority who favor change in the Church. Many of them hold the longest purse-strings, also, and are determined to support the challenges of change and the re-adjustments that will be needed to bring them about.

Wiley looks about him for friendly faces in the congregation and notes their scarcity. After the choir sings a final hymn, he gives the blessing and the service ends. He takes his traditional place at the front steps, ready for the usual comments and thank you's. Many walk out past him in silence, looking straight ahead. Some small groups assemble in the parking lot, pros and cons, apparently, but communications are limited to quiet whisperings and shaking of heads. No riots break out! On the steps, while shaking his hand, some parishioners proclaim their loyalty to his sermon and its meanings loudly, as though to advertise their allegiance to his suggested changes. One elderly man muttered at him in passing..".no to perverts! Not in my church!", as he stomped down the steps.

In the following weeks Wiley confines himself to less rousing sermons but that first Sunday sermon has had its effect. The congregation is steadily shrinking, from week to week until some five weeks later less than thirty people are attending Sunday services, down from a starting number of about one hundred and fifty. A reduction of nearly eighty percent! Wiley is chatting to Deacon Silky, "evidently, the collections are decreasing, yes?" Silky, snorting, "what did you expect! That first sermon of yours tore the very guts out of many parishioners. They left damned scared and were reluctant to come back for more of the same. I don't mean to wag my finger, but I think it would be a better strategy to avoid more of the same .....get back to the familiar. I know many of them will show up again as matter of habit…..just give them time. Meanwhile, to show your smile instead of your fangs....why not start a series of bible studies, having them in private residences....at volunteers...away from the church grounds. On neutral grounds, so to speak! We've had them in previous years and they were quite successful. Wiley…."that's a good suggestion.

Make up a schedule...say on Wednesday evenings for the next three months. That will take us into the Spring.....and the coming of Easter. To bring in the crowds, how about having an Easter sunrise service in the park....up on the mountain. Could you arrange that before some other church gets the same idea. Better have an alternate site just in case others beat us to it. I think the younger people would go for that, especially, but we could arrange transport for the elderly....even push wheelchairs etc. That would bring out the community spirit, eh?"

Silky's countenance brightens, "now you are beginning to get it! Pray to God that there's no windstorm!" Wiley's renewed social strategy of conducting bible study sessions in residences of willing female parishioners is approaching the fourth session. These sessions, away from the direct influence of the church have resulted in a devoted following of seventeen women and spirited discussions. He is now preparing himself for a second assault on homophobia to be directed on the congregation at large which has steadily increased primarily through return. Some additions to the congregation have arrived due to the evangelical fervor of three women who have attended all of his study sessions to date. At his fourth Bread and Wine session , he address the group, "ladies, welcome to our fourth session. This evening I want to turn to the Old Testament and a particularly appropriate story, that of Prince Jonathan and David. As you know, David was the son of Seth, a handsome boy who played the harp and sang the old tribal songs. Please turn to Samuel, chapter 15 and follow me. King Saul, has been rejected by the Lord in as much as he had annihilated the Amelekites as instructed by the Lord yet kept the best of their livestock, planning on sacrificing them to God, much to the distress of Samuel, his mentor who had commanded him to wipe out every living thing as instructed by the Lord. Saul is thus rejected by God as king of the Israelites. God then instructed Samuel that he had found a more worthy candidate and told him to invite Jesse and his sons for inspection. But David, the youngest son was not present, being in the fields tending the livestock. Samuel then told Jesse, bring him here and God said, he is the one who shall be King. Continuing with

Chapter 16, Saul remains distressed at his rejection and his servants identify David as a good musician as an antidote to Saul's low spirits. Saul was greatly improved and is much taken by David who is also a good fighter and handsome. You all know the story of David and Goliath the Philistine the result being that David becomes a real hero, not only to Saul but also to Jonathan, his son.

David and Johnathon made a covenant with each other and became lovers much to Saul's distress. In Chapter 20, Saul, the king says to his son, Jonathan", "do I not know that you have chosen the son of Jesse to your own shame and to the shame of your mother's nakedness"? Jonathan and David meet in secrecy, weep and kiss each other then separate as Saul's wrath is overbearing and he makes repeated attempts to kill David who defects to the Philistines. In Samuel 2, 1:26 this homoerotic relationship continues. At the news that King Saul and his three sons, including Jonathan have been killed by the Philistines, David comments: " "I am distressed for you, my brother Jonathan, your love for me surpassing the love of women". David later became King and ruled wisely for many years. Evidently, because David had many wives he would be labelled today as a polygamist, perhaps as a philanderer, as a bisexual, or perhaps, as a recovered homosexual, reflecting homosexuality as a disease in the eyes of the ignorant". He stops for a moment to allow his information to sink in. "What does this story tell us? Before the arrival of Jesus in Judaic history, homosexual tendencies were not uncommon, that the ancient Israelite authors found no difficulty in that role for David, nor did their Jehovah. Christian history described the role of Judas as the betrayer of Jesus. Initially described as a disgusting piece of human filth, Judas was cleaned up during the Renaissance....in modern times, his kissing Jesus is described by some as homoerotic, perhaps reflecting a homosexual relationship!

Turning to other cultures, the Indian tribes of the Great Plains viewed gay males as 'two-spirited" individuals and gave them particular respect. Similarly, in many Asian cultures there remains great tolerance for gay people...also in the Pacific Islands such as Fiji.

In Chinese history, there was a serial succession of gay emperors who kept male lovers in the palace while insuring that the familial line remained unbroken through the use of concubines to produce male heirs who were similarly inclined....or culturally attuned to that identity. So what can we make of these cultural attitudes? For one, there is an absence of homophobic dogma across many cultures and in many parts of the world. In recent years, we have come to realize that homophobia threatens ecumenical desires to establish a commonality of approach in Christian thinking. Great damage has been wrought by church representatives of all denominations on children of both sexes, reflecting their allegiance to harsh anti-sexual dogmas. The discovery of neurotic behaviors imposed on children by the sexually-supressed has elicited public outrage world-wide and criminal proceedings generated due to violation of accepted public ethics reflected in law. Church officials in high places have attempted to hide, ignore, or falsify documents so to avoid public prosecution and the resulting negative publicity...and, perhaps shame. In my first sermon in our church, due to my concern and zeal for needed change to advance our Christian idealism, I now realize that I may have trod with a heavy foot on organizational concepts and accepted rites. This coming Sunday's sermon will be used as a personal confessional vehicle, in an effort to compensate for whatever damage I have wreaked on the congregation. Please let that be known to other members of the congregation. I would like to see a full house but would be extremely pleased if most of the regulars attend. Let us now stand for a short prayer in the spirit of Christian tolerance. Dear Lord, we pray that these proceedings find favor in your eyes. We are all in need of your continued blessings as we navigate through our sea of troubles. Amen. The Bread and Wine session is over and the group breaks up.

On the following Sunday Wiley glances around the congregation at St. Thomas's, it is the Sunday for his confession. The usual routine with the choir first singing two hymns followed by a common hymn. After everyone is seated, he looks over the sea of expectant faces, coughs, and begins. "It is often said that confession is good for the soul. I truly believe this old biblical adage. Perhaps none of us confess enough and frequently, either to each other, or to oneself, or to our Lord, Jesus Christ. Today I wish to convey to you some of the pain I have personally suffered. Pain that I brought on myself due to my intolerance shown within my family. My father was a non- practicing French Catholic, my mother an Anglican. They married and settled down to raise a family in New Brunswick. Three children arrived, all boys, me being the eldest. I went off to Frederickton to study languages". [He pauses for a drink of water]. "That year my youngest brother quit his last year of high school and ran off to Sudbury, for a job, being at odds with our father over his flamboyant manner and style of clothes. In my second year of university, he committed suicide in Sudbury. Two loyal friends of his accompanied his body back to Kedgwick, causing quite a stir, being transvestites, and loudly proclaiming that intolerance of his sexual orientation at home and the brutality he suffered in Sudbury weakened his will to live. A bottle of Anacin destroyed his liver. He had a caring soul that was ground down by indifference and outright antagonism. I shared the family guilt for his passing at age nineteen". [Another drink of water].

"My surviving brother moved to Toronto, went to art school, and presently works in Montreal as a fashion designer. He is gay and happily coupled with another artist. They recently celebrated their fifth anniversary. My father died several years ago and never mentioned their names. My mother died last year in Kedgwick. According to her priest, she whispered the names of my two brothers with her last breath". Wiley takes another drink of water as tears run down his cheeks. The congregation was silent except for some shuffling, sniffling, and use of Kleenex.

Wiley, recovering himself, "there you have it......a personal confession. If I have moved some of you closer to the Christian ideals that I know you have in your hearts, I am serving the Lord. Tolerance, compassion, and love are the most effective weapons we have to alleviate suffering and to fight the evils caused by bigotry and intolerance. I am asking you to join me in moving closer to the Light. There is much to do and the Lord challenges us to meet his expectations. The hymn "Onward, Christian Soldiers, Onward as to War" refers to our fight against superstition, intolerance, and their related fears. Let us now pray. Dear God, be with us in the coming week as we continue our journey as a congregation dedicated to your purposes. Keep us strong in our determination to do thy will with open hearts and fervent spirits. We make these requests in the name of your Son, Jesus Christ, Our Savior, Amen. I have one more announcement to make. The janitor recently found two large vases in the attic. No one seems to know where they came from. They must have been there a long time, covered in dust and debris. Southeby's has identified them as Early Ming Dynasty and very valuable. They are to be auctioned off as church property and the monies invested in our operations. I view this finding as a near-miracle, timed to the Christmas season and our upcoming events. Have a happy and productive week and I hope to see you all again next Sunday".

5. PRACTICE, PREACHING, AND SEXUAL ABUSE

Setton Major Gile, a retired lawyer and his wife, Dorothy, retired Anglicans from Edmonton, moved to Victoria the same year that Wiley became priest of St. Thomas's. Setton has his heart set on becoming a reverend in his remaining years and has obtained the position of deacon. He is meeting with Wiley in the parish office in the late afternoon. Setton….. "how should I begin this.....the recent party we threw has backfired! Someone snitched to the Bishop about the pot in the brownies. Do you think this will torpedo my chances of being ordained?" "Calm down", says Wiley, I have already put out the fire…..the Bishop called me and I assured him that it was just a vicious rumor. I have identified the snitch trail back to one of the choristers. As punishment, I instructed the choir master to remove her from the choir. When she came in for her next choir practice..... her robes and music had been confiscated and I suggested that she disappear from the congregation for at least six months. Shocked and shunned, she is mortified and neutralized.....and a warden, too! But it has worked!"

Setton, shaking his head, "too bad there has to be a casualty...but the church just cannot afford embarrassing publicity at this time, can it? What with the squabble about female priests and gays.....we don't need it! Anyway, with my potential ordination decision coming up with the Bishop, I can't thank you enough for your friendship and loyalty". Raising both hands upward, Wiley enjoys the expression of his power…."rest assured that your ordination is secure....I have backed you with the Bishop with the righteousness of George Dubya in the war against terrorism! They both laugh. "That obese chaplain who took this ugly rumor to the Bishop.....she'll get hers, too. What a hypocrite! She plagiarizes her sermons off the Internet and verbally abuses her husband in public". "Any idea when the Bishop is considering my ordination?," asks Setton. Wiley squints his eyes and looks at the ceiling, "my best guess is sometime this summer, probably mid-summer....July? Don't fret! It's in the bag! The old feller's a bit unstable, you know, needs to be ushered along in the right direction". Setton squirms in anticipation, "you've made my day! Thanks again, Wiley .....and God bless you for your good works"! Wiley, wagging his right index finger, "remember the old saying...we survive together, or hang separate ly.....or words to that effect. I may have to call on your loyalty some time". "Never fear....you'll have it in spades!", says Setton, without hesitation. "I owe you big time!"

Wiley, thinking expansively, "you know....the Bishop can't last forever…..at least not on this planet! If he insists on gadding about all over the Pacific he could end up like Captain Cook, in a community cookout! Those islanders must be getting tired of SPAM! If I were Bishop, I would spend most of my time fighting the forces that are trying to tear this Church apart .....gird my loins against disloyalty, overly-ambitious females, and.....all the rest. We must guard against shaky steeples and cracks in the bells. Yes! Cracks in the bells!. No sour notes pealing across the rooftops on Sunday morning, Setton! The human ear deserves to hear pure sounds, no discord arising to the heavens!". With a wondrous look on his face, Setton opines, "you have a natural talent for aphorisms, Wiley! Just as Jesus had. Now I must get home and tell my good woman the good news". Wiley stops his move towards the door momentarily, "by the way, Setton, where did you find that huge cross and silk chain that you have hanging in your den? Are you planning on wearing it with your deacon's robes? If so, I advise that you stay away from the river bank, that heavy cross could become a deadly anchor! Furthermore, as you are dreaming of becoming a rector, note that that noun is directly followed by rectum in the Oxford dictionary and there is a commonly-used colloquial noun appropriate to the beginning of that dictionary for that terminus of the anatomy!" He laughs at his own wit but Setton looks at him in confusion turning to a quizzical gaze and he leaves the church office.

Wiley returns to his work on a sermon and the phone rings. "Hello, Reverend Chase speaking. How may I help you?" It is Carolyn calling. Carolyn is a school therapist who holds Wiley in awe. "Hello Reverend, it's Carolynn, I need your help, once again. I have a case here at the school that is causing me some consternation. A young single mother with two small children appears to be heading for a crisis. She was almost an hour late in picking up the children from school yesterday. I've learned that this is often a signal of an upcoming crisis. I have made arrangements to visit her at her home this evening at 8 pm. Could I asked you to accompany me for assistance. Could you come? My apologies for demanding your time at the last minute....and without conferring with you beforehand". "Of course I can come, my dear. Other plans can wait when such needs as these arise. I assume that she had no reasonable explanation for her tardiness? Pick me up here at the church, I'll be here from 7pm on". They both arrive at the address in question and knock on the front door. A pale-faced and obviously distraught young woman answers the door.

Nancy….. "please come in. I'm Nancy Nobadi. I've put the children to bed so we can talk in the living room. Yesterday was the first time that I have not picked up the children from school on time. I have not been sleeping well for several weeks and took a tranquilizer at noon and just collapsed, I guess. No matter what I do, nothing seems to work out and I need some help". Carolyn introduces herself, "and this is Reverend Chase from St. Thomas's, the Anglican church nearby". Wiley smiles and extends his hand. " I'm glad to be here, Nancy, and we are both here to help you in whatever ways are needed. I believe that an essential part of my practice duties includes those in the parish area. If you would give us some idea of your troubles we can see just how we can assist you".

Nancy sighs, I can't go into an extensive account of my circumstances over the past five years ....it is too exhausting and complicated but my immediate problems are bad enough. I arrived here in Victoria a year ago after driving cross-country from West Virginia with my children and finally found this place to rent. The landlord reduced the rent if I would renovate the downstairs suite for another tenant. I agreed and spent two weeks cleaning, painting and repairing.... the place was a mess. The landlord had much stuff stored under the back deck and a family of racoons has moved in. When I asked her to arrange for their removal she was uncooperative and when I called the health authorities they came and condemned the property until a number of problems were taken care of. These includes illegal plumbing, electrical wiring, and drainage problems, all in addition to the resident racoons. When she was informed of these requirements, she got irate, refused to reimburse me for all the work and materials that I had invested in the downstairs suite and gave me notice to get out".

Carolyn shook her head sadly, have you looked for another place to live? Nancy replies, "I only have $900/month for child support to live on....this rent was only $500 if I would manage the property, collect the suite rent, forward her mail to her address in the U.S.A. until I could find a job down the road. I am barely squeaking by now....and the kids have had colds requiring medicines which I had to pay for".

Wiley, "oh dear, you are obviously up against a financial brick wall....and with ill-health too. There needs to be some drastic changes and we intend to help find them. For now, I suggest that you get some sleep .....can you do that? Tomorrow is another day and let's go from there". Carolyn agrees, "make sure that the children get to school tomorrow and keep in touch. You have my phone number if an emergency arises. Be careful with the tranquilizers". Carolyn and Wiley leave the house together.

The next day Wiley returns to the house with some flowers. Nancy meets him at the door, "why are you bringing me flowers? That's not what I need at this time". Wiley, "well, ...one brings flowers to some one to cheer them up, and that's my intention. Did the children get to school on time?" "Of course they did. I think that you should understand that I'm not just another run-of-the mill social case". Wiley remains unperturbed by her show of self-respect, "I fully realise that. You are obviously an intelligent young woman, educated, who has fallen on difficult times". "Exactly, I am an RN, formerly in a major hospital in Virginia in charge of the Pain Clinic (Cancer). Would you like to hear more?" "I am here to listen". Nancy invites him in to the house. They both take a seat and Nancy begins, "while working full-time and pregnant with my third child I discovered that my fourteen-year-old daughter was being sexually exploited by my husband. She was writing suicide notes on the blackboard at school and it took extensive investigation by a psychologist to get at the problem. I was in my third trimester and preparing for a leave of absence. I informed the police who took him away in handcuffs in front of our three-year-old boy. This information should give you some appreciation for my level of fatigue".

Wiley, "that is a calamitous experience and enough to drive anyone to the verge of a mental breakdown. Your financial situation is a further aggravation". Nancy frowning, "you haven't heard all of it! My husband's family is very wealthy and in high society and his two older brothers are well-established lawyers. My husband protested his innocence and the family engaged a law firm of national repute, trying to keep the son out of jail. Four years of legal wrangling followed with my husband out on bail and denied access to the house or the children by state authorities. Wiley asks, "so the State government got involved?" "Yes, they were deeply involved , also probably because

I was in my eighth month of pregnancy and had just taken a leave of absence from my nursing job". She continues relating the outcomes of her predicament.

Nancy gave birth to a baby girl, thankfully healthy, her older, sexually-abused daughter was exposed to a protracted series of psychological examinations and several court hearings, the stress from which has affected her mental health, even now at the age of twenty-one. Several Ministries and the county DA were involved. "My daughter and I were provided with some psychological and psychiatric help". "So what was the outcome of the criminal case, Miss Nobadi?" "My ex-husband was sentenced to six months in jail, filed as a child molester which is a permanent ID in that State, and assigned a legal responsibility to provide for his two children ($900/ month). Wiley frowns, "that judge was rather lenient....he should have got ten years, and sufficient financial support for you and your oldest daughter, at least until she was of legal age. Nancy continues, "that law firm tried every conceivable way to settle out of court, offering the big house in an upscale neighborhood and suggested a large financial settlement which I rejected. I wanted to see him found guilty and labeled as a child molester. I saw him shuffling down the corridor in the courthouse, manacled and in chains, that did my heart good, knowing that he was not going to do that to any other child.

The Reverend Wiley Chase decided to test her moral fibre, "now you have had all this financial and health stress, including PTSD, when you could have owned a nice house and had enough money to pay for all the family psychological counselling on a long-term basis. Was it worth it?" Nancy looks intently at him, "you tell me....you're a priest concerned with morals and ethics". Her response rattles his Reverend demeanor for a moment, "I apologize...that was an unfair question, especially asking that of you in your present state. What a life story....and I've heard many in my practice. I'll leave you now and get busy on your behalf. Have you contacted the Ministry of Children and Family (MCF)?" "I did that more than a week ago when the city authorities were ready to condemn the residence. So far, they have been unable to come up with anything. Presently, I'm on medication for anxiety and depression and fear that I'm getting worse.....not sleeping or eating much. As a RN I recognize the dangers but feel helpless to do anything. I've lost over fifty pounds since arriving here from Virginia". With his concern steadily heightening, Wiley asks her if her MD is aware of her condition. "I phoned him yesterday, saying that I may be close to a general collapse. He said just keep up with the medication". Wiley's concern is steadily increasing, "I will call the MCF first thing in the morning. Do you feel safe enough to get through the night alone?" Your visit here with Carolynn has given me some hope that a solution can be found for suitable housing, says Nancy. Wiley nods, "see you tomorrow then. Goodnight". He leaves with his head spinning. The following day two representatives from MCF arrive at the house and convince her to allow the MCF to take the two young children…..for a short while. She is instructed to sign a legal permission document.

Much happens over the next two weeks. Nancy does an internet search on the medication she is taking, finding out that numerous cases are documented as causing suicidal tendencies and several suicides have been attributed to this medication. She stops taking the medication and starts to feel better within forty-eight hours. She changes her MD and contacts a legal aid lawyer experienced in dealing with MCF. As she is feeling much better, she wants her children back but is informed that is presently not possible. Wiley visits her almost daily.

Wiley, "I'm deeply concerned in helping you secure adequate housing. Not only that, I have a strong feeling that God has put me in your life as a challenge that I must accept". He attempts to kiss Nancy every time that he visits, eventually telling her that he is in love with her. He proposes marriage twice in the next several months while Nancy is trying to regain her children. Carolyn phones and e-mails Wiley that she is severing all professional ties with him due to his behavior. Nancy now has to fend off the attentions of the Reverend Chase, "I cannot complicate my life any further....now that the children have gone into care with the MCF I want to concentrate on getting my health back and registering here as a RN, getting a position, and recovering my kids. Several months pass and she knows that this is a serious breach of parent-offspring relations, especially at their young age and considering what the family's gone through together. "Why can't the MCF help me with housing ?", she asks Wiley. "I thought that you would be able to do something. My retired father has given me his condo here in town and gone to stay temporarily with a friend out of town but that isn't a long-term solution". Wiley jumps at this opportunity, "when your father comes back you could stay with me for a while. I have access to a nice house of a parishioner who spends much time in Hawaii. Think it over. I'm still looking for church-related housing for you but nothing is available presently".

Nancy realizes that the MCF people are dragging their feet on the housing issue. She discovered that her application for subsidized housing had not even been processed. "They have lied to me, saying that the paperwork is in process, on several occasions. Now they are saying that I need parenting skills! Me, a practicing registered nurse who has raised three children under the most stressful experiences that any one should have to deal with! I suspect that their resistance and foot-dragging is a response to my questioning of the management of my two young children. By now they have had four foster-homes in less than six months....and head lice infections from each of them!" Wiley attempts to calm her down, " I think the problem is that you are not a typical down-and out case, you are a professional who dresses well and points out their inadequacies. Your father and your lawyer have advised you to kow-tow to them and you have tried that strategy. It doesn't seem to work, probably because they see it now as a strategy and continue their defensive games". Nancy realizes that the MCF is playing an ego-related game, yes, when they said that I lack parental skills I promptly suggested that I am willing to take whatever course is available. Are there any available? The social worker responded positively saying that several courses are available with vacancies and Nancy promptly requested that course assignment . The MCF then insisted that she must sign a second three-month extension of their wardship of her children. Desperately she signed the paper and waited two weeks before enquiring when the course would start. She was told that her mental state precluded a successful course experience. They lied again with manipulative and dishonest intent. Her father suggested that she take a private course and use that as a lever to reclaim the children. Nancy takes an intensive course over several weeks, with two-hour sessions and has got through two-thirds of it, doing very well. In fact, she was selected by the course-givers to assist in discussions. Meanwhile, the social worker has been resisting giving her regular visitations with the children and cancels the visits frequently....at the last minute. The last cancellation used the excuse that the children were sick. At the next visit she asked them if they had been sick and neither child said they had been sick. Wiley reminds her that her lawyer who has many years of dealing with the MCF told her that you can't beat them. "Your attempt to solve the problem that you've had with them lying in reports of interviews with you by your requests for the use of tape recorders or communication by letter have failed. They have no intention of submitting themselves to recorded accountability in any form, preferring telephone or actual conversation which they can then recall according to their convenience. Admiral CIA tactics!" The social worker assigned to this case does what she likes and treats Nancy in a debasing manner at meetings attended by other MCF staff, including therapists who have noted her laudable behavior. So the power in the Ministry rests with the hierarchy of social workers. Nancy secured one improvement by requesting that her visits with the children take place with MCF therapists present. The first such meeting saw them write a glowing report of that visit in terms of her parental behavior that no doubt raised the ire of the social worker!

Wiley has plans to play a personal role in Nancy's life, "I suggest that we look around to rent a place for you". I can't afford to pay sufficient rent to get a place, says Nancy. Wiley persists," I have been thinking.....I will pay the rent for a year for you....a year lease". Nancy, "why would you do that? I have already told you that I'm not interested in starting personal relationships at this time. You have been assisting me as a professional, a parish priest so let's keep it that way. I appreciate your efforts on my behalf....even if they haven't seem to be very effective. I am not romantically-inclined at this time, as I have told you on several occasions. Surely you have recognized this from my reactions to your attempts to kiss me"! Persisting, Wiley goes on, "I would like to concentrate on finding you a decent place to live....surely that is a laudable concern? Let's start looking tomorrow"! Nancy reluctantly agrees.

A little house in Saanich is found....$1550/mo. and Wiley gets the Bishops aide-de-camp and Setton as references. By this time Setton has been ordained a deacon in Christchurch Cathedral and is awaiting assignment. At the house and planning the move, Wiley exuberates "it's a nice little house and private, isn't it Nancy? You will be happy here and I can visit to see how you are improving!" Nancy hopes that her move will better her chances of recovering her children. It's a change for the better, I hope, she remarks. Wiley gives her twelve rent checks...all dated and signed so give she can give them to landlord. Wiley goes on, "you can use my cellphone...I have an extra". Nancy queries that idea, "that could mean I could read your messages...do you really want that"? Reverend Wiley uses that as an example of his honesty and motivation.....and his patience that she will appreciate his moves. Nancy has some privacy concerns, I'm not sure that you should be letting me into your private and professional life at this time. "I might snoop into your e-mail records"! "But listen, says Wiley, I have nothing to hide. By the way, the pot brownie caper that I told you about is taken care of....and Setton has been ordained!" He chuckles, "I like telling you all the little tidbits, don't I? Just don't get the idea that because several women in the parish and elsewhere are constantly hounding me for attention that it means anything. This parish has so many neurotic women with inferiority complexes, sycophantic and needy, narcissistic, or just plain nuts! I have to be very careful because disappointment on their part can lead to rage or depression, sometimes both!" Nancy responds,"wow, you are talking about your parishioners like that? Are you sure that you haven't led them on, somehow? You know, the father image? I can imagine that the priest as father can lead to easy access to their personal lives".

Wiley goes on to admit that his fatherly concern and compassion has caused him trouble in the past but insists that is over now that she is in his life. Nancy answers," please think of me as a young woman in desperate financial straits, recovering from PTSD and concerned about her two young children. I have enough emotional stress presently and don't need any more. Just what do you mean by trouble in the past, anyway?" A real confessional opportunity arises for Wiley, "I did develop a close relationship with another teacher at the private girls school in Toronto where I was teaching. I had to break it off as she was getting too demanding and controlling. She got into fits of rage when she thought that I was two-timing her. That's the main reason why I went to India as Director of an Anglican orphanage for boys". "So you haven't seen her since....or kept in touch"?, asks Nancy. "Why would I want to! Bessy Wainright was hell-on-wheels". Nancy is becoming more curious about his priestly role, "you've been here as Rector of St. Thomas's for more than three years and there have been no other women in your life? When I think of priests, I think of celibacy and social service, apart from the rites". He distinguishes the difference between Anglican and Catholic priests in the area of celibacy, "admittedly, I've had some close encounters but nothing serious. I've concentrated on my parish work until I met you....and I think that was a sign from God"! Nancy announces her fatigue and suggests that he leave. Wiley responds, "yes, how time flies! I'll see you tomorrow then". He leaves the house.

Nancy is becoming more concerned as Wiley's conversation reveals his persistent motivation for a personal relationship, and one impelled by God. She uses the cell phone and by pure chance, discovers the name Bessy Wainright in Wiley's recent e-mail records and phones her for information. She declines giving her name but asks her if she knows Reverend Chase. Bessy answers yes, "yes, he was a fellow teacher at the private school where I work presently. Is he all right?

Why are you calling me and who are you? Nancy replies by telling her that Wiley has described her as a real harridan that he was glad to escape from. Bessy replies, "so, he is still at his usual tricks, is he and at the same time maintaining a connection with me after disappearing from the school. I should say leaving under fire from the Principal and from several irate parents with seduced daughters. He has given me the impression that he has regenerated himself as a practicing Rector out there in Victoria. Well, you know the old adage about leopards and their spots, he has still got his from the sound of it. You are obviously involved with him or you wouldn't be snooping around, would you?" Nancy assures her that she is not involved in a personal emotional relationship although Wiley keeps dropping hints to that end. She thanks her for the information and hangs up the phone.

The door bell rings and it is Reverend Wiley back at the door. Nancy mentioned that she was just talking to a friend of his in Ontario. Wiley becomes immediately alert, "I wonder who that could be"? At that moment, his cell phone rings and Bessy Wainright is on the line, furious and demanding information as awomen has called her, asking about him. Wiley breaks the connection and turns to Nancy in a rage," why are you causing me problems? Here I am trying to solve yours and this is what I get for it? Are you spying on me"? Nancy explains why she called Bessy Wainright…..after finding recent e-mails between you two. She reminds him that he had said that this relationship was terminated many years ago and that after all that she had been through.....and PTSD, means that she must be able to trust him. Wiley is outraged and calls her behavior perfidious. He reaches out, "give me that cell phone! ". He grabs her arm and tries to wrestle the cell phone from her. Nancy resists, "no, you apologize for lying to me about Bessy Wainright before this situation gets entirely out of hand. Apologize now"! Realizing that she is deadly serious and willing to stand up to him, Wiley tries submission. "Ok, I'm sorry". Nancy is not satisfied and becomes more irritated, "sorry for what? Grabbing my arm or lying to me"? Wiley lamely replies, "both, I guess". "You don't sound very convincing ....is that it"? Nancy looks at him straight in the face. Unused to this sort of psychological trap that he has got himself into, Wiley becomes antagonistic, "come on, now. What do I have to do...grovel at your feet? Remember that an apology is really nothing more than a social lubricant"! Realizing that she is seeing a side of Wiley at odds to his churchly mien, Nancy continues, oh? You learnt that in your ethics courses? U. Victoria gave you a Ph.D. in ethics? I think that the counterpart to an apology is forgiveness? Is forgiveness also a social lubricant? If in all significant human communication apology and forgiveness are merely social lubricants......where do integrity and honesty fit into the picture"?

Wiley realizes that he is digging his hole deeper, "I was being a bit facetious and that's a big mistake with you.....you are just too aware of human foibles and you are tuning in on mine. I should leave now so we can both catch our breath". Nancy agrees, "yes, please go, I'm getting depressed". Wiley slips quickly out through the front door and Nancy realizes that she is falling into another emotional trap, into a manipulator's designing scheme, one brought about due to her PTSD, financial worries, and temporary loss of her children. She quietly sobs. Wiley returns an hour later planning a major show of remorse to get things back under control. Nancy doesn't answer the door bell. The door is unlocked and he walks in calling her name. In her robe, she is lying on her bed clutching a bottle of pills. On the coverlet beside her is a note. "Nancy! Nancy wake up! What have you done?" She is very groggy,bleary-eyed and has difficulty focusing on him. Wiley feels a sudden sexual urge due to her fallibility and leaps onto the bed and turning her over. Ripping down her underpants he penetrates her forcibly, followed by a quick organism. Nancy has passed out as he leaped onto the bed. Recovering himself, and realizing that Nancy is unconscious, Wiley rolls off the bed and adjusts his pants. He spies the piece of paper lying beside her on the bed, noticing that it has writing on it….he picks up the note and reads it. It is a suicide note stating....."nothing is working for me....I'm falling down a darkening abyss, sorry about everything. Wiley you have really let me down!" Wiley is now in a panic. How many pills has she taken?

Is the bottle empty? Nancy is obviously deeply comatose. Wiley is frantic with guilt and possible criminal action. He calls Setton on his cell phone and explains the situation, obviously looking for advice. Hello Setton, "oh my God! I need your advice". Setton, "what is it Wiley, you sound very distraught! Has there been an accident"? "The girl with the dog, as you so cryptically call her, she has over-dosed on sleeping pills". "Where"? "Here in the house we obtained for her". "Is she conscious"? Wiley is panting, "I think she is slipping away. She swallowed nearly a whole bottle of pills. She was laying on the bed clutching a piece of paper". He fails to tell Setton of his aggressive rape of this immobile girl. Setton, "the paper, get it! What does it say"? Wiley groans, it's a suicide note and I am named as a contributor to her stress and predicament". "Take the note and get out of there! Come over to my place, I know it's late but we need to develop a strategy.....hopefully, no one saw you entering the house, or sees you leaving. Leave now quickly with the note!". Wiley puts the suicide note incriminating him in his coat pocket and quickly leaves the house. Without thinking beyond his own fears, he is inviting a criminal case of manslaughter, first degree, with Setton Giles aiding and abetting the crime. Why didn't this priest call for an ambulance straight away and stay with her until medical help arrived? Wouldn't that have been the automatic action of a true Christian?

Nancy woke up in the late morning with a raging headache and a feeling of extreme dryness. Arising from her bed she walks slowly to the kitchen for a drink of water. In doing so she notes her state of vaginal soreness and realized that she has been raped. Her torn knickers are lying on the bedroom floor. Dressing slowly she decides to go to the local hospital for medical attention. Upon physical examination and that of her torn panties in a plastic bag, the MD calls the local police and makes a report. A week later she discovers that she has an STD infection from the hospital findings and secures an appropriate series of antibiotic shots. The local police assign a detective to the case and find that the panties are positive for semen stains, hence check them for DNA. Reverend Chase never contacts her again. Nancy decides to take the case to the Anglican Church, asking the police detective to refrain from further police action at this time. She calls the Synod Committee on Sexual Abuse and retells her situation to the Head, Catherine Scrubbe. Scrubbe is not too surprised at the situation, mentioning that she has the power to defrock those individuals whose actions fail to meet the requirements for priesthood. She requests that Nancy provide a written report of her last encounter with Chase as soon as possible. Nancy is reluctant to proceed at the moment for several health reasons. Several days later Catherine requests a formal meeting involving the Anglican lawyer. Nancy calls Legal Aid and is informed that without her own legal representative at such meetings, she is placing herself in imminent danger as to the legal effectiveness of her case. She declines further communication with Catherine Scrubbe and concentrates her efforts on engaging a more competent lawyer, one skilled in sexual abuse and human rights cases. She finds one who is outraged at the treatment she and the children have suffered at the hands of the Ministry of Children and Family and at the psychological and sexual exploitive behavior of Reverend Wiley Chase. Her new lawyer decides that the first priority is to succeed in returning the children from the MCF.

She manages to do this when Nancy has acquired a full-time nursing position and has moved to a new house close to a grade school for the children. During this period of court procedures, the MCF personnel assigned to the case manoeuver to increase their harassment of Nancy by appearing at the school, demanding interviews with the children and reports on their progress. These activities cease when the judge reviewing the case removes the MCF authority, insuring that the family is secure at home and at school. The school administration recognizes that the MCF has attempted to dupe them with over-extended authority for the children, so the MCF personnel and lawyers are check-mated for any further action. The children do very well at school. Their appetites improve resulting in significant weight gain and normal sleep patterns return indicating major reduction of psychological stress level.

6. JUDGMENT AND PUNISHMENT

Two legal damage cases are prepared, one for the Anglican Diocese and the other for the MCF. The Anglican Church put up a stiff fight to protect their reputation which has undergone serious tarnishing and loss of parishioners reflecting difficulties of dealing with the question of female priests and the acceptance of gay parishioners and their marriage requests. A nominal damage award of 75,000.00 was assigned by a local judge which is put under immediate appeal.

The damage suit against the MCF proceeded to the British Columbia Supreme Court and was greatly assisted by a similarly major parallel case of recent precedence. Both case assessments against the MCF were financially crippling and resulted in some high political appointments being reviewed and terminated. The multiple millions of dollars has had a devastating effect on the Political Party in power.

Criminal proceedings charging Reverend Wiley Benton Chase with rape and attempted manslaughter were initiated with the cooperation of the Area Police Force. He was found guilty and sentenced to five years in a Federal penitentiary. His defrocking was an automatic action taken within the Synod which subsequently retracted their appeal on damages. Several months before criminal proceedings were initiated, Bishop Journeyman suddenly announced his early retirement. Presently, he is the Director of a co-educational private high school in Apnia, Western Samoa. Before criminal charges against Wiley Chase were made, he submitted his retirement from the Anglican Church and was advised by their legal staff to leave the country. That he chose a teaching position in Samoa was hardly coincidental as Canada didn't have an extradition charter with Samoa. However, that changed within two years, resulting in his forced return to face charges assigned to him.

Reverend Wiley Benton Chase (ret.) was found guilty on both charges, rape and intended manslaughter. He was sentenced to seven years in a federal prison and was removed from British Columbia and sent to Quebec. His pre-dated defrocking was precipitated by his convictions. Eventually, due to prison crowding and perhaps reflecting possible Gallic humor by the Superintendant, he shared a double cell with a former Catholic priest who was serving a term of eleven years for serial sodomy of choir boys with sadism and was in his fourth year of confinement. Chase was routinely raped by his cell-mate starting in the latter half of his first year. The defrocked Catholic priest eventually murdered him due to accumulated altercations over numerous interpretations of Christian dogma, according to prison findings.

Several months prior to the onset of charges against the Anglican Church and just before Bishop Ian Roman Journeyman hastily resigned and departed for a position as Principal of a private high school in the South Pacific , Setton Major Gile was elevated to Deacon by the soon to retire Bishop. Eventually, Setton was charged with aiding and abetting Reverend Chase and was defrocked from his ultimate position as a Reverend and sentenced to one year in Federal prison. He served his sentence in British Columbia and was released on good behavior after eight months. Ultimately he became a warden at St. Mathias Church and died of parathyroid cancer some two years later.

Nancy Nobadi regained her health, returned to the nursing profession eventually leaving nursing to author a book with her lawyer, specializing on legal and medical procedures used in child welfare legislation. She still resides in British Columbia and her two young children are top academic students in a Christian school.

After considerable investigation, in Canada, the RCMP discovered a long string of sexual abuse cases scattered throughout the Maritimes attributed to Preston Roundbottom by his Canadian victims who finally described his abuse following the first case of contact with the police and a charge. Similarly, the Indian authorities took up the case as described by alleged victims from a boys orphanage school northeast of Mumbai and boys off the street in Mumbai. Preston Roundbottom has successfully avoided extradition to Canada but may be prosecuted for his sexual crimes in India which continued right up until he was incarcerated in Mumbai. Due to his considerable charity work in league with the Maharashtra State Government, Roundbottom may escape justice based on a combination of foot-dragging and bureaucratic incompetence in Canada and a collusive legal, educational and police environment in Maharashtra State in India.

Waiting for No One

PREFACE

I wrote this originally as a play, then questioned its entertainment value and decided to convert it into a short story as the subject is an existential fictional drama of social significance. The occurrence takes place as a suicide happening on Salt Spring Island in the Southern Gulf Islands located in Southern Georgia Strait, British Columbia. The subject is counter to the usual gamut of modern theatrical productions which generally involve much song and dance……like burlesque. Hence, the short story conversion here. I was told some time later by a resident of that island that such an event actually took place several years earlier but perhaps entailed murder as well.

LUNCH ON THE DECK

The setting is a modest and secluded waterfront house overlooking islands to the east and surrounded on three sides by large Douglas firs, Pacific Madrones, and an understory of salal. The house is professionally designed of yellow cedar with large view windows overlooking the sandy beach through the fir trees, some twenty feet above high tide. A gravel path leads to the beach. The home couple, Joe and Margie are entertaining a couple from Abbotsford, Mike and Phyllis, a farming couple they have known since high school there.

It's a warm, idyllic day in July and Mike is sprawled out in his wicker chair on the cedar deck with the family cat leaning against his long, tanned legs, uncovered by his Bermuda shorts. Phyllis, his wife is nearby, resting on her favorite deck couch and reading a paperback adventure story. The home couple are in the house fixing a lunch for the deck.

I sure miss the cats on the farm since we retired," says Mike. Remember, Phyllis we had four or five but I never got to count them altogether as a couple were off in the barn. Just like the family cat here, Shadow, they were all black as the ace of spades and I couldn't tell them apart. Phyllis pipes up, "don't you remember that one had a white tuft, that was a male." I never had time to give them much notice. Running that dairy farm near Abbotsford was a demanding life and I was on my own when Dad had his heart attack and was permanently confined to that wheelchair.

Phyllis outs down her book for a minute, "you both worked like Trojans on our farm, sunup to sunset, starting right after high school…. well, within five years. A moment later, Joe and Margie emerge from the house laden with sandwiches and coffee. "Lunchtime, Kiddos, says Margie as she sets own the large tray on the spacious deck table. "Are you to talking about the farm? Remember, you are now retired and need to settle back and enjoy your retirement. That condo you bought after selling the farm is sure nice, private, well-landscaped and lots of retirees moving in, coming up from Vancouver for the fresh air and reduced traffic."

Mike tunes in, "yes, and made much money selling their houses down there. The real estate prices have gone through the roof!" They all sit up to the table to begin lunch and Margie pours the coffee. I remember the farm, she says, while you two sowed the land and produced milk, Joe and I took off for UBC and a higher education.

My God! We've known each other since grade school. You two were high school sweethearts but I never let Joe get that close to me….too busy thinking of a career for myself.

She passes the sandwich plate to Mike who helps himself to a couple. Between mouthfuls, Joe starts chuckling, "it didn't take too long, though, did it, Margie! We saw a lot of each other as undergraduates, taking the same science courses and studying together. Then off I went to dental school while you dove into public health and became a nurse. "Wasn't it after graduation that we decided to get serious? No more studying and the wide world waiting out there for us! Well, says Joe, even after marrying, when we both got jobs in Vancouver, we didn't see much of each other, except on weekends! A hectic professional life for both of us. I was really fortunate, going in with Doc McIntyre and be able to buy him out when he retired.

Phyllis was looking somewhat serious while stirring her coffee, "did you two ever think about having children? You know that I couldn't have any. I know I made quite a fuss about that but, Margie you were so compassionate and concerned about that. Mike just balked at the idea of adopting as there were a couple cases in town that discouraged him, And , eventually, me to. You two never had kids, either, I guess we are peas in the same pod.

Most farmers have sons, says Mike, to train and help in the business. Fortunately there as always enough help in the country before better-paying jobs began to rise in the city and dairy farming has been greatly modernized. Joe, looking up at Mike, "I'll give you a little secret, pal, there were many times in that dental office, legs cramping and fighting tension, that I would rather have been up there at the farm shoveling manure and whistling through my teeth!

Margie gives him a light pat, "the grass is always greener on the other side of the fence. I wonder if the cows think that too! Mike nods, "they do, at least some of them. There's always a couple of troublemakers in a herd finding loopholes in a fence, or even making one! But really, says Joe, I used to envy Mike's lifestyle, errant cows or not.

All the sandwiches have disappeared and second cups of coffee are on the go. Phyllis is again looking back in time, “we so young in the early days, young and adventurous. Remember that trip we took together, the cross-country one? Gasoline was relatively cheap and that RV really guzzles it!” “Like an Irishmen with Guiness,” quipps Mike. They all laugh. Mike and I would never have made that trip alone, all the way to Newfoundland and so many interesting places in between. “What fun we all had on that trip, says Phyllis, should we do it again before we shed these mortal coils? Mike, clapping his hands together, “I like that idea! Ever selling the farm and moving into that high-falutin condo system I’ve been itchin’ to run off somewhere. His suggestion is supported by Joe, ”how about taking a two-three week trip down to Costa Rica this winter? A chance to get some sun on our near-hairless pates and check out the parks and ecological reserves?

Now they are all getting excited, and Margie says, let’s go! Someone was telling me that the Americans are busy buying up the place. We should get down there before it fills up with malls and fast food joints! Joe waves a finger, “fat chance that’s going to happen. The Yanks will have to restrain themselves. Any government willing to set nearly one-third of the country aside for parks and reserves has different ideas about the quality of economic growth and the quality of life.

Mike supports him, “I’m with you, Joe, on those concerns, it disturbs me that so many people here in Canada are grossly ignorant of where their food comes from or have a low opinion of a farmer’s life. Margie agrees, not only that, but of the nutritional value of fresh food, organically-produced without a slurry of pesticides on it. The number of kids with allergies I had to deal with have steadily increased in the last two decades. Not only that, they getting allergies at a younger age, giving the ENT pediatricians a field day with inner ear infections.

Mike has more to contribute, ”the way things are going, corporate agriculture will soon be controlling most of our food….at last the kinds that guarantee fat profits! Economic pressures on individual farmers is persistent and growing but the consumers are in a position to turn things around. They should be more concerned about the origins of their food and its nutritional value. There are positive signs here in Canada and in the USA, look at the Saturday markets springing up everywhere. The Europeans never lost them and are more careful what they put in their stomachs.

As a dairy farmer, I was quite relieved when bovine growth hormone was rejected in Canada. It's been rejected in Europe, Australia and New Zealand, too! We dentists over the years have voiced our concerns about diet, too, says Joe. Too much sugar! Sugar is laced into everything to increase sales, not health. I shudder to watch these kids guzzling liter bottles of soda as there can be as much as five tablespoons of sugar in a bottle! Of course, that info is not included on the label. Does anyone read food labels?

At the mention of labels, Margie pipes up "that's what we need! Otherwise one has to trust the food corporation to show concern for public health which remains doubtful. That concern should match their concern for maximizing profits. If the situation is changing slowly in favor of public health, it's due to the rash of food illness outbreaks caused by the processing industry. I don't understand why our governments don't show more concern, put on the pressure for adequate labelling, instead of naively expecting the food corporations to regulate themselves. "I'm not so sure, says Phyllis, that, as a young mother, I would want to be pregnant these days, worrying about the safety of food in general. Makes me wish that we still had our vegetable garden and our free-range chickens. Oh, what one gives up to live in a condo with all its conveniences!

We are so lucky here in rural B.C. says Margie, if we're smart enough to take advantage of it. We buy from the local farmers here on Salt Spring and attend the Saturday markets. It's lot's of fun, too! By the way, says Mike, the fellow who bought the farm has turned it into a co-op, selling shares to allow him to pay back most of the purchase price to his oil-exec father in Calgary. His investors have a guaranteed milk supply for ten years and surplus milk is sold to a cheese and yogurt company and the profits reflected in the price of the shares. He's a smart fellow who has a degree in agricultural economics and loved being a dairy farmer. It pays to go to college! Draining her coffee, Phyllis says, we buy locally in the Valley as much as we can but how about the city folk who are locked up with the big food chains?

We can't solve all the worlds problems, says Joe. Other than by judicious voting choices and supporting NGO's what else can we do? We should be careful about sentimental reminiscing as some areas of life have improved, like some areas of medicine, cancer suppression, for example.

The breeze is coming off the water now, says Phyllis and I'm feeling a bit of a chill. Let's go inside and warm up a little. She and Margie collect all the dishes and take them into the house while Joe and Mike stroll down to the beach and talk about salmon fishing. The sun is beginning to lower in the West and a Great Blue Heron that has been fishing off some rocks takes flight, heavily beating his wings across the water. In the house the two women are busy preparing for dinner.

BREAKFAST ON THE DECK

They are all up by nine o'clock, the two women busy clattering pots in the kitchen while the men share the newspaper. When Margie signals that breakfast is on the deck, they sally out and get ready, inhaling the tantalizing aroma of cooking bacon. Margie comes out with the breakfast tray, "help yourselves to the scrambled eggs, we got them fresh and organic yesterday while we were waiting for you from the ferry, and butter the toast. The bacon is coming along in a minute, along with the coffee. Salt Spring coffee, of course! Too bad we can't grow it here also!

When Phyllis arrives with the bacon, Mile digs in to it. "Hey, this is back bacon and double-smoked! Margie fills the coffee mugs all around, then sits down herself. Joe, smelling the coffee, "nothing but the best! I see Mike that the sea air has given you ravenous appetite." "You know us farmers, we enjoy our eats." They both laugh. Gosh, how the time flies, says Phyllis, we've only been here with you for two days.

We'll have to keep an eye on the clock, says Margie, or you'll miss the ferry, so get your stuff together. They enter the house while their husbands empty the coffee pot then take a last walk down to the beach. The tide is in and the heron is back to check for tidbits, including the occasional young herring. He quarrucks at them noisily and flies off with his slow, rhythmic wing beats. Mike whistles, "I shall remember his call, what a great sight to close this short visit with you."

They are standing by the car. Thanks for the enjoyable but short stay, says Mike. Joe says, "next time plan on coming for a few more days. We have fishing to do!" Phyllis says, "next time it will be longer, we haven't covered everything yet, have we? We're all getting long in the tooth and prone to looking backwards but we still have time! Yeah, says Mike, memories are an essential part of life….and learning from our mistakes that are imbedded in them! Have we got everything, Phyllis? She nods and hugs both Joe and Margie, then gets in the car. Mike gives them a big grin as he begins to drive away. ""Don't forget about that Costa Rica trip, says Joe. I'll get all the info so we can decide on itinerary and reservations. Drive safely through Vancouver." They all wave as the car disappears down the driveway.

As they turn into the house, Margie looks at Joe, "I feel so sad whenever they leave. We have so much life in common. Mike nods, vigorously, "I think that Mike is antsy in that condo after living such a robust life outdoors. I advised him to develop a physical routine …..walking, running, or going to the gym. I see he is getting a bit paunchy but who isn't at this stage of life. I'm glad to have the lawn work, pruning and wood chopping. That's my next job….to fill the woodshed for the winter fires. What are you up to?" "I'm going to spin a few pots ….it always make me feel better after goodbyes. By the time the oven is ready, I'll have some ready to go." They both go about their activities, Margie disappears into her pottery shed as Joe goes in the opposite direction towards the woodshed, looking for his axe.

INTERLUDE WEEKS

This couple is having their routine coffee on the deck when the speaker telephone rings loudly and Margie answers it. "Hello, is that you Mike? You sound different, are you sick?" Mike answers, "Yes, I am. Sick at heart, anyway. It's the suddenness of it all." "what's the problem? Can we help in any way?" After a short spell, Mike speaks, "Thanks, but there's nothing that any of us can do. I find it difficult to tell you but Phyllis has gone. I couldn't wake her this morning, despite my feverish shaking and called 911 for an ambulance. She apparently died in her sleep, quietly…..her heart stopped. The funeral is next Thursday, can you come over? I know that she would like both of you to attend."

"Of course, so sudden. You must be devastated. We could come earlier. Call back after you have thought it over. I am so sorry, Mike! Goodbye." Margie sat there for a few minutes, not moving until Joe came out of the house asking who called. She told him the news. You should have let me talk to him for a few minutes, said Joe. Guess you are too upset. Margie is teary-eyed. "Phyllis passed away in her sleep last night so Mike failed to wake her this morning."

Standing there on the deck, Joe gazes unseeingly at the trees, "what a shame! She didn't have any heart problems, did she? It must have been time for her to go. At least she died peacefully in her sleep and not in some hospital bed, wracked with pain or loaded with drugs. We can get over there as soon as Mike calls back with a time. Life can involve sudden, unexpected changes."

Margie is busy wiping her eyes, "I'm so glad to have had them here for that short but wonderful visit. I wonder if she had any premonitions? She didn't seem overly tired and showed her usual laconic humor. She did mention that she hadn't done any weaving lately. Remember how that loom would crash away when she had the bit between her teeth finishing up a wool skirt or a throw rug for some ones birthday?

Joe puts his arm across her shoulder, "no sense getting maudlin' about it, Mag, she's gone without major complications or pain. The complications are going to be Mike's so I'm concerned that he may be in for a rough time. They were so close, sweethearts even in high school. In that sense, Mike has been a very lucky man as many couples never get that much time together, such a duration of happiness in their lifetime.

Looking up at Joe, Margie says, are you really worried about Mike....how he's taking her passing? I've always seen him as the rugged, independent kind of man so capable of rising to the occasion whenever there was a crisis. I know he was a rock for Phyllis but she was fairly independent herself and well-organized. Perhaps they leaned on each other, knowing each other's weaknesses and strengths. That comes from living together for so many years. They showed flexibility in family difficulties, tolerance, and compromise......with a good sense of humor thrown it."

'I agree, says Joe, it seems that we learnt a great deal from them. The kind of wisdom that's not available in university curricula. Remember how we used to hightail it up to the farm on weekends? The tension buildup during the office week, both yours and mine....it would melt away as the miles flew by as we drove up to Abbotsford. Driving past the high school was always fun and you would take on a new lease on life, collecting the chicken's eggs and the salad greens from their garden. All that fresh air and Phyllis was such a fantastic cook." "Yes, those weekends were great....and the years, too! There must be a good reason why we humans have such good memories. Remembering the good times helps us to get through the bad times to the present.

I think that you and I, Joe, are now trying to get through the present situation that way and I hope that Mike can do that...once he gets over his state of shock."

The phone rings again and Margie answers it, "hello Mike (she turns around to Joe and gives him the 'phone), "Mike, I'm so sad to hear the news. The funeral is on Thursday at 3 pm at the church?

Yes, I know the church, we went there together many times. What about us coming over sooner? Yes, we can come on Wednesday and stay over for a couple of days. There's nothing here that can't wait until the weekend. How are you holding out? I know it's tough but chin up, old buddy, we'll be there in a couple of days. Margie says hello and yes, we'll see you in a couple of days. Goodbye for now."

Turning towards Margie, "he didn't remember all the times we attended that church together. "He's got a lot on his mind, poor feller., says Margie. I'm going to take some baking with us and we can go out to dinner if Mike is ready for it. Oh, don't forget to take a couple of bottles of that blackberry wine.....the three-year old lot that he likes so much, Mike really enjoyed that wine.

What do you think, Margie, I see that you are already on the way....at least in your mind. I'm going to persuade Mike to come back with us after the funeral, otherwise he'll just sit stewing in that condo and crawl into his shell. I's like to see him here fishing, with a nice coho tail-walking across the chuck and ending up as fresh steaks on the barbeque, alongside one of your salads, crusty French bread, and a scotch ale. Well, that should certainly tempt him! Let's decide that when we see how he is bearing up. He may want to stay put and work things out for himself. You know how independent he can be.

"Yes dear, I know that but things can change" says Margie quietly. Right now, says Margie, my latest creations should be coming out of the kiln, nicely cooled and ready for glazing, what are you up to this morning? "Thoughts of fishing remind me to clean and lubricate the reels and hone the fileting knife. See you at lunchtime, my gal? They both rise, Margie clears the table and Joe moves towards his toolshed.

FUNERAL, THEN BACK TO SALTSPRING

The funeral is over at the church and Phyllis is cremated as was her wish. On their second day there at the condo, they couldn't persuade Mike to come back with them. He said that he just didn't feel right about fishing at this time. Joe and Margie stayed until Sunday morning, emphasizing to Mike that they expected him to keep in touch and come over later.

He called two weeks later wanting to know if the coho were biting and arrived the next day. The following morning it was breakfast on the deck, as usual.

"I'm glad to see that you still have your appetite, says Margie. I've made lots of waffles and bacon. Pass me your mug and I'll fill it with hot coffee. You two should eat a good breakfast if you are going fishing. There's lot's of butter, syrup, and blackberry jelly, so dig in! Between mouthfuls, Joe looks at his watch and out at the shoreline, "tide should start flooding in about an hour so I'm taking you to my secret spot known only to me and the orcas. Hopefully, they won't be there. I want you to nail a nice spring salmon, a chinook, their favorite, unfortunately. Last year I landed a fifteen pounder, about this time, too.

"More coffee for you two anglers, says Margie. While re-filling their mugs, "while you fellows are fishing, I'm going into Ganges on a grocery and library trip.

They thank Margie for breakfast and go to the boatshed, organize all the gear, take the skiff down to the beach and attach the out-board. Waving goodbye to Margie on the deck, they start out towards Joe's secret spot. Mike is waving his lucky rabbit's foot keychain and Joe laughs at him. "I don't know whether it's luck or not, Joe says. The fish and you are either there together, at the right time and tide, and the orcas are somewhere else, or you're not. We'll see, Mike.

They spend several hour trolling about, switching gears, using live herring, but no bites, not a single nudge of their lures, in fact and they both are becoming disappointed. Mike, in an effort to generate some positive thoughts comments on the beauty of the area and on the multitude of seabirds clamoring along the shores. They return home at noon as the tide peaked, hungry again and ready for a cold beer.

Margie spies them coming in and sets the outside table on the deck with a plateful of home-canned salmon sandwiches. Sitting on the deck after relieving themselves, they eye the sandwiches as Margie sets down the cold steins and chilled bottles of McKewans Scotch ale. Biting into his sandwich, Mike enquires if this was part of the fifteen pound chinook that Joe caught last year. " I think it is, says Margie, after checking the date on the jar. We ate two thick steaks from the barbeque and I canned the rest for future meals. The fishing gear is put away and the boat hauled up on the beach for another fishing trial later. Time to relax, lie in the semi-shade and read.

Joe plans a hike the next day either up Mount Benson or along the bay beneath it and they did both as Mike was quite enthused with the exercise and scenery. The day went quickly but at no time during their walks was any mention made of Phyllis or their social experiences together as a foursome over a long lifetime.

The next day during breakfast, again on the deck, Joe says, "Mike, I'm determined to see you catch a salmon before you go back. You can't go home skunked but may be it's too warm now although mid-June." He can see that Mike is getting restless as he responds saying, "we gave it a good try but I should get back. I've lots to do…. paperwork and cleaning things up. By the way, I've been thinking, all that money from the farm, I have no intention of ever using it all and there's no relatives, so what to do with it."

Now he mentions Phyllis's name, "Phyllis and I were talking about giving scholarships to the high school and I've decided to go with that decision. Six annual scholarships, two-thousand dollars each to kids planning on going on in school. Three to girls interested in the arts, like weaving and textiles, and three for boys interested in agricultural botany, soil science and conservation. Probably about two-hundred thousand dollars as a self-sustaining investment fund, administered by the school would be sufficient, so I need to get a local lawyer to set it up. Joe looks at Margie for her reaction, "that's very generous and a nice thought that involves Phyllis, too."

Margie is supportive of Mike's plan too. Joe begins thinking. "May be Margie and I should think about scholarships, too! I'm sure the Schools of Dentistry and Public Health at UBC could use such a boost for supporting needy students. Margie says "I I would like to see some UBC scholarships for students majoring in nutrition and food chemistry, diet-related concerns. They would be in line with our discussion during your last visit here with Phyllis." Now that her name has been mentioned, it loosens up the social atmosphere so as to include her which noticeably eases Mike. "What do you plan to do with the rest of the farm proceeds, Mike, that sale left you with a pile of money?

Mike warms up to the subject, "I've been reading a lot lately about GM foods and their seeds. The seed situation is reaching a crisis in many parts of the Third World, aided and abetted by the World Bank and the IMF. When people like Clinton and Gates start throwing their weight behind corporations bent on controlling food production to their own advantage and in such a way as to deny local farmers the right to save their own seeds, I'm concerned as a farmer. They aren't farmers, just a politician and an electronics success. I guess that accepting the propaganda and its neo-liberal concepts comes easy to them.

11 Farming is my identity and I see that doctored seeds aren't doing well in poor or over-worked soils, or during drought…..not as well as the native seeds carefully saved by the locals which are the product of localized natural selection. I've read that Asian and African NGO's are making great progress educating natives in soil rejuvenation, irrigation control and tree-planting so I'm thinking seriously about supporting them with yearly grants. I have to find out how to do that.

Wow! says Joe. " You have been thinking a lot lately. We have always know that you are tuned to Nature, natural rhythms and good husbandry but I'm impressed. I don't know much about GMO business or genetics but it seems to me that the entire planet is getting stirred up about it. Especially in Third World countries where the only food security one has is to grow your own to avoid starving to death. It disturbs me that multi-national chemical and food production corporations have all but taken over food production in America, some 70 per cent, and they are working assiduously in Canada having made big inroads in the Third World. Their seed promises of increased yield have fallen flat in Africa and Asia, causing bankruptcies and suicides among poor farmers connived into the sales gimmicks."

Mike breaks in while Margie is listening quietly, "remember the fight to keep bovine milk out of Canada? American kids are drinking it but it's outlawed here, in Europe, and in many parts of the South Pacific, including Australia and New Zealand. If the Europeans, especially the Italians, hadn't balked at the idea of GM wheat from Canada, our Wheat Board would have let it through. I see why you are concerned, too, but our government appears lackadaisical about public health and nutrition. Also, several federal agencies involved have been systematically whittled down in budgetary support. We've become too damned complacent. The world seemed so promising when we were young….sure problems existed….but wasn't there more optimism in searching for solutions? May be I'm just getting old and tired. This may sound selfish but I'm glad we never had any kids and don't have to worry personally about grandkids, either. What sort of mess are we leaving them?"

Now, now, Mike, try not to be so pessimistic, says Margie. Every generation has its challenges and they change with time and place. We try to blunder through them but their increasing complexity, compounded by pollution, by intake of chemicals that we aren't adapted to process safely, much of them in our food! Drug-resistant bacteria, proliferating viruses….no wonder we're the drug generation! You two are getting me going. Pharmacies are almost as important to consumers as are grocery stores. Pills, drugs, and excessive alcohol, and now we have psychedelic and hard, dangerous drugs. I tend to agree with you, Mike, on children, I've seen so many parents, hardworking and conscientious parents, driven to depression or uncontrollable anxiety by kids hooked on hard drugs. It can tear the fabric of family life apart.

Joe raps on the table with his spoon, "enough of this discussion, it's too damned frustrating. Frustrating because, I believe, that in one's old age at least, one would like to think that you have made the world a better place to live in. Otherwise, other than believing that you have tried your hardest, which may be of small comfort, the question lingers on your mind: have my efforts and influence made any difference? I think it is becoming more difficult to answer that question in the affirmative. Looks like we all agree on the crumbling state of the world and at least now, our present inability to do anything about it. There seems to be major forces at work in the world intent on nullifying our good intentions." On that note, they proceed into the house to view the CBC evening news.

After another breakfast on the deck, Mike returns to Abbotsford thanking his old remaining friends on Salt Spring Island for their hospitality and support, promising to keep in touch. There was no further discussion of possible winter vacation plans to Costa Rica but Joe is still checking on such a trip.

TWO MONTHS PASS AND FALL APPROACHES

The Cunninghams have been waiting for a call from Mike for several weeks but are reluctant to call him due to his anticipated legal and business plans, and don't want to sound overly-concerned.

Finally, Margie calls during mid-morning coffee break on the deck, hello, Mike? A female voice answers the telephone. "Is Mike there, Margie asks, it's Margie Cunningham calling from Salt Spring Island." "Hello, I'm Florence the nurse. I should tell you that Mike has been in a deep depression for the past two weeks and now has the 'flu. His doctor arranged for me to monitor him. I'm a retired RN. He has not been eating properly for some time and has lost a significant amount of weight which I'm trying to remedy. He is adamant about not going into the hospital. Hang on a minute, I hear him calling from his bedroom."

She leaves the 'phone, then Margie hears Mike's weak voice on the extension line which the nurse has connected. "Hello, Margie, I'm in bed with the 'flu." "So the bug has got you, eh? We haven't heard from you for some time and decided to call you. No 'flu shots available yet as it's only mid-September." Mike insists that he will be up in a few days and will call back, hanging up the phone abruptly.

Turning to Joe, Margie says," Mike just doesn't sound right. I wonder if he's on tranquilizers? Why is he depressed enough to affect his immunity, I know it can affect one's resistance to infection but the nurse said that he has lost significant weight……not eating properly for some time?" I have a hunch, says Joe, that he went back to the condo while still mourning for Phyllis, or the sight of all her stuff reminded him……the looms and all the half-finished projects we saw there. All his financial plans must have required much running around, business meetings with lawyers and so on. I think he is desperately missing her and we should have kept a closer watch

Margie pats his hand, "now, don't get yourself in a guilty frame of mind. Right now all we can do is wait for his recovery then make some plans. 'Flu only take about ten days but he has lost weight so recovery may take a little more time. Let's call again next week, in fact call once a week, perhaps we can persuade him to make this trip with us to Costa Rica." Joe is looking solemn and nods in agreement, "the warm weather's down there, the sunshine, would do us all some good if we have considerable time here when the rain starts. You know, drizzle,drizzle!

It's not that bad now, says Margie, "it's sunny today. So we've had some showery days lately. So what! Think of what we had in North Vancouver! Rain coming down in sheets, crowded malls and overloaded parking lots! No Sir, give me Salt Spring any day, even during the winter we have much less rain than the rest of the Coast. Anyway, you're keen to see the rainforests in Costa Rica and the rain and fog down there will be just as wet!" "True, rejoins Joe, but warmer and less rain and fog at the lower altitudes. And the birds, the orchids, and sunny beaches!" "All those brochures have gone to your head! Don't forget, the April showers bring the flowers!"

Margie is ready to go to Ganges for grocery shopping and getting the mail. "Just remember North Vancouver and the lower Fraser Valley and let a smile be your umbrella when the rains come. You could build a pre-winter fire when we get back and after dinner we can sit around gazing in to the flames like a couple of cats, along with our Shadow which reminds me, catfood, I have to put it on the list.

On the next weekly call to Mike, he is doing better and thinking of booting the nurse before too long, otherwise everything is okay. The following week he calls them, a short call saying he is up and about, getting meals on wheels, and sleeping better. Will call again next week.

They are having breakfast in the kitchen as the ambient air temperature is dropping and clouds are beginning to develop. "I've been thinking, says Margie, why is Mike getting Meals on Wheels, if he's recovering he should be fending for himself, being so independently-minded."

"Just calm down, says Joe, sipping his coffee, there's no need to worry. I bet he just wants to get back on his feet by himself. Anyway, he must miss Phyllis's great cooking and his campfire style wouldn't be conducive to gaining weight that he has lost. Mike just has to adjust to his new life, separate from Phyllis, and he has to do that himself. He was intent on allocating most of his unnecessary capital to scholarships and NGO's. I wonder how far he got with that before the depression hit him?"

Well, he was certainly determined to do that when he was here last, says Margie. Do you think he is interested in that Costa Rica trip? By the way, our passports are good for another two years and Mike will need a passport.

Joe laughs, "that reminds me of the passport rigamarole. At least we were all born here so they can't get too snotty with their security stuff. A fellow dentist, born in Britain, plasticized his papers to keep them intact, on the recommendation of a border guard. Although he has been a Canadian citizen for over thirty-five years he was treated like a common criminal when applying for a new passport after his had expired. The bureaucratic female in Victoria demanded that he apply for a new citizenship certificate and fill out two handwritten documents explaining how and why he was driving to Seattle. She also wanted a complete record of his comings and goings to Europe over the past 25 years which, of course was impossible. He was to attend a dental conference in Seattle to give a research paper on orthodontics. Maybe he would have liked to get her in his dental chair!"

Why don't you call Mike and jog him about the trip and passport needs. That way you can find out how well he is doing without sounding too concerned about his health, says Margie. Joe obliges, but Mike isn't interested in any trips, too much to do, and his voice seems thin and wavery. He says, "go ahead and enjoy yourselves" and hung up abruptly. "That doesn't sound like the old Mike."

"I wonder if he is still on drugs, says Margie, remember that he was on tranquilizers the last time we called him. Oh dear! I had my heart set on going south with both of them. Somehow it doesn't feel right to make that trip without Phyllis and I don't want to go without Mike for e both of us would be thinking about him meanwhile and that would spoil the trip. Maybe you're right, says Joe, let's stay home for Christmas. "There will be plenty of time to make that trip in the New Year, even later in the Spring. We'll invite Mike for Xmas, I'll having him splitting firewood and we can get out on some local hikes. Right now I'm off to the toolshed. That big chunk of cedar I found is going to be turned into a mermaid for that big, flat sandstone on the upper beach."

A week later, Margie and Joe have just returned from Ganges. The sun is now weaker but shines through a slight haze. They are bundled up and intend to sit on the deck sipping a mug of coffee after unloading their groceries. The 'phone on the deck rings, "get that will you Joe, I've got an arm full of groceries, says Margie as she walks into the house. Joe picks up the "phone, "hello.....who is this? Reverend Blackstone? From Abbotsford? Oh yes. I recall you now, you conducted the funeral service for Phyllis Stanton. Why are you calling? About Mike? He left a note with our names and number on it? What's happened? Mike's dead!"

Blackstone goes on talking for several minutes while Joe listens in shock. Joe finally thanks him and hangs up.

Margie walks out onto the deck, "who called? That was a long call." Joe stands there oblivious to her question. He is staring down at the decking with a distraught look on his face. "Joe, what's the matter? You look positively stunned!" He finally becomes aware of her presence. "I just can't believe it! That was Reverend Blackstone from Abbotsford. Mike has gone....apparrently put his head in the gas stove. The next door neighbor smelled gas coming from underneath Mike's front door and called the fire department. He had wrapped a blanket around himself and left a note with our names and telephone number on it.

Margie gasps, "how awful! How could he have done that! He must have been out of his mind! A tranquilizer overdose? Didn't anyone at the condo system notice anything unusual in his behavior? That just doesn't sound like Mike, especially with gas! That could have cause a massive explosion that hurt others. Now I do feel that we have let him down. What about his MD? Wasn't he aware of Mike's fallibility?"

"So many questions, says Joe, Blackstone just told me the basic facts, he didn't elaborate other than saying that he visited Mike once a week and said he seemed quite subdued and quiet, as though he was resigned to things, common signs of mourning. The minister did make an effort to challenge him.....to get him to cheer up. I think that he decided that his life without Phyllis was no life at all....perhaps a living hell of personal reminders like all the things of hers there. I think he decided to go after her, wherever she went. We must attend the funeral. Blackstone will call with the funeral schedule. Both gone in just a few months! I hope he has found her! We will miss them both, even more now this has happened."

Margie is standing by Joe's side with tears streaming down her face, finally able to say "I can hardly believe it! They were so happy, laughing and enjoying their visit here in early summer, now both have flown away.

We all act normally as though nothing can change, life made predictable by our wishes, and the assumption of immortality. It's an attitude spawned during youth, one we carry into adulthood, and cling tenaciously to in old age. Then the reminders of mortality begin, friends and neighbors disappear, so do parents and siblings. We begin counting those who are left, wondering who will be next. Are we lucky as a lone survivor in a personal lifespan made significant only by memories of those who played a role in it?"

Joe gets up from his chair and gives her a prolonged, tender hug, saying "what more could I possibly add to that."

LIFE GOES ON IN THE AFTERMATH

This couple returns from Mike's funeral and sees a number of former schoolmates from their school who still live in the general area and have met them on numerous occasions during their weekend visits to the farm. The laudable comments about both Phyllis and Mike echo those given during Phyllis's funeral. Comments and respectful praise come in enhanced intensity due to the short interval between their deaths.

Joe and Margie return to Salt Spring Island and have maintained a rather subdued manner for some time. Again, they are at the breakfast table, looking out at the wind-rustled fir trees. Joe has been lighting the fireplace routinely for the past week in the evenings and Shadow usually joins them, gazing into the fire. Margie makes Joe his usual breakfast of poached eggs and toasts but only makes a slice of toast for herself and refrains from drinking coffee.

"What, no eggs and no coffee?" How come? asks Joe. "I'm just having toast and a glass of milk, my stomach is bothering me., perhaps from all the stress during these past several months." "I don't remember you ever having any stomach trouble, Margie! You have always loved spicy foods, especially Madras curried chicken. You have been gobbling Tums like candy for several days now. Perhaps you should get a checkup with Doc Saunders so make an appointment." Yes, I guess you're right, she answers and reaches for the telephone. "He can see me in two days, at 10 am, now that's a bit of luck. I'm not going to eat much until I see him, no appetite, anyway."

Joe decides to do the cooking…."you don't cook until we get the results. We can eat soup and crackers, I need to go on a diet, anyway, and this is as good a time as any." Don't be silly, she says. "you don't have to suffer for me! One victim in the house is sufficient. I'm making scones for afternoon tea and there's spaghetti sauce and pasta in the cupboard. We're both still getting over the funerals and it is probably emotional fatigue for me. That can bring on all sorts of physical problems, real and imaginary."

Come on now, says Joe, are you suggesting that that you could be imagining your abdominal pain for the last several days? We haven't eaten out and you've not cooked anything exotic either. He rises from the table announcing that he's got to do some work on the cedar block, to start shaping it. Tomorrow, I go into Ganges with you and go to the library for some woodcarving information. Finishing that mermaid is a real challenge, making her tresses look life-like rather than like a Breck commercial.

"Now, now, Margie quips, Breck commercials could be a relief from the news hour! You know, a psychologist has suggested that not watching the CBC news for a month might make one feel less tense. Wouldn't that ploy be an escape from reality, assuming that the news is reality and not partly propaganda?

Hey, that's an interesting thought, Margie! I sometime question the media's intent. Is it to inform us, or to hammer us with day-to-day crisis blurbs with little background information or analysis? If they are leaving the raison d'etre to their consumers, I think they are sadly mistaken. Who has the time or inclination for personal in-depth interpretations of the state of the world? It's almost too much to keep up with what's going on in Vancouver and Victoria, not alone nationally, or internationally. Info bites is what we usually get as though we can store them like a computer! She comments back, that's where good newspapers come in, like the Christian Science Monitor, and the Manchester Guardian with their weekly reviews.

I agree that there's too much politicizing and selective presentation going on even in Canada. As for the American media! Shades of

Randolph Hearst! To change the subject, says Joe, "talking to that young fellow at the funeral ....the one who bought the dairy farm, he gave me a renewed sense of optimism. Forming a cooperative was a brilliant idea, it re-connects the consumer to the land, its products, and to view the land with renewed respect and care."

Margie laughs, "you would be surprised how many children don't realize that milk comes from a cow first, then from a bottle or plastic carton! For us, says Joe,"I wish we had enough sun here for a vegetable garden but I'm not willing to cut down any trees to have one. I could build some cedar boxes and put them around the deck for tomatoes, cukes and salad greens.

Margie thinks that's a good idea, "we could shorten the flower beds or even put them in boxes, too. That would cut down the weeds and we could come out and snip fresh herbs and salad makings right off the deck! That would be a good winter project for you, Joe, and we could also stat a compost box for the kitchen scraps and for kelp off the beach. Not only that, says Joe, "we could have a small chicken house, just two or three hens, for fresh eggs. I read that people in Portland are raising eggs and chickens for meat in their backyards, now that's a way to give the kids experience as to where their dinner comes from! Fresh eggs in the grocery store are weeks old by the time we get them, splashing all over the frying pan when you crack them!"

I notice that the mornings are getting cool now, Joe. The maple leaves are turning, and the showers more frequent and intense. I guess eating out on the deck is about over or this year. Time to start thinking about battening down the hatches for our mild winter. It's mid-October! You sound like a prairie gal, Margie! We may not get much snow this winter and we still have split firewood left-over from last winter. But you are right, Margie, time to haul in the boat, winterize the motor and button up until Spring. They both leave the deck to go about their respective chores.

MEDICAL TEST RESULTS AND AGREED SOLUTION

Margie's test results are back in ten days from the laboratory. Doc Saunders calls, ...come in for a chat. She goes in alone while Joe is splitting logs for firewood with his single-bladed axe and wedges. When she returns at lunch time, "Joe, let's have a bowl of soup on the deck! The sun is coming out and I see some blue sky"!

Joe is showing a sweat and throws down the axe on to the chopping block. "Some of that chili you made yesterday with some French bread?" Coming right up, master. She brings out a steaming tray within five minutes and they settle down to smell the aroma of the chili. "No butter for me, Joe. Doc Saunders says I must reduce my fat intake as much as possible, at least for a while and some additional testing. Are you being somewhat skittish about your test results, Margie? Do you intend to keep it a secret from me and worry me some more? I'm sorry, Joe but I'm finding it difficult to talk about the test results but talk I must.

Joe is stirring his chili and watching the stream rise from the bowl. Well, out with it, nurse! Have you got an ulcer? Oh, I wish! That can be treated and go away. Brace yourself now....this isn't going to be easy. She pats his forearm, her face showing both sadness and sympathy. Doc Saunders believes that I have a possibly incurable condition. The tests show that I have a series of small tumors on the bile duct for which, presently, there is no effective treatment. Surgery is no option and tumors there usually indicate that the cancer will spread to the liver. He gives me two to three months at the most, probably less time, and hospitalization and painkillers will be inevitable.

Joe is sitting there, immobilized, his spoon poised in mid-air. Finally he looks her straight in the eyes, well, that's it then, isn't it. If you are unwilling to go through several weeks of agonizing pain, dulled by massive drugs before you go.....we'll go together! If there's no chance for recovery, I don't want to go through what Mike did. Look what it did to him, no, no, no! Not for one minute, watching you fade away into the distance. I want us to decide how to end it for us, together, without complications. He slaps his knee vigorously. We'll go together! I insist! Don't try to talk me out of it! I'll find a way.

Margie is overwhelmed by Joe's reaction as she had no idea this would be his position. She was developing worries about his potential health problems after her demise but his suggestion tends to relieve them. I'm not going to give up trying to persuade you, Joe, but soon I will be too weak, I will not have the strength , anyway. Margie, we're going to plan this just like a holiday trip…..only one from which we don't return, at least to here.

First we must decide about the estate. I suggest that we ask our lawyer to act as our executor…..that we follow the same plan as did Mike. Remember we talked about scholarships to UBC and the BC Cancer Society needs support, too. A new wing is planned for Jubilee hospital in Victoria, dedicated to cancer treatment and research. Canvassing for public support has begun. We could make a significant donation.

Margie agrees with the donation concept, " but what about this place….our haven in the woods?" "You have no close relatives and those you do have are in Toronto and Ottawa and are well-established. My only close relative is Cindy, my shirt-tail niece in Alberta. The last letter we had from her was really depressing but there was no request for help despite that her husband is wheel-chair bound from a logging accident, with spinal cord injury. With three small kids it must be tough sledding even with insurance and they are renters, too.

There! I think you have the solution then! Let's leave them this place, lock, stock and barrel. No rent and they can raise the kids out of the city. They will be very surprised having the opportunity to move here. The climate must be very tough on her husband, being unable to deal with snow and ice conditions. See how neatly things fall into place? The legal paperwork needs to be done, wills and all. The lawyer can get our wish list registered, then we can sign it. Are you content with that?

Margie is brightening up, "yes, I feel good about it….a perfect solution for distributing our goodies. Reminds me of that local poet's last reading at the library: there's no pockets in the funeral shroud for the stuff of your travail. I want to donate to the new library in Ganges now on the plans but I remain concerned about your suggestion for coming with me when I go." "Forget such concern, Margie, it's probably based on your guilt feelings, anyway. Believe me, I have no desire to stick around here when you are gone. Do you understand that?" She nods her head. Good! Now to get ready for our trip! In the meanwhile, not to get bogged down with self-pity, feeling sorry for ourselves. That is just ego and we must raise our minds and hearts above the maudlin. Think like Buddhists but leave the reincarnation bit out of it for now.

What comes after passing, if anything, will come regardless of what ego-driven notions one can pick and choose from this life. Haven't we had a good run, Margie? At least as good as we have been capable of having. Both successful in our vocations, serving humanity with professional concern and compassion. That's not to be sneezed at, relative to the selfish concerns of many others. Our planned donations will serve to hand on the baton……to try and make the world a better place for all, a happier, more just and sharing world. Good fortune to those who try, I say! They embrace tightly for several minutes.

Several weeks later, all the legalities have been put on record. Doc Saunders is monitoring Margie's condition closely, matching her personally-defined pain level with increased drug intake. She is holding up well but at breakfast she is swallowing a handful of pills. Sipping her glass of milk, she says, "I'm feeling very existential these days and am not afraid of dying. Must be all the Buddhist literature and meditation tapes available from the library. Of course, we are both listening to the tapes together, usually in front of the blazing fire accompanied by Shadow, our black cat."

It's too bad that we didn't start listening to meditation tapes and practicing meditation a long time ago, says Joe. Looking out at the sunset over the water after our evening meal certainly integrates with meditation. But meditation by itself doesn't go far enough, clearing the mind, controlling the breath and sitting comfortably is more effective.

Too bad I didn't start real meditation technique years ago as it would have made my dental practice less stressful.

Margie agrees enthusiastically, "also I find that even the everyday moments seem to be injected with more zest, more enjoyment. I actually feel more alive and appreciative of routine living. The bird calls seem sweeter and more poetic. Sometimes I feel that the fir trees are humming along in the breeze." That sounds downright spiritual, says Joe, keep up the good work!

Now, on the inevitable subject of "how and when." I've been developing a strategy so listen carefully. We both know the carbon monoxide is an odorless gas that can put you to sleep without pain or discomfort. We could sit in the station wagon as if we are going on a trip….both kitchen and garage doors closed and the lights in the garage left on. Simple as that!

Margie, thinking, "well, we could be sitting there for some time as we have very few visitors. Days, perhaps weeks! "No problem, says Joe, "we know the hydro guy comes to read the meter once a month on a Wednesday and that Wednesday is in two days. We could go then, the garage lights will be on, he will be expecting his usual cup of coffee and a chat, and fondle Shadow who is attracted to him. He'll be alerted when we don't appear, the garage lights on. We can leave a note on the front door asking him to get the power shut off. That will get him thinking and he will look through the garage window, and he will see us in the car. Also he'll be looking for Shadow who usually comes running over for a pat and tickle behind the ear. Besides, he knows where the front door key is hidden. And the engine will probably still be running as the gas tank is full."

Joe, you are making this into a real adventure and I don't want another week of these drugs as they are now pulling me down and interrupting my sleep badly. Also I'm getting very nauseous and starting to vomit severely. Okay then, that's that, says Joe. "I'm going to make sandwiches for the trip, says Margie……just like old times when we drove up to the farm on the weekend. There's sourdough bread, Freybe's herb-laced lunch meat, butter lettuce and blue-cheese dressing. I'll fill the large thermos with milk, too. Joe chuckles, think of all those sandwiches we ate while driving up to Abbotsford! I'm going to dig up some of our tapes for the trip and put them in the glove compartment!

The next day, Tuesday, about noon, they are sitting in the wagon in the garage. Joe has attached the vacuum cleaner hose to the tail pipe securely with tape. He starts the car, "pass me a sandwich, love. Oh, says Margie, I forgot to feed Shadow, I'll be back shortly. She goes into the kitchen and returns a few minutes later. "I gave her an entire can of chicken liver and filled her other dish with the remains of the whipping cream and put them both outside by the front door." "Did you lock the door, too?" She nods and settled own in her seat. "What will become of her?" Oh, the hydro guy makes such a fuss of her. I bet he takes her! Now let's get on with our lunch.

Turn on the radio, Margie and put one of the CD's in the slot. Oh, you thought to put in some extra pillows, Joe, how thoughtful of you. Put one on my shoulder and rest your pretty head, my love. Ah, Arty Shaw as he turns up the volume to drown out the engine. Not much traffic on the highway, sweetheart, I feel like we're driving nearly thirty years ago! Yes, Joe, our last trip together in this dimension. A thump is heard over the radio music. Shadow has entered the garage through her cat door. "Here's Shadow! Shadow leaps up to the windscreen and looks in at them, then settles down against the bottom of the window between the two windshield wipers. "I think she wants to go with us, Joe!" "Who knows what cats think but she seems to be going asleep.

The Egyptians held them in great awe and reverence, even worshipped them and gave them extra-ordinary powers. I'm getting a bit sleepy, Margie, how are you doing? The air in here smells a little like downtown Vancouver on a hot summer day. Hold my hand, Margie, like we are the Strangers in Paradise. Are your eyes getting blurry, too? Yes, and it's starting to get dark in here. Same here, my love! We don't have to go through what Mike suffered. We are like Romeo and Juliet, Cleopatra and Mark Anthony, Launcelot and Guinevere, Tristan and Isolde. The list could go on, so we are among the lucky ones. Oh, Joe you can be such a romantic, squeeze my hand. I think we are nearly there and I love you so much! It's been a wonderful life together and such a lovely last trip. Are we driving into a lighted tunnel? I see a brilliant light at the far end.

Their voices become muffled and the lights in the garage seem to become gradually dimmer as the music slowly fades away.

Into the Wild Blue Yonder

PREFACE

An literary acquaintance suggested that I should engage in writing a story that reflected the sexual angst reflected in the modern mind, one on the onset of sexual identity concerns in youth. I chose to use my own pre-teen and teen years in Southern California as a geographical compass, greatly reinforced by considerable reconnoitering through the internet on the subject of male homosexual behavior. From modern television accounts of youthful sexual behavior, the present story although pure in motivation is probably somewhat naïve.

ADOLESCENT INTEREST IN AVIATION

It is spring, 1947 in Southern California and a teenage boy is commencing his junior year at his high school. Living in West Los Angeles several years before the onset of the Korean War which will be soon identified as a U.N. Police Action, Jeremy has discovered his interest in aviation. He had joined the Air Cadets when fourteen, in junior high school, eventually obtaining a uniform, which he was very proud of, attends Saturday classes at the local airport in Van Nuys given by retired military pilots and those active in the Civil Air Patrol. His parents have encouraged his flying interests, think that the semi-military exposure, including uniform and marches in local civic parades will keep him out of trouble. They are both strict Methodists and the family, including Jeremy's younger sister attend church faithfully every Sunday. His father is a senior carpenter in set construction at Republic Studios.

Jeremy's school grades improve with exposure to the Air Cadets and moving into high school. He attacks with vigor the orientation and teaching manuals supplied during his Saturday classes at the local airport. His self-discipline develops, with time-related organizational abilities becoming more necessary, he is concentrating on both school work and Air Cadets now. Jeremy's hobby interests reflect his interest in flying. When fifteen and now in high school, he builds model aeroplanes for controlled wire flying but within that year, upgrades his interests to free-flying models with more powerful engines and joins with two other classmates in flying them in the San Fernando Valley which is a near-desert valley a few miles northeast of home. There, in that valley, his flying desires are encouraged as their models, nearly three feet in wing length, often get caught in thermals, requiring chasing after them in the Model-A owned by a participant.

While most of his classmates are obsessed with girls and possible dating adventures, Jeremy's experience with the opposite sex has been on hayrides and picnics organized by his church, monitored by his parents. His father is pleased with Jeremy's model-making interests.

His mother checks Jeremy's wallet one evening as he is taking a shower and discovers a small photograph of a nubile, nude woman there. Confrontation results following his stepping out of the shower, towel-wrapped, his mother producing a harridan-like reaction to her discovery. Jeremy explains that a schoolmate had given copies to several boys at school, in the locker room after gym. Following confiscation of the snap and attempts to plant the seed of guilt in her son, parental discussion follows with both parents deciding to encourage his flying interests even more so as to avoid any sexual problems. They can't consider punishing him further due to his high academic record at school. The bobby-sox fad and school dances are becoming raging interests at high school and hip-gyrating Elvis has recently hit the song scene. Blue suede shoes have become a definite need of the socially-dominant teenage boy's shoe closet.

Jeremy keeps busy with Air Cadets, continuing his meetings at San Fernando Valley Airport, near Van Nuys. A major written exam developed by several pilots is given in the Spring, 1948 shortly before Jeremy's sixteenth birthday and the top student will receive a free flying course in preparation for a pilot's certification and license, second and third prizes are hour-long air rides. He studies hard and awaits the results at the next Saturday meeting. Having had several 20 minute air rides in the landing field area, Jeremy wants the first prize.

As the chief instructor steps up to the podium, every student there, including two girls, wait silently with baited breath. Looking about the room, the instructor smiles and looks at the paper held in his right hand. First prize goes to Jeremy Witherspoon who obtained a 98% rating on his examination. Second prize goes to Tom Lansome, for a 90% rating, and third prize goes to Ralph Kettering, for 86%. We will inform you three winners when the arrangements are made for collection of your prizes. The rest of you students, keep up your good work and try again next year. Jeremy is stunned at his good luck and sees his goal of obtaining a pilot's license drawing near.

At home, his announcement over dinner generates parental enthusiasm. They both congratulate him on his achievement. When will you start your flying training?, asks his father. They will let me know shortly. It will take at least four months before I can fly solo and I have much to learn about navigation, communication, and weather interpretation in the meanwhile. His two air model friends regard him with awe and also disappointment as he will have no time for model flying now. Jeremy has encouraged them to join the Air Cadets for some time but the marching and uniforms are interpreted as jeopardizing their free spirit.

Two weeks later, Jeremy gets a letter from one of the instructors, Carol Simmings, informing him that he has been assigned to manage his flight training course which is financed by the Civil Air Patrol and the California Air National Guard (CANG), in which Simmings has both memberships. They meet the next Saturday at the airport. Jeremy recognizes Carol as a background instructor at Air Cadets. Over a cup of coffee, he discovers that Carol, an athletic blond 25 year-old, is a second lieutenant in CANG who flies fighter jets. Jeremy is overwhelmed with his good fortune. You are a fighter pilot! Carol chuckles, yes in F-86's, "that shows you what you can do if you really try." He goes on to explain his background. I am a silver-spooned only son of an aeronautical engineer who graduated from Georgia Tech then married my mother from Virginia and he took a job with Lockheed in Burbank, becoming a major player in management. He was involved with building that two-engine plane, the AT-20 that Amelia Earhart flew into the Pacific. We lived in a big house in Pasadena, close to Cal Tech. I was sent back to Virginia to a private academy for high school boys age 14, I think that was a parental decision reflecting insufficient time to invest in me. My father was busy cranking out the twin-boomed Lightning, the P-38, during World War Two.

After Virginia I came back to California, that was in 1941 and enrolled at Stanford, studying history. I suspect that my father's influence with the military kept the draft off my neck. I remember that uniformed Army Airforce generals and colonels were at the house on occasions during my summer holidays, also some politicians. I was commissioned in the Army Air Force in 1945, from my ROTC training at Stanford, combined with my civilian pilot's license that I got through the USC Flying Club, just after the end of the war. They put me through military aviation at Nellis AFB, including jets. My first jet ride was in an T-33 trainer, then the F-80. Now with the F-86 coming on line, I've finished training for it in my reserve status. That's the attraction for me, training is never ending as new models emerge each with more complicated instrumentation and more power. Right now I'm doing shooting and bombing range practice.

Jeremy's excitement shows on his face as he imagines himself flying in Carol's footsteps. Carol notices his dream-like trance and reminds him that much hard work lies ahead for both of them if they aim for solo flying within four months. "My Cessna 140 we'll be using is an easy plane to fly, stable and with sufficient power but there is much to learn as many pitfalls lurk behind the pilot, many environmental changes can occur quickly, demanding cool nerves and lots of awareness and planning routines, so let's get started by checking out the 'plane and I'll show you first the pre-flight inspection routine and the instrumentation panel from the pilot's seat". They then return to the AC facility and Carol assembles a pile of instruction manuals. On the way to drop off Jeremy at home, Carol asks him about his last name, Witherspoon. I work at Republic Studios with a guy by that name who makes sets and I do the painting, blue sky, clouds, and greenery stuff as well as indoor sets and making phony cowboy villages.

Arriving at the house, Jeremy`s father is cutting the front lawn and walks over to the car. Both get out, Carol shaking father`s hand and laughing, ``so this is your son! What a surprise! I`m assigned to assist him in his quest for a pilot`s license. Looking at Jeremy, his father laughs, "I'm cutting the lawn, that`s your job, son! You`ll have to figure out your lawn task if you intend to go flying! He smiles at Carol, "what a coincidence, this is, see you at work tomorrow!" Jeremy waves goodbye to Carol and proceeds into the house with his pile of manuals. His dad finishes the lawn and goes inside to listen to Jeremy`s animated conversation with his mother, describing his flying instructor and his background which he wants to follow. Both parents listen intently, nodding their approval at their son`s good fortune, and feeling proud. Carol has given Jeremy a month to study his manuals and they go over some interpretations during the Saturday Air Cadet meetings in Van Nuys.

The flying starts on a smooth summer day, and they fly beachward, climbing to four thousand feet over the sea where the off-shore islands, including Catalina Island come into view. Jeremy is enthralled as

Carol casually mentions that he intends to put the `plane into a spin. He pulls back the throttle control and shoves the stick forward, taking his feet off the pedals. Jeremy is suddenly looking straight down as the horizon rotates around them. At 1500 feet on the altimeter, Carol rams the throttle forward, slams his right foot on the aileron while yanking back the stick.

Jeremy`s eyes are wide-open as is his mouth. The `plane comes out of the spin about one thousand feet above the ocean and climbs again steadily to their former altitude as Carol heads north towards Santa Barbara. Did that frighten you, Carol asks. Jeremy swallows hard, "admittedly I was a little scared but knew that you were in control and that we were perfectly safe". Good comment, says Carol. Before too long with you at the controls, we will practice that manoeuvre until you know that you can regain control with confidence. Now we are going back to the strip to practice some partial landings and take-offs, to give you the feel of control.

With the fuel gauge down perceptibly, they land and call it a day. I want you to go over flying procedures for take-off and landing until they are firmly bound in your head, says Carol as he drops him off at the house.

Next Saturday Jeremy is given the controls to make turns, dives and pull-ups. He is establishing the feeling of control and the `plane responses to his manipulations. A week later, he is allowed to take-off from the strip with Carol ready at the controls, landing is a bit more difficult especially with a little cross-wind, but he reacts smoothly to maintain control which pleases Carol. After three weeks of such practice, Jeremy has developed confidence in his abilities and is totally confident with the instructor role that Carol is playing. Carol is quite impressed with the accomplishments to date as Jeremy`s performance outshines that of his former students. Jeremy is a natural but Carol refrains from expressing that thought to avoid possible over-confidence in his student. He is starting to feel like an older brother.

Further practice over the course of the summer finds Jeremy ready for solo flight in September. He is itching for it and Carol plans it after an AC meeting. With all the instructors and students standing about, Jeremy goes through his pre-flight inspection, climbs into the `plane and proceeds to the outer strip after getting radio permission from the little tower. He takes off smoothly and climbs to fifteen hundred feet, circling the strip five times before requesting landing permission and coming in for a landing. Climbing out of the plane he is hugged by Carol amid the clapping from the onlookers then everyone enters the building for a celebrating Coke. After another five solo flights including some windy weather, Carol signs off on his pilot`s license when the results come back from the written exam. Now the emerging difficulty is rental expense so as to accumulate his flying time as aviation fuel isn't cheap.

Carol keeps in touch and phones him several weeks later asking him if he was interested in joining the CAP, and if he was interested, would he be ready to commit on short notice to any emergency situations that might arise in Southern California. I may need a spotter and you would get some experience in rougher terrain that you have experienced to date, he said. Jeremy agrees enthusiastically and joins the CAP even though he has no `plane of his own, as a potential spotter equipped with binoculars. Carol calls him at home on a Friday evening several weeks later, saying that a flight was missing from Bakersfield to Palm Springs and he was assigned the mountainous area southwest of Bakersfield, to leave promptly at daylight the next day which happens to be a Saturday. He picks up Jeremy at 5 am and outlines the search protocol while driving to the strip. I`ve been assigned the cut through the south end of the Sierras below Bakersfield and two other `planes are assigned the lower hills leading on to the desert.

Carol`s Cessna 140 is fueled and ready to go so they leave quickly as dawn breaks into morning light. They approach his search area by first flying over Riverside and then proceeding north. It is a clear day and arriving in the foothills area, Jeremy is listening to the radio. No other planes are yet in the general area as they begin climbing up through the convoluted pass towards Bakersfield. They make five searches through that assigned area without spotting any possible wreckage and Carol, after talking on the radio with Search Operations is asked to descend further towards the desert and assist the now single search plane assigned to the foothills.

After an hour of combing all the adjacent minor valleys and hillsides, Search Operations instructs them to proceed on to the desert on a general track directed at Palm Springs which has some high mountainous areas surrounding it that enclose the Coachella Valley. By now they have been in intensive search for over two hours without any success and Carol takes a heading towards Palm Springs.

Twelve minutes later, the engine starts to cough sporadically, although the fuel gauge indicates two-thirds full. Carol adjusts the throttle somewhat, assuming possible carbureter problems from dust pickup but the sporadic nature of the ignition effects suggests to him that spark plugs or magneto might be the source so he calls in withdrawal from the search and head towards Palmdale or Lancaster. As they have sufficient altitude and the distance is less than sixty miles, he assures Jeremy there is little danger. If we can`t make it there we can always land on the dry salt lake at Edwards AFB which is close by but I`m reluctant to land there for security reasons. Anyway, I know there`s a good mechanic at Lancaster so we`ll head for there. This is a good experience for you, how to handle an emergency. Radio Lancaster and inform them we are having engine trouble and will be arriving within thirty minutes. Jeremy transmits the message which is acknowledged. The engine continues sporadic splutters at several minute intervals until Lancaster appears through the propeller whirl. Landing without difficulty, Carol taxis over to the service center and shuts down the engine.

The mechanic has been informed of their arrival as he has his radio on full time while working in the shop and emerges to meet the `plane. Discussing the problem with Carol, he removed the engine cowling for inspection. I don`t think it's the plugs, he says, after Carol said a full inspection and routine maintenance had been done a month ago. He checks the magneto which is overheated although electrical connections are undamaged, locates his electrical instrument then askes Carol to start the engine which fires up with difficulty. That`s it, the mechanic says, an unreliable magneto and I can lay my hands on one before morning. It is now approaching 11 am. So we`ll be here overnight then, says Jeremy, I`d better call home and let them know we`ll be back tomorrow by lunch time.

The mechanic tells them that a small motel and coffee shop are located within a ten minute walk and they depart to return in the morning. At the motel, one small unit is available with one double bed so they sign in and proceed to get some lunch. After lunch, there is not much to do in Lancaster but they walk around the small town to stretch their legs. The afternoon sun now bores down so they return to the motel and its air-conditioning after grabbing some magazines in the office.

We`ll be outta here in the morning, says Carol, no sweat. That reminds me to take a shower, I never managed one this morning before we left on this search. I`ll take one too, says Jeremy. After showing, and laying on the bed in their shorts they feel refreshed, and mull through the magazines, some of which are well-thumbed, one being pornographic.

Carol picks one up and starts looking through it, laughing at some of the poses and shows them to Jeremy. I`ve never seen such stuff and it`s very erotic, says Jeremy. I feel rather tense, even after that shower, must be psychological stress affecting me. Sometimes I get back pains when I`m studying too long. Do you have them now, asks Carol. Yes, I do but a long rest may help to get rid of them, says Jeremy. Carol looks over at him, you weren't scared of that ignition problem, were you? I can give you a back massage if you would like, something I learnt after playing intensive hand-ball with fellow pilots. Just roll on to your stomach, lay your head down on the sheet and try to relax. Jeremy obeys willingly as Carol adjusts him towards the middle of the bed, saying that gives his knees more room.

He proceeds to massage Jeremy`s supple body, starting at the neck and shoulders, then proceeding, with the palms of his hands, to pressure the spine in both vertical directions. Is that working, he asks

Jeremy. Yes, keep it up as I`m beginning to relax and feel better. Carol continues for another ten minutes and Jeremy can feel something hard pressing against his buttocks as Carol sways back and forth, pushing on the spine. Well, how`s that, then, says Carol, enough? He climbs off and Jeremy moves over to give him more room on the bed.

Jeremy rolls over on to his back and puts a magazine over his crotch. After a few minutes, Carol notices that the magazine appears to be moving slightly, rhythmically, up and down. Mischievously, he reaches over and takes the magazine which was hiding Jeremy`s swelling penis. Jeremy is laying there, staring at the ceiling, his mouth slightly open, and emitting several small gasps.

Carol reacts immediately, recognizing his reactions and gently reaches over to extricate the now throbbing penis from the enclosing shorts, almost in a trance. Grasping the penis with his right hand he begins to stroke it gently, until it is totally rigid with the head bursting with redness. Just relax, Jeremy, I`m not going to hurt you and perhaps you need it. You may probably enjoy this beyond your wildest, sexual dreams. Leaning down while running his left hand over Jeremy`s thighs and testicles, he takes the penis into his mouth and licks around it with his tongue. Jeremy responds by light moaning and increasing chest heaves and responds by running his left hand through Carol`s curly, blond hair.

Carol`s sucking movements, followed by taking down the shorts completely to the knees, become more emphatic and include the testicles which makes Jeremy whimper. He makes no attempt to reject Carol`s actions, in fact, is thoroughly enjoying every stroke and tongue movement. Carol kisses him on the neck, his left ear, his lips travelling to Jeremy`s lips which he nibbles and sucks gently. He then returns to the penis, eight inches of pulsating, teen desire, and envelopes it once more into his welcoming mouth. Another series of sucking movements whereby the penis is taken to the full depth of his mouth, followed by renewed nibbling of the head and along the length of the member.

Jeremy is now moaning without any inhibition and he reaches out to find and grasp Carol`s member that is showing equal excitement. At that moment, Jeremy, moaning in quick succession, ejaculates, spurting into Carol`s mouth in great volume. Carol continues his sucking and tongue movements, the white semen dribbling out of his lips and running down his chin. They rest for several minutes after Carol wipes his face on a towel. Did you like that, he asks, hoping that Jeremy was accepting this as a joyous experience. Laying there, mouth slightly open and still breathing rapidly, he answers, yes, with conviction. Now in camaraderie, hand-in hand, the couple lay on the bed that has transported them into an enriched, expanded personal relationship. A relationship, non-exploitive, lacking any guilt, and revealing the potential range of masculine, physical harmony.

Jeremy breaks the silence, "I've never had an orgasm like that before and I`ve been masturbating in the shower since I was ten. That was a mind-exploding experience! Where and when did you learn to do that." Well, replied Carol, some of us tried it in college, in the fraternity, but that was just experimentation mixed with hazing and guilt, threatening our concepts of masculinity and social status. Actually, I have had little experience with homosexual activity, but I do remember group masturbations under candle light after Lights Out at that academy in Virginia. I never participated. Those sessions were organized by aggressive, high social status seniors most of whom were hoping to get into West Point. I never had any social life with girls there because that academy was for males only, or at home on holidays. At USC I spent most of my time chasing my self-image of masculinity, reinforced by flying and before becoming a jet pilot. There, the usual butt-slapping and towel antics in the shower room as shown by many young men, suggests the homosexual edge to their social relationships.

I had no desire to chase after girls. I did have several mechanical episodes with sorority girls as the result of dares and bets but they were not satisfying emotionally, after panty raids on sororities. I did that to keep my status in that fraternity during my junior and senior years.

My status there was also bolstered by my academic performance as it helped keep up the fraternity average GPA. Since starting military flying I think that the possibility of death from military flying makes me reluctant to develop a heterosexual relationship which, for me, would be rather intense. The thought of leaving a widow and possibly small children without a father due to a flying disaster for me was a feared end to personal life. I guess, in my mind, the desire to fly fighter jets is directly opposed to the possibility of creating suffering in others in my world. What do you think?

Well, I've had almost no experience with girls, either, replies Jeremy. I've been more interested in aeroplanes and flying. I do remember instances in high school like personal challenges to commit masturbation together. They happened in the change room next to the gym, dares made to see who could "shoot" the furthest but I never fell for it. Another of my classmates used to come out of the showers with his penis tucked back between his thighs and with his fat belly bulging out to imitate pregnancy. It got hilarious laughs in the showers.

I can understand your point of view about death. Existence morally involves exploring one`s desires, ambitions, and goals without generating suffering in others, either the general public or one`s own family. Simply put, it's the "do unto others……" adage. I guess that you have been non-sexual other than masturbating yet you've accomplished great things. I'm presently studying existentialism in grade twelve now, so these thoughts are most instructive for me. I have no guilt over our mutual sexual experience, it's been so natural. I guess that events come into one`s life perhaps to test character and ethics. I honestly liked what happened and I appreciate your emotional and technical attention to my expanded maturity. If we keep this to ourselves, just as a matter of privacy, we can go on to expand, to continue growing.

In this culture, I suspect that such expressions of love are totally taboo and could lead to harassment and jeering from most people, also my parents. Am I making sense? I think that we both have many air miles to accumulate and there is excitement in the anticipation of future events that will string through our lives, providing we use common sense and a sense of ethics.

Carol sits up in bed, and looks directly at Jeremy in admiration. "I`m surprised at your degree of insight and maturity at your age. I appreciate your reaction to my unplanned, instantaneous expression of desiring behavior. I have kept a careful lock and key on my sexual desires by intense physical activity in sports, particularly handball and swimming, added to my preoccupation to being a jet fighter pilot now in reserve status in the Air National Guard. Perhaps my interest in the Air cadets is to give teens the opportunities that I have had in becoming a pilot, a social responsibility that takes me out of myself. I have developed a regimen in my activities and these occupations of mine are dovetailed with my job in the Studio, decorating sets that your dad makes, perhaps as a source of recognized delusion. Anyway, we both have an expanded connection that I sincerely hope we can both cherish in support of one another. We can fly together, we are a good team, and use my plane on weekends whenever you want. That will allow you to gather your flying time and I can watch you grow into an accomplished airman. How does that sound"? Jeremy slaps his knee, wow, that`s sounds great! Let`s take another shower, this time together, and then go out for some dinner, I`m getting ravenous.

That evening, they retire to bed, explore each other and cuddle for a few minutes. Jeremy asks: your Cessna 140, when did you get it? It's a long story, replies Carol, in my third year as a military pilot, training completed, my parents both died in Burbank one late evening last year, a head-on crash with a drunk. Ironically, the drunk survived but with a badly broken back, he's permanently confined to a wheelchair. As the only offspring with no close relatives, I had my parents cremated and buried at Forest Lawn, according to their wills and everything was left to me. I sold the house, other belonging, and banked the rest. When I decided to transfer my commission to the National Guard, I bought a new condo in Santa Monica and purchased Sally. Sally? What is that, Jeremy asked. Chuckling, Carol replies, that's my Cessna 140 my only girlfriend! Guess you've not noticed that name behind the cowling flap! I bought it right off the assembly line two years ago. I'm too wound up at the 'plane to notice such things, says Jeremy but that coincides with my going into Air Cadets. They then hug, kiss and fall off to sleep.

Daylight in the desert comes early and both wake to check their watches. It is seven o'clock so they rise, get dressed and go out for a quick breakfast. After eating they trot over to the 'plane and find the mechanic busy installing a new magneto. He works early to avoid the heat of day, even on a Sunday, although he admits that he usually takes Sunday off but is showing his appreciation for their CAP search work on the weekend. The magneto installed, Carol fires up the engine and revs it for several minutes, then shuts it off. Guess you were right, he tells the mechanic, I had my suspicions about the magneto, also. The mechanic grins, "great minds think alike, he says, while wiping his hands after installing the cowling. Send me the bill, says Carol, and I intend to add a little extra for your prompt work on a Sunday. He gives him his calling card for the National Guard along with his mailing address. They get set for take-off and fly towards Riverside, then through the cut in the mountains to Los Angeles. The 'plane flies smoothly and Jeremy gets to fly all the way to their home strip in Santa Monica and land. H

His parents are anxious to get filled in on their adventure, well the flying part of it, anyway. Carol phones from his apartment just before sunset saying that the 'plane and pilot were found in the desert just short of the east side Coachella mountains and Palm Springs. He landed out of fuel and smashed his landing gear and propeller in the desert sands, suffered a few cuts and bruises, and a non-operative radio.

School proceeds as usual with some short-term practice flights with Carol, concentrating on take-offs and landings. Graduation comes quickly. Jeremy and his parents plan the budget for his university schedule at UCLA and he mails in his application for admission.

GRADUATION AND SOME LONG-TERM FLYING

His father's brother who is a successful businessman with no sons, buys Jeremy a used two-door Ford sedan to commute to university as he plans to stay at home for at least the first two years. Carol takes his two weeks of summer leave from the studio matching film production schedules and that at the Guard. There is a week-long State Congress of the California Civil Air Patrol in conjunction with air races at Palm Springs and Carol invites Jeremy to go with him for two weeks and to do some flying as far south as Arizona and New Mexico. Jeremy has no scheduled summer job but is on call at the Santa Monica airport for odd jobs. The extended flying trip south has him all excited, especially the chance to accumulate his flying time. His parents agree as long as he stays close to Carol, and when Carol arrives he pledges that. Before they leave Jeremy reads his acceptance letter from UCLA.

They take a course to Palm Springs east from Riverside to fly along highway 395 to avoid the air congestion in the Southern Los Angeles area arriving at Palm Springs in mid-afternoon. Jeremy calls home and begins a daily call for parental info. The Air races and the CAP sessions are in a hotel near the airport and Jeremy gets the opportunity to understand how the organization works in the first three days of their visit. The air races are over in the following two days so they plan their flights southward spending hours in the swimming pool and tanning another day before leaving. Jeremy is curious about further sexual adventures with Carol and learns to give fellatio to him on several coached occasions and Carol reciprocates.

One evening their playing becomes very hot and steamy stimulating Jeremy to ask what else they can do. Carol mentions anal sex cautiously, assuring Jeremy that being careful, using a condom and lubricant, we might both enjoy the experience and there's no reason why we can't reciprocate. You mean like alternating under or over positions, queries Jeremy. That's for sure, says Carol, reciprocation is the real secret, I think. "As both of us are novices, which do you prefer first, over or under"? Jeremy hesitates for a few seconds, okay, you go on top first and I will take you but be careful and use lotsa lubricant, after all, I've never done this. Okay, but neither have I, says Carol, so we are both curious neophytes. I'll wait until you give me the signal, says Carol smiling, my experience is entirely visual, from TV films I've rented. By the way, use my camera for a visual record of our flying adventures.

That same day after lunch, they return from lunch, take a dip in the pool, Jeremy takes some snaps, then they return to their room. Jeremy throws himself on the queen-size bed and takes off his bathing suit, laying there on his stomach with his head turned, grinning in anticipation. Carol follows quickly and they embrace and kiss fervently. He rubs Jeremy's back gently, his right hand travelling downward over his beautiful, tight buttocks and kisses him all over from the neck downward to include his thighs. Then he gently runs his index finger up from the scrotal area tracing the crack in Jeremy's cheeks and nibbling his cheeks. He does this several times, increasing his finger pressure until he contacts the anus. Jeremy begins to gasp and Carol nibbles his cheeks again, spreading them to expose the nearly virgin anus and begins licking the crack vigorously with his exploring tongue. From Jeremy's quiet moans he knows that things are going well and he remembers the action that he has seen on gay porno films.

Adjusting his stance between Jeremy's legs, he parted the buttocks to expose the small anus, surrounded by fine hairs, and begins licking the whole area, increasing his tongue vigor in response to Jeremy's reactions. Then, reaching in the side table drawer, he grabs a condom package and a bottle of lubricant, both of which he had purchased that morning. What are you doing now, asks Jeremy, turning his head to look around at Carol who is fitting on the condom on his erect penis that matches the size of his, and watches as it is saturated with lubricant. I'm getting ready for penetration and now will lubricate your anus liberally, then begin probing which you will feel shortly. He applies the lubricant, rubs it into the peritoneal area and anus, with his index finger, exploring the opening. Jeremy gasps louder, as the finger begins to slide into him, in then out, in repetitive fashion, going deeper on each thrust. Next Carol adds his adjoining finger and notes the anus expanding slightly, as though to invite entry. I think that you are nearly ready for entry, he says. Oh, my ass feels red hot and ready, replied Jeremy, do it!

Carol begins rubbing his stiff member up and down the ass crack, then probing for entry. He pushes to finds the anal opening. Grasping both cheeks with his hands and pulling them apart, he prods gently in the right place and Jeremy responds by wriggling and arching his ass a little, anticipating entrance. The penal head slowly enters accompanied by Jeremy's increasingly louder gasps and is furthered by persistent rhythmic thrusting until the entire length of the penis is fully buried in Jeremy's ass while Jeremy increases his squirming, with both hands gripping the sheet tightly. Now they are both groaning in syncopation as thrusting becomes more vigorous.

After some ten minutes Carol gives a loud gasp and says, I'm coming, I'm coming. Jeremy can feel the pulsating, and ever-stiffening penis ejaculating in the condom as Carol collapses on top of him. Laying there, both gasping for breath, they begin chuckling together as Carol nibbles at Jeremy's left ear. After several minutes he pulls out slowly, still half-erect, takes off the condom and wipes off his member with a kleenex as Jeremy rolls over onto his back. Waving the used condom merrily in one hand while clutching the used Kleenex in the other, Carol says, see what I could have given you! The condom is nearly one-third full as Jeremy gazes at it with a heightening smile as it is tucked into another Kleenex and tossed beside the bed. Laying there now both in more normal composure, Carol asks how was it for you? For me it was absolutely fantastic, thank you so much, I never had an inkling that anal sex could be so good, and so tight and throbbing, better than one's hand.

Jeremy matches his response, I agree, it was simply marvelous after you entered me so carefully and increased your stroke tempo like a symphony conductor! You have a magic touch, now I must try to match it, perhaps tonight. I had no idea that anal stimulus could feel so good, almost as good as ejaculation and lasting much longer, too. I've just got to try it on you when you are ready. Now I know from my health class diagrams why the penile length matched the distance from anus to prostate gland. The nerve connections must include penis, peritoneal area, the anus, prostate, and connections to the brain via the spinal cord. No wonder it feels so good! They both lay there in convulsive laughter. Your constantly surprise me, says Carol, you sound like a medical analyst!

Now I feel like a short nap before another dip in the pool. What a great time we are having, flying and making love to each other, says Jeremy. Nothing in school could possibly match our experiences together. Well, says Carol, look at it this way, we are both in school but studying ourselves instead of books! They both laugh and lay there resting further.

That evening after dinner they are both eager to return to their room for more play but first take another dip in the pool. Towelling off back in the room, Jeremy looks appreciatively at Carol's slim, toned body, hugging him from the back and reaching forward to fondle his penis. It's so great that we have matching cocks, in size and both are circumcised. The uncircumcised ones I've seen at school in the shower look really ugly! We both have curly hair too, although yours in black, laughs Carol. Are you ready for Freddie, says Jeremy. That's the name I'm giving to my penis, at least for tonight. He strokes Carol's shoulders, his arms, and buttocks. So nice! I can hardly wait! I get to ride my instructor! Throwing down his towel, Carol turns, hugs him and throws him down on to the bed and lays beside him. Jeremy fondles his penis, then Carol's, then begins a studied interplay of fellatio and body kissing, until Carol's penis and his own are stiff and throbbing. Turn over now for Freddie! Carol obeys, and says, now be careful, just like I was this afternoon. The condoms and lubricant are in the side-table drawer. Jeremy pats him on the cheeks, gently biting him like eating a hamburger.

He grasps Carol's erect penis, from behind and sucks on it with enthusiasm, alternating that with licks on Carol's ass-crack and testicles. Then spreading the buttocks, he dives in with his tongue and explores the peritoneum and anus until his tongue ached from all the action. Carol, breathing hard, arches his back up to Jeremy's face. Get the lubricant he gasps, and Jeremy leans over to retrieve a condom package and the bottle of lubricant. He squirts a goodly shot of lubricant onto the ass-crack and runs his hand up and down several times while feeling for the anus with his index finger. Spreading the cheeks apart, the almost hairless anus looks very inviting and he begins rubbing it vigorously then penetrating it slightly with two fingers. Carol responds by contracting his cheeks and anus simultaneously several times which excites Jeremy even more. I think I'm ready, says Carol, do you have the condom on? I've never used one before, replies Jeremy, tearing open the package and fingering the condom with both hands. Well, look at it and see that it opens up to slide on your penis, says Carol. Oh, done, now I'm ready, mutters Jeremy as he sights on his target and begins probing, again with both cheeks spread wide with his now well-lubricated hands.

Carol can feel the prodding as it nears his anus, then settles on it with increased pressure. Jeremy increased his pressure and slowly, the head of his cock begins to enter. Oh! What a feeling, he says as he continues, his penis slowly entering and Carol slightly moving his hips as though to help him. Beginning now to stroke, and with each move, his penis adds more depth of penetration until his thighs slap noisily against Carol's cheeks. Driving in and out, over the whole length of his penis, from cock head to thighs, he establishes a steady rhythm that is punctuated by Carol's grunts of appreciation. Then faster, for a few strokes, then slowing, then faster again, this time reaching a crescendo of strokes and his gasping breath announcing the onset of organism. Jeremy then collapses on Carols back, sobbing quietly.

The couple relax in quiet for a few minutes then silence is broken by Jeremy, shall I pull out now, I'm still stiff 'though. Carol replies huskily, go some more if you like, I'm enjoying it! They both laugh and Jeremy continues for another several minutes until his penis starts to relax and he pulls out slowly, grabbing the box of Kleenex, removing the condom, and wiping his recovering cock. He tosses both wrapped Kleenex over the side of the bed as Carol turns over and grabs him into a wrestling hug. "How was that", I thought it was just great and you performed like a maestro, what talent you have!" A wide grin spreads across Jeremy's face, that was the cat's meow, he responds, I'm so proud of myself! So happy that you are so pleased also, we are learning to drive each other to absolute bliss.

Can we improve our talents even more, enquires Jeremy. My God, says Carol, your untiring ambition is astounding, and yes, we can try but so far the experience has been nearly overwhelming. I'm sure glad that we are both vigorously healthy and energetic. If our relation continues to grow in absolute trust and fidelity, we can look forward to doing this without condoms, what is called "bare-backing" in the media. Perhaps that means that we fuse completely. Perhaps we should take some unusual pictures, says Jeremy, but from Carol`s frown he realises that would be a bit much, at least at the present time. Remember, says Carol, pictures may get into the wrong hands, you never know.

The next day they pre-flight Sally, and prepare to fly south to Phoenix. The weather is sunny and calm, typical of the desert country during the summer unless a front comes in with thunderstorms. Flying over the Salton Sea they can see the shrinkage caused by irrigation demand in the upper valley. They then turn east to Phoenix and land after a two-and-a half hour flight to stretch their legs. They take-off again, Jeremy does the job, and head northeast to Albuquerque, a three-and-a-half hour flight over some very mountainous terrain. Local altitude is over six thousand feet. With a tricky cross-wind, Carol takes the controls and lands the 'plane. We stay here the night, says Carol, as six hours flying is quite enough in a Cessna 140 due to the noisy cabin. With headsets on, it's not so bad, is it? After mooring the 'plane in the directed spot, they call for a cab to go to town and check into a motel with a pool, and to grab some southwestern food. Their room off the pool has two double beds stimulating Jeremy to suggest rampant skylarking that night.

After eating and a swim and relaxing rest, they settle down in their shorts and listen to the black and white TV for a short while then Jeremy makes his dutiful call home. If it hadn't been such a long day, we could've found a gym and worked out any knots, says Carol. I don't have any knots, says Jeremy, but I would like a back massage before going to sleep. The high altitude here is affecting me. Carol leaves his chair, picks up Jeremy from his chair and deposits him on one of the beds, pulls off both their shorts and rolls Jeremy onto his stomach. Same menu as yesterday, sir, he asks. His partner grins and settles down for his anticipated massage, and the additional hard pressure on his butt cheeks.

Yesterday's routine is shortened and within 20 minutes they are both relaxing and looking at the ceiling. We are getting more sophisticated, aren't we, says Jeremy. Less fiddling about and hesitation makes the love act even more intense and interesting. Do you think that our bodies are physically and psychologically becoming more like one? Our trust in each other is building, if that's what your getting at, replies Carol. Time to brush our teeth and slip under the sheets, and chat about tomorrows plans. In bed, between the sheets, Carol continues, if the weather holds, we could fly to Las Vegas but that's a five hour trip. We could fly down the Grand Canyon on the way but that might add more time. What do you think? The Grand Canyon sounds very exciting Jeremy murmurs as he begins to fall asleep. Carol quietly kisses him on his cheek then quietly turns off the lights and falls off to sleep himself.

Next morning, Jeremy wakens before Carol so quietly turns and slides his upper body downward under the covering sheet, nearing Carol's thighs. He moves the limp penis around, getting it into his mouth then stroking and licking it with his eager tongue. His efforts begin to pay off and the member begins to enlarge. Encouraged by his efforts he increases his actions and the cock becomes fully erect as Carol begins to shift and open his eyes to see a bobbing head underneath the sheet. Reaching down with his right arm wrapped around Jeremy's chest, he throws him upward then onto his back.

Fully awake now, he rolls on top of Jeremy and plants several deep kisses on his mouth.

Are you ready for breakfast, you sneaky sucker! I'm going to nail you, feed you a big, thumping sausage. Jeremy giggles loudly and turns onto his left side as Carol throws his right leg over him. Jeremy folds both legs and projects his ass towards his partner who presses his stiff cock against the inviting buttocks. Spitting a large gob of saliva onto his right hand, he slaps it into the ass crack, beginning to rub it vigorously. Jeremy's cheeks relax in anticipation as the thrusted member seeks its entrance. Heh, what about lubricant, Jeremy says and Carol reaches for the bottle and applies it liberally to the ass crack and his cock, then pushes with much sighing and intent. What follows from this new position is predictable and some fifteen minutes later Carol joins with Jeremy's moans to announce his coming. He comes directly into the ass without wearing a condom and it feels so good that he almost screams in delight. Oh, my God, I got so wound up that I forgot about the condom, he says, almost sheepishly. But there is no health danger as we are both pure in heart and body, and have no background in the usual behavior of many male lovers that I've read about.

Jeremy now sits up and looks at him straight in the eyes, saying I agree, no danger as long as we swear total fidelity to one another as part of our friendship. Carol nods in agreement and they both swear fidelity to one another and kiss to make it sure. They both lay back down, holding hands, and Carol says that actually shooting my semen directly into you is psychologically more significant in the union as no barrier exists in love-making, also the contact is much more intense on my penis as you will see yourself. Jeremy nods, yes, that condom is a nuisance to put on and is a barrier which we don't need. I'll discover the added intensity myself before too long. We just made a serious oath and if it is broken, by either of us, it can totally destroy our friendship as the trust and faith in it will be destroyed. The trust and faith is most important to me and should be likewise to you, so keep that in mind in the future. Now, how about breakfast and some hot coffee?

They find a small restaurant and enjoy eating the local diet specialities with their orange juice and coffee. When we return to the motel and before packing up to leave, I want to go over possible flight plans for today, says Carol. You want to fly over the Grand Canyon and I suggest it's best to fly west to Flagstaff, that's some 345 miles, or just short of four hours flying, and stay there overnight, then go north, fly the canyon north to the south end of Lake Powell and Hoover Dam and return to Flagstaff. That trip would be nearly 400 miles and four hours flying. Next day fly south-west to Lake Havasu City (130 miles and an hour and a half flying) then turn west towards San Bernardino and home to Santa Monica, so our last flight from Flagstaff to Santa Monica would involve another 380 miles or four hours flying. At home we can go to my condo for a days rest and that will give me a chance to show-off my place and attract you to visit whenever you feel like it.

How does that plan sound to you? Okay, you have it all worked out and I can keep adding to my flight time and navigation experience, says Jeremy. This whole trip will have given you experience in radio, radio compass and ground navigation practice, and flying over desolate expanses, and some at fairly high altitudes. Places like Abuquerque can be dicey in a small plane. Yes, I see that, says Jeremy, and I am really thankful for all your help as an experienced pilot. Well, let's get at it then, says Carol, back to the plane and off to Flagstaff. We should top up the fuel and check the engine oil level for this due west flight, the weather is holding stable. They check out and take a cab to the strip, pre-flight and take-off with Jeremy in control. Carol lets him fly almost the entire trip and land at Flagstaff. They get there at by mid-afternoon, tie-down the`plane and head for a motel in town.

After a quick lunch and checking in, they use the pool for a short swim to loosen up, then hit the queen-size bed for a while. Jeremy is tuning in well on cross-country flying, using the compass, radio compass, and chart reading of topography. Now he has other things on his mind and looking at Carol with a gleam in his eye, "are you ready for action now or do you want to wait `til later". Carol grins, I thought that all that flying you did today would slow you down but I see you have the bit between your teeth. He reaches over and rubs Jeremy`s chest and stomach, then ventures further down to a flaccid penis. Let`s wait until this evening, buddy, and venture downtown to check out the place. Flagstaff has an interesting historical background and much art and pottery activity, let`s look.

They spend the rest of the afternoon poking about until the sun begins descending in the west, finding a neat restaurant full of historical knick-knacks where they descend on the tantalizing menu with much gusto. Back at the motel, another short swim, and by now the bed looks very inviting to both of them. Ripping off their swim shorts and making sure that the window blinds are secure, they both leap into bed and hug each other with joyous chuckles. Jeremy is already getting hard and stimulates his partner to match his own now fully-erect and throbbing cock. Carol turns on his side motivating Jeremy to close in behind him and throw his left arm across Carol`s chest and down to his genitals while kissing his neck and shoulders. He then throws his left leg over as Carol folds his legs somewhat towards his chest as he feels the probing stiffness.

Jeremy has the lubricant under his pillow and retrieves it without delay, cupping a goodly amount he slaps it on Carol`s cheeks and rubs it vigorously into the ass crack, feeling for the anus and rubbing the entire perineum as his breathing increases. Carol is obviously ready as he arches his spine, tilting his ass up towards the probing cock which has found the entrance and is presently rubbing up and down in between the occasional thrust on target. The head begins penetration as Jeremy begins to gently rotate his hips as his penis sinks slowly in. He emits light moaning sounds as he begins stroking, gradually increasing both length and frequency of stroke, accompanied by slapping sounds as he penetrates each stroke to its fullest. Carol is now beginning to grunt and groan and his vocalizing matches that of Jeremy who is now clutching Carol`s left cheek and moving towards the peritoneum where his fingers also find the base of his own cock, rock-like and sliding.

Nearly twenty minutes pass, then Carol begins rolling onto his stomach, with Jeremy following without losing connection. Stroking continues as Jeremy clutches Carol`s left shoulder, pulling on it as he drives his penis full length into his ass and churning it around by hip movements. By now they are both groaning aloud and Jeremy begins sucking and biting on the neck and ears until, with a loud cry, I`m coming now, he pumps furiously, then collapses onto to Carol`s back with heaving, gasping breaths passing his ear. They lay still for several minutes and Jeremy makes occasional thrusts in short bouts until his penis begins to soften. Grabbing at the Kleenex box on the side table, he slowly pulls out, catching semen drops on a Kleenex and wiping his member. With another Kleenex he wipes Carol`s ass crack, down to his anus, noticing the fine blond hairs radiating outward and across his buttocks.

Carol rolls over onto his back, smiling, how was that! You have really cottoned on to technique, even with hardly any practice, you`re a fantastic lover for me. I`m going to have to concentrate myself just to keep up with your technique! Jeremy laughs broadly, I`m so glad that you feel that way and I always try to improve myself at everything I do. That was the best orgasm I`ve ever had, even better that the one I had from you blowing me the first time! Bare-backing is so great as long as you`re with the right person. We are a great pair of lovers, you and I, how lucky we are to have found one another, and both of us flyers! Great rewards follow from true hearts and maximum trust, I suppose. A quick shower, yes? Then we should get a sound rest as we have a four hour flight tomorrow over some very rugged and possibly gusty situations. They will really test your cockpit abilities but I will be there too, on guard for any difficulty. Now, shower and to bed, buddy of mine. Jeremy nods in agreement, soon darkness comes and they are both asleep.

The next morning, Carol is awake first, checks his watch, it`s nearly eight, and rubs Jeremy`s shoulder from which he comes awake with a sigh. Oh, time to get going, ace, we have a good four hour flight today, perhaps a bit more depending on winds and the canyon, so rise and shine. Carol gives him a long, deep kiss on his cheek, then directly on his mouth. That should get you going, he says as he leaps out of bed, heading for the bathroom to relieve his bladder. Jeremy is close behind him to do likewise. Both shave although Jeremy`s whiskers are scant and short, leading to a teasing comment from the twenty-five-year-old. They dress after a little horse-play leading to minor wrestling on the bed before dressing and heading out the door for breakfast.

Upon return Carol goes to the office, explaining that they will be back in the late afternoon or early evening for another night stay before flying back to Los Angeles. Today, Carol says to the receptionist, we`re flying up to see the Grand Canyon from the air, and Lake Powell. Sounds exciting, replies the girl, to see the Canyon from the air. He returns to the room, gathers up Jeremy and their bags and makes sure he still has film for his Pentax. At the plane, they pre-flight as usual, and taxi over to the fueling station to top up the tank and check engine oil. The weather check shows no problems, and Jeremy takes off without any problems despite some mild gusts of side wind. Carol nods approvingly, as the plane swings north, headed for Lake Powell at 3500 feet of altitude.

Nearing the south end of the Powell Lake, they turn to follow the canyon down towards Hoover Dam. Carol instructs Jeremy to follow the river course, and get set to decrease altitude as they enter the Grand Canyon, and be ready for possible gusty winds, especially downdrafts. Feel you way along, like a bird in flight, and prepare to gain altitude if necessary. The trek through the canyon is impressive, especially when they drop down towards the river below and see the surrounding massive cliffs appear to close in on them from above. Carol takes many snaps of the canyon walls and the thread-like river below that enlarges as they descend. Jeremy is really wound up saying this must be like a combat mission but with nobody firing at you! Carol laughs, we`re flying much too slowly for combat but this kind of flying is much more fun that driving a jet hot-rod with a big fuel appetite and not much more than an hour in the air.

What you should look out for is a soaring vulture, there are a few California condors in this area with a wingspan nearly ten feet and weigh up to thirty pounds, so if you hit one the impact would be devastating, especially if it came through the cockpit. They originated in the Pleieistocene era and were even bigger then. You know about birds, too, says Jeremy. Well, they are flyers, too and we shouldn't deprive them of the common air, so keep a sharp eye, says Carol.

At the downstream end of the canyon, they turn south and Jeremy sets up a heading back to Flagstaff where they arrive at half-past five, to watch the sun beginning her descent into darkness. The nightly routine continues as does that in the morning, the pair sharing with boundless enthusiasm. Calling home that evening, Jeremy tells them they are expecting to arrive at Santa Monica in the late afternoon in two days and will call them then. Carol sets up the compass track for their last leg, back to Los Angeles, another four hour flight, heading first for Lake Havesu City, then San Bernardino, then through the cut in the local mountain range towards the Pacific Ocean presently over the horizon. Again, Jeremy has the controls for some three hours then Carol takes over in anticipation of increase air traffic as they approach the coast but he gives landing controls over to Jeremy as they approach Santa Monica after he has radioed the tower for landing permission and runway number. Landing is a snap for him and he taxis over to the tied-down position as directed by Carol.

Grabbing the bags, they go to Carol`s MG roadster, put down the top and throw in their bags. He drives to his condo, showing Jeremy the best route to take. Showing him around in the condo, including the sea view out the west-facing sliding doors and veranda on the third floor, he points out that the beach is only half a block away, and sees that Jeremy is quite impressed, especially with the large framed photograph of him climbing out of an F-86. He stands beside him, arm around his waist, saying that could be you before too long, you know! I feel like you already, says Jeremy, giving him a kiss on the cheek. That evening, after a long, hot shower for both, Carol takes him to great Chinese restaurant nearby for dinner before they relax in the condo. There, he grabs two beers from the `frig, pours them into his fancy beer steins and hands one to Jeremy who takes it eagerly, saying my parents being Methodist have no alcohol in the house so I have only had such an opportunity several times at a friend`s house.

He sits down, putting his stein carefully on the drink pad provided on the adjacent side table, takes a few sips, then shows his appreciation by taking several good gulps. Carol watches him from a nearby chair, smiling, well, you`re starting university in a couple of months and beer-drinking becomes a major obsession for many guys, some to their academic downfall. However, you are different, self-controlled and disciplined, so you will have no problems. I am your guardian angel! Jeremy laughs, yes, that`s true, and I expect you to be hovering over me at every sign of danger! But not like my mother, `though! They both laugh and drink their beer. I`m planning to live at home for the first two years, at least, Jeremy continues. That will save money and allow me to study without the noise and interference I hear goes on in campus housing.

Carol nods in agreement, at USC I had my own room so avoided much of the fraternity shannanigans as that crowd looked at me as a loner and spoilsport, so that was to my advantage. When do you register and what will be your major? Registration is in the first week of September and I`m planning on history and political science as a split major, what do you think of that, answers Jeremy. I majored in classical history specializing in Greek culture. Your selection sounds great and it will expand your general knowledge of society and its organization, as well as all the mistakes and lunacies our race has got embroiled in during the past, creating great suffering. That suffering applied mostly to entirely innocent people, including children. I`m looking forward to assisting you in any way possible, including keeping up your excitement and closeness! You are welcome here at any time to keep me company and lessen my oft-times loneliness which certainly has been blown away, so to speak, by our now-completed summer flying adventure. Beers finished and a quick review of the bland TV offerings, they prepare for bed. Jeremy has already surveyed the bedroom and the fancy queen-sized bed which also has a sea view and entry to the veranda. They shower and fall into bed in each others arms and soon are fast asleep. It`s been a long day and the beer made Jeremy drowsy.

The next morning, he awakens alone in bed. Carol is in the kitchen in his dressing gown, coffee odor begins to fill the air, and he is at the kitchen table making notes. He looks up as Jeremy appears, scratching the few sprouting hairs on his chest. Oh, coffee! That`s what I need. Sit down here, says Carol, jumping up to retrieve mugs from the cupboard, milk and sugar`s coming too. I have frozen waffles ready for the toaster! Yummee, says Jeremy looking at the paper on the table. I`ve been collating all our flight data for you to show your family, says Carol. Do you realise that we have flown nearly 1900 miles in the last ten days! That`s starting to look like a continental trip and I`m already starting to think of another trip next summer, besides some shorter trips beforehand. How about New Orleans and the Everglades?, or Mexico! Ole! Time will tell, won`t it. Meantime we must get on with the expectable stuff.

Expectable stuff! When can we go back to bed, quips Jeremy. After a good breakfast, Romeo, I`m putting on the waffles, can you eat three? I`ll get the dinner plates out, the butter, and a jug of Canadian maple syrup. Jeremy folds the paper and returns to the bedroom to dress, returning in five minutes to find a heaping plate of waffles on the table. I made six waffles so take as many as you want, while I pour the coffee. Both sit at the table and munch away, slurping down the coffee between bites of waffle. After breakfast, call home with a time of return and I will drop you off and go to the CAP office to catch up on the news. Be sure to take my telephone number, I have yours. God, it`s going to be hard to go back to the routines, back to work at the studio in four days. I have to check back in at the Guard too, probably some routine training stuff to do. You have your car so you can be over here lickety-split but call first to make sure I`m in.

They finish breakfast, brush their teeth and Carol opens his dressing gown provocatively to show his rising cock. This happens nearly every morning, he says, ever since I was six but it`s taken some time to know how to use it productively. Jeremy giggles, may be because I didn`t start masturbating until I was ten means that I should catch up, and he goes to the bedroom, taking off his clothes. Finishing his coffee with a gulp, Carol follows him quickly, removing his dressing gown, throwing it in a corner and leaping on the bed next to Jeremy. This is a great bed, Carol, so soft yet firm, and bouncy! His penis is rising rapidly, making Carol make clucking noises with his teeth, reach down to engulf the throbbing member in his mouth and to slowly slide it down his throat, return to nibble the head and roll his tongue around its peripheral ridge which brings cries from Jeremy. His own penis has behaved likewise and is aching for action. Lifting Jeremy`s legs to his shoulders and putting a small cushion under his back to elevate his hips, Carol reaches for the lubricant, pouring it on Jeremy`s peritoneum, testicles, and shaft along with his own member.

With a gentle, caressing right hand he stimulates the anus, followed by fingering and ringing rubs until Jeremy begins moaning. Leaning forward on his knees, Carol thrusts almost instinctively at the vital spot, his penis sinking slowly into the treasured interior. Jeremy reaches up and caresses Carol`s nipples, gently pinching them, raising his head then to invite kisses from above. Carol responds strongly, their tongues intertwining and exploring each others mouths and lips. The stroking increases and Jeremy puts both hands behind Carol`s neck and begins matching the copulatory rhythm with hip movements of his own, including squeezing his anal and cheek muscles in coordination with the thrusts of Carol`s cock. Within a few minutes both began involuntary gasps and moaning, followed by violent kissing, then, with an audible cry, Carol ejaculates and collapses on top of his partner who frantically nibbles his ears. As soon the heavy breathing dies down, Carol reaches for the Kleenex box, and slowly withdraws, catching his now softening penis with a Kleenex, then with another sheet, carefully wiping Jeremy`s anus and peritoneum. With eyes half-closed, Jeremy produces a long sigh, that was a new position and I really like it because we are face to face and can kiss in wild abandon, also I can play with your nipples!

They both lay there relaxed and chuckling. Finally, Carol says, your comments are so engaging, so starkly frank, that you just overwhelm me with your personality. What more could I say, I have fallen for you with my whole being and life has changed for me dramatically, for you, too, no doubt. Romeo and Juliet had nothing like this, despite all the drama surrounding that Shakespearian play on love. I hope you don`t think I`m being melodramatic? Jeremy has been listening quietly, no, no, I feel the same way, so it must be normal human emotion. We are just two very fortunate guys, spiritually fused, and embarking on a tremendous adventure that we must be sure to protect and defend, regardless of any opposition. We are the One! Your natural wisdom is showing and it surely comes from the heart, replies Carol, we have to be careful though.

They arise in preparation to return Jeremy to his family and his anticipation of starting university. On the way over to the house, Carol, looking over at Jeremy on several occasions, finally says, let`s be very controlled at this parting at the house, I don`t want your parents to think that our flight instructor-student relationship has changed profoundly. Both of us must carefully avoid any clues that might alert them. That would surely generate enormously negative reactions on their part that would have destructive effects on both of us. We have done nothing wrong, nothing evil, we have simply found one another and are in a state of grace.

Jeremy is listening attentively, nodding in agreement several times. They approach the house, park by the sidewalk and both climb out of the car, and walk up to the door, Jeremy holding his bag rings the bell. His mother answers the door with the younger sister behind her, both smiling happily. His father is still at work. The usual greeting routines and conversation occurs then his mother thanks Carol for bringing back her son safely after such an experience. Carol declines staying for coffee or tea, saying that he has catching up to do with his organizational activities and leaves Jeremy to download all the travel info. He gives him a brief hug and pat on the back and departs to his car. A more complex, interesting life has arrived for them both.

Jeremy immerses himself in schoolwork as Christmas draws near. His six-cylinder, two-door Ford sedan has proved to be a good buy and is economical to run. He still has his part-time job at the airport which is handy, for his expenses are now increasing. Fall exams are now over and he has done well, high grades, B's with a sprinkle of A's Carol takes him out for short rides in the Cessna almost every other weekend so as to continue his experience, and they spend a few hours in the condo also. The Korean War broke out that summer and Carol has been involved in intense combat training sessions at Nellis AFB, in southern Nevada, all Fall. It is rumored that he might be re-activated in the Tactical Air Command (TAC) along with several pilots. The air war in Korea so far has been in the U.N.'s advantage, with the USA using its F-80 fighters and B-29 bombers on active duty. However, since the arrival of MIG-25's in Korea, mostly flown by skilled Russian pilots, the bombers have been badly mauled with heavy casualties during daylight raids. Two F-86 Wings are sent to even up the losses and B-29's only fly night missions.

Carol is given notice to prepare for transfer to active duty in the TAC in Korea, and he spends Christmas dinner with the Witherspoon family. In late January, his orders are cut and he prepares to fly to Seoul by military transport within three weeks. He hurriedly settles his affairs, breaking the news to Jeremy in the condo during several visits after the holidays, which results in several tearful discussions. Carol gives him the keys to the Cessna and writes a check for three thousand dollars to cover Cessna expenses in keeping it flying and maintained. Two weekends before his departure in mid-February, he spends the Sunday at the Witherspoon house. In private with Jeremy's father, he gives him a sealed package containing his will which leaves all his possessions to Jeremy, condo, Cessna, and bank accounts, telling Witherspoon that in the event of his possible death in Korea, that he will be notified by military authorities and can take charge of all arrangements. He does not mention the nature of the will but stresses that, having no close relatives, he is putting this responsibility on Witherspoon. His wishes are acknowledged and attempts are made to lighten this event by both of them.

Jeremy senses that Carol has a premonition of death but dismisses that idea by looking forward to an active correspondence with Carol until he returns, probably as a war hero. His Spring term is underway and he finds time to see Carol on his last weekend, and Carol gives him the keys to the condo and telling him that all maintenance expenses for the condo have been paid in full for an entire year, using dated checks given to the property manager. Use it if you need to, he says. Jeremy is rather overwhelmed, not primarily by Carol's generosity regarding the 'plane and condo, but by his fearful concerns for Carol's safety. Well, replies Carol, I'm a fighter pilot and there's a war going on in Korea, so I must go and do my duty It is expected of me and think of all the public expense that has gone into my military flight training. We'll write each other long letters during my combat tour which will last at least six months before I return. In the mean time, I expect to hear that you will bomb all your courses and keep Sally occupied. They have a tearful farewell after a great Chinese dinner and an emotionally-drenched last bout of love-making before Jeremy slips reluctantly out the door to return home and to his books.

A long letter arrives from an APO in South Korea two weeks later, informing him of the situation which is getting graver, militarily by the day. Carol already has been baptized in combat, having been assigned to a squadron, has his own F-86 and ground crew, and has racked up seven missions so far, mostly hammering railroad yards and trains. Jeremy re-reads the letter many times and shows parts of it to his parents, only one un-numbered page he keeps aside in a secret place, and writes back promptly. Their correspondence continues for almost three months before no further letters arrive.

POST-COMBAT ADJUSTMENT

An official telegram arrives at the house, addressed to Jeremy's father, followed by a personal letter written by the squadron commander expressing his sorrow that First Lieutenant Carol Delano Simmings, having completed twenty-seven combat missions had been shot down by ground fire. According to his wing leader who followed his downward flight, he was not seen ejecting from his steep diving, flaming aircraft. His failure to respond to radio calls during his dive, was probably due to injuries. He was a dedicated and accomplished fighter pilot whom we in the squadron will sorely miss in respect for his comradery, combat prowess and damage done to the enemy.

The sudden death of Carol greatly disturbs the Witherspoon family, especially Jeremy who is so grieved that he almost quits university but both his parents console him and encourage him to bear up to the catastrophe and stay with his academic studies. Several days later, his father opens the sealed manila envelope to find the will and Carol's lawyer's card enclosed with instructions to call him. He does so, telling him that he is following Carol's instructions from their last meeting. The lawyer and he meet two days later in the lawyer's office where the two military letters are seen by the lawyer who now is certain that he must follow the legal procedures. He introduces himself as Clancy Muldoon and sets up a meeting between Jeremy and his father where he goes over the will in great detail, explaining Carol's wishes. As Carol's remains are not available, being consumed in the exploding F-86 on impact, his wishes to be cremated and his urn placed next to those of his parents remain unfulfilled although at the cessation of the Korean War a query to military authorities on the possible recovery of his remains is officially discouraged.

Carol's will is lengthy, listing all his property, including bank accounts, is read by his lawyer who states that the value is considerable, amounting to more than several hundred thousand dollars that also includes the entire apartment house(Goldstone Manor) which consists of 22 units. Apparently, Carol had purchased this real estate soon after its construction, using a fractional mortgage from the Bank of America, based on his financial power. Several months later, he arranged with his lawyer, Clancy Muldoon, who had rented one of the six, three bedroom penthouses apartments, to become his business manager as well, and signed ownership for that penthouse over to Muldoon for property and legal services rendered ad infinitum, reflected as one-twenty-fourth of the overall real estate value of Goldstone Manor. Carol's judgement was clear as Muldoon is an ex-Catholic priest who had gone on to law school and settled down to practice in California from Loyola University some ten years earlier and a good friend of Carol's.

Muldoon explained the details of his instructions as regent of the properties. Jeremy was to receive twelve thousand dollars per year, one thousand per month, until his twenty-second birthday when he will come into legal ownership of the majority providing that he has graduated from UCLA. If he fails to graduate with a Batchelor's degree and resulting diploma shown to Muldoon, further adjustments in his share of the properties will be made but such adjustments are withheld unless found necessary by Muldoon in the alternative. In the interim until graduation, he is also to have the 1948 MG roadster, the Cessna 140, and use of Carol's penthouse apartment. Should critical financial needs arise that exceed the twelve thousand dollars a year, more funds are to be released at the discretion of Muldoon who is to manage the invested funds judiciously and add to them additional net investment profits generated from rental income above those applied to the apartment house mortgage, salaries for maintenance and improvement, such as maid and landscape gardener existing contracts. Are there any questions, asks Muldoon.

Jeremy, you are a very lucky boy and I hope that you appreciate the opportunities that Carol has given you. Mr. Witherspoon, until Jeremy gains his twenty-second birthday, we shall become quite interactive regarding all these investments. I shalle begins maningH provide annual accounts for your perusal and signature. That's about all I have to say at this time. They rise, shake hands and Jeremy and his father leave the office. His father wishes to see the apartment before going home so they go there for his inspection and he is quite satisfied with the location and state. In fact, he is rather overcome with the size and quality of Goldstone Manor and its grounds.

Jeremy remains somewhat stunned by the size and nature of his potential inheritance, particularly with his upcoming ownership of the Cessna 140, the MG roadster, long-term use of the apartment, and the annual income which should get him through school without difficulties. At the house, his father explains to his wife just what their son has just been awarded from Carol's will and she understands even more the appreciation and affection that Carol obviously held for Jeremy. Jeremy now realises his responsibility to meet Carol's expectations of him and becomes determined to meet the challenge to the best of his abilities. He completes the Spring semester with very good grades after spending every other week at the apartment, studying hard and remaining very conscious of Carol's investment in him. Clancy Muldoon keeps an eye on him when he is there and they become good friends, talking about history and philosophy, topics that Muldoon is quite literate about, being a former priest.

Over the summer, apart from flying the Cessna, Jeremy spends most of his time at the apartment, and he sets up a small shrine in the spare room that Carol used for his paper work and artistic efforts at watercolor painting. He also has a considerable collection of Buddhist literature there. Jeremy arranges the small shrine surrounded by photographs he found of Carol's boyhood and beyond, and those snaps that they took on their extended flight last summer. He also hangs Carol's medals on his F-86 photograph and pledges his total abstention of sexual thoughts beyond those that describe their erotic relationship and flying experiences. That room becomes a locked, private space known only to him although his family is invited to use the apartment when he is flying on weekends.

He continues steadily with his academic work and abstentive sexual thoughts throughout the next two years, beginning to think more extensively about his sexual identity and occasional desires. The possibility of engaging in further homoerotic experiences simply disturbs his well-being and he comes to the conclusion that such potential experiences, either thrust upon him or solicited by him would be entirely distasteful and do blasphemous damage to his memory of Carol. His relationship with Carol has become an icon of intense, undying homoerotic love that could never be replaced. He remembers a discussion with Carol on Spartan and Athenian cultures as they reflected homoerotic and sexual values which Carol had included in his minor on classic history at USC.

In late August, prior to the new academic year, he decides to consult a doctor, a psychiatrist about his sexual experiences amid concerns that he may be driven to some irrational social responses on campus that might lead to his demise. He enters the office of a psychiatrist in the nearby medical building, takes a deep breath and enters in order to make an appointment. The nurse is very tactful, asks no questions as to his desire to see the psychiatrist and an appointment is made for Saturday of the following week and he goes home feeling relieved that he has committed himself to possible analysis.

At the prescribed time next Saturday he meets Dr. Rufus Claymore, a middle-aged pony-tailed fellow wearing a sweater who waves him in to his couch, smiling, and shaking his hand, notices that the palm is cool and dry. He recovers to his chair and assembles his writing pad and pencil. "I would like to have a brief verbal account of your self-defined dilemma, you must have one seeing that you are here, also some general data on your background, then we can proceed with some direction. I know that boys of your age group can generate some angst, I've raised three boys of my own. Jeremy admits that he has some difficulty with his sexual self-image, is a second-year student at UCLA , and has embarked on a semi-independent life with his own apartment and car but sees his parents quite often. "You look like a healthy, intelligent young man, is school a problem? Jeremy shakes his head in answer. With no difficulty there and you are sleeping and eating well, there must be a reason for your apparent disturbance. Are you sexually active with other students, of either sex, or with both? Jeremy responds abruptly, saying no several times, no sexual activity with others at all.

Dr. Claymore studies Jeremy's face for possible clues before asking, have you had any sexual experience, apart from the normal masturbation behavior of growing boys? Jeremy now shows that he has touched on the underlying case history and proceeds to relate his relationship with Carol. This takes some time and Jeremy doesn't omit any details. Claymore writes a few comments down on his scratchpad then says, do you feel any guilt about that experience, sexual or otherwise? No, not at all, says Jeremy and I have a deep respect and love for him even though he is no longer here. Where is he now, then, asks, Claymore. Jeremy now breaks down, sobbing, and Claymore waits patiently until he has regained control of his emotions. Jeremy then says he was killed in Korea last April, blown up in his jet fighter in enemy territory. Claymore studies him further, you have had a very intense, sexual experience apparently surrounded by mutual love and affection. I suggest that the psychological intensity of your relationship with this courageous pilot reflects your previously naïve state of mind about sex.

Sounds to me that you two had more going for you than many of my married or previously married adults. I'm glad that you have no guilt, for that is a very strong point in your favor. Homosexual behavior in an innocent psychological state also showing social and moral values is perfectly normal, in my view. A few of my patients have had sexual doubts because they have feelings for both sexes and I've told them, how lucky can one be! Twice as much potential fun and experience as the rest of us. I would like you to go home now, think about my comments, and make another appointment for same time next week. Meanwhile, as you are on campus, examine your degree of interest in coeds, even if it's just a faint spark. We'll talk about heterosexual concerns next week. Jeremy shakes his hand and leaves after making another appointment with the nurse._That medical visit told Jeremy that he has found a sympathetic and wise counsellor, also a father of much experience.

At the next visit with Dr. Claymore, he is shown a sheaf of Rorschach prints and asked to comment successively on what he sees in them, one by one. Claymore is busy taking notes and nods appreciatively as the last print is commented on. Have you thought much about my request that you examine your potential interest in the opposite sex, he asks. Are you afraid of girls, afraid, perhaps of their potential triggering of emotions that you have little experience in dealing with? Do you remember any incident in your teen or earlier years that may have embarrassed you about sex, either at home or at school? Yes, says Jeremy, when I was about twelve a playmate gave me a photograph of a nude women and my mother found it by snooping in my wallet while I was showering. When I came out of the shower, towel-wrapped, she screamed at me in her rage and disgust, raved about filthy ideas at my age. She also told my dad but nothing further came out of it. Oh, that's interesting, did you feel guilty about it? Yes, I did, and was embarrassed in front of my parents for more than a week, replied Jeremy.

Your parents, are they very religious and are they generally strict with you? Well, we went to Methodist church faithfully every Sunday, and to church social events like hayrides for boys and girls, and church picnics. Do you attend church regularly now that you are living independently? No, and not often when I was actively flying with my pilot instructor on the weekends. Well, that's enough for now, says Dr. Claymore. You have been very open with your experiences and emotions, I wish that degree of forthrightness was as common in my other patients. I think I have enough material to give you my analysis and advice during your next appointment which may be the last one that you may need. I'm really impressed that you earned your pilot's license at such a young age. That is commendable. See you next week.

Intuitively, Jeremy begins to think that he had a sexual block for females which discouraged him from going to the high school prom or in general, getting involved with girls in high school. At the next appointment, Dr. Claymore assures him that he has no basic hang-ups, no neurotic tendencies, and encourages him to not think otherwise.

That encounter with your mother served to produce a mental bloc that infringed on your developing social awareness as it relates to sexual images and your self-image. Your description of the relationship you had with Carol Simmings is fundamentally sound and healthy as it was based on care, respect, responsibility, and knowledge (technical, at least, and to do with flying). It was not just emotion and sexual lust. It expressed an inter-personal and creative capacity that you both dedicated yourselves to.

You have a significant capacity for intense love as shown from your personal account and that is not common as it was not based on ego or narcissistic tendencies. I recommend that you read some of the works of Eric Fromm, a fellow psychiatrist and acquaintance of mine who is also a socialist, and philosopher. He has been teaching at Bennington College but recently left the U.S.A. for a seat at the University of Mexico, due to political harassment by Senator MacArthy, the communist seeker. Two of his books in English I suggest that you read and assimilate. He writes two titles down on a prescription sheet, Escape from Freedom (1941), and Man for Himself (1947), the latter being a study on human ethics. I also know that he is working on another book combining many of his published concepts in both German and English to do with love and loving as an art.

I suggest that you actively consider developing social relations with girls of your age group and intellectual interests at UCLA. After all, about half of the human population on this planet are of the female sex. Social opportunities should come naturally at university, and you are a stable and intelligent fellow, so just follow your head and heart. It will lead you in the right direction, the direction that will assist you in finding and maintaining personal happiness. Should you feel impelled to discuss any of Fromm's concepts I would be happy to engage in talks…..not charged of course, and preferably in our spare time.

Jeremy's broadened psychological stance lasts through to the first half of his senior year. He takes a number of Air Cadets up for short rides, as do the older pilots, and encourages them to study in preparation of gaining their licenses, as did Carol, and has some casual dates on campus. After Christmas holidays in 1958, he takes notice of an attractive coed also majoring in history who has attended the same classes and invites her for the occasional coffee. Over their conversation, he mentions that he has a pilot's license, a small 'plane and flies whenever he has the chance, usually on weekends. She becomes very interested and enthused, so he invites her for a weekend spin on a Sunday and takes her up the coast to Santa Barbara for lunch, then a further flight along the coast south over the Channel Islands, and lands on Santa Catalina Island for dinner before returning to Santa Monica before dark.

Jennifer is fearless in the air and Jeremy urges her to take the controls for a few minutes on the way back. She does so with some trepidation but then realises that it's just like driving a car, only off the ground. A potential friendship has developed and that is encouraged further by more short-term weekend jaunts.

AN AWAKENING

One weekend he asks Jennifer to go to dinner and an early movie which she accepts without hesitation. After the movie he invites her to his apartment. Just for a short while, I want to show you my place. I stay there one week then one week at home with my family. As long as I get home before dark, she says. The movie is a Hollywood rendition of a Norsesmen saga, invading England, with all the expected pillage and murder typical of that history. At Goldstone Manor, Jessica is quite impressed at the apparent luxury, and with his penthouse place on the top floor. Your family must be very rich to give you such a place to study and be alone, she comments. Oh no, replies Jeremy, they are quite average, my father works at Republic Studios as a set foreman and my mother is a housewife. I also have a young sister, still in Junior High School. That doesn't match with the luxury of this place 'though, does it? I've been very fortunate as the fellow who taught me how to fly and get my license was a jet pilot who was shot-down and killed in North Korea. Come, I'll show you his photograph.

He takes her to the office room, unlocks the door. That's him climbing out of a F-86 jet fighter That's the fighter who that died at the age of 26, a first-lieutenant named Carol. Jessica looks intently at the photograph, saying he was young and good-looking, wasn't he? Jeremy nods sadly, he was such a good friend, almost an older brother to me. He came from a very wealthy family and his parents died in a head-on crash here in Burbank. Carol was their only son and inherited all their wealth. As he had no close relatives, he made a will, leaving me with this apartment, my MG, and the Cessna which was only two years old. I'm so fortunate. Now I'd better get you home before the sun sets.

He walks her up the pathway to the front door, thanks her for the delightful evening, and kisses her gently on the forehead. Jessica smiles shyly, then kisses him back lightly on the lips, turns and waves goodbye and disappears in the house. Jeremy turns, blinking, and returns to his MG and the apartment. He obviously is developing an attachment to this girl….and it's so natural, he tells himself. Why should it be otherwise? She is very attractive, poised, intelligent, a history major…..and I think that she likes me! He prepares for bed and a long, restful sleep before the Monday morning commute to the UCLA campus.

This couple meet at lunch time and discuss their flying adventure to the Channel Islands. Jennifer wants to learn how to fly and Jeremy promises her further flying adventures and says he has some manuals she should read. They agree to meet on the following Saturday at her house in North Hollywood so he can meet her parents. The academic week goes swiftly for both of them and arrangements are made for Jeremy to meet her parents Saturday afternoon. He mentions Jennifer to his parents mid-week and they are happy that his intensity of bereavement for the absent Carol is waning and encourage Jeremy to step out and develop his social relations as he will be graduating before the summer. Their appreciation for the economic boon provided by

Carol for their son remains strong and they have a solid relationship with Clancy Muldoon who periodically shows his determination to meet his legal and personal obligations to Jeremy, as desired by his former great friend. They are also most happy that their son is probably going to graduate with academic honors, from his grade records so far. Their only concern is that Jeremy has missed many Sundays at the family Methodist church and they have been often reminded of that fact by the minister.

Jeremy and Carol had several discussions about religion in the days prior to Carol's planned active duty transfer to Korea and Carol has indicated that he is inclined to support the Buddhist ideas, including reincarnation of spirits in the absence of a defined God. Since his departure to Korea, Jeremy has been reading some of the Buddhist literature and likes that the religion started some 500 years before Christianity and has an enormous collection of literature, including that on medical practice based on natural sources, meditation, and nerve stimulation through needles. However he has refrained from discussing religion with his devout parents. Several weeks after the notification of Carol's demise in North Korea, he had three dream episodes involving Carol who seemed to talk to him. In all three cases, Carol urged him to lower his grieving obsession and get on with life, saying they will meet again in the future.

Next Saturday arrives and he drives to Jennifer's home in North Hollywood, taking Laurel Canyon Blvd which is full of curves through the mountain range separating the San Fernando Valley from Northern Los Angeles. She lives just off that blvd just across the Los Angeles River, turning east to near Studio City. Finding the house is easy and he arrives there about two pm and his MG at the front side walk is spotted by Jennifer who runs out to meet him. Holding his hand, she leads him through the front door into the living room where her parents are waiting to meet him.

Jennifer's father rises from his chair and approaches smiling, bidding him welcome. That sentiment is echoed by her mother as Jeremy shakes her hand gently also. So you are a pilot that has his own plane, is that right, says Mr. Renton. Jeremy nods, smiling, I guess you had a full account of our last flight over the Channel Islands. There have been others? asked Celia, we haven't heard of any others. Jennifer pipes up, yes Mom, there was a short air ride around the airport before but I didn't want to worry you. Jack Renton laughs, our daughter has an independent mind and was in the girl scouts as a leader, too! That doesn't surprise me, says Jeremy, she seems rather fearless at new experiences, at least flying in small planes. Anyway, my Cessna 140 is almost new, very safe, and I have racked up nearly 2500 miles so far, and my longest trip with my instructor was over 1500 miles with me doing most of the flying.

He decides to expand further, saying that he and Jennifer met during common classes and they are both majoring in history, so have common intellectual interests in the human record. Jack Renton then explains that both he and his wife are high school teachers, he is the principal at North Hollywood High and Celia also teaches there. I also majored in History at UCLA, with a minor in Civics but now I am tied to the Principal's desk dealing with all sorts of problems as the area is expanding rapidly, new families coming in etc. I went to North Hollywood High, says Jeremy, and I vaguely remember you as my Civics teacher. Do you remember me? Rick admits that so many students passed through his classroom that he has few specific identities in his memory, although some of his senior students never graduated because they had joined the National Guard and were activated to Korea and nearly half of them were killed.

Celia has been listening quietly and now gets a few words in. I taught school before we married but stayed home to raise Jennifer until she was ten before I ventured back to teach home economics and hygiene, luckily where Jack teaches, before he became the principal. Well, we seem to have a lot in common, don't we, says Jennifer, three history buffs and Jeremy tells me he likes to cook! They all laugh. By now Jeremy and Jennifer are sitting on a chesterfield placed between parental chairs at her father's bidding.

I see you have an English sports car, an MG, and red, too, says Jack. When I was in college I drove a Ford Model A which was reliable, cheap to run, and had a rumble seat for extra passengers! Those were the days! Hot-rodding over Coldwater Canyon to the beach with my buddies, and that was where Celia and I met, at Paradise Beach, then we later found our own paradise! Your mother was one of the first girls at college to wear a two-piece bathing suit, Jennifer! Her mother Celia jumps up, asking if a cup of tea would be welcome and looking at the nods, looks also at Rick with her eyebrows raised then she goes to the kitchen to put on the kettle. The others smile and relax.

Jeremy is reluctant to go into any details describing his good fortune and is relieved that such questions don't arise. Perhaps Jennifer has already give them some information, perhaps to tone down her mother's bulldog attitude to her several boyfriends starting in high school. Celia returns with a tray of tea and they move to the kitchen table to enjoy it and a plate of her chocolate chip and raisin cookies. Stirring his tea and nibbling a cookie, Rick asks Jeremy what his plans were after graduation. I know that Jennifer wants to find a teaching job, hopefully not too far away from us.

Jeremy looks a bit perplexed then comments that his original dream of becoming a military pilot has soured somewhat….so perhaps a commercial pilot but driving around in one of those big, lumbering giants must be like driving a truck or bus, compared to the excitement of my Cessna. May be I'll eventually become an instructor pilot for teens who, like me, have an urge to fly. I really have no definite plans other than to travel and broaden my mind, based on my education in history.

Both parents nod with interest. It's now close to four-thirty and Jeremy looks at his watch saying that he should go and drop in on his own parents. They live fairly close to you, the other side of Lankershim blvd near Toluca Lake. My dad is a set foreman at Republic Studios so he has a short commute to work. Everyone rises, Jennifer's parents thank him for visiting and urge him to come again soon and Jennifer goes to the MG with him, and waves goodbye after they hug and kiss.

She watches his car disappear down the avenue then returns to the house where she wastes no time in asking her parents if they like Jeremy. I think he's an intelligent, solid guy who has a fine future at whatever he wishes to do, says Jack and her mother agrees emphatically, saying he is the best fellow of the bunch so far! Mother! You sound as though I go around lassoing guys and you know that's far from the truth! I may see them but have dropped them shortly on their heads, right Dad! He laughs and hugs her, that's my gal! I suggest that you see more of this guy 'though and find out for yourself. Your mother and you should plan for a quiet dinner here with him, I'm all for that!

Sorry to pop in on you without calling first, Jeremy says as he walks in to his parental home, I was close by visiting Jennifer and her parents and felt an obligation to drop by here, too. He goes on to describe the visit, they live fairly close near Studio City and both her parents are teachers at North Hollywood High, her dad is the Principal, and I remember my class with him in Civics. How did the visit go then, askes his father. When I left, I had a good feeling, says Jeremy, her parents are good people, seemed to like me and are from local families here in Los Angeles County.

This meeting should be paralleled by one with all of us together and I'll talk to Jennifer about setting one up. His parents agree and they chat about the latest family news. His young sister comes home during that conversation, and asks for a ride in the MG. She is now approaching her thirteenth birthday and loves the MG. Back at the house, Jeremy tells her that he is saving his Ford coupe for her when she has earned her driver's license. You have to wait for two years, he says, and I'll keep it in storage for you until then. She yelps in joy and runs into the house as her brother drives off back to Santa Monica.

Back at Gladstone Manor he meets Clancy Muldoon leaving the elevator and stops to chat. He is very contented with Muldoon's work. Due to the Korean War which lasted until July, 1953 his stocks in Lockheed and Boeing have more than quadrupled in value, followed closely by his investment in Republic Studios. You are going to be a very wealthy young man soon, says Muldoon, how's college going, you should be graduating this June, no? That's in the bag, says Jeremy, and I expect to graduate with honors, too. Muldoon slaps him on the back, saying that's great, Jeremy! There's other news I should tell you, Mr. Muldoon, I've met a fellow classmate at UCLA, also a history major and she also likes to fly. She is very attractive, intelligent, and has a daring bent like me and I've just come from her house visiting her parents. I'm beginning to see her in my life on a serious basis, but we shall soon see. Muldoon shakes his hand, smiles enthusiastically and leaves, waving.

That evening after eating, he settles down, calls Jennifer and they go over the visit, both happy at the outcome. He mentions that his folks now know about that meeting, the result being that he feels closer to her than before, and his trepidation about possibly starting a relationship with her is fading. Jennifer expresses her similar feelings and they are both anxious to see each other soon on campus. Putting down the phone, Jeremy realises that he cannot replace Carol but Jennifer is steadily becoming his primary interest. He has no interest in gay culture, particularly the neurotic, behavioral symptoms he sees exhibited at UCLA, or in the rising gay political movement that has recently emerged. He regards his sexual experiences with Carol as just the outcome of maturation, both psychological and sexual despite the intensity of that experience dovetailed with the excitement of flying. His rising heterosexual urges are focused on Jennifer and he is gearing himself to explore them further with her. Looking at Carol's photograph, he wonders how his life would have developed had Carol survived Korea, returned a well-decorated hero, and continued his career in the military. Would they have been able to continue and develop that relationship to mutual satisfaction? His memories swirl in his mind and are then stalled by thoughts of Jennifer.

These muses don't conflict with one another, he tells himself, his love for Carol remains a strong, lamenting memory probably similar to many such instances in the warrior state of Sparta in ancient Greece, he thinks. Am I bi-sexual, he asks himself. Mentally, he travels back over his extended encounter with Carol who he now realises entered his life as a model, a jet pilot who took a personal interest in him once they started his flying lessons that led to him earning his pilot's license. That an emotional relationship expanded beyond that for instructor and student due to both sensing that a psycho-sexual interface arose, triggered by his arousal in that motel in Lancaster that Carol had detected and reacted to.

Was it the result of them together overcoming that partial engine failure, the emergency situation that they both reacted to with cool, level-headed behavior? Jesus! I'm only twenty-three and have my whole life ahead of me. My decisions must adequately reflect my search for personal happiness and faulty decisions could prove disastrous. Luckily, my encounters with Dr. Claymore and reading the Fromm books that he recommended gave me a sound grounding. Finally, before going to bed he becomes determined to follow his attraction for Jennifer and find out where it leads.

During the Spring months their relationship steadily builds and becomes more intimate, as hugging and kissing become like second nature to both of them and short flying trips around Southern California become routine, now often with Jennifer at the controls at intervals. Both sets of parents are becoming good friends, having parallel desires to see this son and daughter develop a serious relationship. After weekend flying, Jeremy and Jennifer would stay in the apartment for several hours. This became habitual with resting on the couch or bed and accompanied by passionate kissing that finally led to exploration of their bodies. Not by fumbling around but by agreement that it would increase their bond which was, by now, well-developed.

On the first such occasion, Jennifer removed her summer dress and brassiere, kicking her sandals off to the floor. Sitting there, upright on the bed, she encouraged Jeremy to strip down to his shorts and waved him onto the bed. He knew that she had nice breasts from their profile showing through her blouses but was fascinated by their pertness in the skin. Cupping them with his hands, he kissed her passionate, then began stroking them as if they were sculptures. These stroking movements were followed by more kissing as he moved his hands down across her stomach, rounding a finger gently on her umbilicus several inches above her panties. Jennifer giggled which further encouraged him. Wetting a finger, he returned to the umbilicus then followed upward with wet finger circular rubs of her nipples. This excited her as he quickly saw as they became very erect.

They kissed some more and Jennifer gently rubbed his neck and back, then onto his chest and nipples which showed the same reaction. Jeremy laid back on the pillow, panting while Jennifer could not help seeing his erect penis poking out of his shorts. She reached down and retrieved it, holding it gently saying, I've never seen this before, just the hanging models in anatomy charts and the bumps in guys pants and bathing suits. This is astounding, and magnificently large, beautiful and awe-inspiring to me. She continued stroking his penis, exploring the swollen head with an index finger until Jeremy began groaning. Sitting up, they both look into each others eyes, realising that they have approached a point of decision. Kissing him gently all over his face and neck, she whispers in his ear that they should stop now and continue another time. They both get dressed and Jeremy drives her home frequently rubbing his right hand along her left thigh and knee-cap as though to continue the stream of emotional events they both had experienced on his bed.

They did continue another time, in fact numerable times, the adventure deepening with added experience without underwear. The mystery of Jennifer's vagina was explored with wetted index finger, searching for her clitoris, and finding it, gently massaging it to bring her to climax. She did the same for Jeremy, experimenting with fellatio, and bringing him to climax. That tastes a bit salty but has an interesting taste, she said. Over the course of the next several weeks, they became expert with their tongues, nipples, penis, and clitoris became familiar sites for mutual delight and both agreed that penetration with all its potential complications should wait until they were publicly united. Jeremy asks Jennifer if she has read Marco Polo's book on his travels to the Orient and gets a negative shake of the head. I remember a singularly interesting description of his involving his marriage to a Mongolian girl of high social status. That was insisted by Kublai Kahn when Marco was about 27 years old. He worked for the emperor for over twenty years before coming back to Italy.

So what's your point, asks Jennifer. Well, when the marriage date was set, the couple was separated. The girl went to a nun's retreat, like a convent, and Marco was sent to a monastery. There they were both massaged and sexually manipulated several times daily, bringing them nearly up to orgasm with no relief. The monks and nuns apparently were expert at doing this and it was a pre-marriage privilege given to those of high social status. The purpose was to maximize their sexual response potential so that at the event of consummation after the marriage ceremony their orgasms would be greatly magnified. Perhaps, by our activities, we are following an historical sequence of behavior that was well-developed more than a thousand years ago in the Mongolian Empire started by Genghis Kahn! Jennifer laughs, I hope it worked for them and will for us, too! Marco Polo never mentioned in his book whether it worked, but the frustration in the interim of training must have been considerable, smiled Jeremy, as he kissed her passionately several times, in between her giggles.

In their continued exploration of each other, they lay on the bed side by side having conversations about courses at the university, sexual stories they hear at school about others, the latter mainly from Jennifer who has been in a girls dorm throughout her time, and comments on the slutty behavior of some. Males apparently commonly enter the female dorms, especially on week ends with the collusion of their girl friends. Jennifer has been coming home on week ends but still hears all the rumors and antic descriptions most of which are centered on first and second year students. I realised some time ago that some girls go to college to snag a suitable husband in time for graduation, possibly abetted by parental desires to justify their educational expenses, she comments. Luckily, my end of the second floor dorm involves academically-minded girls, third and fourth year girls which kept the noise and fracas down. Jeremy's eyes widen, I have no idea that sort of thing was going on since I have lived off campus altogether, hardly with a social life.

Have you have any sexual experience……may be in high school, asks Jeremy. I was very careful to avoid any compromising positions but was embarrassed a couple of times on infrequent dates, Jennifer says. Like what? Once, in a movie, I was holding the popcorn and my date put his hand on my knee then slid it up along my thigh, nearing my crotch while looking seriously at the screen, so I threw the popcorn in his face, got up and left, catching a bus home. Another time, I was on a double date to the local drive-in on a Friday night and my date was driving his dad's big Buick sedan. The couple in the back seat were wrestling around throughout most of the film and about five minutes before the end the girl kicked at the side window so hard with her bare feet that the four boys in the next car starting howling and banging on their doors so that people were putting on their lights and tooting the horn. We slunk out of there as soon as the overhead lights went on and I said to all three of them….never again, count me out! I think it was a Doris Day movie.

It is now early Spring, 1954 and their weekend flying trips continued, along with relaxation at the apartment. In April, nearing Jeremy's birthday in mid-month and Jennifer's coming in early June, a week before graduation, Jeremy buys a one carat diamond engagement ring and gives it to Jennifer two thousand feet above the Dead Sea desert on a Saturday before his birthday, saying her acceptance would be the best present she could ever give him. His hands on the controls are perceptibly shaking slightly until she slides the ring on to her finger and leaning over, kisses him several times, saying it fits perfectly. At that reaction, he calms down enough to gives a Tarzan call at the windscreen. Jennifer responds likewise, with a Jane yodel, then says that she accepts the ring as a birthday gift. They return to Santa Monica, first circling her house several times with Jeremy jockeying the throttle, causing some of the neighbors to peer skyward at this small erratic plane above.

Time starts flying by now and life for both of them is growing more complex as finals approach and both mothers get involved with marriage plans to take place shortly after graduation. At school, all the girls that Jennifer knows on campus ogle her ring with fascination and several in sororities begin showing up with rings too. Jeremy shops for a pair of wedding rings in Beverly Hills jewellers, finally selecting a plain gold ring for himself and a one carat diamond, surrounded by five smaller emeralds, in a South American setting for Jennifer. When he tells Clancy Muldoon that he is engaged and getting married after graduation, Muldoon volunteers to be his best man which is accepted gladly. Jeremy also invites Dr. Claymore to the wedding.

Before proposing to Jennifer, Jeremy had engaged in several long personal bouts on whether to discuss his previous relationship. Lack of memory guilt accompanied by a transitory phase in his development of maturity in his search for self-identity lead him to ignore any need for confession. Time will tell if he has made the right decision. Their psychological and sexual attraction appears to guarantee success. They are both writing honor theses for their degrees, and considerable discussion takes place with both of them agreeing that their main interests were in the sociological underpinnings of academic history. Jennifer prepares a paper on female emancipation in cultural milieu and Jeremy decides to write his similarly on homosexuality.

Both papers are received with enthusiasm in the Department of History and given excellent ratings. Jeremy had given a draft to Dr. Claymore for comment and was pleased with the response, suggestions and added psycho-analytic comments which he added to his final manuscript. There remains no doubt that both will graduate with honors and there are Departmental offers to submit their names for Phi Beta Kappa.

Both sets of parents attend graduation, along with the young daughter than a celebratory dinner is arranged and paid for by Muldoon in a restaurant in Santa Monica. Three weeks later, the wedding is held in the family Methodist church in North Hollywood with parents looking on with great pride. Jennifer and Jeremy have moved most of her personals into the apartment several days before with the aid of her parents who are wide-eyed at the residence and both sets of parents agree to give them time to themselves. During that week in their apartment, the happy couple consummate their marriage, spend much time at the beach, and feel blessed. Their confidence in each other has maximized and they begin to contemplate their future, initially with the urge to convert their honor papers into a short book illustrating integration of historical academics with their sociological grounds. Such interests are temporally put aside as potential honeymoon locations are gone over with much discussion.

Muldoon arranges a date for legal transactions in accordance to the will instructions, paper signing and official records of transactions completed. He announces that they are now worth more than three million dollars, along with an estimated yearly income from earnings of approximately two hundred and seventy thousand dollars before taxes. He retains his responsibilities as estate manager and the newly married couple embark on a four month world tour arranged with several tour companies by him.

They start from New York to Europe on their first leg, followed by North Africa as far west as Morocco, back to Spain then on to Rio de Janeiro, touring as far south as Southern Argentina, then to Chile and Peru to see the Incan relics, followed by a flight to Panama City where they catch a cruise across the South Seas, stopping at Tahiti, Fiji, then on to New Zealand and Australia, before catching a steamer back to Los Angeles carrying a load of coconuts, mangos, and bananas. By this time, they have worn out several pairs of shoes and sundry travel apparel, and have made love on a track that encompasses more than the mileage measuring the earth's circumference. A deluge of sent mail has accompanied their travels. Taking a taxi home to Santa Monica they rest for five days and Jennifer announces that she is probably pregnant. With that news they telephone parents, announcing their return and a possible baby next June which arouses much joy and anticipation. Who knows what lies in store for this couple in the coming years?

The Agony of Eddie Dolan

PREFACE

This is a modern situation reflecting the Oedipus myth of Greek literature. Our modern trials and tribulations parallel those described by the ancient Greeks despite our technical and scientific progress, possibly because we have not yet learned to deal effectively with our psychological mindsets. Oedipus tragedies although rare, still occur in modern society despite all our communication electronics.

Eddie is born in Vancouver, the son of Ian Dolan and Shirley Templeman. Ian, his father was de-mobilized from the Canadian Army in 1946 at age 21. He married Shirley who had just turned 16 and Eddie was born a few months later in 1947. The marriage went well for several years and Ian got a job in a local paper mill. He then started drinking hard liquor which caused many arguments leading to his violent, abusive behavior. He increasingly physically abused his wife until she became much afraid, leaving after he became extremely violent while drunk and she never came back. Eddie was nearly seven years old. With the aid of a scurrilous lawyer, Ian filed and received a divorce based on desertion. He transferred his physical abuse to his son, who stood it until the age of 15 when he was physically strong enough to object effectively but was determined to graduate from high school which he did with good grades. Then he enlisted in the military a day later.

OPTIMISM AND FLIGHT OF FREEDOM

Eddie was sworn in to the Canadian army in Vancouver and shipped to Calgary for Basic training. During weekend passes, Eddie and two buddies, also from Vancouver, find a haven in the city called The Mountain Pass and spend several evenings there drinking beer. There, on their third night, Jimmy nudges Eddie, saying "have you noticed that gal in the far table, she keeps looking over here. I think she has the hots for you. Time to make a move, buddy, give it a try. I think she was here last night too for a while. Eddie is feeling the social pressure from both his pals and Mack challenges him to do something about it. "I just want to sit here, enjoy my beer and relax", he answers. Mack now gets obstreperous, "ok, if you don't make a move I'm going to have to show you how it's done." Defensively, Eddie says "My dancing skills are zero but I see her looking over this way. I seldom went to hops in high school…..didn't have any good clothes anyway." Jimmy rises to the occasion to show his skills with the girls. "watch me work," he says and casually saunters over to her table. "Hey, pretty lady, you should be on the dance floor…..with me. How about a dance with a new soldier boy. We're just finishing Basic Training here and we three are from Vancouver."

Joanna smiles up at him at his come-on. "My name is Joanna. A dance? Sure, why not. I've been sitting here staring at my drink too long and need to stretch my legs." She gets up and they move over to the small dance floor for a slow two-step emanating from the trio on stage. Jimmy is enjoying this experience with a girl older than those he interacted with in high school. "You're a good dancer, even making me look good on the floor, I could keep this up all night."

Joanna smiles at him tolerantly, "well, practice makes one perfect they say. Does your buddy with the black curly hair dance?" She is obviously probing for information on Eddie. As the record finishes, Jimmy tells her that Eddie is kinda shy and says that he can't dance. "Would you like to come over to our table, I notice that you have been eying him ever since we arrived." I want to lay a bet with my other buddy that you will be dancing with Eddie before we call for another round."

That sounds interesting, says Joanna. "Ok, I'll come over for a short while." Jimmy takes her back to the soldier's table and introduces Mack and Eddie to her. "I want you to meet my buddies". He points at Mack, "this guy trying to grow a moustache is Mack and curly head is Eddie." Eddy jumps up and pulls out a chair for her and she sits down. "Hello you fellows, I don't need another drink right now, Jimmy," then she looks across at Eddie. "Eddie with the curly black hair.....you remind me of someone I once knew. Would you like to dance? I promise not to tread on your toes." Jimmy is whispering about a bet with Mack. Eddie gathers his nerve, "I'm willing to try not to tread on yours. Hopefully the next song is a slow one." Joanna laughs and rises to meet him and they proceed to the small dance floor as the trio swings in to another slow two-step. Moving on to the floor, they begin dancing as Eddie becomes more self-confident. "You are sure a good dancer, Joanna....you make me feel like Fred Astaire!" They both laugh, feeling the spark of attraction between them and another tune starts up from the trio.

Another chance to get stepped on, Joanna? "Sure, dancing is more fun than just drinking beer and you are a natural dancer once you settle down to enjoy yourself." Her comment rises his self-confidence even further. "What do you do in Calgary, he asks. "I work for the Royal Bank as a teller, getting to handle everyone'd money. I like the job because I feel that I'm helping people to manage their money, pay their bills, and plan for the future, she said. "We all need to look at the future.....the past can be useful to avoid more mistakes but I don't think one should let the past shrink your spirit or weaken your optimism"

Eddie is surprised at her upfront manner and her expressed intelligence. "I agree with what you said, use the past as experience but don't let it keep you fearful of the future. Hey, you are really something. Sometimes I surprise myself by making a meaningful observation too. I think that you're bringing it out in me and you make me feel so calm and confident, just in your nearness. I think the others might be thinking that I'm hogging you.....this is the third dance in a row! So what!, the girl replies. "Things come naturally and what good can come from thinking otherwise?" Eddy nods in agreement. "Let's split from this place, grab a coffee somewhere, I'm sure your pals wont mind." Going back to their table, they announce their plans as Jimmy is busy counting bet money. Mack winks at Eddie, "see you back at the barracks then," as both Eddie and Joanna laugh and leave the beer joint.

They find a nearby coffee house and settle down to further explore each other. Thank God this is Friday, says Joanna. "I don't have to work tomorrow. I must have drunk too much beer in that club.....or maybe it was all the dancing." " That was more dancing than I did in high school and you made it so much fun. I'm so relaxed with you..... like I've opened a door to another world and I like it. I think we are kindred spirits destined to meet each other. What do you think of that idea?" Joanna is looking pensive as she studies her cup of coffee. "I believe in destiny......things happen for a reason, usually beyond our recognition or understanding. Perhaps there are Gods up there determining our fate.....it's certainly an effective ploy for humans to avoid blame for undesirable situations they find themselves in, areas of interaction they may have had a hand in bringing on themselves." Eddie responds, "if those others are Gods they must be capable of cruel and sadistic powers and be dangerous."

Eddie is now on a run of ideas as he stirs his coffee, "I don't believe in Gods who can interfere with human beings and put them in situations that destroy their happiness, or even their sanity. From my short life to date, experience tells me that negativities causing unhappiness, tragedy, and suffering come from human behavior. Even diseases like alcoholism can be laid to human weakness, causing others to suffer for it. My father is an alcoholic and an abusive parent to me. Looking back, I often wonder how I managed to make it through high school without major physical or mental damage. I guess we can be tougher than we think we are.....something drives us to overcome adversity. But I don't think that ability reflects a fear of death, necessarily, rather a seed of optimism deep in one's soul, perhaps faith, that urges us on to a better life."

Joanna is quite impressed with the depth of his comments, "Eddie, you show a wisdom uncommon for your age. Perhaps that personal suffering that you allude to is character-building and can be turned into advantage and a heightened sense of justice and fair play? I feel that you and I have met for a reason.....that we are pilgrims on a common path and journey. We should see more of each other.

Summer is here and there is much to enjoy in fostering new friendships. I have really enjoyed your company and would like to see more of you. I don't mean to be bold but I invite you to a picnic on Sunday. Would you come?" She looks anxiously at his face for signs of acceptance.

Eddie grins broadly, "that sounds great! But how can we do this? I don't have a car, don't know where you live, or even if you are a free soul!" Joanna laughs, "you are so cute and charming! I do have a car and I'm single......a free soul. Suppose that I pick you up at the Camp gate, say, between ten and ten-thirty. We can drive out into the country. I know a quiet little lake where we can feed the ducks and have lunch. I'll bring everything we need, you just bring your appetite.....and your good looks! They both laugh in anticipation of a good time. Joanna looks at her watch, "it's getting late now so before the Gods throw stardust in our eyes we should find my car. I'll drive you back to the Base and be on my way. Help me find my yellow bug.....it's a VW.

Eddie is at the Camp gate by ten o'clock and sees the yellow VW pull up a few minutes later. He waves eagerly and climbs into the bug with a wide grin. It is mutually infectious. As Joanna pulls away on to the main street, they are laughing like children going to a picnic. Joanna turns her face towards him, "did you have a hangover Saturday morning? I sure did! Not used to drinking so much beer in a short time." Eddie replies, "I had a buzz on but the coffee and chat we had cleared my head somehow." My pals were worse off than I, as both missed the breakfast chow line. Guess we all had a good time at that club. Do you go there often?" Actually, no, says Joanna. "Friday night was my first time out of the apartment for months. One of my co-workers at the bank mentioned that she was there recently with a date and enjoyed it. So, feeling bored, I launched myself out the door, looking for excitement. Guess what! I found you and now we're on the way to my favorite little lake to feed the ducks."

Eddie eyes the picnic basket in the back seat, "looks like we'll be feeding a lot of ducks, perhaps also a gaggle of geese. I'm getting hungry already." Joanna chuckles, "I hope you are hungry. I roasted a chicken last evening and made a potato salad. That might be a change from the military chow. Do you like wine? There are two bottles of white wine chilling in the cooler bag with ice." Raising both hands, "a bottle for each of us! This will be a fun day for sure." They are now in the country and approaching the lake and picnic grounds. Eddie surveys the view, "if we come here again I want to bring fishing tackle…..there must be fish in this lake. I haven't fished since I was a small boy and that's now a distant memory when my dad was still being nice to me." They park and find a shady spot, a picnic table under some alder trees near the water. Eddie heaves the picnic basket out of the back seat and carries it to the table. "Phew! This thing weighs a ton!" He is grinning in anticipation.

Bringing up the tablecloth and kitchen gadgets, Joanna laughs, "don't you know that females bring everything but the kitchen sink to an outing? It's your job to fight off the ants when they discover the hoard of goodies. Also to carve up the chicken and eat most of the potato salad, not leaving much for the critters." Eddy shows some mock concern, "you have to help, too! Before we eat, let's walk along the shoreline to maximize our appetites. I see some ducks have seen our presence and are waiting for their share of the bonanza. Shall we feed them first?" Joanna nods vigorously, "the poor dears must be hungry as we seem to be the first visitors here this morning. I'll get the bag of stale bread from the basket and we can have them quaking in appreciation." You sure have things organized, says Eddie as he points across the lake. "Look, I see a couple of swans over there. I wonder if they have a nest or young. The young are called goslings, aren't they? They look like a pair. Maybe they have a nest in those reeds and are still incubating eggs." "I understand, says Joanna, that geese mate for life and if one dies the other becomes solitary. That's more than you can say for humans……at least in our society. I'll get the bread." She returns with the bag of stale bread and they get busy feeding the ducks then take a stroll along the shoreline before returning to their picnic table.

"Are you ready to eat, Eddie? If so, please carve up the chicken while I get out the plates and utensils. Oh, and the corkscrew gadget is in the side pocket of the cooler." The food is laid out on the table shortly and Eddie uncorks a bottle of wine, "I'll pour the wine then we can toast each other's health and good fortune. What a beautiful, sunny day for us!" Raising his glass and grinning happily, "to us, to everyone, happiness and prosperity! Do I sound like the local mayor? The ducks are looking prosperous, well-fed and some look sleepy. Now to attack this chicken!" They tuck into the food with gusto, relishing each other's company as they eat. "More wine, Joanna? What could be better, roast chicken, potato salad, wine, and a lovely lady to share it with. Thanks for all your planning and cooking efforts, I really appreciate them." Joanna is sampling her salad, "let's face it, life can be so tedious unless shared with others. Let's finish this bottle of wine and spread the blanket in the shade. The sun is getting high now, perhaps so am I!" They put things away and lie next to each other on the blanket.

Joanna picks a buttercup flower. Do you like butter, Edie? She puts the flower next to his chin. "I learnt as a child that if it reflects the yellow on to their skin it means they like butter. You surely do!" Eddie laughing and leaning on his right elbow, "of course I like butter, doesn't everyone?" He takes the buttercup and holds it against her chin. "See, so do you! Julia Childs, the TV chef, says butter is good for you and essential in French cuisine. I read that the Russians found a frozen mammoth in Siberia having buttercups in its teeth, perfectly preserved. They ate some of the meat, too!" "Please, groans Joanna, not after such a good lunch! Anyway, poor mammoth, it must have ventured too far into the swamp, intent on nibbling clumps of buttercups…….then, oops! I hope it wasn't a mother mammoth with a baby to look after!" "Perhaps an ancient Siberian tragedy but there were many in Siberia since the time of mammoths, mostly among humans sent there by Stalin for opinions and actions not supporting State policies." "Eddie! Don't tell me that you are interested in political history? What have you been exposed to in your military training?" Shaking his head slowly, "not much. Mainly how to march, obey, pile out of bed early in the morning at 5 am, and to make up one's bed with hospital corners. I read a lot in school, though. Perhaps I'll go to university after my three-year enlistment, start climbing the ladder of success. What do you think?"

She nods enthusiastically, "I'm sure that you will do well in life. I see much potential in you. You haven't kissed me yet so I know you have potential." Eddie kisses her on her cheek. Then as she turns her face fully towards him he kisses her tenderly on the lips….a long, lingering kiss. "Wow, some of your potential is realized! One kiss deserves another, Eddie. Take one from me." She throws her arm across his neck and kisses him with mounting ardor, saying that's one step out of the way! Eddie is dealing emotionally with their amorousness, "let's put things back in the car and take a hike around the lake. I see there is a well-defined trail and we can work off the big lunch." Joanna agrees promptly, "yes, let's do that. When we come back with a developed thirst, we can open the second bottle of wine." They disappear around the lake.

Upon an hour later and with the second bottle of wine fully drained, they watch the sun descend towards the tree line as they prepare to return to town. "Let's go to my place, says Joanna, I want to show you my apartment and there is the rest of the picnic left over for dinner. Half the chicken is still there to challenge. I can drive you back to the base later. "You are reading my mind, says Eddie, besides you have given me strict orders to insure that all the goodies are eaten up. I bet you just happen to have a couple of beers in your 'fridge too! I could get used to all this on a permanent basis. I had no idea that Calgary would prove so interesting!" Just wait! She says. "This may be the beginning of a beautiful friendship…….I think the Gods are smiling on us." They arrive at Joanna's apartment in an older, well-kept building sheltered beneath mature elm trees. Her place is on the top floor, rear that looks out on a small park. Joanna unlocks the door of 311 and they enter carrying all their baggage.

Eddie looking around, "where should I put the hamper?" "On the kitchen table is fine as I will deal with the contents later." She disappears into the bathroom, coming out shortly after flushing the toilet. "Would you like a beer or coffee?" Eddie had stepped out on to the balcony and now returns, "you have a neat place here and so private. I see that you have a humming bird feeder." "Actually, two feeders, one is around the corner under the eaves. Those lucky birds, they keep me busy filling up their drinks for nearly four months then disappear south- ward, probably to Mexico and Central America, while we stay here shoveling snow." "Well, says Eddie, they earn the trip. For such little birds to fly all that way, there and back, is surely one of Nature's marvels. Also consider the Monarch butterflies….. they are even smaller and more fragile."

"You really surprise me with all your comments. You are interested in natural history. I can imagine us as butterflies…. fluttering around each other, looking for nectar." She approaches Eddie, putting her hands around his waist and looks intently into his eyes. "We are searching for the sweetness in each other, don't you think?" Eddie takes a deep breath, "I think we've found it. That door must lead to your bedroom?" "I was going to make some coffee but that can wait. Follow me, soldier, there's some reconnoitering to accomplish. I think we both have urges that demand satisfaction." She points him towards the bedroom door and they disappear inside.

An hour later, Joanna strokes his face gently, "I knew that you could be a tender lover. What a fantastic release! In my limited experience I have known a man to sob so passionately. This is surely the beginning of a beautiful friendship. Perhaps we both have accumulated many unfulfilled emotional needs and have discovered the delight in meeting them." "Let's throw ourselves into it, I don't have to be back on the Base until reveille at 6 am in the morning. Let's have that coffee, perhaps a snack or two then go on from there." Eddie has discovered his central mind-body connections and is celebrating the intensity of his recent experience. "I'm with you, says Joanna, first some coffee than some more pillowing as the Japanese say." "Ah so on that, says Eddie, that's the only Japanese I know." "That's totally sufficient, Eddie!"

OFF TO PETAWAWA AND TECHNICAL SCHOOL

By the time Basic Training is nearly finished, Eddie and Joanna have established a vigorous and ecstatic affair. He is spending most of his off-duty time at Joanna's apartment. His pals are teasing him, envious of his good fortune, and missing him at their carousing escapades in town. The results of screening tests have returned and he is to be sent to Petawawa for three months of intensive training in combat electronics. He is wondering how to break this news to Joanna who he now calls Jojo.

"I have some news, Jojo, but it isn't all bad. I'm going to Ontario, to Camp Petawawa for three months technical training and am getting my first stripe when I get there.....as a private first-class." He braces himself for her reaction which he suspects will be sorrowful. "Oh no, I knew this couldn't last she wails, getting teary-eyed. That's the military for you!" Eddie hugs her and tries to soothe her down, "now, Jojo it's not the end of the world. Consider this as a test of the strength of our love for each other. I'll 'phone you every night and write you long love letters as well. Let's not spoil the remaining time we can enjoy with each other. I must catch the train on Wednesday as classes start on the following Monday, so we have four days before I must leave for Petawawa. Let's go out to dinner tonight to start things off." He hugs and kisses away her tears yet is moist-eyed himself. "I guess we have to wait and see, meanwhile I'll miss you terribly and I don't mind admitting it. The past several weeks have been heavenly and have changed my life for the better. Gods forbid that I should lose you so soon!" "Don't think that way, Jojo, you aren't going to lose me. It will work out. As you would say, the Gods are on our side so think positively! Where would you like to eat tonight? How about that little Japanese restaurant we found last week? Then we could go to a movie." Joanna begins to brighten up, "yes, that little Japanese place and see a movie. You will 'phone me every night?" "Every night and flood you with love letters. Jo-Jo I love you fiercely and intend to defend our relationship with all my might, come hell or high water! What more can I say? Now, what movies are showing in town? You pick one without violence, explosions, and cops chasing at high speed through heavy traffic. Perhaps a love story like ours, that would suit me." Joanna busies herself looking through the newspaper.

Eddies orders are cut and he is scheduled to catch the express leaving for Ottawa, via Toronto at 10 am on Wednesday morning. Joanna can't get excused from work on such short notice so they have a tearful goodbye on Tuesday evening in the bug by the Main Gate. Promises are exchanged and repeated several times followed by a prolonged kiss with clutching arms.

The trip east is uneventful, across the rolling prairies and wheat fields until Ontario turns the vistas more green. His transfer to a local line to Petawawa from Ottawa is slow but Eddie's rising excitement to enter his new base and get settled down occupies most of his thoughts.

He arrives at CFB Petawawa approaching midnight on Thursday and is put in temporary quarters overnight where he throws himself on a cot and sleeps soundly for ten hours then reports to his formal unit where he is assigned a barracks room. That evening he 'phones Joanna from the barracks telephone. He has a handful of change to feed the meter. It is 9 pm local time but 7pm Calgary time so Joanna has finished eating dinner. "Hello Jojo, It's your long-lost lover, lost for two days anyway, I'm settling down here and start school on Monday. The barracks is filling up with other students so I can't talk for ever as a long line extends behind me. Not much privacy here so I'll have to find another 'phone to call you from tomorrow. I'm going in to town tomorrow. The base is right on the doorstep of town. Everything here is lush and green, not like Calgary but similar to Vancouver. How are you doing?"

Joanna tries not to show her oncoming depression, "I'm concentrating on my routines, work load, and watching television after dinner until bedtime. Just like I did before we met….sliding back into the rut. But I'm not going to feel sorry for myself, at least not yet. I want you to do well in school and I know that you'll give it your all. That's you, my darling. That's why I love you, my darling. Take care and call me tomorrow or whenever you get a chance in the evenings. My thoughts are with you always……kisses and hugs. Eddie is getting elbowed by the fellow behind him. "Same here Jojo, goodbye for now." They keep up their daily 'phone calls and letters begin to fly in both directions. Some eleven weeks go by and Eddie is preparing for final exams as the instructors review the students weekly tests and provide their findings to the major in charge. He calls Joanna at the end of week eleven, telling her that the chief instructor

Has asked him to consider staying in Petawawa on the instructional staff. "It means a promotion to corporal, a second stripe, by the New Year if my performance is maintained. Things are buzzing here with preparations for overseas assignments for many. How do you feel about that?" After a few moments of silence, Joanna's voice becomes tense, "That means you may not be stationed in Calgary ever again.

How do you think I feel? Three months is torture enough. If your new job at Petawawa is more or less permanent, should I consider getting a transfer closer to you…..what do you think? I could check around in the RBC for upcoming vacancies." Eddie's hopes are upwelling, "is a transfer really possible, that would be great! Let's wait until my potential position is clarified, then we can plan to be closer. Have patience my love, we may be together again before too long if the Gods are willing. We are both willing ourselves that opportunity….. kisses and hugs, Jojo. Must go now, goodbye my love."

A week later, the exam results are listed and Eddie has passed at the head of his class of 50. The major guarantees his instructional position and promotion to corporal. His leadership and assistance qualities shown to other students has impressed the officer also. Two days later Eddie is contacted by the local Red Cross office telling him that his father has died in Vancouver and his aunt in Abbotsford has requested that he attend the funeral. He calls Joanna about his father's death and says he has five days of compassionate leave, "I'm catching a flight in the morning and will stop in Calgary to see you afterwards. I'll see you in a couple of days, Jojo. Must go now and prepare to travel. We'll be together soon, Jojo and I'll call you from Vancouver for my flight to Calgary. The Gods are with us! Bye now!

At the Calgary airport two days later, on Friday, his evening flight has landed and he emerges with his travel bag and Joanna leaps on him in the luggage area, "I'm so glad to see you, honey, and you look great in your first class uniform. What a soldier I have again at last! Do you want to eat something in town?" Kissing her five times all over her face, Eddie says you must have some scraps at home, let's go and relax, I have things to tell you."

They return to the apartment where Eddie relates the events at his father's funeral which was also attended by his aunt and uncle from Abbotsford. Aunt Miriam was called by the Vancouver police. His father had lost his job at the factory on the Fraser River and was living in a rooming house in East Vancouver. He was knocked down in the middle of Main street in a drunken stupor according to the police and several onlookers. Aunt Miriam gave me a package of photographs they found in his room and the rest of his meager clothes she gave to the Salvation Army. The funeral was basic, he was cremated and his ashes scattered out on the farm in Abbotsford. Joanna listens quietly, "that was a terrible tragedy. What a waste of life but alcohol can do that to its severe victims. There was nothing that you could have done to help him, Eddie and you are lucky to have survived that father/son ordeal as well as you have. Things could have gone bad for you too, like drug or alcohol addiction, bad company leading to criminal activity……who knows? You must not generate any guilt feelings but look ahead to your future, hopefully with me." Eddie nods vigorously, "my future is definitely with you, my love. We have two days before I must report back to duty at Petawawa. We must make the best of it. Joanna makes some sandwiches and coffee, then they go to bed.

Eddy is still in bed when he awakes to the aroma of fresh coffee. Stretching and yawning, he calls out to Joanna, "Jojo I'm ravenous, tell me when breakfast is ready." He disappears into the bathroom to take a quick shower, coming out in five minutes wrapped in a Turkish towel to hear Joanna shout 'Breakfast is ready! She has been up a while and as Eddie sits down at thekitchen table she pours his coffee and then returns with a plate of hotcakes with two poached eggs on top. "eat up soldier boy, there's more batter." She brings her smaller portion to the table and sits down across from him, watching him wolfing down his breakfast. "We both had a good, restful sleep …… finally, and I want to discuss things over a second cup of coffee." With a mouthful of eggs, Eddie mumbles, "we have two days to talk about the future, let's deal with the present for a few hours, eh?" She waits for him to clean his plate, rises to re-fill their coffee cups, then sits down, studying his face. "Perhaps both the present and past need some airing. You lived with your alcoholic father. What happened to your mother after she left when you were five? You never talk about her, is she still alive?" Joanna is curious as she now knows that Eddie has an aunt and uncle in Abbotsford.

His plate now cleared, Eddie leans back sipping his coffee and patting his stomach. "My God you look good in that silk robe and I bet you have nothing on underneath it!" "Your mother, Eddie!" "My mother….yes, I hardly remember her, just as a shadowy figure in the house. She left when I was starting kindergarten at age five but I do remember violent arguments and things being thrown about and smashed. I was always put in my bedroom by my father and the door closed. I did peek out once and she was on the floor with a chair raised over her head, crying. After she left, my father often lost his temper with me for no particular reason as I was careful not to antagonize him, even helped with housework, including dishes. That didn't prevent me getting regular beatings which I took until I was nearly sixteen. By then I was tall for my age and strong. I remember he raised his hand once to strike me across the face but I grabbed his wrist and looked him right in the eyes, saying "that's enough, any more of it and I'm leaving." He turned abruptly, left the house and came back hours later, dead drunk, and passed out on the kitchen floor. I struggled and got him to bed. He never touched me again, it was a stand-off and he knew I wouldn't take it anymore.

That was halfway through my junior year and we lived together, yet apart, until I graduated from high school. A month before graduation I was down at the army recruiting office talking to a sergeant who encouraged me to graduate. Despite my home life, I had good grades so was sworn in on the last day of school. I never went to graduation exercises and had my diploma mailed to me here at Calgary. I was free at last and never looked back. His drinking had grown steadily worse and he began missing his shift work at the mill on occasion. Joanna has been listening carefully, "no wonder you show no feelings over your father's death. He just beat any love out of you….love for him anyway." Eddie continued, "I have no feelings of guilt but do have some of sadness. He did open up to me once about his wartime experiences in Germany. H showed me a large scar on his right leg due to a hand grenade but he killed three Germans in a trench in the process of getting wounded. He had a peculiar look on his face then so I intuitively realized that he suffered from that experience. Aunt Miriam said he went downhill fast after I left and she knew where I was because I sent her a card during Basic Training.

"Now, I have some background to tell you, soldier boy, after I pour us both another cup of coffee. I used to live in Vancouver, too. I married very young, eloped while in high school to get away from my parents. I was barely sixteen and had a son shortly after getting married. My husband was an ex-soldier too, nice at first but became a drunken and abusive husband. He beat me badly several times and I became very scared of him but couldn't go back home as my parents had all but disowned me. I had enough money for a bus ticket to Calgary so left when I was 21. With a sleazy lawyer, he had me declared an unfit mother and got a divorce, claiming desertion. I never saw or heard from them again and went to night school to finish my diploma and then got a junior job with the RBC, working myself up to a teller's position. We have both suffered at the hands of abusive alcoholics so we have much in common. My son would be almost the same age now as you, Eddie, and that now makes me feel rather ancient, almost 34.

"Come on now, you aren't ancient, Jojo. In fact you don't look even 30 and very attractive, so you have taken care of yourself. Anyway our age difference is irrelevant isn't it? We are both just a couple of loving kids. Enough of the past, let's now talk about the future. You mentioned the possibility of getting a bank transfer to be closer to Petawawa, is that possible? That would be great, even if we have to commute some distance, maybe on weekends." Joanna's face lights up after all that talk about background misery for both of them. "There's a good possibility as I have accumulated enough years of seniority as a teller. At least somewhere in southern Ontario, as close as possible. I'll put in for a transfer on Monday so wish me luck. Otherwise, we will remain dependent on 'phone calls, letters, and infrequent vacation visits and that would surely challenge our relationship. Dammit! I'm coming after you as soon as I can." She throws her arms around his neck and kisses him with gusto. He returns her kisses, "that's settled then. You know that my father's death has allowed us to strengthen our bond at a pivotal time, so I guess I should be thankful to him in a way. Life is full of ironies, isn't it?" "Yes, she answers, ironies and recompenses. We must learn to use them as stepping stones to fulfillment of our dreams and our goals in life. How about getting dressed and stepping out for some exercise and fresh air, perhaps a latte down the road?"

Later in the evening, they eat at a Chinese restaurant then, for sentimental reasons, go to the club where they first met and dance away the late evening. Back at the apartment, Eddie throws off his shoes and slumps into a chair. "I'm bushed after all that dancing. You dance me off my feet, where do you get all the energy?" Joanna, kicking of her heels, "I've been saving it up for nearly three months and there's still some in the reserve tank! I think we should retire before the clock strikes twelve and make passionate love. Then I can fall asleep in your arms. The morn comes so swiftly, so a poet said." Eddie chuckles, "you are constantly surprising me. Bring on more surprises! I'll race you under the covers!" Joanna dims the lights and they move into the bedroom and the door closes.

The next mid-morning she is up and busy in the kitchen. The clattering of pots and pans seems not to disturb Eddie and she shakes his toes. "Up and att'em cowboy, there are things to do, shower and breakfast, or should I say brunch. You have to report back for duty, for your new assignment, and your ticket says a 2 pm take-off. The ride to the airport will take 20 minutes or more, so shake a leg!" "You sound like a sergeant, says Eddie groaning and yawning. Is the coffee ready?" "If you'd wake up you would smell it! It's been on the table for nearly ten minutes. I'm frying eggs and ham. Do you want toast and jam with it?"

Leaping out of bed, Eddie says "give me time for a quick shower, Jojo, then the hungry lion will be roaring for food. Yes on the toast and jam. I doubt if I'll get more than a bag of peanuts on my Air Canada flight." They have a scrumptious breakfast with much conversation and are too busy to realize that time to leave for the airport is fast approaching. Eddy, between mouthfuls, "I hope you get a transfer before too long, meanwhile we must remain satisfied with 'phone calls and love letters. I'll be waiting to hear from you those magical words…..I'm packing, I'm coming, I'm on my way to see you soon, my love. I must be patient and get on with my new assignment." Joanna, looking up at the kitchen clock, "less than 40 minutes before the drive, Eddie, is your bag packed and ready to go?" Loaded and locked, says Eddie. " I'm ready for the firing range and have my sights squarely on your cute apron. I'm going to rip it off you for a last fling!" Joanna screams with mirth, "gosh! What is a girl to do!" "You know the procedure, says Eddie, this one will have to do for a while, then we can be together without many breaks." They retire quickly to the bedroom for a brief connubial sojourn then leave for the airport after hurriedly dressing.

A month passes. Eddie is doing well, taking on his first class of trainees. The chief instructor, the major, monitors his sessions weekly and has recorded laudable progress report to file. One evening as Eddie is making his usual 'phone call to Joanna, "hello, Jojo, my love, how are things going? You have good news! Spill it! The transfer has gone through! Great, to where? Close to me! Where? At Trenton, next to the Base! I can hardly believe it! You're leaving Calgary on the 20th, that's four days from now. The moving company will deliver your goods here within ten days? That is perfect timing, as you can be here in time for us to hunt for an apartment and move in your things on the first of the month. You will be able to start your new job on the Monday. 'Phone me when you hit the road, drive carefully and 'phone me along the way so I know where you are. I'm so excited! You will be so busy wrapping up there but keep me posted, Jojo. I've got my own quarters now on the Base, with a telephone so here is the number, 538-2728-5952, love you immensely, Jojo, hugs and kisses from your Eddie."

Three days later, Joanna makes her last 'phone call to Eddie from Calgary. "The movers loaded everything this morning and are on their way." Due to the frantic planning and time frame, she begged off a going away scene at the office other than accepting a set of place mats for her new apartment. "I'm hitting the trail first thing in the morning and staying in a motel here overnight. I should be in Petawawa in three days, barring any problems. I'm sharing the driving with a female engineering student going back to U. Toronto and discovered her ad in the local paper. We have connected and should be able to drive eight or more hours daily with stop-offs for meals and breaks. The bug is comfortable for sleeping as the right front seat fold back. If we make ten hours per day and average 55 mph, it should take us 3-4 days. Sally has it all worked out, that's the students name. The weather forecast is for fine conditions through next weekend so I should be in Petawawa on the 24th. Sally is a trooper, going in to her final year in Mechanical Engineering and is the practical type, and has a good sense of humor. I'm comfortable sharing the driving with her and she wants to share the costs, too. Must go now, I'm giving away some things to a neighbor and she is at the door. Until we connect again, Eddie my love, darling of my life, sayanara." She hangs up the 'phone and runs to the front door.

The next day at noon while Sally fuels the car, Joanna uses the public phone. Luckily, she has caught Eddie after morning classes and in his room. "Hello Eddie! You are in your place! I've got a slug of coins to feed the meter. My God, this country is so wide! We went through Winnipeg by driving through the night. Little traffic on the road at night. Now we're approaching Saulte Ste. Marie and plan to stop for a bite to eat. The bug is faithfully humming along. I had thoughts of trading it for a Jetta station wagon in Calgary but the new price is not cheap and I was concerned about buying a used one for this trip. The total distance is about 2000 miles, so we should make it within 3-4 days. Sally says that we should be in Toronto by late this evening and I'm planning on staying there overnight for a hot shower and some rest before driving on by myself. Maybe staying at her dorm, then driving on through Ottawa to Petawawa in the morning. If that works out, I should be there by late afternoon, depending on traffic, so sit by your 'phone after classes. I'm really happy to have Sally share the driving with me….she is a real hoot and is now waving so must go. See you soon, soldier-boy." She hangs up the 'phone, putting her reduced amount of change in her pocket and runs to the car.

She phones again the following morning, "hello Eddy, wake up, I'm your morning bugler. You must be getting up anyway, my ears are humming from all this driving and I can still see the highway lanes with my eyes shut. I stayed last night at Sally's dorm. Students here have nice facilities and the cafeteria food was good this morning. A hot shower took the kinks out. I should be in Trenton late this afternoon and will call you when I arrive." Eddie has been showering and putting on his uniform for breakfast in the Mess. "Jojo! You are a genuine racing driver! I'm so happy that you two made a safe trip so far. I will finish classes at 4 pm so will be hanging by the 'phone waiting to hear your sweet voice close by. My heart is beginning to pound with all this excitement. Drive carefully through Toronto as the morning rush will be underway." "Bye, my love, says Joanna, see you soon." Sally has given her a Toronto city map and outlines her route to Trenton. They hug at parting and promise to keep in touch, Sally giving her the hallway 'phone number and her postal address. She leaves with a smile and waves as she descends the stairway to the parking lot.

JOANNA ARRIVES IN TRENTON

Late that afternoon she arrives in Trenton and follows the road sign to Petawawa, a short distance away. She parks at a gas station just outside the Main Gate and finds the public 'phone. Feeding a quarter into the slot, she dials Eddie's 'phone number, listens to the ringing while crossing her fingers, "hello soldier-boy, I'm just outside the Main Gate at the gas station across the intersection. Can you meet me here?" "I can hardly wait, we can eat then get a motel." Joanna laughs with happiness, "you can hardly wait….neither can I, for a good massage and what other talents you can show me! In five minutes? Make it two, 'bye for now." Eddie grabs his hat and runs towards the Main

Gate, recognizing the yellow bug across the street. Helopes across the intersection, opens her door and gives her a big kiss. "I spotted the bug, "I'm so happy that you are here safe and sound. I would feel like a pretzel had I made that long drive." Joanna gets out of the car and gets another big kiss and gets swung around several times, Eddie then saying, "what do you want to do now?" She replies, "let's find a nice, quiet motel, I need a hot shower, then dinner….then a long rest."

Clapping his hands together, Eddie says, "I know just the right place, there's a motel just down the road, of under some shade trees and very quiet. A girlfriend of one of my students stayed there for three nights and she raved about the place, and the price is reasonable, too." Lead on, MacDuff, says Joanna, "I've had enough trail-blazing for some time. I'm just a local girl at heart, not well-travelled, not inclined to be nomadic, but I do know what and who I need. Get my drift? A hot shower, a light dinner, and a soft warm bed with you in the middle of it!" They both climb into the VW and prepare to locate the anticipated motel. Eddy is in the right seat, "turn here, it's about half a block ahead on the right. See the big fir trees surrounding it?" They pull into the driveway, go to the office, register, and go to their assigned room.

Joanna looks around. "this will do fine. Now I' going to slip into a hot shower while you decide where we can eat a quiet dinner." Peeling down to her undies and bra, she disappears into the bathroom with her toiletry case. Sitting on the double bed, Eddie scans the local yellow pages for possible restaurants. As yet he hasn't eaten away from the base. He hears Joanna shut off the shower and begin drying herself off, "I've found a likely place….a Thai joint and they should have a good selection of light courses. Are you game for that?" As she emerges from the bathroom , wrapped in in a towel and using another to dry her hair, "that sounds great. I'll slip into something from my suitcase. A little food in the belly will crank up the furnace, don't you think, followed then by a sensitive back massage?" His eyes widen, "I get what you mean, Jojo, your comments can be so visual. At least that's how they affect me but then, perhaps I've a one-track mind when you're near me!" They both laugh as she throws her hair towel at him as he reaches out to grab her and plant a big kiss on both cheeks. A few minutes later she is dressed, hair brushed and tied, then they depart for the restaurant.

Later, back at the motel, they lock the door, undress quickly and slide into bed. "I've a delicious bottle of massage oil in my cosmetics case. Would you?? Eddy retrieves the bottle as Joanna rolls over onto her stomach. Dripping the oil carefully along her spine and across her shoulders, Eddie begins to work it into her skin. She groans with delight, "oh, that feels so good. Sleeping in a car challenges one's posture and causes aching bones and tense muscles. Push more intensively, yes, that's doing it! Ooh! Eddie now says, "getting a particularly tense muscle and you are transferring that condition to me. Turn onto your back so I can massage your neck and forehead. Then I'm going to take you to the stars!" She rolls onto her back, "I'm not quite ready for astro travel, so massage my feet, my ankles, my toes, yes, like that! I love feeling your fingers slipping between my toes." Sounding like a spaceship commander, Eddy says, "buckle-up, helmets on, get ready for blast-off! Look out moon, here we come!" After their love session they both fall into a deep sleep, wrapped in each other's arms.

The morning sun comes streaming through the bedroom window and awakens them. Eddie, rubbing his eyes, "thank God it's Saturday.... no school until Monday." He pats Joanna on the shoulder, "are you waking up or am I talking to myself?" She yawns, "I really needed that sleep to make up for that trip but we have things to do.....can we start looking for my apartment. I'm supposed to start work here in Monday. I'd like to find a place before the movers arrive, then they can transfer all my stuff straight into the place. I hate this moving business but this is a very special case. No wonder the nomads and gypsies have a modicum of belongings to carry around." Well, says Eddie, "I think the North American Indians were limited by their transport technology, at least until they got horses from the Spanish explorers. You can't carry much tied between two poles that you drag around."

"I have a big truckload of stuff and I'm anxious to get it in place. Can we scan the ads over a coffee. The office might have a newspaper." Eddy dresses and goes to the office. Chatting with the desk clerk, she tells him that there's a vacant apartment in her building that just came on the market yesterday. Eddie jots down the address and her directions, thanks her, and returns to their digs. "Heh, Jojo, get dressed and let's check this vacant place out, the desk girl lives there and said it just came on the market." Joanna hurriedly gets dressed, saying, maybe we can beat any others. Hopefully it's a nice place." The desk girl say it is nice and we don't have to check out here until noon, says Eddie.

Soon they are out the door and driving quickly down the street. "This place is by the river and she said it has a nice view. Turn here, it should be about a mile down this road. There it is!" He gestures with his right hand as Joanna slows down and looks eagerly. "Looks quite nice and what a view! She exclaims, and the hills start in back." She parks the VW and they find the manager's apartment on the ground floor and ring the bell. As it is still quite early, he appears in his dressing gown, listens to their search need and states, "yes, a vacancy just came up but I've had no time to advertise it yet. How did you know?" Eddie explains talking to the desk girl at the motel who lives here. "Wow, this is the fastest connection that I've ever experienced, say the manager. Here is the key, it's on the top floor, number seventeen, that looks out on the back of the property." Eddie takes the key and they run up the stairs to the second floor, open the door and walk in. It's nice and airy, with a beautiful and private view off the balcony. It's fantastic, says Joanna, "I hope the rent isn't exorbitant." "Well, let's find out, says Eddie and they return downstairs and knock on the manager's door again. The rent is only slightly more than she was paying in Calgary so she is pleased to take it. She takes out her wallet and gives him the first month's rent. I will be working at the Royal Bank here as Head Teller starting on Monday, the first of the month, she says. The manager is pleased to have a bank employee as a tenant, with almost no effort on his part.

They drive back to the motel, thank the desk clerk, and arrange to stay there for two more days. The manager calls the motel and says he has a fold-up bed she can use until her goods arrive so that saves them two days of motel bills. “I’m getting hungry, says Eddie, I’m taking you to the Grenadier Arms for fish and chips, and a pint of ale.” “We’ve had no breakfast and it’s lunch time, so I’m ready for a meal,” says Joanna. After lunch they survey the town of Trenton, locate all the facilities, and read up on the town’s history. The population hovers about 15 thousand, many civilians working on the military base. The Royal Bank building is on the main street, not imposing but has a solid look without a lot of fancy glass. The adjacent Ottawa River has some pleasant riverside promenades backed up by tennis courts and landscaped areas that are quite park-like.

They are both very content with their anticipated life together, having found that the national park is quite close with several lakes and many hiking trails. “I really like this place, says Joanna, we can hike, fish and camp every weekend during the summer. I bet there’s lots of ducks to feed, too! We are going to be so happy together here, you and I. The gods are surely looking out for us!” “If you are ready for another short drive, says Eddie, we can get some sandwiches tomorrow and poke about up in the park. Would you like that, Jojo?” She takes a deep breath, I like everything here, soldier boy. We can’t stay out too late tomorrow though because you have classes on Monday and I must report to the bank for my new job. I’ll call you from the bank on Monday at noon with my office telephone number and we can connect outside the base after work. I have a feeling that, as in Calgary, you won’t be spending many nights on the base once we get settled in.” Eddy grins, “no, not if I can help it! Your big bed is much more comfortable than my army cot!”

The furnishings arrive on Wednesday as Joanna has telephoned Calgary and given them her new address in Trenton. Joanna and Eddie spent most of Wednesday and Thursday evenings putting the final touches to the apartment. Joanna had been warmly welcomed at the bank. Despite her newness, the bank manager, in view of management guidelines, has made her head teller based on her length of employment in RBC and the recommendations that accompanied her transfer request. Joanna sighs, "a place for everything and everything in its place. Well, almost. The five boxes of books can stay in the hall closet until we figure out some shelving. Eddie has a suggestion, "we could get some bricks and pine planks. I can build shelves. How about putting shelving in the living room along that empty wall?" Joanna nods in agreement, "that's a good idea but there's no rush. Let's get settled in for a while and enjoy our new home. There's room in the hall closet for your civilian clothes and I'll share the big chest-of-drawers with you, at least one drawer for you. You have storage on base for your uniforms etc., yes?" Right on sweetheart, he rejoins. "What are you making for dinner, I'll volunteer myself for dessert." She smiles coquettishly, "does that mean you will do out and get dessert, or that you are offering yourself as dessert? Sometimes I get confused as to your appetites. How I love the confusion! I'm making a beef stew for dinner so you decide on dessert." "Can we have two desserts, says Eddie. I'll pick up some chocolate ice cream." He takes the car keys and disappears out the door, returning in twenty minutes. "That stew smells heavenly, so is it ready? I'm starving!"

After dinner and a bowl of ice cream, Eddie, sprawling in the big armchair, "I want to show you the pictures my aunt gave me. I haven't open the package yet and this is going to be a surprise as I don't remember there being photographs in the East Vancouver house." He opens the package as they both sit on the chesterfield, drawing out a sheaf of prints. "Most of these must have come from my aunt's house.....pictures of my father in army uniform, on the rifle range, and boarding a troop ship to go to Europe from Halifax." Here's one showing him on crutches. Joanna is peering over his shoulder. "I remember he had a big scar on his right leg which he got from a German hand grenade, then he shot the young soldier who threw it and two more in the trench before he realized how badly he was injured." Joanna says, "many soldiers were injured over there but the unlucky ones died." Edie continues, "he never talked much about his war experiences but he did open up once when I was about twelve. How could I forget that! He had tears running down his face as though he had suddenly lost all his power. I realized that his armor had chinks in it when he suddenly yelled for me to get to bed, then proceeded to get drunk. That was the only time when I felt close to him, when he showed weakness. I think he was a strange, lonely man with much hidden suffering."

Joanna breaks in,"let's move on. Show me some more pictures before you get hung up on bad memories." "Yeah, yeah, here's one of me on a swing in a local city park. I must have been about five.... just before starting school. I was a cute kid, wasn't I?" "You still are, lover boy! "That's my mother and father standing either side of the swing chains but the sunlight doesn't show their faces very well. My dad was still okay in those days but his temper and drinking must have started soon after that day in the park. I remember a huge fight, broken furniture, my mother screaming on the kitchen floor and my dad holding a chair over her head. I saw this from the crack in my bedroom door. I was really scared and dived under the blankets shaking until I fell asleep. When I awoke the next morning she was gone.....gone forever." Eddy has become almost frozen, his face taut, and biting his lower lip. He didn't notice that Joanna was looking intently at the photograph.

Recovering, he pulls out the remaining pictures and spreads them on the chesterfield cushion. "These were taken years later at Aunt Miriam's place. She and Uncle Steve had a small farm near Abbotsford, up in the Fraser Valley. He did a lot of welding for his neighbor farmers, working out of his battered old trucks, smoked heavily, like a chimney, and died from tuberculosis. Most of these pics were taken at the farm on weekends when I was starting junior high school. My dad used to drop me off there and disappear until Sunday night and we would drive back down to the city after dark...... him reeking of booze. Joanna has been watching him closely, seeing the pain in his eyes and wants to have a break. "This is getting too depressing, I'll get us some more ice cream and a coffee." She jumps up, goes quickly to the kitchen and clatters the coffee mugs and bowls onto the counter. "Old photographs can be reminders of bad memories, can't they? May be we should get a camera and start a new collection, showing happy events. I have no pictures of my life in Vancouver and your bad memories are about to change."

She returns with the bowls and coffees on a tray and sets it on the coffee table. "Here's a suggestion Eddie, before winter comes we should take lots of snaps on weekend trips so we can sort them out and start building our collection." Eddy agrees enthusiastically, "after coffee, let's go to bed early because we must get up early. Both of us with new jobs starting Monday with our new jobs, no time for depressing thoughts. I don't want to see those photos any more as I'm feeling a little anxious, too. Just remind yourself on occasion how lucky we are, here in our own love nest, both with jobs and a bright future. Drink up and let's hit the hay." They do so and retire for the night.

Several week later they have settled down completely and their jobs are going well. On a Friday evening Joanna suggests that they could get the shelving materials next morning and get the books out of the hall closet to make room for shoes and hiking boots. Eddie agrees and suggests that after doing that chore they should go up to the park and check out more trails, take snaps with their new camera, before the winter season starts. It is now October and becoming chilly with occasional showers but no snow yet. This will be their first extensive hike in Algonquin Park. As the weather is still clement, tennis shoes and some bug repellent arte all they need. Eddy says, if we intend to hike during the winter we must get proper hiking boots and rain gear, perhaps snowshoes? They leave for downtown Trenton and return with their purchase of decorative bricks and pine boards which stick out of the side window of the VW. Joanna sighs contentedly, "It will be great to get rid of those boxes and have books on the shelves. Shall we do it now or wait until after lunch?" Eddie answers, "I'll set up the shelving before lunch but first must haul out the boxes so the books can be sized. The big books like encyclopedia volumes and dictionaries belong on the bottom shelves." He begins unpacking the boxes containing the largest books as Joanna calls from the kitchen that she is preparing sandwiches with extras to take with them on the hike.

Busy taking out the encyclopedias, Eddie calls out, "do you have any book ends stashed somewhere?" She answers, " there should be two pairs located in a box, brass ones shaped as racing schooners with heavy bases." He looks through the other boxes and finds them in the lightest box filled with paperbacks. "I've found them , he calls, and proceeds to organize them, putting them in alphabetical order on the lowest shelf. He notices in volume T-Z, the last volume, that something is sticking out so he opens it to see a photograph fall out onto the carpet. "Jojo! How did one of my snaps get into the last volume of your encyclopedias? I thought I had put them all back in the package that night we looked at them." Joanna comes out of the kitchen, wiping her hands on a kitchen towel and picks up the photograph from the carpet. "That's peculiar, she says, looking at it. It's very faded and there is a side tear on it but it sure looks somewhat like one you showed me weeks ago. A small boy sitting on a swing?

Eddie takes it from her saying "I'll return it to the collection and gets up to do so, retrieving the package from the top of the chest-of-drawers in the bedroom. The swing photo is on top of the pile in the package so he suddenly realizes that there are two identical photographs, despite the shabbiness of the one that he retrieved from the encyclopedia…….a five-year old boy sitting on a swing, that part of both snaps is clear and identical. He utters a confused and anguished cry, one seemingly coming from the depths of his soul, and it expands into a loud shriek of understanding. Joanna comes quickly, standing there beside him, "what's going on Eddie?" He looks at her, his face transfixed in horror then he throws down the snaps and dashes out of the apartment, running down the road in a headlong run towards the Main Gate of CFB, Petawawa. Joanna is stunned, standing there she picks up the two snaps. Yes, they seem identical. Was the frayed one hers? That's impossible. Did she stash it years ago in that volume. Could the boys in those two photos be the same one? Could Eddie be her long-lost son? No wonder he fled into the street and disappeared. She has no clear memory of putting that photograph in that volume of the encyclopedia. So many years have past since she was convinced to buy that set of encyclopedias from an attractive young male student with black curly hair, a university student trying to meet his tuition expenses.

THE AFTERMATH OF DISCOVERY

Eddy has found his way back to his barracks and disappears in his quarters for the remainder of the weekend. He fails to respond to repeated knocks on his door on Sunday morning, some students have questions on the assignment due on Monday. Although Eddy is usually away for the entire weekend and overnight during the week, he was seen entering the barracks by two of his students, Gil and Ned, just before noon on Saturday, wild-eyed and stumbling in civvies.

Monday morning, after breakfast in the mess, the class assembles for the day outside the barracks waiting for Eddie to appear and march them to the classroom. He fails to appear and doesn't respond to Gil pounding on his door several times and calling out his name. The head instructor is alerted, and the major appears promptly to investigate the delay. He opens the door and finds Eddie sitting on his bed. Eddie is weeping, and in a weakened and strained voice he cries out," I'm blind, I cannot see….can't see to put my uniform on. The major calls for an military ambulance that takes Eddie to the Base hospital. The head nurse confirms that he is blind, puts him to bed and calls for the duty MD who examines him and prescribes dehydration procedure while blood samples are taken. Eddie refuses to eat for two days and is put on fluids. The base psychiatrist is called in for observation.

Captain Stavros arrives the following morning. "I would like to talk to you for a while, do you mind?" He brings up a chair to the bedside and sits down after introducing himself. Eddy nods at the psychiatrist's request weakly. "This is your third day in the hospital. Can you tell me why you are refusing solid food? I realize that you are blind and this can be a very frightening experience but I assure you that this condition is only temporary. In my trade we call it a conversion reaction and it can be caused by a highly-charged emotional experience. You will recover your sight soon, I'm sure, and eating solid food will accelerate your recovery. Your blood results indicate that you are in excellent general health, hence your fluids have averted any complications from dehydration.

Your blood chemistry is stable and quite normal. Can you tell me when this vision loss took place and what might have caused it?" Eddie doesn't answer him and the MD sees that he may be oblivious to the external world. Assuming that his words might be getting through, "I'll check on you tomorrow. Perhaps you should consider what I have told you today and that you will be willing to talk to me in the morning. Hopefully, by then I will find you eating some solid food and starting to feel better. Good bye for now. Try to relax and organize your thoughts. If you have any difficulty sleeping, just ask the nurse for a pill." He leaves the ward after informing the duty nurse to give Eddie a sleeping pill if he asks for one and to consider this patient as under suicide watch.

The next morning, he returns to sit in his chair. "Hello, Eddie, can you hear me talking to you? Please nod if you can hear me." Eddie nods, saying that he managed to get some sleep after getting a pill. "When I woke up this morning I ate a little oatmeal along with some orange juice." Captain Stavros is pleased with the reply, "that's good! I would like to see you gradually increase your solid intake for the rest of the day. I know that hospital food can be uninspiring but look at it as fuel for your body and you will see that your body will respond positively to it. Are you having any headaches? I see that your blood pressure has dropped a little and is now quite normal." "I'm feeling a bit better now, no headaches and my dizziness has subsided but I still feel quite weak. Before I felt external to my body and didn't need food or drink."

"Do you think that you might have been punishing yourself? Punishment that you were bringing on to yourself for some reason?

I understand that you are instructing in the Communications School, is that correct? I hear that your performance there has been exemplary. Can you think of any reason why you should be punished?" Eddie doesn't answer. "Are you confident that you will succeed in this assignment?" At this question, Eddie responds, "I like my job and have been looking forward to a promotion around Christmas time although nothing seems to be worthwhile now."

Stavros waits a few minutes, then says, "would you be unduly disappointed if that promotion failed to materialize? I've been in the military for some twelve years and have decided that promotion is dependent on many factors not necessarily related to one's abilities or performance. This is not a perfect world for any of us, don't you agree? Eddie is becoming more eager to converse with his psychiatrist. "I haven't had much experience other than in high school but even there teachers were nearly always fair about grading. I guess it comes with knowledge and experience." "I'm impressed with your answer, Eddie. You are obviously an intelligent fellow and quite mature emotionally for your age. I see why you were selected for instructional duties with others of your own age group. I'm pleased with our talk today. Starting tomorrow, I would like to chat with you once in the morning and again in the late afternoon. Would that be acceptable to you? I think that we are making progress and the more progress we accumulate, the more likely that the delay in the return of your vision will be shortened. See you in the morning, Eddie and try to eat more solid food." He rises from his chair as Eddie makes a last comment, " yes, more progress, I want my sight back. What am I good for, otherwise?" Stavros leaves to talk to the duty nurse.

The following morning Stavros returns, "good morning, Eddie! How are you feeling this morning? Did you have a good sleep? "Not bad, says Eddie. "I did wake up several times and had a bad dream…..a nightmare." "Tell me about your dream. Do you remember it clearly? He picks up his notebook in preparation to take some notes. Edie takes a deep breath, "it was a very clear episode. I was hiking on a forest trail that I was unfamiliar with. The trees were tall and stately and the birds were singing as I came to a pool in a glade. Sitting on a rock was a beautiful girl dressed in leaves and flowers. She took my hand and led me to a door in a huge tree. The tree trunk was massive. She opened the door and she invited me inside. It was cosy and warm there and smelled of fresh cedar oil. The odor was intoxicating.

She smiled at me invitingly but when I put my arms around her to give her a tender hug she turned into a hairy, black monster, like a big spider. I turned and ran outside and I could hear the monster crashing through the undergrowth after me. I slipped going down a steep path, hitting my head…..then I woke up. It was a very vivid dream and I was perspiring heavily when I woke up. The nurse was standing there with my breakfast tray."

"That was a terrifying dream, wasn't it? But you managed to escape the monster's clutches. I want you to keep that in mind, that you got away although you hit your head on a rock in the escape process. What did you have for breakfast?" "Oatmeal again. I like oatmeal. Also some toast and orange juice.

After eating I could feel energy flooding back into my body. I must have spent much energy in that dream, hiking and then escaping from that monster." Stavros has been busy making notes and looked up then to say, "I'm pleased to hear that you are eating a significant amount of solid food, keep it up and drink lots of liquids, juices, and perhaps some green tea. Do you like green tea?" Eddie shrugs, "I have always taken coffee with cream and sugar but I don't crave it now. Perhaps I should try green tea. May be the monster won't return if I drink enough green tea." Stavros returns to the dream, "are you worried that the monster might return? If it does come back, remember that you know how to escape its clutches but in escaping try not your hit your head on a rock and try to roll when you fall."

"On another topic, the school has substituted another temporary instructor for your classes until you can return. Two of your pals, Gil and Ned, have been asking about you at the front desk. Perhaps you should wait for a while before seeing. Wouldn't it be more satisfying to see them when you have regained your vision?" Eddie agrees, I don't want to see anyone right now, in this condition. It has been tiring enough talking with you but I do appreciate your concern for my health. If my blindness is temporary, how temporary? I want to get back my sight." "We must be patient, says Stavros. "I must go now, other patients to look in on. We'll talk again this afternoon. Try to eat a substantial lunch…at least some soup and fruit, okay?" "Okay, but can I have a radio to listen to since I can't read?" "I don't see why not says Stavros. I'll arrange for one with the duty nurse." He leaves for the front desk.

He returns at 4 pm, "I see you have a radio. Are you listening to the local radio station on FM" The AM here in the hospital is not very good due to electronic interference." "I was listening to the local news about sleeping pills. Someone died two days ago here in Trenton. The coroner report mentioned suicide from an overdose. Other than that news the weather report was good." Stavros was quick to suggest that Eddie not listen to local news but listen to music that he liked. Stavros has been talking to Ned and Gil. Again, he broaches Eddie's personal habits, "I understand that you haven't been sleeping on-base for some time. Do you have a girlfriend in town with whom you spend much of your free time? According to the nurses, you have had no telephone calls enquiring about your health." Eddie remains silent and closes his eyes so Stavros quietly leaves after hearing Eddie murmur that he wants to nap.

He checks in at the front desk and informs the duty nurse to call him if Eddie shows any difficult behavior during the night. He then calls the school and arranges to talk to Gil and Ed after classes. Meeting them at the school. He introduces himself as a psychiatrist, treating Eddie in the Base hospital. He emphasizes that any information they can give him about their buddy's behavior might help him to recover his health. "As you already know he has lost his sight but it is temporary. His recovery depends on locating the source of his condition that precipitated his loss. He is suffering from what we call a conversion reaction. They are not uncommon, particularly in war-related victims. People, both military and civilians expose to horrific sights have responded by temporarily losing their vision, as if they were trying to erase their experience of the external world. I think Eddie has had such an experience and it is my job to expose it to the light and steer him out of his darkness." Gil looks at Ned quickly, "we are both anxious to do whatever we can to help him as Eddie is a great fellow, generous with his time, and a good soldier." Stavros homes in on his intuition, "I know that he spends much time off the Base from the gate security records. Does he have a girlfriend in town? Has he mentioned any names to you?" Gil answers promptly, "he has a girlfriend in Trenton and he is madly in love with her. That's all we know about it as Eddie is very private emotionally but is always ready to assist us at school and has a great sense of humor." Stavros thanks them both for their honesty and goes home.

Over a scotch and water he recollects the comment that Eddie had made after getting his radio.....about an apparent suicide in Trenton. He calls the coroner, giving his identity and medical reason for the call, asking for the name of the recent suicide victim and was told that her name was Joanna Templeman, that she was a teller at the RBC and new to Trenton. The coroner also mentioned that there was no evidence of foul play. The bank manager had called the police after going to her apartment on Tuesday at noon after she failed to show up for work. He had also noted that her behavior on Monday seemed very subdued and unusual for her normal bubbly self. He went to her apartment thinking that she might be seriously ill and unable to notify anyone. Her VW was there but she failed to respond to his persistent knocking at her door so he alerted the manager who came upstairs with the pass key. They both went in, calling out her name to no answer then found her lying in her bed, dressed as for work but apparently cosmatose, so called the ambulance. The coroner confirmed that death was due to an overdose of sleeping pills and that the body was in the city mortuary awaiting potential burial plans. Stavros thanked him for the information.

The next morning he 'phoned the head nurse requesting that Eddy be transferred to a private room as soon as possible. The transfer was made within the hour and he arrived to visit Eddie at 1030 am. "Well, Eddie, how are you feeling this morning?" Eddie replies with a question, "why have I been transferred to a private room, am I contaminated as well as blind?" Stavros hastens to reassure him. " I have other medical reasons and we need to be able to talk in complete privacy, not in the general ward. Did you eat breakfast?" "Yes, most of it and a double serving of fruit juice. I'm feeling stronger now and had a good sleep last night." "Good. Now I must ask you an important question, you mentioned a recent fatality that you heard on the local radio. Do you have any reason to believe that this death is related to your blindness and associated physical condition that brought you into this hospital?" "No, I have no such belief. Why should it have any connection to me?" Stavros hesitates a minute, then says, I understand that you have a girlfriend here in Trenton, is that true?" "What are you trying to tell me? I'm getting nauseous."

Stavros puts his left hand on Eddie's forearm, "I want you to steel yourself for some bad news. The sooner we get this out of the way, the sooner you will recover your usual state of health. Are you up to it?" Eddie leans up in his bed, "was that suicide in Trenton a woman and was her name Joanna Templeman," he asks in a rising voice. "Please tell me!" Stavros pats his arm, "yes, that was her name. She worked at the Royal Bank here in Trenton." Eddie is turning rather pale and beginning to shake. Stavros calls for a tranquilizer, quickly inject him in the forearm and instructs the nurse to start a suicide watch and to call him at any signs of uncontrollable behavior, then he leaves the ward after a few minutes.

He returns the next morning. "Are you awake, Eddie? Still feeling sleepy?" Eddy moves slightly at hearing the psychiatrist's voice. "I'm still a little hazy, that was shocking news you gave me. I had a gnawing feeling that something bad had happened to her." Stavros begins to re-start his questioning, "Did you two have a violent argument last Friday that caused you to leave? I gather that you returned to the barracks from the security records and that your appearance from them was followed by your ensuing blindness that you discovered upon waking the next morning. There must have been a very emotional scene, one that you couldn't endure. Is that the case?" Eddie responds, "there is nothing that can be done about it. It's the story of my life. I seem to be incapable of escaping overwhelming personal torment."

Stavros begins to soothe him, "now, Eddie, calm down, I'm not trying to torment you. I'm dedicated to help you to recover being the person I understand that you were before this situation. You are a bright, capable young man, looking forward to a promising future. But you must help me to set you back on the path to peace of mind. Are you willing to do that?" Eddie remaining reluctant, "I wonder if that is possible. There is so much pain involved. I feel totally victimized. How could this happen to me, after all the misery I've been through I my short life?" Stavros remains persistent, you may have good reason to feel victimized in your life. I'm not prepared to question that at this time. My job is to help you understand why you feel that way. I'll return in the morning, hoping that we can proceed from here. I think this is enough for one day. I want to leave you with the thought that by trusting me with your feelings and the situations that are associated with them, that I'll be able to get you back on your feet. Meanwhile, go over what we have covered here today and try not to feel sorry for yourself. We are going to climb out of this swamp and get back on solid ground." He leaves the room is instructs the nurse to continue the suicide watch.

Tuesday morning he returns, first checking with the duty nurse. "Hello, Eddie! The nurse tells me that you are eating well since we talked yesterday and that you ate all your breakfast this morning. That's what I like to hear! Are you ready to go on from yesterday's talk? If so, I would like to hear more about the emotional scene on Friday afternoon. What started it and why was it so traumatic for you?" Eddie sighs, "I still feel like a victim. So many horrible things have happened to me. I would feel more comfortable recalling my earlier life with you, then to approach the present as a final blow." Stavros interjects quickly, "whatever makes you feel most comfortable, Eddie.

I understand how difficult it is to talk about one's personal life but talking will help to find the solutions."

Eddie sits up in bed, takes a deep breath and reaches for the glass of water on his side-table. Stavros guides his hand to the glass of water. "I think that my very early childhood must have been fairly normal but that changed when I was about five years old. I was about to start school, I remember that. My parents started fighting after I was put to bed. Usually I slept through most of it but one night the noise got so loud that I woke up. I got out of bed and peeked through the bedroom door. My mother was on the kitchen floor screaming with her arms covering her face while my father, straddling her, had a chair raised above her head. Don't kill me, she screamed. I must have yelled because my father came over and told me to get back into bed and keep the door closed. The next morning my mother was gone and I never saw her again,ever. When I asked my dad where she was and when she was coming back, he became very upset, saying, we don't need her and her sassy mouth.

Stavros looks up from writing his notes, "and she never came home, ever again?" "She never came back. My father told me never to mention her name. He was reasonably kind for a while but then he started to drink systematically. First, just on weekends, then, by the time I was ten, he would start drinking as soon as he came home from work. I tried to help by setting the table for dinner, washing the dishes and running errands to the grocery store…..that sort of thing. Then he started beating me for no obvious reason. He would fly off the handle easily and I stopped bringing friends to the house. We lived in a tough neighborhood in East Vancouver and all us boys had scratches and bruises, partly from climbing about in vacant lots full of garbage and in disused buildings that were subject to being torn down. The teachers at school never questioned any of us. I got used to his beatings but I finally rebelled when I was about fifteen. I was big and strong for my age and when he raised his hand to clout me across the face I grabbed his wrist. Looking him straight in the eyes I said, no more of this stuff, I'm not going to take it. I'll leave! He turned away and left the house, coming back late at night, dead-drunk and I helped him into bed. From then on it was a stand-off. We lived in the same house, went through the daily routines and after the evening meal I would retire to my room to do homework and go to bed. He didn't object when I made dinner for us….sometimes he grunted his approval, and he sometimes asked me about my schoolwork."

Stavros comments, "I'm impressed that you stayed so long and took all those beatings. Didn't you have any relatives that you could talk to about it?" "Just my Aunt Miriam and Uncle Bert who lived up the Fraser Valley near Abbotsford on a small acreage. Aunt Miriam came down to Vancouver several times and I was taken up to their place on some weekends but nothing was said about drinking, the loss of my mother, or some of my bruising. My father would come back to pick me up on Sunday night, reeking of booze, and we'd go back to the house in Vancouver. Despite my home life, I did well in school. Guess I was determined to graduate and get out looking for a job by myself. I visited the army recruiting office several times before graduation and the sergeant advised me to graduate then come in to see him. I didn't go to graduation, no decent clothes anyway and volunteered the next day, having my diploma mailed to me in Calgary during Basic Training.

That's when I met Joanna… in a small nightclub in downtown Calgary along with a couple of my training friends who were also from Vancouver. We hit it off straightaway …..it was like magic. We had so much in common, our poor backgrounds, abusive experience, and the shared determination to find a good life. She was very attractive, slim and athletic, and psychologically matched with me despite that she was a little older. We had much fun together, just a couple of happy kids exploring each other and enjoying out times together. I finally found someone with whom I could have a close and emotional relationship. Then, after Basic Training and testing, I was sent to Petawawa for schooling in electronic communications. We were determined to maintain our closeness despite the distance between Calgary and Trenton. When I was offered a permanent position here as an instructor, she became determined to transfer closer to me and was lucky enough to get a position right here in Trenton. We settled down here in a nice apartment and her job at RBC was great, as she became the Head Teller there shortly after arriving." Stavros, looking at his watch, "sounds like you two were head-over-heels in love for her to make such a drastic change in jobs. What were the circumstances that lead to your blow-up?"

Eddy is showing reluctance to continue and comments that he is getting tired. Stavros gets the cue, "you have a right to be tired. Going over bad memories can be very taxing if emotional connections remain strong. I appreciate your feelings of victimization, losing your mother at a young age and being physically and emotionally abused by your father. He was a most unhappy man, wasn't he?" Eddie decides to go on, "yes, very unhappy. I became sorry for him as I grew older and could see what the drinking was doing to him. By the time graduation was approaching, he began missing shift work at the mill. After a few weeks here, my Aunt Miriam contacted me through the Red Cross as I had sent her a card. My father had died and I got several days of compassionate leave to attend his funeral. He had lost his job at the mill and had moved into a flophouse in downtown Vancouver. He was knocked down on an intersection of Main Street, walking across the intersection against the lights, apparently drunk. The cops and several bystanders testified that he was staggering drunk when hit severely by a delivery van and killed outright." "you are doing splendidly and I'm pleased with your willingness to relive some of your more important bad memories. Let's continue tomorrow, we are making great progress." He leaves for the front desk, cancels the suicide watch and goes to his office to go over all the notes he has collected.

The next morning Stavros is anxious to continue and comes to Eddie's bedside, "hello, Eddie, have a good night?" "Not a bad one, I woke up several times then drifted off to sleep again." I see that you ate a large stack of hotcakes!" Eddie replies, "that's one breakfast that I learned to make at the Vancouver house while going to high school." "You obviously were a resourceful kid and one your father should have been proud of." Eddy nods, slightly, "I was thinking last night about my father. He once showed me a big scar on his right leg. H said it was from a German hand grenade, that he got the German who had thrown it and that he wiped out several more in the trench before he realized how serious his wound was and was treated by a medic, then sent to a field hospital. He then got moody and I think that he suffered from combat stress that never left him….dogged him for the rest of his life."

Shaking his head, Stavros agrees, "that sounds quite likely. There was scant attention paid to veterans returning from WW2. In fact, there was a definite stigma attached to combat fatigue and little appreciation for its outcomes. We now acknowledge that condition and call it PTSD, or post-traumatic stress disorder. Due to the reluctance of higher military figures, it wasn't called a disease but a disorder which makes it sound less serious. Now I want to continue with your life account…..to bring it up to date. I want to focus on the emotional experience that led to your present visual difficulties. Yesterday I asked you if you could describe that Friday afternoon event and what led up to it. I need to appreciate why this emotional experience was so traumatic that it led up to a lapse into a conversion reaction."

Eddy is growing uncomfortable, squirming in bed and clutching the edge of his blankets. "This is very difficult for me and I feel so embarrassed and guilty. How could I get myself into such a horrible mess?" Stavros responds quickly, "stop chastising yourself. Self-punishment is often associated with an inflated sense of wrongdoing. It would be more productive if you would explain the situation as you see it and wait for my reaction to it. That's my job, to help you understand why you feel that way and to cast my interpretation of such events in a more useful and acceptable light. Eddy is showing signs of resentment and resistance which he then overcomes, "okay, it has to come out, sooner or later, doesn't it." Stavros goes on," only in terms of reference to your healing process, not for public viewing. As a psychiatrist I am bound by principles of practice to maintain strict patient confidence. You have trusted me so far and look at the progress we have made together!"

Eddie thinks for a few minutes, "yes, I appreciate all your efforts on my behalf, so here we go. I was helping Joanna to build some shelving for several boxes of books that were stored in the hall closet. She was in the kitchen making sandwiches that we planned to take on a hike that afternoon. I was stacking encyclopedia volumes on the lower shelf when a card caught my eye. It was sticking out of volume T-Z and I picked it and opened it and a photograph fell out on to the carpet. Looking at it I was somewhat confused as it looked familiar. Several weeks earlier I had brought back a package of photos from my father's funeral that my Aunt Miriam had gathered. I retrieved that package to compare the dropped snap with the one in that package. Although the former snap was badly faded and torn and the sunlight in both pictures partly obscured the adult faces, I realized that me sitting on the swing at age seven was identical in both pictures.

Initially, when the snap dropped out of that book I had assumed that, for some obscure reason, it had wandered from my package of photos." Eddy begins to shake violently and Stavros quickly reaches into his medical bag and prepared an injection into Eddie's forearm. Eddie slowly slumps down on to his pillow and becomes comatose. Stavros leaves for the front desk, informing the duty nurse of the situation and leaves to return later. She goes to Eddie's bed, sitting beside it for several minutes monitoring his condition, then makes a couple of notes on the clipboard at the foot of his bed.

Stavros returns later that afternoon. "Are you awake now, Eddie?" Eddie's eyes flutter momentarily, then his unseeing eyes open. "Is that you doctor Stavros? What happened to me? I thought I was flung into a burning pit! Oh, yes I remember now, my head is clearing. Yes, that photograph.....the room started revolving around me as I was screaming and Joanna's face was looming close to mine. I don't remember anything else until waking up on Monday morning, crying and trying to get up in preparation for school." Stavros remains somewhat confused, "why did that photograph overwhelm you to the point that Joanna's face appeared so large and frightening? Just what did the photograph depict? Can you tell me now?" "It was a photo of my early life, as a five year-old sitting on a swing with my parents on either side of me. The horrible realization suddenly crushed me. The only way that Joanna could have had that copy in her book from years ago was if she was my long-lost mother!" Who else would have a copy? He starts sobbing violently as Stavros's face suddenly shows the implication and Stavros waits to see if he will calm down.

After a few minutes, Eddy begins to stop crying as Stavros waits, observing him. "We cannot stop now, Eddie, now things are starting to fall into place, like a jigsaw. No wonder you regressed into a state of shock. The realization that you and Joanna were lovers, mother and son. Incest in our culture is a very strong taboo emanating from the Old Testament. The guilt fell on you like a ton of bricks. Now we can start on the path of recovery. I'm sure that you will regain your sight. You are doing extremely well, a great patient and with courage. I'll drop in tomorrow but in the meanwhile, keep a clear head. I want to stress to you that you are not guilty of any serious crime. Yes, you have been victimized in the more distant past but perhaps not by more recent events. Rest, listen to some relaxing music and be proud of how far we have gone in search of effective treatment. He leaves to return to his office and some intensive analytical summation of all his has now gleaned from Eddie's life story.

At ten the next morning, Stavros is back. "Ah, Eddie I see that you are wide-awake even without functional vision. Did you have a good night of rest?" "Yes, I slept soundly and had a great dream that I would like to have again." "Tell me about it, Eddie! "I was back in that forest, walking along, down a trail lined with large ferns on either side. I heard some music getting louder, like pan pipes playing. You know the ones that Pan the Greek god played. I didn't see anyone playing these pipes yet the music was getting quite loud and was quite entrancing so I sat down next to a small, murmuring stream. The melody filled me with a great calmness. When it finally subsided, I stood up and strode out of the shady forest into the bright sunlight….

as if on wings. Then I awoke. It was a marvelous feeling and I felt the energy flowing through me and wish I could repeat it again."

Stavros was quite ecstatic about this dream, "I would like to see that dream regenerated in you in the next few meetings. Firstly, I want to reassure you that your blindness is temporary and that condition is not rare. Secondly, you are not guilty of anything! You went into that relationship with a pure and joyous heart. Dismiss any guilty thoughts that you have, either about your father's demise or, more importantly, about Joanna. Would you try to do that?" Eddie answers, "yes, about my father but what about Joanna, she was my mother! She used me! She was a twisted, dishonest, and scheming person! She disgusts me now that I see her for who she really was!

Stavros is getting concerned, "now hold on there, Eddie. I'm not surprised that you want to blame her for putting you in this predicament. That isn't a surprising reaction, on your part. One creating feelings of betrayal, dishonesty and exploitation. Perhaps she had those very feelings after you left the apartment. That might explain why she took her own life, punishing herself. I would like to explore that motivation with you. I hope that when I'm finished you may be able to see your mother in a different light. With more understanding, more compassionate. If so, that would greatly assist in your complete recover.

Eddy is quiet for a few moments……then, "do you mean to suggest that she may be as innocent as I am? Stavros claps his hands together in agreement, exactly! Listen carefully. Your mother was strongly attached to you on first sight, wasn't she? You happened to resemble your father physically and perhaps psychologically, at least during the first years of the marriage. Those years were when your parents were deeply in love….before the troubles that started and led to complete alienation and severe fighting. Perhaps your mother was attracted to you because she was prompted subconsciously by those fond memories of their first years together. These fond memories were driven underground , compounded by the loss of her young son, after she received threats of loss of life. She may have been successful in obliterating those early memories after she left, trying to find a new, less dangerous life for herself. Meeting you, think of the odds against such a meeting! And starting a relationship that was equally satisfying psycho-socially and sexually and serving to regain those feelings for her from the early marriage years. Remember that she was only sixteen when she had you! Likewise, you found someone to lavish your love and affection on. Someone who returned it without reservation or rejection, unlike your father.

I'm willing to give Joanna, your mother, a chance for redemption and I'm asking you to consider the same. Think about it! Can you give her that chance? That photograph that spilled out on to the floor may have caused a flood of memories and, like you, she realized that you were her long-lost son, now lost again forever. The pain of that recognition, compounded by guilt, exploitation….the feeling of stealing your innocence. The load was too much for her, hence she turned to suicide to relieve her agony. I want you to think about my analysis, my best interpretation of her possible motives. We shall never know for sure but I feel there was a natural purity and innocence in you meeting by chance in Calgary. That's what the Greeks called fate, conducted by the Gods on Olympus. You two had developed a relationship that proved to be beneficial to both of you. A source of great happiness that was smashed by the discovery of that snapshot.

I have thought up a technique I would like you to develop after I leave today. In a quiet moment and when you feel like going over our talk today then close your eyes and visualize your mother's face smiling at you, just as you remember Joanna, then open your eyes and expect to still see her. Do this until you get weary. Have a good sleep and I'll see you tomorrow." "Before you go, says Eddie, you have given me much to think about, Dr. Stavros. I'm indebted to you for your concern and desire to see me back on my feet. I will really make an effort to follow your suggestions." Stavros waves and leaves.

Later that very evening, Stavros gets a night call from the duty nurse informing him that Eddie got out of bed, shouting, I can see, I can see now! Stavros rushes to the hospital. " Where is Eddie, is he back in his room?" The nurse nods teary-eyed and Stavros rushes to the room that Eddy has been occupying for several days. "There you are, Eddie! Jumping about like a five-year-old. May I guess that you have taken my advice and thought about your mother's motivations? I have gone over them repeatedly myself and feel that I'm on the right track. Since this afternoon, you seem to have changed your initial assessment of her role in your recent life. Did the visualization exercise help?" Eddy is pumped up with newfound joy, "yes, I'm starting to feel closer to her. Not as a lover anymore but as a son to his mother. The tragedy remains that we have lost each other permanently, at least in the present life. Perhaps we shall meet again in the next one. Many people believe that we shall meet our loved ones in the next life.

Stavros is self-charging his analytical confidence, "there is always that hope despite our generally-accepted conceptualizations of reality in modern times. As Hamlet, the Prince of Denmark said, there are more things on heaven and earth, Horatio, than are dreamed of in your philosophy. But keep your emphasis on the present life, Eddie and on the NOW. Forgive me Eddie, I had several belts of single malt scotch following the telephone announcement of your sight return, so you may see me right now in a changed light. None of us is perfect and the last several days have proved earth-shaking for both of us. You know Shakespeare had much to say to us moderns, following that tremendous contribution to human thought provided by the Greeks. You are well along in your recovery, Eddie. In the morning we can have a final chat and I will likely discharge you back to your duties in the Communication School before too long. Returning to your class responsibilities will accelerate you complete recovery."

Stavros is certainly feeling the effects of his scotch and his elation that Eddie, his patient, is recovering. He goes on, "I'm willing to bet that you will be hiking again in the real forests in Algonquin Park. There are fantastic hiking trails there and in our local area. I visualize you hiking through the forest this coming summer when all the tourists show up, including campers and hikers, including university students. Coming around a bend in the trail you are following, you sight a girl resting in the shade, next to a small stream, and leaning back on her backpack. She's wearing a sweater with a leafy pattern, her cheeks showing the bloom of youthful vitality. She is obviously in tune with the forest environment. She looks up with an inviting smile and pats the ground next to her, signaling you to sit down. As you sit down beside this attractive girl, she offers to share her bag of trail mix with you. You notice the sparkle and intelligence in her bright blue eyes, and her possible interest in you as a hike-mate. You take it from there! See you in the morning!"

Solo Sailing to Mexico

PREFACE

Even in so-called modern times, sailing south from Victoria to La Paz, Mexico is a venture demanding serious planning due to weather and sea conditions, poor port facilities, including navigation and radar buoys, and these potential difficulties can be greatly compounded by solo sailing. My account may prove useful to others entertaining similar ambitions.

MY HISTORY WITH MULTI-HULL SAILING

I secured my first trimaran while working as a scientist at the Pacific Biological Station in Nanaimo. A sailor acquaintance wanted to sell his 26 ft. Piver Mariner, order to buy a larger trimaran he eventually called Windspeed, a 32 ft. Kristofferson. I gained multi-hull sailing experience first on the 26 ft boat, custom-built in Washington for a surgeon, then shared experience with Ian on his Windspeed. I learnt most of the potential foibles that are exaggerated by the superior sailing speeds available on multi-hulls, relative to classic designs and also appreciated the superior stability and roominess, both on deck and in the interior, that such designs afford one. I developed patience and tolerance with self-identified "expert racers" in local clubs who often felt the need to challenge my boat by improper manoeuvres or dangerous attempts at driving me off-wind.

Here's an example for you, I took my new wife sailing off Vancouver once during a strong and stable outflow wind from the Squamish estuary. It was joyous sailing abeam of this wind in both north and south directions. On my third northern trip, a 32 ft. racing boat with gossamer sails approached me from the north on the downwind side and within 16 feet of my amah. I simply gave him a cheery wave and from his large destroyer wheel he looked down his nose with a straight face. "Watch this, Dalia," I said. I proceeded north for about 100 yards, then turned about abruptly, tightened up all rigging and bore down on him with a three-foot wave surging from my rudder. I needed both hands on the tiller to hold her steady. He saw me coming and, screaming at his female companion for assistance, he began tightening his rigging and giving me constant glances. I bore down on him at about twelve knots, passing him with a speed difference of at least three knots. Within a few minutes he was a speck on the horizon and my ale-filled stein still rested on the side seat. I never spilled any drink in that cockpit.

On another occasion with this 26 ft. Pivor Mariner, I was sailing to Vancouver from Victoria. As I departed Porlier Strait I noticed two sailboats coming out behind me, some 500 yards back. The first fellow could not gain on me until within a few minutes he was gaining somewhat, then began falling back once more. He did this at least three times, denoting that he was using his motor to decrease the distance between us, then hoping after shutting it off, he could keep up. The fellow behind him seemed to be using the same tactic but, in his case was it me he was determined to catch or the ego-stricken single hull sailor he was following?

I found another Kristofferson for sail, newly finished except for the interior on Gabriola Island. Two Norwegian background ship builders had produced it for a customer living on the island. I discovered that he had married during construction and that his wife was quickly pregnant so the house had to be enlarged rather than finish the 32 ft Kristofferson which was a close relative of the other Kristofferson that I had sailed on. Inspection showed some water damage with the transom from rain during the previous winter as it sat on his lawn. Otherwise the rigging, sails etc. were new and unused. My sailing pal inspected it with me and we both decided it was a good buy. As he owed me a substantial sum that had been required to recover his boat from marine salvage in Port Hardy after we both had spent eighteen days upside down in it coming south from Haida Gwai in a ferocious summer storm, unannounced by marine weather agents until several hours before it arrived from the south Pacific. But that is another true story.

I motored this Kristofferson down to Victoria and had it put on the hard in the vicinity of the port, near the embarkment facility. My carpenter friend had repaired his Kristofferson there and it was now back in the water. Ian extended the length of my vessel by two feet, built a new transom and an extended aft cabin top which allowed for sleeping quarters in the aft cabin which I declined as there were two large beds, one on either side of the main cabin and I built a table and storage compartments.

Kristofferson was a Norwegian ship designer who eventually lived on Quadra Island. Although multi-hull interest is very slow to develop in Canada, he discovered a large number of his design in Australia where they were enjoying their own, exclusive club races. Conservative attitudes in marine culture in Canada remain frozen in place, assisted by the economic costs applied by marinas for double spacing…..unless one can secure an outside berth. The French have pursued multi-hull designs, both catamaran and trimaran with significant commercial success and the technical advances made there have now trickled down into single hulls by flattening and broadening the hull and using suspended bomb weights to avoid turnovers. Suspended bomb weights have been quite a headache for the racing crowd as damage due to grounding has resulted in some major failures and mid-Atlantic drownings.

Personally, I prefer trimaran hull design as the catamaran design has major weakness. Many commercial models have insufficient headspace under the cross deck and this exaggerates the energy impacts of swells coursing at angular transects across the boat. Hence, a large rapid swell containing a significant amount of energy may flow past the upwind amah, cross under the deck and slam forcefully against the inside face of the downstream hull, driving upwards and slamming vigorously against the cross deck at the rear. That is when the headspace is of sufficient volume to allow such hydraulic action. That circumstance was emphatically shown in an expensive French catamaran bought by an American couple when they neared upcoming seas at the mouth of the Mediterranean, past the Straits of Gibraltar. As the upper and lower deck configurations were separately manufactured, then fastened together, the hammering on the aft deck resulted in the vessel beginning to come apart. Luckily for these two, obviously competent sailors, they managed to turn back and recover their investment.

OTHER PREPARATIONS IN READINESS FOR THE TRIP TO MEXICO

With the major hull and cabin roof changes made, I finished the interior carpentry, and took the vessel to Vancouver for more modifications. The wooden box mast was replaced with a high tech aluminum mast from N. Carolina. The stainless steel quarter-inch rigging was carefully inspected as were deck fastenings, some of the latter being supplemented, particularly those designed for towing. A French designed furling jib was installed by a professional rigger's company in Vancouver. An HF radio system was added to one of the backstays, also a VHF radio and GPS, with alternate control in the cockpit. A freshwater generator was added to the interior plumbing, along with a complement of seven batteries along the floor boards and a starting battery in the aft cabin. A radar system for improved visibility was suspended by a custom fastening off the aft cabin roof adjoining a backstay. The opportunity to use HF radio in conjunction with a lap computer and small printer gave long-term weather reports, decoded from either Alaska or San Franscisco. The drogue system was a small drogue for limiting undue speed from the aft, and a 28 ft. cargo parachute that could be set off the forward bows, with appropriate floats, line lengths and hardware. The dinghy was an eight foot inflatable powered by a five hp motor. Basic foods were stored in lockers in the main cabin and a propane cooking stove and a heating stove were included. I custom-designed and built a freezer-cooler unity for the front cabin in the bow. On the aft cabin roof I set two German solar panels. I designed and had custom-built a sliding, stainless steel outboard retracting system. I seemed all set. As I was now 65 years-old, having retired two years earlier I was itching to go.

I had hoped that my wife would accompany me by retiring from her teaching job after nearly thirty years of trying to educate and civilized children. However, she had a very good grade at her school and wished to take them on through the next grade as the grade two to three transition she thought was extremely important. So, I resolved to solo down to Mexico and see her at Christmas during holidays. She realized that I had the bit between my teeth so she acquiesced to my nomadic desire. I named my trimaran Halobates which is Latin for salt bug, knowing that an oceanic species is present with a circumpolar distribution. This satisfied me as it reflected my biological research background and academic training.

DEPARTURE AND THE BEGINNING OF THE SAILING ADVENTURE.

I departed on August 5, 1995 first sailing west to overnight at the small USGS at Neah Bay inside Cape Flattery and asked the obliging CG to phone my wife saying that I had arrived safely and was leaving for the outside waters in the morning, providing that winds failed to rise substantially. I hoped that would reduce her concern and begin, in me, the habit of calling in whenever I went into port. I slept well, had a good breakfast of porridge and set sail for the outer waters.

Cape Flattery was passed without any incidence, winds were low, about 8-10 knots and from the north so it was easy sailing along the rugged outer coast. I marveled at the scenery, and felt much respect for the coastal natives who regularly plied these waters in their canoes searching for whales to harpoon or halibut to catch on their bone hooks. Those waters around Cape Flattery can rise up quickly to match wind velocity changes so their many-manned stout sea canoes would have been necessary with probable painful reminders now and then.

I decided to sail some distance off-shore, at least ten miles, calculating that my safety chances off-shore were possibly much better than trying to dive in to minor inlets along the coast should the weather blow-up. Aberdeen was about 200 miles south so, even if I wanted to, I would not close with that potential anchorage before nightfall, so I set the self-steering and went to sleep, leaving the navigation lights on. The next morning I was still more than a 100 miles north of the Columbia estuary and the wind shifted to the southwest and began to blow, increasing to about 25 knots with a building swell. I decided that should the wind build any further, I would prepare to launch my parachute drogue and sit it out. The wind increased and the drogue was launched. The vessel rode easily like a sea gull with the jib furled and the main partially battened. Before I retired I noted the GPS position. The wind stayed stable all night and when I rose in the morning and checked the GPS the vessel position had moved northward some 150 meters. From that data I assumed that the drogue was working well and possibly, the vessel movement was due to a low, northward current. I stayed there for another night and checked the position again in the morning, the GPS indicating a northward movement of less than 250m. I was content with my strategy and the wind died down late that afternoon so I retrieved the drogue and stowed it and set sail southward. I headed for the Columbia estuary outflow, some 100 nm away.

I traversed the area in front of Astoria, Ore. and Vancouver, Wa. keeping a look-out for commercial traffic. No activity was seen. The wind shifted towards the west at low velocity so the sailing was without any difficulty. The surface water appears to be unusually warm and many chum salmon were surfacing about, seemingly aimlessly. Then a pod of N. Pacific dolphins appeared and started playing around the vessel, playing hide-and-seek with each other between the hulls. They continued this play for nearly ten minutes then abruptly disappeared, to come back about 20 minutes later....but were they the same ones? I breathed a sigh of relief once past the Columbia area and the next morning I was surprised by being buzzed by a four-engined aircraft, probably on patrol duty. As I was sailing at least 15 nm offshore, I was quite surprised. Between mouthfuls of oatmeal I radioed them and was asked my destination, origin and identity. I provided that quickly as they circled around, San Franscisco is my destination port. As I was at positioned quite offshore, they must have realized that I was a serious sailor who knew the ropes as they rocked the wings with" safe sailing and over and out," and droned off north.

That afternoon a light fog approached so I switched on the engine, reefed the jib, switched on the navigation lights, and set up the GPS with the automatic steering. By darkness the fog was very thick and I sat in the cockpit with a handy flare nearby and dozed. Suddenly I became alert, coming out of my half-sleep I seemed to see a white angel hovering above the boat! Then it was gone, then it reappeared on my crosstrees as I strained to make it out. It was an adult barn owl, perched there and looking at me. I must admit I was a bit scared at the first appearance until I realized what it was, then it flew around the vessel in circles then re-perched on my mast. A few minutes later he did the same thing again, disappearing for several minutes before returning. This time it alit above my head on my radar housing so I shooed it off. Again it circled and repeated its moments of disappearance then returning. By this time I thought that the poor owl was lost in the fog, no visual cues other than my vessel. After resting there for several minutes it left, never to come back.

Another scare in the fog about thirty minutes later when a large freighter passed me on my starboard side, about 70m away, doing about five additional knots. I shone my big flashlight up into my main sail as he passed and assume that he had seen me from my radar reflector. But he was fairly close….so I wonder! Two scares in the same night in dense fog. How lucky can one be? The fog lifted the next morning and GPS put me offshore north from Eugene, Oregon and the wind started to pick up. By that afternoon it steadily built from the northwest and I decided to go into Newport harbor which I was familiar with from my student days at OSU, especially the river bar which can be dangerous. I called the Newport CG and expressed my desire to enter port if the bar is navigable. The reply, it is right now but things will change, where are you? My position is nearly due west at about ten miles now, I answered. Come on in and line up behind the two large commercial vessels that are awaiting escort. I did so, noting that the fishing vessels were large, steel trawlers, so I was to go in behind them. Out came the CG cutter and escorted the big vessels in one at a time then radioed me. I followed them in at full throttle, staying close to the north jetty as the local current swept vigorously towards the south jetty, this I knew from fishing from small boats. Entrance was fine but the bar was rapidly becoming snarly and obstreperous.

Safely inside, I proceeded to the marine on the south side and tide up with a sigh of relief. That evening I decided to cross the very high bridge over the Alsea River to snag a fresh fish dinner in the Whale's Tail, a good seafood on the old town waterfront. By the time I crossed the bridge, on the very narrow sidewalk and against blustery winds with auto traffic roaring by, I was more concerned than crossing that bar in my boat! But the fresh pink shrimp, that was really something! Fortunately the wind had dropped substantially for my return trip to the marina and a good nights rest.

The marine research center that had been built several years earlier was prominent on the south side and I regret not going in to see who was working there. I knew that the director was a deep water crab specialist who had come up from California after losing the battle against installing that huge nuclear plant in Humboldt Bay as he was concerned about rising coastal water temperatures due to the cooling system. He apparently decided to leave the state.

I know that bar can be very dangerous. The School of Oceanography at OSU had a research vessel that listed at the entrance, nearly turned over passing that bar while going to sea and that aged the participants on that cruise considerably. Later on, it was exchanged for a modified naval minesweeper and the tippy vessel transferred to Anchorage University in Alaska. As I remember, the only oceanographic scientist on staff at Corvallis who didn't get seasick was June Patullo. I met the first Director of that Oceanography school when he was first appointed to the OSU faculty in Science. He had a small aluminum boat from which, in the bay, he was looking at saltwater progression up river with a modicum of instruments. On the same day I was also sampling from small boat. I had a small zooplankton net which I towed on the incoming tide about at the river-seawater interface and was surprised to collect almost a quart of settled zooplankton (Acartia tonsi), a pure culture, in a few minutes.

Approaching Bandon the next day, I decided to go ashore as the wind might blow up again. It proved a rather exciting entry through rough water but I bee-lined in towards the lighthouse, first homing on the clanger. By then it was dark and I was somewhat confused with the paucity of navigation lights and the presence of an old, brokendown jetty on one side. Only one red beacon was discernable which looked like it was on a near headland. I radioed the CG station and told him where I was and was told to simply follow the red beacon. Would you give me a magnetic steering from my position to make sure, that red beacon still bother me? He refused, so I cautiously proceeded to motor in slowly past the beacon and spotted the masts in the marina in the slight moon. Suddenly I was almost on the beach so stopped and reversed, maneuvering around that spit to find the entrance on the far side. As my vessel only drew 15 inches, my long keel was touching the sand as I reversed. In to tie up and sleep.

The next morning I went up to the local coffee shop which was filled with commercial fishermen having breakfast, so ordered and got my own request. Finding an extra place at the long table, I sat down amongst them. “When did you get in,” asked my neighbor as he was busy eating. Last night was my reply. You’ve been in here before then, he answered. No, this was my first time, I replied. At that last comment, food-laden forks all around me became held in mid-air for a few seconds. Then my neighbor informed me that was quite a feat. For your information, a fellow came in here several years ago at night and beached his 60 ft sailboat even though he had been around the world with it before coming into Bandon at night. I thought to myself……another good reason for sailing a trimaran!

Off again the following morning, I was jubilant to have a 10-12 knot wind behind me as I proceeded towards Cape Blanco. The sailing was great, with a 4-5 foot swell urging along at an average vessel speed of ten knots. That afternoon the situation began to change. Suddenly my benign aft wind shut down and was replaced by a rising wind from the southwest. Within a short time the water started getting ugly, the new wind kept rising over 25 knots against the existing swell and I decided to go in to Crescent city which was more that 20 miles shoreward. As I turned beachward, the jib shook quite violently then lifted off the deck to stream with several very noisy, violent snaps. It had come off the deckfast! By now the wind was exceeding 30 knots and the new swell developing from the southwest. The jib gave one more agonizing shriek then the lower half simply ripped off downwind and was gone.

The furling line with the gear attached at its lower end began swinging about as the vessel pitched, colliding twice with the cross-deck between the main hull and the starboard amah. I knew that if it came through the front windows in the increasing bad weather that I would be in serious trouble. What to do? I tied off the rudder, grabbed a spare line and clambored up onto the main deck towards the main mast base with the line between my teeth. I watched that piece of suspended metal, hurtle about several times, the third time it came from behind me and whistled passed my ear, coming forward to hover some two feet in front of my face. I grabbed it and tied it to the mast base and slid back into the cockpit. There, I smashed my ribs against a main winch severely, possibly breaking bones. The pain started immediately and I began having difficulty breathing without considerable pain.

The possibility of recovering vessel control with just the main sheet, with the upper jib remains flailing about, and my rib problem appeared doubtful and my efforts were unsuccessful, anyway. Hence, I managed to drop the main to halfmast, positiond alee and crawled inside to radio a mayday on the VHF. Some one answered on the emergency frequency to a shore station……I heard, I'll go to him, it was possibly a commercial fisherman. However, no further messages came over the VHF and I then realized that the transmission distance was probably too great, so I sent a Mayday on the HF radio which was answered by the Coast Guard. I gave him a terse description of the difficulty and also mentioned that the waves were rapidly exceeding ten feet and were beginning to break on top, like surf. Standby, was his reply. A few minutes later he called, "we're coming out with a helicopter to take you off the deck," to which I replied that I wasn't ready to abandoned my vessel. Then call me back every 30 minutes with your GPS position and situation, he said. I did that four times, noting that the rigging was beginning to work, the waves were still growing, as was their surf. Finally, he decided to send out the cutter to my position.

By that time I was in extreme pain on my left side, and breathing was difficult. It took that 80 ft steel cutter almost five hours to reach me. In the meantime, a huge freighter showed up and called me. It was a Pakistani Captain (from his accent) and he stayed a safe distance, about half-a mile seaward of me. The CG HF then failed and we began communication vie VHF, relayed. My VHF suddenly came to life hours later as the cutter called me, "we have you in sight, we are coming up behind the freighter and plan on towing you from his windward side. I acknowledged that message, then called back to suggest that the tow preparations would seem safer if made from his lee side……this was agreed.

The cutter came up within 50 feet with five seamen hanging on the rails and viewing me in the cockpit now. I suggested on the VHF that they prepare a double tow line to be connected to the tow fastenings on the amah bows and a table was brought out on deck as they busied making up the line. Waving, a seaman began throwing a monkey fist which landed on my front nets and I scrambled as best as I could to retrieve it. Clutching it in my right hand, with my left locked through the deck netting and crawling to the starboard amah, I looked with horror to see the seaman dumping the one-inch diameter tow line half into the sea…..which promptly sank. With great effort and with my right hand I managed to haul in the line and attach it. The other half of the tow line followed as I crawled across the nets onto the port amah and did likewise with the line.

I had hopes that one seaman would leap onto my vessel to give me a hand as they knew my ribs were injured but no such luck. Perhaps I had exhausted all my luck for the time just having them come out from the station. Then the tow was about to proceed as they all disappeared into the cutter. The captain began the tow, first by instructing me to stay on the rudder and follow their track. He took off at nearly twelve knots, climbing across each wave at an angle, then turning to run down its far side at ninety degrees. My trimaran was literally flying through the water in skips and jumps and a line parted midway about an hour later and had to be replaced, then the tow recommenced. After about three hours I was becoming hypothermic from the constant dousing so tied the rudder straight and returned to the cabin, informing them through the VHF. I stood inside until we arrived in calm water, nearing Crescent City, hanging on to the interior grips so as to minimize my movements which were very painful.

At the dock, two seamen tied up Halobates as a third fellow, a medic, checked my ribs. Don’t think anything is broken, he said as he stashed equipment in his bag. By that time. I could hardly stand up and hoped that they would take me on to the base and throw me in a hot shower to revive, but no such luck. "Where can I go, I asked, I'm definitely hypothermic and need to get warm." There are a couple of hotels on the far side of the area, just walk that way, you will find them, then they left for the CG station. I staggered over a mile in the dark to a local hotel behind the marine facilities, checked in about four am, drew a hot bath and laid in it for an hour before starting to revive enough to crawl into bed and fall asleep. I woke nearly at noon, checkout time being 11 am, got dressed in my still damp clothes and went downstairs to the desk. They must have known that I was the salvaged mariner and the manager assured me that I wouldn't be charged for an extra night…..unless I stayed that night. The local paper was full of the CG exploit, the daring rescue through mighty seas and the manager was pleased to take my desire to meet with the CG captain willingly, taking me to the CG station in his Cadillac. I was curious to meet the captain, also to thank him for the arduous, lengthy tow that he and the crew had accomplished. He was the captain of the station and a ranked captain.

The hotel manager dropped me off at the marina where I had my first rested chance to view the damage. The remnants of the jib were hanging forlornly while several people were taking photographs. Climbing into the cockpit I realized why, when approaching the harbor, I was unable to steer with the rudder. The rudder had been cleft in half, probably from hitting a floating log as it was substantially constructed. I set about planning repairs and discovered that fiberglass construction and materials were practically non-existent commercially. Luckily, one of my visitors viewing Halobates was an amateur boat-builder and was finishing a multi-hull of his own. From our discussion, he wanted to get some advice on finishing his keel and I gave it along with a detailed sketch on how to rig a large parachute drogue if he was caught at sea and had to ride out a storm. He was so thankful that he invited me to use his shop at home and took me to get fiberglass and plywood to make a new rudder. He and his wife were practicing Christians and I was truly thankful for their assistance.

It took me several days to rebuild that rudder, and I laminated a sheet of quarter-inch thick stainless steel within it bridging the fracture area found in the original rudder. Another fellow at this marina, a mechanical engineer on faculty in San Francisco on his annual cruising holiday on his converted troller, helped me to remove the jib remains, re-attach the furling line and hang a storm jib. I found the two-inch bolt that had been used to fasten the furling line to the deck! It had rolled under the lashed jib cover on the main bow and had no threads. No wonder it rattled and came off! The fellow who rigged it in North Vancouver (located beneath the Second Narrows bridge) was obviously incompetent. It should have been locked with a nut. However, I blame myself, as I had failed to inspect the work when completed, assuming naively that it was done properly.

Once again ready to sail south, I intended to sail into San Francisco to visit academic friends living near Berkeley. Five days later, with the new rudder installed I headed out to sea. I was showing more caution about positioning myself more than a few miles offshore, in fact, drew some comfort seeing the shore as I sailed southward. I sailed into Humboldt Bay and stayed overnight after coursing up the channel for some distance to a marina. The following day at sea I approached a gathering fog so motored in towards Fort Bragg, homing in on the radar beacon but failed to find the clanger. Figuring that my radar sight was somewhat off as the fog descended and seeing a large number of rock piles scattered about I began circling without much luck, so called the CG and gave them my GPS position. Do you hear any rocky nearby? He said into the VHF. I certainly did! Stay where you are! We'll send out a small boat to guide you in. A few minutes later, "we are at the beacon, can you see us? Yes, I replied, barely and I'm coming over to you. They lead me in, through a winding channel, through a narrow high-walled entrance to the marina which reminded me of Southeast Asia where I tied up and thanked them. Rising the next morning after a poor sleep, I saw that all the noise was coming from a bevy of large, noisy sea lions sprawled all over the dock and reluctant to move. I stayed just long enough for the fog to lift to good visibility and the sea lions to leave on a foraging spree.

As I approached Point Reyes and neared the shoreline I motored towards the Point, an impressive jumble of massive rocks against an even more massive mountain face. As the wind had shifted to the north I hesitated going into San Francisco knowing the tricky current patterns and wind vortex characteristics associated with the Golden Gate bridge required novice caution. So, like Captain Cook, I decided to anchor overnight behind Point Reyes, partly out of the wind. I did so, but as I had failed to check the fuel content in the cockpit tank, the motor sputtered as I approached the hungry rocks but I managed to transfer enough fuel quickly to motor safely around the Point and anchor on the downwind side against a sandy beach. The wind rose to above 30 knots overnight as Halobates and I, and a host of sea birds rode out the storm. I stayed there another night until the calm. After breakfast I went forward to free the anchor, a large, 20 lb. Danforth, to find that I failed to dislodge it by hand. I firmly believe that a single sailor should be capable of hoisting his anchor by hand, otherwise stay home. Starting the motor and edging forward against the shortened anchor chain did the trick, angular tension. Stowing the anchor and chain in its bow compartment, I proceeded south into San Francisco Bay.

Passing by that ominous prison island with a nice tailwind, I shot across the bay doing twelve knots as I approached the entrance to Berkeley Marina. As the entrance neared, I dropped the storm jib, swung the main boom in, and started the motor, ready for reverse, if necessary, wondering if my speed drop would prove sufficient. It was, as I motored in below the indicated maximum 5 knots, found a nice outside berth and tied up. What a fine marina! I stayed there for nearly a week with friends. Even went to the horse races with the identical twin brothers. When we talked together, I had no problem telling them apart as one was a retired high school principal and the other, a clinical psychologist with a matching wife who suffered from Alzheimers but still made an effort to get into my head!

GETTING THE FURLING GEAR REPAIRED

As the bay area has many marine facilities, I decided to get my furling gear inspected at the south end. Asking my friend in Berkeley if we could visit the area south of Oakland to find a suitable location, he looked at his watch. Impossible to do it today, he said. The traffic is already thick even though there are six lanes in the highway below their house on the hill! So we went early the next day, found a suitable location and I planned to bring Halobates there the next day, passing under the Bay bridge into the canal. The rigging shop fellows were quite curious about the furling gear. They climbed the main mast and checked the entire furling line and gear. I showed them the mischievous bolt. "Jesus Christ!" they said in unison, "you should get that idiot who did this. Not only that but the size is insufficient for Halobates anyway. You need the next size up." They did the job and while they ordered and installed the new gear I had the next door sailmaker make me a new three-quarters jib. While waiting for completion, I phoned the N. American head for the French furler and outlined my case, including fortunate survival at sea in a major storm. He was sympathetic but had no authority over retail sails with installation. Returning to Berkeley and staying one more night with my friends, we shared a fond farewell as the retired principal expressed his desire to sail with me, further down the sea of time. His own wife with Alzheimers died next year and they are now both buried in the local Jewish cemetery.

During my stay at Berkeley Marina, I met a fellow alongside who was also in the Korean debacle. Interestingly enough, like me he was stationed on Okinawa at Kadina AFB at the same time but unlike me who was crewing on a B-29 dropping bombs he was a military air controller so saw me come and go on my combat missions. We went into town for a lunch in his Jaguar 120 and I also wanted to check a sales item at a local store. There I found a new, packaged 7-day Soviet clock with all the nuclear submarine decals on it…..for $60 and installed it on Halobates. For lunch we went to a restaurant called Reuben's, had an enormous corned beef sandwich, and feasted on a heaping bowl of the best pickled cucumbers I have ever eaten! Sherman's in Palm Springs trails miles behind with their pickles and is more mean with them, too!

I departed San Francisco on the south side, hugging the shoreline. I observed a few sailors in the Bay during my stay and none seaward of the Golden Gate bridge. Enquiring of local sailors at Berkeley Marina, I was told that hardly any one ventures outside and most boaters go upstream into the backwaters during the summer. My comment that as a potential local sailor I would plan to sail to the offshore islands, the Farrallons, if just to look for a Great White shark!

A terse comment followed, describing the knock-down and loss of a 60 ft ketch a few hundred feet west of the bridge although the crew if five were saved. Is the wreck still on the bottom?

For the rest of my journey I was determined to consume the sea miles avidly. Again I went offshore some distance, past just inside the Santa Barbara Islands and several oil-drilling platforms, I persisted southward. Passing inside Catalina Island and abreast of Laguna Beach evoked family memories of that now congested, hotel-ridden ex-village and sighted the horizon for the first signs of Mexico. Passing the enormous hulks of a nuclear-powered aircraft carrier and several menacing-looking destroyers probably playing a military exercise game, off San Diego, I started picking up a high tailwind, racing past Ensenada. My knotmeter read out at just over fifteen knots so I was quite jubilant at escaping the ominous military aura of San Diego.

About 200 nm south of San Diego the wind dropped dramatically to almost a dead calm, forcing me to motor with my GPS/navigation control system. Nearing Cedros Island, some 300 nm south of San Diego, my fuel supply was running short so I stopped in there to wake up the inhabitants. They were very obliging, as the local taxi had a fuel supply that he was willing to share....for the right price and with Yankee dollars. Money can get you anything, anywhere, at any time! Leaving them smiling, also gifting them with a new pack of cigarettes I found in a closet, left there by my wife. I went on south.

Passed innumerable beautiful sandy beaches and the wide expanses of bays used by the Grey whales for berthing and preliminary rearing of their young.

Coming near to Cabo San Lucas was evident by seeing several large sportfish boats trolling for those spectacular gamefishes, the Black marlin. I entered the port and found a berth amongst such boats, mainly American and noisy. Starting up their powerful motors at six am, ready to go out for a half-day of fishing. The largest marina was also American-owned and the entire town was pervaded with the atmosphere of Las Vegas, although gambling was not yet in its heyday there. With money one could get anything…….anything one desired was for sale!

My wife flew down over Christmas vacation and I was looking for her. First in the Port Captain's office where she had thoughtfully left a message two days earlier when she arrived. He found it after scuffling through his desktop papers. Luckily, being a linguist, she had no trouble dealing with the Latinos, speaking fluent Spanish which they greatly appreciated, coming from a blonde, white female! Her message indicated that she had gone to a small resort in San Jose Del Cabo so I high-tailed it there by bus. We enjoyed that classic little town with its good restaurants and small shops, spending half our time there and then back onto Halobates in Cabo San Lucas, sailing locally and swimming, before she flew back to work in cool, rainy Victoria.

My next short trip was to leave Cabo San Lucas and its thumping music, and sail around the peninsular to La Paz the capital of Southern Baja, passing inside Cerralvo Island to enter La Paz Bay. Sailing in at about ten knots on a caressing wind, I managed to miss the discrete channel by a short distance and ran up on the sand. Despite my quick attempts to back off against a falling tide, I was stuck there! A few hours later as the tide turned, a couple of college-age deckhands working on a huge motor yacht at the large marina just inside the bay, came by from fishing and we managed to push Halobates off by waist-deep shoves. I promised to take them out sailing to reduce their boredom on the yacht. Sailing in with considerably more care through the narrow, badly-marked channel, I anchored in front of a pretentious hotel and boardwalk restaurants and cafes. I had arrived at my final destination……at least for now! As more American sailboats began to arrive and the thumping, simple rhythms began to appear, I moved my anchorage over to the quieter inside of the adjacent island, using my inflatable for transportation in to a nearby marina, also owned by Americans.

I stayed there until early April when I flew back to Victoria and home. I was reminded of the poem by Robert Browning: Oh, to be in England, now that April's there….although as an ex-Brit my family left England in 1947 when I was but fourteen for Hollywood, California. There, I was subjected to the drama atmosphere, going through high school before enlisting in the USAF. In La Paz I met some interesting people, some long-term American escapees, some Mexicanos who had returned to their homeland from the north, and some wearing slick suits engaged in questionable activities.

I played tennis with a Mexican real estate agent with a father retired from banking. The son was constantly endeavoring to attract me to real estate and I became somewhat obliging as he would protect me from the gouging of local businessmen when I was doing maintenance on Halobates. I would phone him in indignation and, handing him the phone for a few minutes, the businessman would become more obliging at a much reduced price. He finally got me to spend the day cruising around in his Jeep Wagoneer looking at available property on or near the beach in the general area of La Paz.

I saw some very tantalizing coastal properties at prices far below those north of the border but when I asked him on three occasions who owned the property for sale, the answer was either a politician or police chief, in all cases reclining in jail for several years, found guilty of fraud, bribery, or stealing public money! Have things changed since then? I left for Canada that April after leaving Halobates on the hard at the big, luxurious marina, planning to return the following October.

Another local acquaintance, an American-escapee who had lived in La Paz for many years and spoke Spanish fluently, regaled me with an incident that usually took place at Christmas time, involving the local police. This season saw them looking very avidly for income source. He was stopped by a motorcycle cop for speeding in town…a frivolous charge which he contested. He was given two alternatives: pay the cop immediately $100 or have his license taken, then he could retrieve it at the police station for even more fine. He chose the latter and gave up his Mexican license to the cop who then drove away. He then drove immediately to the License bureau and applied successfully for a new license, then drove home.

On property considerations, I ran across an American woman who had a beautiful place on the beach, landscaped, swimming pool, and a live-in maid. Her mother lived in San Francisco, became diagnosed with cancer so her only daughter went north to take care of here, leaving the maid to care for her own place. Maintenance checks for her property that included the maid's salary were mailed from her local bank in La Paz. Her mother succumbed after some four months and she returned to La Paz to find that the wrought-iron gates were closed and locked. The maid wouldn't let her in, claiming that the property was now hers since a single payment from the bank failed to show up. It took this distraught woman over two years and two lawyers to pursue the case to success, regain her property and evict the maid. Apparently, under Mexican law, a servant can effectively claim land ownership if a payment for work goes missing.

I stayed for Christmas in Victoria and the coming of Spring. That March I purchased a new outboard (9.9 hp), a high thrust, four-cycle unit to replace the two-cycle unit that drank fuel like an Irishman drinks Guinness. I flew down to Palm Springs with it and stayed at my sister's place for several days, then she drove me south to Tijuana where I caught a bus to La Paz. That was a revealing bus ride. Several stops along the way and inspections by Mexican army personnel, including a barely seventeen-year-old sporting a semi-automatic rifle striding manfully down the aisle with a fierce look on his face. My new outboard arrived two days later, on another bus, had been broken into and everything except the actual motor stolen….manuals etc. This should have been a warning for me....but I seem to be a slow learner. Installed on Halobates in the dry dock, I took the time to inspect the hull for any signs of decay due to summer heat. I found one small area under the starboard cockpit which showed signs of separation and arranged to have it repaired.

I purchased the necessary materials at the marina office and instructed the attendant on how to do the repair work which he, being totally inexperienced, was thankful for. I then paid the bill and returned Halobates to my favorite anchoring spot. That evening, going over the bill, I discovered that the manager, always in a suit and tie, had billed me for a gallon of fiberglass resin and some other extras so I went back to see him. He did not speak English but the assistance of my worker on the repair job (in Spanish) failed to change his mind. Finding that the marina and the associated hotel and restaurants were owned by three brothers out-of-town, a friend advised me to see the Hotel manager "as he is the point man for the brothers. Do you know the brothers? I would be very careful."

I went to see the manager who put me off several times before me getting a firm date and time to get an official answer, as he seemed sympathetic to my account and bill evidence. To add a bit of leverage, I mentioned that I write articles for the American tourist associations brochures.

Arriving at the hotel at the prescribed time and asking for his whereabouts at the desk, I was told that he was in an important meeting upstairs with the brothers who had flown in from the mainland. I wrote a short reminder message for him and asked a bell-boy to take it upstairs. He did so promptly, breaking in on their meeting to give him the message. He arrived in the lobby ten minutes later in his slinky grey suit and tie, smiled and drew out his wallet which was stuffed with one hundred dollar bills and gave me one, while apologizing for the inconvenience. I insisted that the money was not important as I was ready to tear it up in front of him, that the issue was honest, business management. He left to return upstairs.

Feeling somewhat victorious, I walked over to the marina where I met a young fellow, a pilot, who spoke good English worked in the office and knew of my billing. Where is the manager? I asked. "Oh he left suddenly two days ago and the female book-keeper left yesterday, taking more than half the financial records with her. She was busy financing her father's serious hospital bills from here and she cannot be found. I'm quitting soon and going home begin flight training for passenger jets." Good luck to you, I replied, this is a dangerous place, isn't it. "Did you know that the three brothers own this entire place and just returned from San Diego after machined-gunning an entire family also in the drug business? You have been playing with fire! These are the Sinaloa brothers!"

I had planned to leave Mexico in early March, taking Halobates back to Victoria so considered leaving earlier but ended up staying until late March. My 8 ft Nissan inflatable with 5 hp o/b which I had bought with the 9.9 hp two-cycle Nissan was stolen one night, tied up to Halobates while I was asleep. The police weren't too interested but did inform me that a new regulation had just come into effect requiring all commercial sportsfishers to have a standby 5 hp motor for safety reasons. Thee months later, a telephone call from the local marina I used for commuting informed me they had the inflatable (it had Halobates painted on it). Give it to some needy sailor, was my reply. Meanwhile one of the brothers had been killed by police.

I motored back along the coast all the way to Victoria with that new engine, stopping in only in Santa Barbara and San Francisco for fuel. Had I decided to go offshore some 500 nm before sailing east it would have been foolhardy without at least one other competent sailor, possibly two. That trek would have added at least another thousand sea miles to the journey whereas, my return trip along the coast took 2000 nm.

END

White Shark Encounter

The summer that John transferred to Oregon State at Corvallis from his California university, who met and roomed with another ex-military fellow, he from the USN, off campus. Both were studying biology, John fascinated by fishes and Bob by predatory birds, like falcons and eagles. At the end of the school year, Bob became restless and left school to take a temporary position with the US Fish and Wildlife Service. He loved to hunt and play with guns so his new job attracted him. He was assigned to a research vessel, a contracted halibut schooner captained by a Russian having experience with fur seal biology. Two other students were also on the boat crew.

Their job was to follow the southern annual migration of fur seals from Alaska to sub-tropical waters. This migration takes place offshore. The strategy was to come close to a migrating group and to shoot a number of them as they porpoised out of the sea, collect the dead bodies before they sank and remove their stomachs for dietary analysis. Also, teeth were sampled for age analysis, and length and weight, and sex were recorded. Shooting required a very sharp eye and fast reflexes, enjoyed by all.

One of the students managed to shoot and kill a young northern sea lion travelling along with the fur seals. That evening, Bob tied a stout rope to its body and hung it over the side.....just to see what could happen. After anchoring close to the Santa Barbara Islands, the crew ate dinner and eventually went to bed. Deck lights were turned off. About two am Bob was wakened in his bunk by vigorous thumping against the side of the vessel, thumping close to his head. Waking up, he slipped into some clothes and went out on deck to see what was happening. It was a dark night, a quarter moon only, and as he stood at the rail he could hear the thumping continuing adjacent to where he had tied the sea lion. Straining his eyes to see in the poor light he heard a steady hissing sound at intervals, followed by more thumping. This hissing sound raised the hair on his neck and soon after he could see a large triangular fin arcing through the water, the origin of the hissing sound.

He then realized what was making all the sound, pounding and hissing, a large shark. Shark, shark he screamed at the top of his voice as he ran to turn on the deck lights. At the flood of lights crew began stumbling out on deck as the shark tore off behind the halibut schooner in a rush of white water which culminated in a huge layer of sea foam some thirty yards behind the boat. The captain appeared, swearing volubly in Russian as he surveyed the commotion which went on for some time. The crew had positioned a large $3 thousand dollar fine mesh gill net behind the boat to catch forage fishes with the intent of comparing their catches with the stomach contents of the fur seals. "Get back to bed everyone," he commanded. "We will deal with the net in the morning. The net was a complete loss.

After breakfast, the net and its contents were quiet so they gradually hauled the net system which was securely wound around the shark in multiple layers in close to the side of the boat. The net was badly ripped but still intact enough to hold the suffocated shark. The captain identified the shark....a large white shark. It was too heavy to simply hoist on deck using the available deck winch so, lashing several coils of heavy line around its body, they hauled it up sufficiently to begin chopping it in half with fire axes which was heavy work, particularly when trying to sever the massive spinal cord. On deck, the two pieces were put together and measurements made. It had a fifteen-and-a half foot long body, was a female from partial dissection, and the stomach contained the remains of five fur seals accompanied by a rubber tire of some two feet diameter. The captain estimated its weight at approximately fifteen thousand pounds. Almost as heavy as a small car and possibly charging one at nearly thirty miles an hour!

"We'll cut out the jaws and send them to the Smithsonian museum and dump the body further out to sea," he said. At this intention, Bob, after viewing the size of the front teeth in the upper jaw, levered two large teeth of the jaw with his scout knife and secreted them in his pocket. At the end of the summer, Bob returned home then came down to see me before that start of the school year and to recount his adventure. He showed me one of the teeth which I wanted to keep but he had given the other tooth to his father, a practicing dentist in Portland. I managed to borrow the other tooth long enough to examined it carefully under a dissecting microscope. To my surprise, I found that the nearly two-inch long, triangulated tooth edges were lappetted in serial fashion and each lappet was hollow-ground. One could easily slice a sheet of newspaper with the tooth so I warned him to be careful with his prize.

Several weeks later, I heard that his father had taken his tooth to the office and shown it during coffee break in his dental-medical building to his cohorts. Along came a surgeon who examined the tooth, saying, "I bet I could operate with this." Everyone laughed but when he ran the tooth edge against the palm of his left hand below his thumb he opened it up to a spurt of blood and ran upstairs to care for his wound. Coming back down some minutes later, he had put four stitches in his left hand and showed his wound to the gaze of his compadres. No wonder white shark bites are wide and clean, serving to chomp the victim, then let go to watch it die from blood loss before safely enjoying the meal without victim resistance! Bob became a dentist himself and surely, retained that tooth, as did his dad. That was the first white shark captured on the West Coast of North America. As I remember, that was in 1957 or 1958.

A Motorcycle Ride

PREFACE

Riding a motorcycle can give one some very exciting times apart from dealing with moronic motorists. The new realm of enhanced communication through cell phones, Facebook etc. can have some disturbing outcomes. Other events involved with liquor and reduced inhibitions are predictable despite the efforts of appointed guardians of civilized behavior, our police.

In 1990, high schoolers in suburban Toronto were preparing for Graduation with all the aspirations, particularly for the anticipated grand party that evening. The boys having established their dates and buying orchid corsages, get fitted with a rental tuxedo. For the girls, new hairdos, new fancy dresses and shoes, and all the cosmetic details involved in primping in preparation for the party that evening after graduation. Matilda Spencer and Christopher Duggan are involved. Matilda has several boy friends and Chris is one of them.

Graduation goes smoothly with Matilda giving the student address, her theme being jump into life with great anticipation and enthusiasm, reflecting the support of one's parents in following one's dreams. A general ovation follows then the bestowing of diplomas by the principal begins with the long line-up, followed by every graduate throwing their mortarboards high into the air.

That evening, the graduation party is held in the gymnasium all decorated up with school banners and party miscellania. The school band and music instructor have organized a dance list which is supplemented by a school quartet specializing in aping the styles of several rock and roll bands. The dance proceeds as expected and later on, the quartet takes over and the excitement mounts. Teens begin slipping out the side doors for illicit booze stored in their cars, returning with flushed faces and more jumping about to the music. By this time most parents have gone home, leaving the several teacher guardians to hold down the fort until 11 pm when the festivities shut down.

Matilda and her three admirers have been imbibing surreptitiously too, with the latter three begining to show competitive behavior for the right to take Matilda home. On the way, they decide to have a few more snorts from the bottle, just to empty it, and drive to a secluded area south of town, a traditional area for necking and making out. Before too long, the boys begin exchanging positions in the back seat with Matilda who is enjoying all the attention and the sexual atmosphere as her body is caressed and clothing is being removed by all four participants. The most dominant boy, a star athlete on the football team for two years takes the lead, ripping down Matilda's panties and climbing on top of her to the encouragement of the others, desirous of their opportunity. She offers no resistance as all three boys climax in her in turn, in fact they all consider this action to be part of the rite of adulthood.

Matilda has wondered all school year when this sexual experience would happen, and all three boys now realize that masturbation is not the real thing. There is no guilt expression either, as they feel a common social bond that's their secret to cherish. As midnight has past, they all begin readying to return home, first to drop Matilda off at her house, than the football athlete drops the other two boys off at their homes before returning to his palatial home with his new Chevrolet convertible, destined for college. They see little of each other during the summer as they have temporary jobs that keep them busy, scattered about the province.

Matilda registers at a private college near Lake Superior, the athlete has a scholarship at Notre Dame in Indiana, Chris starts his academic studies in Toronto, computer technology, and the third boy has enlisted in the army. Their paths never meet again. Matilda shows signs of pregnancy by mid-August and after a catholic family showdown she stays home for delivery with all its difficulties. A year later, the bouncing baby girl has worked her magic and Matilda attends college majoring in Business Administration, graduating four years later while her mother takes care of the child, named Stephanie. Now with a five-year old child she wants to become independent of her generous parents so accepts her first job in Calgary in the growing oil business, then transfers to Victoria for a lucrative position in hotel management. Years later, after collecting several years of experience in Toronto, Chris moves to Victoria, taking up a position with the provincial government managing their computer records.

Chris stays single after several disastrous relationships and buys himself a large motorbike, commonly called a hog. At the age of 34, sixteen years after high school graduation, he is now a confirmed bachelor, drinks much beer and rents an apartment downtown. He has become entertained by Facebook communications, creates his own personal social identity and trolls the medium for sexual encounters. He soon discovers that his effectiveness is much enhanced by concentrating on younger girls and there he contacts Stephanie who is sixteen, adventuresome, and has discovered sexual activity, first with high school boys with their fumbling around and amateur performance, then with older men. She runs across Chris's social description which includes motorbikes, and is attracted due to her self-imagined, sexual concept of bikers.

She dares to send him a message, describing her attraction to 'bikes and wanting to ride on one although she is only sixteen. They plan to meet in the large city park, next to the children's zoo on the following Saturday afternoon. It is now summer so she shows up there in shorts, sandals and a summer blouse. Stephanie is physically attractive, tall and buxom for her age and as Chris rides up on his 'bike she is quite excited, showing her anticipation with a big grin. He parks his 'bike, looks her up and down. Leisurely dismounting, he takes off his helmet and shows his perfect teeth in a casual grin. "You must be Stephanie?" That's me, she answers, " I was wondering if you would show up. That's a beautiful 'bike. I really like maroon and you have leather saddlebags, too!"

"If you're ready, put on this spare helmet, it should fit you and I'll give you a short ride. We can't go too far as you aren't dressed for the highway." He gets on the 'bike, kicks up the stand and motions her to hop on behind him, finding the foot pedals and holding him around the waist, beneath his open leather jacket. He drives slowly around the park, over to the beach road for a short circuit, then spies a small lane behind the cricket field, shaded by large trees and drives down it to the brush terminus. Meanwhile, she has been moving her right hand down his bare abdomen, locating his umbilicus, then further down to meet the elastic band of his underwear. Chris stops, turns off the ignition and kicks down the rest stand as she gets down herself, leaning against the bike and patting the broad leather seat.

Chris is breathing heavily and takes off his jacket, showing his biceps and quadraceps which she touches while biting her lips. "This is getting hard to take, Stephanie!" If it's getting hard enough, why don't you take it, then!, she replies. Chris whirls around, turns her and bends her forward over the broad seat of his motorbike. Pushing her forward so that her hips are square over the seat he tears down her shorts and panties to reveal her plump buttocks and smacks them several times to the tune of her joyful yelps. He puts her left hand on the right handlebar and tells her to grasp the right foot pedal with her left hand. "That will steady your while I go to work, he says.

She looks back over her shoulder to see him applying a over-size black condom to his penis and it barely meets his lower abdomen.

She squeals in delight, "go for it, Chris, I want it. It's so big and hard, give it to me with vigor." He spits on his right fingers and applies the mucous to her vagina, rubbing it a few times. Finding her clitoris, he gobs on it also, rubs it gently for a few minutes then begins to enter her, when she starts moaning. Sinking deep into her vagina, he stirs with considerable force and she groans in rhythm to his thrusts for nearly fifteen minutes when he finally ejaculates. They rest for several minutes then he withdraws, taking off the used black condom and throwing it into the bushes. He lifts her up from her position and turns her face towards him. "That's what you wanted, wasn't it?" Yes, she answers feebly, that's certainly what I needed as she pulled up her shorts as Chris re-buttoned his jeans.

"I'll take you back to the zoo, then I must leave to do some chores." Could you take me home, I'm having some difficulty walking, she says. He nods sympathetically as she tells him her address. Drop me off just around the corner, she murmurs. Waving goodbye, he roars off down the street. Stephanie limps into the house, showers and falls into her bed. It is only 4 pm.

Her mother arrives home from work to find her in bed. "are you sick, she says as she walks into her bedroom. No, but I feel really sore down below, Stephanie says. Her mother throws back the douvet to discover that the bottom sheet is red with blood. "What happened to you, ?" Stephanie thinks quickly, I was raped in the park by a scruffy guy reeking of booze. He came out of the bushes . clamped his dirty hand across my mouth and dragged me into the bushes and raped me……then disappeared. I had trouble getting home. Her mother is aghast, calls 911 for an ambulance and calls the police reporting a rape.

The ambulance arrives fifteen minutes later and takes Stephanie to the hospital, The Royal Victorian and her, mother follows in her car. She is examined within a few minutes, the MD calling for surgery. Twenty minutes later a gynecological surgeon repairs her vagina torn in two places. The local police specialist in rape calls at the hospital and gets a complete deposition on the "description" of the rape and the raper, and the location in the park. The next day, Stephanie calls

Chris on her cell phone, leaving him a message, telling him she is in hospital but has had surgery to take care of vaginal tears and bleeding. "My Mom is on a rampage and is determined to see some progress on the perpetrator identity with intent to get him charged and I'm going to be here for another day. Please come and visit me here before I leave for home, I promise that your identity I'll keep secret and I want to see you again."

Chris is relieved that she has steered the medical difficulty to a fictitious character that the police are looking for and decides to visit her the following morning, hoping to make sure he will be safe. Going to the hospital, as he mounts the main steps, a woman leaving the hospital passes by him, then stops. "Do I recognize you?" she says. She looks at him closely. "Aren't you Christopher from my high school?" He looks at her closely, gradually recognizing Matilda, the honor student from the back seat of that convertible after the graduation party and all the booze. He is somewhat flummoxed but control himself. "Why, I'll be darned!, he says, Matilda, my high school flame! "Are you living in Victoria?" Yes, I am, she says, I've just visited my daughter who came in here three days ago with a medical problem. "What are you doing here and do you now live in Victoria"? Chris thinks quickly, as the hounds of hell seem to be baying in his ear, "I've been here for some time, and am here to visit a chum of mine who had a motorcycle accident a couple of days ago. What a surprise to meet you here! Do you think about old times?" No, she replies, that's all in the past and I have a sixteen-year old daughter to care for. Chris swallows the rising lump in his throat, "well, nice to have met you again, good luck to you and your daughter, I must go in and see my pal."

Matilda turns to descend the stairs to the parking lot while waving a casual good bye. Chris watches her leave after entering through the swinging doors then decides to leave himself as the feeling in the pit of his stomach increases. Going back to his apartment, he changes his cell phone for another number and cancels his Facebook account. Spending the next few months when on the street, looking over his shoulder, he arranges to transfer his job to Vancouver. He realizes within two days of his encounter with Matilda that Stephanie, the product of that back seat sexual fiasco seventeen years ago in Ontario, might be his daughter. He knew that the football star, eventually in the NFL, had killed himself while racing his Italian sports car and friends from high school had informed him that the other fellow who went in the army was also killed, in a roadside bomb explosion in Afghanistan.

Stephanie, since the age of eight has bugged her mother on a number of occasions about her potential father, who was he, where is he and why don't we know him? The grandmother and her daughter have been tight-lipped in the face of such questions in the early years, finally telling Stephanie that her father had died just a few days after her birth from a serious illness and he had no relatives that they knew about. Hence, the family's social reputation was secure.

The Dancers, Letitia and Pacis

PREFACE

This fictional story stems from the Greek myth of Galatea and Acis, latinized by Ovid in his poetic books in Metamorphoses. Galatea and Acis were lovers on Sicily. Out of jealousy and his unsuccessful love for Galatea, the cyclops Polyphemus kills Acis with a rock. The resulting profusion of blood turns into a river then called Acis and Acis becomes a river god. As in another Greek myth, one concerning Oedipus which I have brought into modernity (The Agony of Eddy Dolan), the present story seems as appropriate to modern times.

Two young dancers meet during intensive training in formal ballet in Chicago under the watchful eyes of Robert Joffrey and Gerald Arpino who had recently founded a small but modern ballet troupe. Both teen dancers had well-recognized classical ballet talents and were attracted to express their talents in the modern ballet forms developed originally by George Balanchine. Latitia Seaborne , a Bostonian late teenager received her early ballet training in Boston, supported by her well-to-do parents in the shipping trade of Norwegian background, emigrating from Iceland. Gratia was a striking natural blonde discovered by Joffrey from his teaching classes in New York City. Pacis Faunly was born in Texas, in the sleepy town of Brownsville, on the Gulf Coast west of Houston. His father, an assistant port captain, moved the family to Chicago on a promotional opportunity when Pacis was ten. His father was one-quarter negro, his grandfather being a freed slave, and he had married an Apache Indian girl. That combined heritage gave Pacis striking good looks, piercing black eyes, black curly hair, and a light dusky skin. He showed much interest in dancing from an early age which progressed into ballet lessons in Junior high school, followed by professional coaching. He was an outstanding gymnast in high school, showing strength and endurance far beyond his gymnast cohorts.

Although Joffrey and Arpino had little money, they planned to start a ballet company in the future. To this end, they assembled a small troupe of dancers, six in all, in 1956. While Joffrey returned to NYC to generate funds from his teaching expertise to finance this tour, Arpino took this small troupe, which included Letitiaia and Pacis as the youngest couple, on a two week tour, hauling their modest equipment in a U-haul trailer towed by a station wagon. This small troupe was not the only impoverished dance company phasing into modern dance in America. The tour started from a five-day polishing performance in Chicago, then went south to Indianapolis, Louisville, Nashville, Memphis, ending in New Orleans for nearly a three week long touring and travelling performance.

Their production lasted slightly over an hour, ran for two nights in each toured city before Memphis, three nights there, and five nights in New Orleans. The production received considerable local interest from their four twenty minute dance skits, all of which were conceived and choreographed by Joffrey. Letitia and Pacis danced in two skits with NYC themes: Moon over Manhattan and On the Brooklyn Bridge. Both wore complete, skin-tight body suits, Letitia's was white, made luminous by phosphorescent dye and Pacis's suit was jet black silk. The first skit was a duet featuring them as aspiring lovers, and the second skit involved all six dancers in a flowing pedestrian stream of office workers and shoppers. The young couple stood out amongst the dancing group on stage. The music was taken from various sources, including jazz, and reflected the upbeat and youthful city life in America.

Their performances generated an increasing public interest as they proceeded on their tour with national attention received by the time they performed in Memphis and New Orleans. Due to their close teamwork and coordinated strivings for perfection, the dance duo, Letitia and Pacis, became good friends and spent time together, relaxing and commenting on their backgrounds leading to modern ballet, including their parents support and interests. Both mothers had showed psychological connections with water. On the beach during summers in Massachusetts, Gratia's mother liked to sit quietly on a promontory overlooking the surf and sea horizon, reluctantly joining the sand castle building when asked by her husband and Gratia. Similarly, Pacis's mother would get enthused for camping beside the Rio Grande after the Spring rains when the wildflowers abounded. "Sit quietly and listen to the river talking to you", she would advise Pacis as a small boy when they still lived in Texas. She also told him that her ancestor was Grandfather Stalking Wolf, a Lipan Apache chief. That both maternal parents in the Greek myth were associated with water nymphs makes for an interesting connection with pounding surf and the singing and gurgling of the mountain river heading for the sea.

The Memphis show attracted dance enthusiasts from throughout the cultured South, especially New Orleans. One enthusiast from New Orleans bought front seat tickets to all three Memphis shows and appeared at the stage door as a semi-permanent attraction, wildly-bearded and holding bouquets for Gratia when she appeared. Festus de Polycrops had a substantial estate along the Mississippi River above New Orleans and featured a black silk patch over his blind right eye from a late teenage auto crash while speeding. In his last bouquet in Memphis, he added a handwritten letter to Gratia, informing her that he was no longer capable of dancing ballet due to his injuries which included significant loss of balance and coordination. Gratia was somewhat frightened by his overbearing demeanor and feverish adulation of her although she accepted his flowers with grace.

Festus de Polycrops anticipated continuing his attention when the dance show reached New Orleans and met her again there at the stage door with a large bouquet of red roses after every performance with an invitation to dine with him in the French quarter. Her agitation at his persistent attention caused Pacis to thrust him vigorously aside on the fourth night as they and the other dancers left for a group dinner at the Court of Three Sisters in the Quarter. Festus was greatly enraged at Pacis's behavior, particularly galling was his obvious ethnic inferiority, his dancing skill, and apparent closeness to Letitia. At home after several mint juleps, Festus worked up a seething fit of jealousy, abetted by his failed attempts at courting Letitia and compounded by his own loss of dancing ability. He decided to eradicate Pacis as the source of his failed attempts before the show leaves New Orleans so he stalked them to the restaurant after the last night's show, armed with a pistol but evening crowds posed much difficulty for him.

Parking his red Ford Mustang close to the Court of Three Sisters restaurant, with an eye view of the entrance, he waited. They arrived once again at this restaurant, their favorite place to dine, this time as a lone couple. Entering to dine and emerging nearly an hour later, they appeared hand-in-hand and began walking down the street towards their hotel. Festus followed slowly in his Mustang, slowly enough to miss the green light as the couple were obviously waiting to cross the intersection. As the pedestrian walk sign began to flash and they stepped off the curb, Festus gunned s his motor, driving forward with a squeal of tires. Pacis reacted with quick reflexes, pushing Gratia back on to the curb but was slammed against the curbside end of the Mustang grill, bouncing off into the gutter and laying there without moving. Festus gunned his hotrod through the red light, looking back through his rear mirror to see a crowd gathering at the intersection. Now panic-stricken and fearful of capture, he sped through town on to highway No. 10 (north) which runs alongside Lake Pontchartrain.

Several witnesses of the accident noted his car description and license plate identity and related that info to an approaching patrol car. The police sized up the situation, called for an ambulance and set off in chase. Festus thought he had escaped but several minutes later he spied flashing red lights rapidly approaching from behind him and increased his speed to over 80 mph as he proceeded alongside the shore of Lake Pontchartrain. The patrol steadily gained on him so he stomped his accelerator to the floor, reaching over 100 mph. Driving that fast was made difficult by his need to pass minor traffic proceeding northward towards Baton Rouge. On one such passing attempt he lost control, flipping over the embankment. Turning upside down in an aerial arc, the Mustang slid into the lake to disappear in a cloud of bubbles and mud spray. The patrol car approached, waved down by the last car passed at high speed. Both negro policemen climbed out, surveyed the ruptured embankment and the sliding tracks into Lake Pontchartrain, and called for a wrecker and a diving crew. Hours later, the Mustang is dragged out on to the mud bank with muddy water streaming from the fractured windows and collapsed windshield. An inert body, covered in black mud and showing one open, sightless eye, is maneuvered into a black plastic, zippered body bag and transported to the city morgue.

At the city hospital, a dazed and bruised Letitia was comforted by a nurse outside the emergency operating room. Inside, the anesthesiologist and two surgeons discovered that Pacis will survive with several broken bones and a severe concussion, the aftermath being a partial and permanent loss of fine balance and reduced control of muscular coordination Letitia solicited the assistance of several prominent local lawyers and successfully sued the de Polycrop estate for financial aid, both for hospital bills and loss of potential dancing income. Their common ordeal strengthened their building relationship and they eventually married and returned to the ballet company in Chicago. Letitia became a major star performer and Pacis, after much agonizing physiotherapy secured a position as an assistant instructor and choreographer to both Joffrey and Arpino in the developing and prestigious Robert Joffrey Ballet Theatre which was invited eventually to the White House by Jaqueline Kennedy in the early 1960's.

Meetings in Europe

During several scientific meetings in Europe I met many interesting individuals from different countries but three people stand out, probably because I spent some personal time with them after meetings, both in travel and in their homes.

While returning from a scientific meeting in Kuopio, Finland I travelled by train through Sweden, stopping first at the Drottningholm Laboratory north of the capital. A scientific discussion with the Director there, a well-known ornithologist, animal behaviorist, who had published an outstanding paper on the spawning of the European pike, and the environmental stimuli that led it to its upriver spawning grounds. As we chatted, a scientist knocked and came into his office to go over his intended trip to Paris for giving a paper. The Director listened to his plan, asked him how much expense money he needed, including which hotel he was staying at. The hotel name, locale and travel expense estimate was approved by his Director who agreed with the itinerary and costs. Opening his desk drawer, he retrieved his check book and wrote out the required amount, signed the check and gave it to the scientist who thanked him and left forthwith.

This transaction amazed me who was required to submit to a host of paperwork and approval from headquarters in Ottawa and a time delay of several weeks. In fact, my eventual trip to France two years later took almost a month of bureaucratic machination, resulting the French government becoming rather irate at my inability to clearly state expected definitive and prompt planning as several governmental groups were attending. Finally, some three weeks before the meetings, the French Minister of the Interior telephoned me with a desperate query. "Will you be presiding over these meetings as the time element was growing short" he asked. My response, "I'm still waiting for approval from Ottawa". He then suggested that he could directly call his counterpart in the Canadian government, calling for expeditious action. I hastily discouraged that suggestion as the bureaucrats will undoubtedly assume that I had precipitated that call and plan for later punishment. Fortunately, the paperwork came through within two weeks of the meeting date so I could reassure the French that I would be attending and officiating. I swore never again to represent Canada in international meetings.

Travelling across Sweden by train on a Saturday revealed the countless examples of outside saunas emitting tell-tale smoke as the menfolk engaged in their steaming rituals. I experienced my first Scandinavian sauna ritual at a Drottningholm lake. The university research facility there was fairly new, and the first priority in development was the construction of the large, wood-burning sauna.

Reaching Malmo on the southwest coast of Sweden, I was greeted by several scientists from the local university and also met a Swedish engineer who had developed synthetic milk for the UNESCO and WHO. By so doing, he produced a solution to the general butter surplus that had resulted from governmental economic policy in several European countries (partial underwriting of production costs). Literally, many thousands of tons of butter were being stored in refrigerated warehouses and accumulating over several years. His product used the butter fat with other agricultural components to provide a synthetic milk capable of an unrefrigerated shelf life of months, even in African and Indian climates. He also specialized in food packaging, having developed the familiar pyramidal cream container at his several factories. He was also very interested in crayfish and had financed a hatchery and rearing system in Malmo which I was happy to visit with him. I had supervised a live shipment of mature crayfish from the upper reaches of the Pitt River below Pitt Lake a year before to Malmo.

He invited me to dinner the next day in his large farm house full of oil painting, starting out my visit by driving me around the estate. He pointed out a number of alien tree species that were growing luxuriously despite dire warnings from government forestry experts, mentioning that university students and their professors visited every year to inspect these trees. He also had imported a large number of wild pigs from Austria which we ran across at dusting spots and the large males were quite intimidating. On a trip to the USA he had seen the rail crossings used to prevent straying across highways by cattle and applied them for his wild pigs, constructing several road crossings of rails to keep them confined. Much to his consternation, within two days the pigs had escaped into the adjacent farmlands and were raising major problems. A major recovery program resulted which took several weeks before all were recaptured and the rails were replaced with iron gates. The nimble pigs had simply trotted over the rails and escaped. "I have something special for dinner," he said and I visualized an exotic Swedish dish. At the dinner table that evening, the butler brought a large silver tray and lifted the steaming lid to reveal a large Atlantic salmon. "I had this wild salmon flown from Norway," he said. It was not a patch on the magnificent 50 pound chinook from the BC Central Coast that I had previously eaten, the over one-inch steaks which when broiled could be seen to exude fountains of oil in their self-basting. This fellow had accepted a major director position in the FAO in Rome and invited me to accompany him in an advisory position for fisheries management/research which I declined due to my distrust of major bureaucratic organizations, world-wide. He was most disappointed as was I ......eventually.

I met Rheinhard Spitzy for the first time in Finland, at the University of Kuopio at a meeting of the IAA, the International Association for Astacology, the study of freshwater crayfish which Spitzy had founded, reflecting his interests in hydrobiology. I had attended the second such symposium held at Louisiana State University at Baton Rouge, Louisiana two year previously where I gave an important research paper and was elected President of the IAA, due to the activism from Scandinavian scientists there. These symposia are held every two years and are published in hard copy.

The third biennial symposium was held in France, at Thonon les Bains in 1978, on the edge of Lac Leman (Lake Geneva). On the last day of meetings, I was invited by Rheinhard Spitzy to visit him at his alpine estate in Austria near Maria Alm. I took the overnight train from Geneva to Salzburg and was there picked up by his eldest son, a lawyer driving west from Vienna. We had some interesting discussions during that drive to Maria Alm, as his son was a dedicated communist and wanted my reactions to his interests. More interesting was our lunch at a traditional inn where I was introduced to sausage and sauerkraut in sour cream. The sauerkraut was like eating ice-cream, fermented and aged in oak barrels, far from the vinegary concoctions sold in North America. The lawyer son returned to Vienna after dropping me off at his father's residence and concluding some legal business in Salzsburg.

Rheinhard met us in the driveway and took me into his residence which was the historical weekend residence of the Prince-Bishop of Salzsburg, his hunting lodge, where he speared bears while refraining from blessing his population. 1453 was dated over the entrance. As he spoke fluent English without a trace of accent I was curious about his background. During my three day stay we had many discussions, some about freshwater crayfish which he was most interested in, reflecting the horrendous population losses of European crayfish due to the introduction of Cambarus clarki from Louisiana which is the carrier of a shell disease which has decimated the European species throughout the continent due to their almost complete lack of resistance. The initial imports of C. clarki apparently were traced to Italy and the lethal disease spread northward, accelerated by imports to Germany.

From my queries about his language expertise which also included Spanish and Portuguese, discussions ranged from his early diplomatic services in the German Embassy in London where he made many British cohort friends. There, he was executive secretary to the German Ambassador, Joachim von Ribbentrop starting in 1936. They both returned to Germany in 1938 and von Ribbentrop became Minister of Foreign Affairs in Berlin. Rheinhard was with Hitler and Ribbentrop at the meeting with the British Prime Minister, Neville Chamberlain, at the Reichstag. The comment by Hitler following the exasperated comments of von Ribbentrop: "It's only a scrap of paper" was heard by Rheinhard at the fuehrer's elbow, while watching the P.M. descend the steps to his waiting limousine while waving the paper containing the Anglo-German Agreement of Non-aggression, a reflection of the Munich Agreement and all its dithering relative to the fate of Czecho-Slovakia.

I assume that this and other duplicities, including his low opinion of von Ribbentrop as an ignorant bumpkin with strong cravings for high social status, were involved in his transfer from "diplomatic work" which included negotiations with American Companies in Germany after the outbreak of war in 1939. By 1941 he was working with Admiral Wilhelm Canaris, Head of German intelligence ….the Abwehr and by 1943 with Walter Schellenberg and Prince Max Ergon zu Hohenlohe in the Reich Security Main Office in Berlin.

As a full colonel in SS Intelligence and a member since 1932, the year of my birth, he became Head of German Intelligence in Spain and Portugal. I was quite surprised to hear that he was involved in assassination attempts on Hitler, particularly Operation Valkyrie after which he fled into a Spanish monastery for some time disguised as a monk. He showed me photographs to that effect, saying that he was the only planner who escaped detection and destruction. As British Intelligence directed radio messages to him nearly six months before the end of the war, exploring possibilities, he was advised by them to avoid returning to Austria as that was designated as an American zone and the Americans had him on the Nuremberg list, primarily due to his lack of cooperation. I suggest those communications reflected his diplomatic friendships while operating in London, starting in 1936. Rheinhard had a rather low opinion of American government officials, no doubt reflecting his personal social background and high caliber education, possibly reinforced by his British counterparts in London.

He fled to Argentina with his family, wife and two small children, early in 1948. According to Rheinhard, they lived in the outback in a large estate richly forested and adjacent to a large river. He surveyed the timber for its potential commercial value and built a river boat to distribute Coca Cola products along the river. His photographs of his high-born wife stirring the cooking pot over a forest fire and his comment that his children never saw a bicycle until they returned to Austria after some ten years in rural Argentina maintained my curiosity. They returned to Austria in 1958 following family deaths there, trading some castle belongings on the Rhine for his present holdings near Maria Alm.

Although he had three Alps behind his present estate, I declined to hunt chamois with him and spent that second day with his youngest son who had recently graduated in Israel with a M.Sc. in Physics and desired to earn a doctorate in the U.S.A. I recommended Cal Tech in Pasadena or M.I.T. in New England while I was dry fly fishing in one of the large trout ponds below the main house and caught a nice three pound Eastern Brook Trout for lunch. That evening, although skunked on his hunting trip, Rheinhard and his attractive wife held a dinner (roast chamois) with some two dozen guests, one being a Hohenlohe princess who regaled me with the antics of court life when she was a debutante in Germany. Seating me at his right side, Rheinhard tactfully asked me if I agreed to table conversation in German to which I declined as my German skill was almost entirely directed at biological science. Tapping on his wine glass, he announced "Herr Doctor-Professor Mason would prefer English spoken during dinner". He had insisted in labelling me in that manner on several social occasions, despite my objections. Of course, everyone spoke fluent English, much to my relief. Continental Europeans have the advantage of close geographical cultures which allow their offspring to absorb linguistics almost painlessly at an early age.

During dinner, a guest asked the young physicist about his degree in Israel. He answered that it was an enjoyable experience and that he left several very close Jewish friends there when he returned to Austria. There was a sudden disruption of conversational hum for nearly ten seconds with some food-filled utensils poised half-way in their trajectory arc to the open mouth before the conversational hum returned.

The older son took me for a drive in the adjacent Alps and in to Maria Alm, the local village where I had the opportunity to examine local specimens of native crayfish in the nearby lake. When his father organized the IAA, the first meetings were in Austria. The front cover of that first edition displayed a medieval oil painting depicting peasants knee-deep in that lake at night, holding flaming torches to facilitate catching the crayfish in hand nets. The present stock must have been perilously low due to the crayfish plague and C. clarki was in that lake. Rheinhard told me that the Prince-Bishop of Salzburg had ruled that several hundred kilos of crayfish were to be delivered to him on an annual basis and local monks had devised methods of preparing live crayfish for discerning palates by having them crawl through troughs of several concoctions of flavorings before being steamed. The local fishermen/peasants came up with a sad tale of low catches so as to reduce the Prince-Bishop's take. He responded by announcing that if the stock was perilously low that all fishing was to stop until recovery was determined. The peasants then came up with his expected tithe with alacrity.

During that drive, we passed several Mountain Ash trees with ripening berries which Rheinhard's eldest son mentioned were being guarded with shotguns by the local farmers who make schnapps. That alcoholic outcome is drunk from a shot glass quickly, followed by several swigs of beer. I told him that these trees are common in coastal B.C. and asked how they decide when berries are ready to gather for fermentation. Put a berry between thumb and fore-finger, he said, squeeze and count the drops, two to two and a half drops is ideal for making schnapps. That fall in Victoria, I tested his formula, getting three to four drops from a local tree. Schnapps, anyone?

Returning to linguistics, I promised myself while waiting for my plane from Vancouver to Paris for the meetings at Thonon les Bains, that I would only speak French while in France. Promises, promises… ..I gave two papers in English, spoke French to a Polish Professor (Kossakowski) who spoke no English and was repelled from speaking French in Thonon les Bains with locals after the second day there. I had great difficulty understanding them, exacerbated by their rapid speech and nasal tones, deciding that my French was to blame. However, asking them to slow their delivery typically resulted in a smirk and even faster delivery….so I gave up. From those meetings I took the train to Geneva, intending on a flight to Bern. Stepping out of the train station I hailed a local fellow and asked him in French about some places I wished to visit in the city. He replied in French, we had a five minute conversation without any difficulty, then said goodbye. Walking down the street I realized that my French was passable to him and his was fully understood by me. Later I realized that my French was Parisian mode and the southern French provincials dislike moneyed and demanding tourists from Paris although they seem to be the main source of livelihood in that spa town.

During lunch between meetings on day two, I had three federal ministers at my table, the conversation turning to Lac Leman and their ecological difficulties there. I had noticed the evening before, while strolling along the lake shore, that impressive amounts of algae were winrowed along the beach, suggesting nitrogen enrichment, eutrophication possibly from sewage. As there was a valuable lake whitefish stock for gourmet applications in expensive restaurants, a stock in decline, several ecological events had happened. The stickleback population had exploded and they carried (resistantly, due to their large lateral armor plates) a parasitic copepod that also seriously attacked the fry of whitefish that fed in the shallows. A hatchery was producing fry for liberation but was not too successful. One minister suggested that the deep cobble banks used for spawning of whitefish were becoming organically saturated and suggested that by plowing them the agitated cobbles would be again available for the adhesive eggs. I gently advised not to do that plowing which might merely stir up the hydrogen sulfide produced below…..and that would efficiently kill developing eggs and fry. One possible way to enhance whitefish fry survival was to introduce crayfish to the lake after suitable aquaria trials involving stickleback reproduction in nests constructed by the male being raided and destroyed by egg-eating crayfish. I never heard whether or not that suggestion was followed. As the French and Swiss were cooperatively managing lake resources, progress towards solution would seem potentially rather slow.

Another interesting fellow at the Thonon les Bains meetings was a Spaniard whom I had met at Baton Rouge, Louisiana two years earlier who had introduced C. clarki into a coastal river-lagoon system in southern Spain with much success. Archduke Andreas Habsburgo-Lorena attended the Thonon meetings and invited me to drive down to Spain with him, inspect some crayfish projects and advise on them. I accepted, meeting him in Bern to begin the drive southward, after meeting the Spanish representative to the WHO there. His custom Volvo sedan performed well on that drive through Southern France and up into the Pyrenee mountain range, then down into Spain.

While driving through the immense pine tree forest on the Spanish side we encountered a band of hand loggers relaxing on a large log while eating their lunches of bread, cheese, and wine flowing from their wine sacks. Andreas enquired if there was a restaurant where we could have dinner and was told that their village was nearby and could satisfy us. We drove down to the village while Andreas informed me that, many generations ago, a Spanish king had given a large forested tract to this village which had developed a conservation routine including hand-logging, milling, and production of furniture.

We had a delightful early dinner of fresh trout and local wine before leaving the friendly and hospitable villagers and returning to the main road.

We stopped while still in the sub-alpine area at a small stream where Andreas was involved in testing the introduction of Pacifastacus leniusculus from Canada. As the stream was far too small for that species, I recommended that P. trowbridgii would be more suitable as it is found in smaller and hilly streams. P. leniusculus is found in large rivers, including their oxbows, and in large lakes (introduced there) as in Lake Tahoe in California.

Further along, we encountered a heavy rain storm producing two to three inches of water on the road, so intense was the downfall that all drivers except Andreas had parked to await the cessation. Andreas continued to drive at high speed down the steep and winding highway to my rising concern which drove me to turn on the radio. A news flash resulted, King Carlos had another offspring just born, a boy, which stimulated Andreas to exclaim in a rather grumbly tone that now he would never get to be king with some three offspring in front of him, compliments of Carlos. In surprise, my reaction was to scold him mildly by pointing out that such an inheritance involves a complete lack of privacy and personal freedom defined by established protocols aimed at maintaining the royalty tradition. You would just be a pseudo-leader primed to keep the multitude entertained along with obligations to open this and that event, show yourself in established public routines, with every utterance from your mouth scrutinized by government hacks for possible application to political whims. After several minutes he somewhat reluctantly agreed as we neared the town of Merida on the expansive plain below us.

Before entering Merida we were driving along a back road through bean fields and came up behind a farmer astride his donkey, obviously going home after his days work. It was in the early evening and as the light was fading I opened my window to hear a melodious and partly wild stream of guitar music emanating from the farmer. "Slow down for a few minutes and listen," I suggested and his playing dexterity, musical mood, and harmony with the descending light was almost magical to me. Later I discovered that the best Spanish guitarists were not those musicians entering the commercial world of concerts, tapes, and records but locals who were satisfied to play in their own areas, usually in the local taverns for free drinks and food, mainly on the weekends.

Andreas was a close relative of the Emperor of the Austrian-Hungarian Empire, Charles 1 and his wife, Zita. His older sibling, Otto von Habsburg (1912-2007) also grew up in Spain, was fluent in seven languages and wrote some forty books after earning his Ph. D. at Louvain in 1935 at the age of twenty-three. He was very active in politics and helped many Austrian Jews escape from the Nazis. The Empire came to a close in 1918 at the close of WW1 when it was broken up into many national identities. The Emperor was evicted from the palace in Vienna, went to Madeira in exile and died there in 1922. Andreas told me an amusing story about Charles. As they were leaving the palace, loading into their carriage with few belongings, including jewelry, Zeta demanded to know where they were going as they passed out of the palace gates. Reaching into his jacket pocket, Charles extracted a cigar, clipped off the end and began searching his pockets for his lighter case, discovering a folded sheet of paper. It was a deed to a hunting estate belonging to a Count who was in a card game the evening before with Charles. He lost the bet and forfeited this deed in recompense. Lighting his cigar Charles then read the deed, rapped on the carriage roof and informed the driver where to go. Otto von Habsburg, as first son got this estate in Austria, along with the primary titles of his family.

Once we arrived in Madrid at Andreas's condo alongside the Madrid Country Club, I explored his place while he went back downstairs to check his mail with the porter. Walking out onto his large second floor sun deck and looking at the greens, I heard a rustling in the profuse ivy covering the adjacent walls. To my surprise, a very attractive blonde was climbing down onto the railing from her place above. Halfway down and as I turned towards her she says "oh, you're not Andreas" and climbs back up and disappears. I refrained from telling Andreas of this brief encounter but assumed that her climbing antics were well-rehearsed. We ate at the Country Club restaurant that evening and I enjoyed sliding steamed Moroccan surf clam necks down my willing throat.

The next day we went to the edifice built to commemorate the civil war that rendered Spain into a military dictatorship, ruled by General Francisco Franco (1939-1975), 36 years. The entryway crowned by fascistic statues reminiscent of Soviet art continued in the broad interior which led to the side-by side burial of Franco and the Republican leader. That afternoon I went to El Prado and saw the fine art collection that included portraits of Andreas's ancestors and understood why he was sometimes stopped on the streets of Madrid with queries on his resemblance to those portraits. "This is your last evening in Spain as tomorrow you fly back to Canada," said Andreas. My reply, I would like to see some authentic Spanish gypsy dancing. That stuff is for tourists, he replied but we'll go anyway.

We first stopped at an exclusive residence surrounded by high walls and an impressive set of wrought-iron gates. Andreas disappeared inside and returned a few minutes later with a friend who climbed into the back seat of his Volvo. From the short flash of interior light I noticed she was an ash blonde. The barking dogs noise receded as we drove away. At a very fancy nightclub a show was proceeding in the main show room and we waited for some ten minutes in the ante-room where I noticed several photographs of the grinning mug of an American politician surrounded by young show girls. So, not only did he plan and finance the overthrow of the Chilean leftist leader, Salvador Allende, who shot himself in the palace before any assassination attempt could be attempted. The American politician had a penchant for show girls and expensive clubs although that interest is now reserved to the secure United States as travel to Europe is rather risky for him due to the questionable legality of his political shenanigans which have been well-documented.

Then the last foot-stomping and loud singing faded away and lights went up in the main room. To my astonishment, the three long tables leading to several small tables immediately below the stage was populated exclusively by Japanese businessmen and their wives. This explained the serial flashing of camera lights all around the room, as piston-like, the camera men stood up for their shots emulating a large working machine. Suddenly a loud high-pitched scream in Japanese erupted from a Japanese man holding up a yellow flag. The entire group stood up in unison and quietly filed out of the building, climbing into two large busses that roared off into the night. It was a seemingly alien spectacle to me, quite bizarre.

We had a reserved table close to the stage and before the performers returned I had the opportunity to drink in our female guest. She was a German princess, an ash blonde with intensely deep blue eyes, graceful, well-poised and intelligent in her conversation. A stunning and breath-taking image who was in Madrid to develop her divorce from her ultra-rich husband prince while looking after her two young children. Apparently, he owned nearly twenty corporations in Europe and also owned the CN tower in Toronto. My blood pressure was certainly rising and was further enhanced by the re-appearance of the performers on stage.

The onset of the guitars from three players reminded me of the bean farmer outside of Merida and the sudden appearance of the principle female dancer was accompanied by her haughty gaze out at the audience. Her performance was emotionally overwhelming to me, so well coordinated with the guitar rhythms. It was a soul-searing performance that revealed the humanitarian depths of her psychic being, an almost god-like artistic expression of the distance between the higher human and its ape-like origins. I fail to remember what happened during the rest of the evening as I was totally caught up with that performance and her movements, like viewing a revolving, flashing and hypnotizing jewel. The guitar accompaniment blended exquisitively with her movements.

My last night in Spain. Only sensing the artistic design, workmanship and atmosphere of the Alhambra in Granada could have competed with that experience. The following evening I was back in Canada, leaving Archduke Andreas Habsburgo-Lorena at the Madrid airport after thankful fairwells issued by both of us.

He expressed his pleasure at our social and intellectual interaction, commenting that I treated him as an equal, not his usual social interactions with many people in Europe who were awed or subdued knowing of his aristocratic background.

Motorcycle Sagas

Riding a motorcycle on busy, rainy streets amongst self-driven automobile drivers who act like the proverbial rabbit in Alice in Wonderland can be rather exciting….in fact, borderline suicide in large cities for the motorcyclist. Commuting to work in Vancouver, B.C. in rainy, blustery weather conditions requires steel nerves and hyped mental alertness. While on the First Narrows Bridge, in the inner lane and in heavy commuting traffic, fighting blustery winds, a large Cadillac jumped lanes, pulling in front of me suddenly without any warning and causing me to nearly lose control against the opposing heavy traffic.

I noticed a sign in his rear window: I LOVE MY GRANDKIDS! Well, at least he admitted by sign at least that he included others with his self-love, although the familial connection was probably ego-connected, primarily.

I decided to follow him into the city and he led me a merry chase but failed to pull into a underground parking area where I was determined to smash all his lights, punch a hole in his radiator and leave a prominent gouge in his driver's door…..just to feel better about his dangerous and uncaring behavior. After several block changes he found a parking place on the street….for a couple of quarters, no doubt……a cheapskate also and disappeared.

I found a parking place a few yards away for my 'bike, walked over to the Cadillac, read his proclamation once more while holding my thirty-inch solid steel bar in the left sleeve of my leather jacket but was stymied by the flux of pedestrians walking by to their jobs. After walking passed his chariot several times, hoping at least to see him return, my motivation to produce havoc subsided and I, too, left for my office in the Sears Tower. Had he entered an underground parking lot in the vicinity the sheer joy of macerating his Cadillac would have made my day.

Recounting this episode to a friend, a Director of Mental Health, stimulated his account of a motorycle ride the previous summer. Being a semi-professional racer in his former years, he kept an off-on road bike for week end joys. Riding from the North Shore up past Whistler and intending to go to Kamloops for a prominent motorbike jamboree, he enjoyed the curvy, narrow road devoid of traffic, both commercial and not. The mountain scenery before dropping down on to the flatlands is also most pleasant. Breaking out there, following a large curve, he came up on eight Harley-Davidson riders, riding two abreast in neat configuration. They are following a red Mustang which endeavored to pass a medium-sized 'bike in front at every opportunity between the numerous curves, passing at speed over the double line to fade back as the curve approached. This dangerous harassment continued five times then the first couple of Harleys rode up to the Mustang, the leader depressing his right, gauntleted hand at the driver's window visually suggesting that he desist his activity. The Mustang driver apparently rolled down his window and said something, accompanied by a vigorous middle finger. The two Harley's then fell back. At the next straight stretch the second rider roared up to the Mustang, casually reached back into his leather side-case, extracted a long piece of heavy chain and just before the next curve he swung it side-ways across the Mustang windshield, resulting in the windshield shattering completely as the curve was entered.

Not surprisingly, the Mustang driver lost control, drove through the side barrier and flipped upside down, then cascaded in several loops to come to rest at the bottom of the gulch, still upside down. Soon after, the car burst into flame and became a funeral pyre which the Harley drivers watched for a few minutes with my friend with them before moving on to turn north at Cascade Creek. Rod on his Kawasaki turned south towards Kamloops on route 99 with thoughts of Karma echoing through his helmet.

Entering Kamloops, he located the Jamboree field and began inspecting the rows of bikes lined up in neat rows. Among a few 'bikes dating back several decades, he suddenly spied a WW1 camouflaged British Army 'bike that still looked in good condition. A tall, lean and elderly fellow approached him. "You like my motorcycle," he said in a clipped English accent. Rod nodded enthusiastically, saying that he was amazed that such a machine was still operable. " I brought this machine back with me after eventual de-mobilization, returning here two years later to my small ranch in the local area. Many other chaps I volunteered with failed to return and those married left widows and children who returned to England."

So you were in the British Army, asked Rod. "Yes, for several years after the war. I lived in the same barracks with Laurence until he was killed on his 'bike on a narrow, winding lane. "You mean Laurence of Arabia?" Yes, that Laurence. He was a clever chap who designed a speedboat for rescuing downed pilots parachuting over the Channel after we were transferred into the newly-organized RAF from the Army. He also designed the RAF insignia that is still in use. Rod was over-awed by his account and its immediate contact with history. "That is a most interesting story for me.....what sort of a man was he?" The old man studied the ground for a few minutes then spoke. "He was a damned jolly fine chap! But there were a lot like him in the old days."

Rod was still curious, commenting that this old fellow seemed rather elderly for 'bike riding. The old man snorted and waved a finger at Rod. "I'm eighty-five years old and fit as a fiddle. I just finished riding this machine to Vancouver, had to do that as they informed me that they were cancelling my license. I drove in, found the headquarters, pounded on several desks while roaring a few objections. They retreated, retracted their decision and I rode home in contentment. I think that age is as much a state of mind as of accumulated years!

Rod shook hands with him and they shared watching some racing heats before he returned to Vancouver before nightfall. Stopping at that fateful curve to again view the charred remains of the Mustang hotrod and its occupant, the thought once again flashed across his mind: Karma has no time limits and can apply at a moment's notice.

A-Hunting We Will Go

Most boys in Western culture are subjected to the hunting drive originating from their nomadic ancestors, particularly stimulated by growing up in semi-natural environments containing wildlife. Sticks and stones, slings, bows and arrows, spears, nooses and, more recently, the advent of gun-powder and guns, are securely enlaced in the primary historical role of the human male as hunter; an activity he swiftly discovered was effectively transferred to others of his own kind.

The relatively recent advent of the conservation movement, perhaps stimulated by the massive and near annihilation of wild game species (including fishes and birds), rationalized by modern man's attempts to control harvesting through attempts to rationalize stock management protocols reflect questionable effectiveness due to poor understanding of stock dynamics in complex environmental relationships exacerbated by human population growth and parallel landscape and seascape destruction.

Not surprisingly, nomadic hunting cultures are nearly extinct, having been replaced by farming of both plant and animal foods, and the development of village life which has now resulted in huge cities typified by traffic jams, smog, noise and light pollution, and much human death but insufficient to counteract population growth. World-scale wars have been driven by competition for territory and its useable assets, coal, oil, grass, slave labor etc. and now freshwater looms as an additional asset. Large-scale war, killing off hundreds of millions of humans have been compensated by surging population reproduction to maintain continued population growth.

Population growth is fed now by corporate agriculture and its obsessions with poisoning the soil and related organisms (some called "pests") and reducing the economic costs of human labor (jobs) with machines and agricultural genetic manipulations touted (without proof) as increasing yields and biological control. Weakened soil productivity and increased pest resistance are of no corporate interest beyond profit margins driven by GMO technology.

There is much scientific evidence that GMO technology and its haphazard genic transfer protocols have already produced hazards to human and other mammalian healths, documented in hormonal and internal organ disruptions, weakened immune systems, and allergic reactions, the latter most readily seen in young children.

Is it not ironic that chemical corporations whose economic success originated in production of warfare-related poisons such as Asian-Orange defoliant are now using their contents, such as glycosphate to lace their patented seeds, touting weed control as one of the useful outcomes.

Considerable evidence has accumulated to document that such promises of higher production, and better weed control are hollow, jeopardized as such claims are by increased chemical resistance of weed and insect pest species that require even higher concentrations of chemicals. The increased suicide rates of Third World farmers due to poor GMO seed performance is another concern as they cannot save the seed or afford to buy more.

BGH, (bovine growth hormone), another corporate success, although outlawed in more than 70 countries, including Canada, is contained in the milk of American children. The argument that BGH improves the milk production of cows by some 30% is nullified by the reduced production of milk in the overall life of the cow which loses some three years, precipitating its demise to the slaughterhouse for hamburgers. Dairy farmers in the U.S.A. should do their math.

Modern man in industrialized Western countries retains the desire to escape into the woods and fields, often to persist in claiming his native rights to hunt wild game but also to appreciate the fresh air, exercise, communication with Nature, and to pursue the ancient excitement of the chase and kill rituals. His hunting desires are abetted and eased by automatic loading of shot guns, high velocity, automatic firing of rifles, now further powered by 50-caliber rifles capable of piercing three inches of steel.

Psychiatric authorities have suggested that the size of private armament collections, rifles, machine guns etc. might be related to personal concepts of penile size inadequacy although other inadequacies may be involved. The thrill of knocking down crows on fence posts or causing the explosive disintegration of fur and flesh of ground squirrels is hardly associated with hunting animals for food since the local grocery store has remedied the need for it.

One of my co-workers spent most of his managerial employment time on his office computer, calculating powder loads for his various shooting activities and loading his own ammunition. When required to undergo field inspections he always took along some shooting hardware just in case a luckless crow was spotted on a convenient fence post. He accumulated many deer, moose, and elk prizes, than expanded his aspirations to include African game. He came back from Africa proudly carrying the magnificent canine teeth of a hippopotamus. "You shot a female hippo?" Yes, he answered, quite legally, as I paid more than three thousand dollars for the license. I detected a somewhat defensive attitude, particularly after my comment about shooting at barn doors and hippos.

Curiously enough, his son at UBC who graduated in economics had fallen in love there with a beautiful Indian girl who was working on a doctorate in sociology. They married that summer and prepared to move to Central India where she intended to research village life adjacent to a large national park for her dissertation. Their small residence was located on the edge of the park and while Phillip spent his time playing with the young Alsatian dog they had brought with them and reading books, his wife spent most of the day in the adjacent village filling her notebooks with sociological comment which she transferred to her computer at home in the evenings. They became habituated to taking walks along with the dog on an established trail on the edge of the national park after eating. She came home one day with a heavy load of data to process and after eating declined to accompany him on the walk. Phillip and the dog left alone.

They timed their walks so as to arrive home before sunset which in that latitude happens rather suddenly, precipitating total darkness. That day, darkness had fallen but Phillip and the dog were not yet home. About half-an-hour later the dog was scratching at the door, looking for entry. She waited some twenty minutes and after calling out into the darkness, got no reply and phoned the Park manager in her developing panic. He assured her that nothing could be accomplished until the following day at daylight and promised that he would arrive promptly at daylight with two assistants.

Following along the trail they arrived at a well-stomped area of reddened mud and swampy ground, spying one of Phillips hiking boots protruding from the muck. From there, the scene of encounter, the two animal guides traced the tracks of the bull elephant and the dog back into the bush but the elephant was long gone. Apparently, the dog dove into the bush and surprised the bull elephant feeding, harassing it by barking all around it. The elephant became incensed with rage and chased after the dog who ran out of the bush on to the trail where Phillip was standing and he received the elephant's wrath, being stomped to oblivion while the dog then ran home.

This incident registered strongly on me although I hesitated to console Phillip's father, the obsessive shooter of anything alive in his gun sights but wondered if that tragedy changed his hunting habits as I prepared to retire and seek a peaceful life sailing with Karma echoing in my thoughts.

END

Reflections of a Canadian Aquatic Scientist

TABLE OF CONTENTS

THIS ENGLAND, THEN OFF TO HOLLYWOOD

My very early memories in England are hazy and scattered. Perhaps going to school on the first day at the age of five in 1937 is my first clear one, hanging on to the door knob of the school while my mother issued calming and reassuring words. She left when the teacher came to steer me to the classroom. Belmont School, about a fifteen minute walk from home turned out to be quite interesting, mainly because the first things we leaned was to weave raffia place mats, then to learn to make woolen snakes with cotton reels. The next skill was learning how to knit with two needles to make pot-holders and scarfs, the latter taking much time and effort in order to avoid dropped stitches and holes. As I already knew the alphabet and numbers up to twenty, beginning reading and arithmetic were my next challenge. My older sister, Belinda was reading the newspaper before she started school and that motivated me to start reading. Belinda attended a Church of England school and was taught by nuns and became one nun's favorite pupil although in somewhat later years she called her "doubting Thomas" as Belinda had difficulty accepting the usual religious dogma. I was two years younger and was spared that experience but seemingly she developed a better education than did I despite that and breezed into Secondary School eventually with flying colors.

My father was brought up strict Church of England and my mother was Catholic, attending Church schools as a day student. The institution that she attended consisted of both a teaching convent and a monastery. She often wondered in this school for girls why an occasional toilet seat was left up when she went to school on Mondays, until older girls explained the significance. Apparently both of our parents had enough religion and the subject never came up until Belinda, now called Linda, and I became aware of Sunday school as a potential obligation. We asked our parents one day why we didn't go the Sunday School as most of the other kids that we knew seemed to. From parental looks with raised eyebrows we waited expectantly for the answer. Finally our mother broke the silence saying if you want to go, go! But where we chorused. Just pick a place that interests you both and keep me informed, she replied. We set about that task. Linda suggested her school but I said definitely not……all that ivy on the walls and an ancient, creepy look about the place. Across the main thoroughfare intersection from her school was a small hill with a red-brick two story building at the apex, with white windows and a cheery look about it and no ivy. Let's try there, was my brotherly command, and we did on the very next Sunday. The Sunday school rooms were off the main church although we got to visit there during sermons occasionally, and I was impressed. The established routine of coloring pictures of biblical scenes while listening to their accepted meanings proved boring but opportunities to explore the building led to the discovery in the basement of a dumb waiter, large enough to climb into and from which the other kids could haul you up to the third floor and back down again. Now that was the cat's whiskers!

Boys will be boys and Roger and I discovered a fold-up poachers shot gun in our father's private closet in the common hallway. Roger took it out against my consternation and walked with it into the living room. I followed remonstrating and he aimed it at me as I was standing close to the diamond paned windows. A loud bang followed with a rush past my head, resulting in the disappearance of a window pane. We quickly returned the shotgun to its closet storage and found other things to occupy our boored minds. To our surprise, the next day our father lectured us both sternly and took us to the police station to show us the cells. I suspect that our mother had attenuated a more violent paternal reaction by pointing out his carelessness with the weapon. Apparently, a cyclist passing the house at that explosive moment received some pheasant shot in his neck and had to have the lead removed from shallow penetration. The glass pane was replaced promptly and the opportunity afforded by the large next-door house that housed RAF officers probably came in handy. Fortunately, nothing became of this incident beyond prison cell inspection and I avoided any statement that would have described my position during the firing. Also, my father was very occupied with his official duties. When the war started we were surprised occasionally by the sound of explosions but they seem to be always in the distance. We lived in Uxbridge at the end of the Tube and our back garden wall was a six foot high red brick barrier demarking the large RAF Camp on the far side, behind some enormous oak trees. Incidentally, there in the RAF Camp the planning and conduct of the Battle of Britain took place.

English Sundays in the winter were my dreaded times before discovering Sunday School. Until Sunday school was discovered, drizzling rain or intemperate showers would keep me house-bound. Then, unless the weather was atrocious, Linda and I would don our mackintoshes, boots, and rain hats and go off joyfully to the church. One Sunday the rain was intermittent and not too harsh so we prepared to venture outside. Just as we were ready to open the front door, a heavy downpour commenced forcing us to wait. Our mother appeared from the kitchen, and in an unusually-imperious tone told us to stay home as she was tired of boiling hankerchiefs and doctoring our winter colds. About that time the rain stopped completely and we got ready to leave in regained anticipation then the air-raid sirens began wailing as we opened the door. Hah! Your children aren't going anywhere now! We glumly began to shed our outer clothes when a couple of minutes later there were three successive bomb explosions. One bomb completely demolished the block of houses where our two Sunday school friends lived. Had we gone to pick them up we would have been gone too. We had no idea of the damage or specific location of that first bomb until going to school the following morning and surveying the rubble. The other two bombs fell in the RAF camp, one destroying part of the hospital wing. As an eleven-year-old, I spent much of that day thinking about Sunday School and our narrow escape from being blown up with those families. Upon getting home that afternoon from school I announced that I was finished with Sunday School. Why, my mother asked? Because we would have been killed, I said and if God is going to allow that sort of thing and he knows everything, I'm not impressed with his lack of interest despite all that stuff about him knowing every hair on your head and every sparrow hopping in the street. As she then turned to stir a pot on the stove I couldn't see if she was smiling or not but she said no more.

A few weeks later, preparations were made for Linda and I to go north to Lincolnshire, where my father's family and ancestors had lived since the Norman Invasion in 1066 A.D. after first landing on the Isle of Wight to the south. There in Dersingham we stayed six months with our great aunt Mary in her country house with the thatched roof and the living room festooned throughout its periphery with the heads of foxes. She had no electric light but she did have a large sheep dog which she fed by boiling a sheep's head once a week. The entire family had been fox hunters and my Squire grandfather was Master of the Hounds from his estate called Calceby Manor. Grandfather had a large racing stable and actually raced in the Steeplechases. Obviously a very determined racer, he used to sit in a manure pile up to his neck, overnight, to lose weight. He died rather young, about a decade after a serious riding accident involving the rescue of a Lady acquaintance he was courting whose horse bolted during a country ride. He managed to retrieve her from her saddle on to his but lost his own balance in the process, receiving a serious head kick from her mount.

He died when my father was about ten, after marrying my grandmother, a nurse, who assisted him in partial recovery but promptly sold the estate a year before WWI and moved into Louth, buying Greystone Manor which was turned into a private hospital when she died in 1947. My father never recovered from the loss of his father or his initial way of life, having ponies of his own and a personal bridegroom. He was doted on by his father who was also a major in the Lincolnshire Cavalry. My father used to ride around the estate and the farm labourers would doff hats or pull fore-locks if not wearing hats. Although a good academic student, his mother refused to finance him to university….told him to get a job. He joined the Metropolitan Police Force in London, rising rapidly. During the war he was an Aliens Officer, Head of the Uxbridge Police station and chaser after Nazi sympathizers in league with MI-5. I hardly saw him during the war as he would come home to sleep, then leave on his duties. Only on one occasion do I remember him talking to me about his work. It was the event when he arrested the head of the British National Socialist Party, the millionaire steel magnate who was sent off the Wormwood Scrubbs, Osgood Mosely.

In the early summer of 1939, prior to the declaration of war, the family went on holidays to the Isle of Wight when I was seven years old. This is where my ancestors had landed in 1066 A.D. There sitting on the sandy beach and playing, our parents close by in beach chairs, I heard my mother say a few words, "Bill, there's a bobby coming down the beach and I guess he is looking for you." Minutes later, after a short talk and a salute, the bobby left and we children, me, Linda, and Roger, were told that we had to get back to London immediately. War was officially declared the next morning.

The air raids started a couple of years later and became progressively more severe, including buzz-bombs followed by V-2's. This prompted a parental decision that Linda and I should go north to Lincolnshire. When Linda and I arrived at Great Aunt Mary's house, I was disappointed not to see horses in the paddock. She was 84 years-old at that time and told me that the last horse died a year ago in retirement and that she had his hooves filled with lead to use as door stops. Why did you stop riding, I asked? I was thrown into a hedge, she replied. Then why not just get back on and ride, I asked? She looked at me amused, son, I've been riding since the age of five, when a horse can throw me it's time to quit riding. All the stuffed fox heads adorning her living room were trophies that the first person on the scene of the kill gets, along with the bloody brush wiped across one's face! GA Mary rode side-saddle in long skirts and riding boots.

After walking to church on Sunday, she would announce a cross-country walk before going home. Linda and I dutifully followed….. over hill, over dale, through fields, over styles with GA Mary, shorter than I and very slight, thumping her silver-headed cane rhythmically as she strode the miles. We would get home by mid-afternoon, Linda and I thoroughly fatigued, and GA Mary would get busy with a meal.

In the evening, she would give us a hot mug of cocoa and a candle each to take upstairs to bed. Sitting in front of the roaring fire while the cocoa cooled sufficiently enough to drink, I would look up at the fox heads, their glass eyes shimmering against the light from the fire and, after a few days, began to recognize their individuality.

On one occasion, after church, GA Mary announced that she was taking us to the Sandringham Estate owned by the Royal Family, particularly to Saint Mary Magdalene Chapel where they often worshipped. At the chapel I ran ahead and stood in front of the altar. Standing there I became very light-headed and felt waves of vibrations emanating from my shoes, rising up through my body. As they approached, I said that I feel very peculiar and described why. My GA Mary looked down at the red carpet and noted that I was standing on the brass plate commemorating Prince John who had died approximately at my age and was buried in the cemetery outside. Perhaps if you were to stand off that plate you might feel better, she said. I did just that and the vibrations ceased immediately. Many years later I realised that was my first psychic event which was followed several times later in life.

In the summer of 1945, my brother, Roger, and I were invited to go on holiday with friends of my mother, down to Dorset and next to the sea. That was our first real holiday since the war began and we revelled on the hills, accompanying the local milk-maid in her work of milking and delivering milk. Fishing with a hand line on the gravelly beach gave us plump mackerel to take back to the caravan to cook. We had a real gypsy caravan to live in…..and many fond memories. I spotted an adder sunning on the stone wall adjacent to us and he quickly disappeared into a crevasse. We sat out in the back garden of a local pub with refreshing, foaming glasses of cider to keep us busy on VJ Day, my first experience with the effects of alcohol at age thirteen. Our last family holiday had been in the early summer of 1939 when we went down to the Isle of Wight and had to return home the next day as World War Two was then declared.

During the war I had a morning paper route before school. I would arise at 6.30 AM, grab some toast and cycle down to the tobacconist shop to pick up my morning papers, about 50 to deliver. In England, unlike the United States, a paper-boy had to get off his bike, fold the paper neatly and walk up the garden path and posted it in the letter box. V-One bombs, locally called "buzz-bombs", were fairly common and could be heard approaching from their buzz. When the buzz ceased, a few minutes later you would hear the explosion. Once, during a rather heavy period of air-raids during the buzz-bomb days, as I was delivering the paper to a letter-box, the door opened and the lady smiled, took the paper from me and said: "if the bombs come any closer, you may knock on the door and come in for a while!" That's how conditioned Londoners got to the bombing experience.

On one such occasion, as I was pedalling back home to get ready for school. It was still dark and I was stopped by a bobby and chastised for not having my backlight working. I guess the battery had finally given up. I suspect that he was suffering from disciplinary action as he told my father with some relish that he had caught me while doing his morning patrol. I caught hell also from my father! "A policeman's (son's) lot is not an 'appy one! Delivering newspapers early in the morning during bombing raids wasn't commended enough! I did have two exciting things happen during the war. A nearly intact German fighter, a Heinkel I believe, was placed next to our school and the huge swastikas on it were certainly formidable. A Spitfire force-landed in a field next to me. The pilot got out and walked over to me dressed in his heavy wool clothing and boots. Damn, he said and in broken English, for he was a Polish airman, I almost made it back but ran out of fuel. From where we were standing, Northolt Field was visible. That event occurred during the Battle of Britain.

The routine of schooldays during the war were sporadically broken by air raids and I estimate that I accumulated about six months sitting in bomb shelters at school. We had no reading lights in the bomb shelters so other than singing, clapping rhythmically, or playing guessing games such times were boring. Food became rather short even with ration cards and I really missed fruits. We kids used to raid the local Justice of the Peace's orchard for plums and apples, as much for excitement as for nourishment.

One day I had a tantalizing red apple which I took to school and put in my desk. When I lifted the desk lid half-way through the lesson to retrieve a text book I spied the apple and carefully took a single bite. The teacher, a stern Scot with ears like a fox heard the snap, located the source of sound and demanded to know what I was doing. I confessed straightaway and was sent to the headmaster's office to await punishment. There I waited in trepidation, eying the set of Calcutta canes he had in a rack. He was over six feet in height, an artillery army captain from World War I, with a nervous tic that showed one side of his front teeth spasmodically. A few minutes later, he walked in, having talked to my teacher, and had me stand at attention while he carefully selected from his cane collection, taking one after another and swishing them through the air until he found one that he preferred. I thought, maybe I can keep my trousers on, if so, it won't hurt too much. To my surprise I was told to hold out my right hand, palm up and fingers outstretched. There had been some changes in corporeal punishment. He brought that cane down with a mighty swish and it caught me mid-palm, just missing my thumb, then told me to get back to class. My entire hand was numb for the rest of the school day. I couldn't hold a pen or pencil so simply sat there in several classrooms silently thinking that buttock bruises would have been preferred.

I detested that teacher for the next two years and often hoped a bomb would drop on her. At that school, there was a secondary building, of wood, that was located under a large pine tree and the first time that I heard it sing in the wind I was mesmerized by the sound as other large trees were oaks and beeches which sounded quite different and not as musical and poetic to my ear. Little did I know that pine, fir, and gigantic cedar trees would appear later in my life in routine locations.

The general situation in Uxbridge did not change much during the year after the war, some foods were still rationed and people were still reeling from the wartime conditions. Veterans were showing up with one leg, battle scars, and were trying to get back to work. When arrangements were made to emigrate my best friend's mother said…. oh, the rats are leaving the ship, are they? My aunt and uncle living in California had encouraged my parents to leave England in late 1937. My father applied for release from his position in early 1938 but it was refused. Well, he said, I shall submit as many requests as necessary, to which his superior said, we shall keep filing them in the waste-paper basket. You are not going to leave, no paperwork will be processed.

We managed to leave in April, 1947 travelling first to Cardiff, Wales for medical inspections then boarding a freighter going to Texas, the SS. Chirripo, sleighted eventually to load bananas. I enjoyed that ten day trip through the South Atlantic, flying fishes, and all I could eat in the Officers Mess. I would routinely go through the entire breakfast menu and got to know the cooks well. I went through the entire ship, watched the grimy stokers shovel coal into the boilers, in the engine room, putting my hands on the immense but slow moving drive shaft, up on the bridge, in the radio room, and also accompanying the bow watch at night, seeing the phosphorescent wake of large oceanic sharks turning aside from the ship's presence. There were only twelve passengers on the ship so we kids had it to ourselves. That is surely the best way to travel, by freighter. A North Carolinian was on board bringing his wife's mother, the wife being a GI bride. I asked him what North Carolina was like and he generated much excitement in me by describing the mountains as being so high that you had to lie on your back to see their tops.

We landed in the United States after passing through the Gulf of Mexico, to Brownsville, Texas a rather desolate port west of Houston with many dead fish cast up on the muddy banks, probably from ship's bow waves. We took the train from Texas to Los Angeles and the landscape looked very foreign to my English eyes. But I still have a soft spot for Texans, despite their brash and nonchalant behavior. I was also fascinated by their tobacco chewing and spitting accurately into spittoons. The train stopped somewhere, for reason that we knew not, at this small station, probably for water, and we were allowed to alight for a few minutes. During that time, an old and grizzled Texan gave us a big bag of oranges for the train ride. After reaching Los Angeles that morning, aunt and uncle were waiting for us in the large railway station and invited us for breakfast in the local restaurant. Upon hearing that the egg ration, if you could get it, was one egg a month, my uncle lost his appetite.

They very generously had a house for us located on the edge of the Los Angeles River, under the Hollywood Hills, with a large walnut grove on one side. Three major studios were within walking distance and the front garden was dominated by large cacti and other succulents. The Hollywood hills were right above us and a streetcar went from North Hollywood to downtown. We used to go to films at the Grauman's Chinese theater near Hollywood and Vine after a ten minute ride on that streetcar, settling down in luxurious plush seats. After such a significant change of scenery, climate, and culture these changes proved challenging for all of the family, especially 102 degrees of heat on Xmas day.

Our block on Aqua Vista Street proved to be an interesting area for we had three film directors there, and the fellow who wrote the book "Twelve O'clock High" lived half-way down the block. He was a B-17 navigator who survived the 50% mortality of those air crews pounding Reich industrial targets, and moved on when the film was made. One art director who was trained initially as an electrical engineer at MIT and his wife, a Smiths College graduate lived several houses away. We knew that they had difficulty having a child then she started taking male hormones, grew a moustache, and got pregnant. Everyone waited expectantly for the result as the husband was a very short, slight man and she was physically formidable and tall, a Brunhilda. That spring they had breakfast on their adjacent patio with the boy in his playpen on the lawn. The boy never made a sound all summer and the general feeling was that he was incapable of speech. People walking down the street to take the streetcar began talking to him and within a few weeks he was gabbling, starting the conversation himself as people approached. Apparently, his parents never talked to him during the critical period of language formation. Another director who remained unknown to us had a negro valet, good-looking and with a rich Paul Robeson voice. He would sing on his way to the streetcar and served dinner only in pink tights, I was told.

High school days for me were quite boring. I was placed a year behind my chronological age with the reasoning that I had no knowledge of American history. Well, at least from the American point of view! Actually, I was significantly ahead of my classmates in math, English, including spelling and writing essays, and science although I had spent several months in air-raid shelters during one school year. As an excellent speller, I became rather distraught when the results of my first spelling test came back with a 70% grade. I then realised that American spelling was different and that I had to submit to it. Classmate boys ragged me constantly about my clipped English accent which they liked to imitate. In Hollywood I bumped into stars on many occasions. Most were quite noticeable despite attempts to look disguised and some were easily spotted from their stage postures in public, life being but a stage to them.

At school, gym coaches took on the obligation of teaching me sports. Do you play basketball? Of course not, that is a girl's game in England. How about football? I play soccer, primarily, as inside right. No, we mean football, we'll show you how to play it. When the guy with the football approaches you tag him. I tagged the first such player with a flying tackle that knocked him to the ground, gasping for breath. Both teams stood around the casualty in a ring looking agitated while I looked on nonchalantly. The coach came up and was told what happened from a chorus of complaining voices. Why did you do that, he said. Well, you told me to tag the player carrying the ball, so I did! By tag I meant to touch him on the hips not throw a rugby tackle at him was his exasperated reply!

The next opportunity occurred during baseball season, a game which we called rounders, a leisurely played girl's game in England with little contact and a rubber ball. I was instructed to wear a large, unwieldy leather glove with which to catch the ball. Gamely I tried but finally threw down the glove to use my bare hands. Coach cautioned me, you may damage your hands without a glove, son. Sir, I played cricket without gloves except when batting I wore knuckle gloves, see my two bent little fingers? That resulted from learning to catch a cricket ball which is much harder that your baseball. I continued to play baseball without a glove much to everyone's consternation.

Another parochial behavior surprisingly concerned a history teacher who stopped me one day on the stairs, asking me if my white sweater with the blue and red stripes outlining the vee was my old school sweater. If it is, he said, you should not wear it to this school. Was it a concern for disloyalty? I assured him that it was just an ordinary sweater that I had brought from England. He left me with some reassurance. During that period, the MacArthy hearings and loyalty oath demands of university professors and many in the film business were ongoing. I suspect that a second rate actor who headed the Actors Guild and became a dedicated activist for that phony MacArthy was selected to become the President a few years later, based on his aquisitive behavior that led him first to the Governership of California. Before that history, I remember during Nixon's run for that position, a grade school teacher being interviewed on the main street of Redlands, his former home town, for her comment on Nixon. She revealed that she had taught both Nixon boys in the second and third grades and commented that his brother was an average kid but Richard was a bully, liar, and a cheat. That episode seemed to bring sidewalk media enquiries to a close in America.

My social development with girls was much retarded due to my background in English schools. However, my calmness and good manners really floored several girls in my classes and I often got goo-goo eyes shone at me. I was very shy around girls and a little terrified of them so didn't go to the graduation dance. The only dance

I knew was the waltz! My teachers were very supportive in general perhaps motivated by my excellent grades. One teacher of biology I took great exception to although the girls practically swooned over him. He was about thirty-five and good-looking, in fact, a pretty boy. When I found out that he went to the basketball team home games in his class-A marine uniform as a Reserve captain I was rather disgusted and I earned a C grade in biology among all my A's. A number of my classmates were sons and daughters of Hollywood stars, therefore social stars in their own imagined right.

I read books profusely, all those of Aldous Huxley, for example. There was a sizable British element in Hollywood and I realised that the longer they were from Britain, the more outrageous became their accents. My father played cricket at the Hollywood Cricket Club and I met Sir Aubrey Smith, the club president on Sundays at games play in Griffith Park. He would dodder about on his cane congenially interacting with people. In later years I read The Loved One, a short farcical novel about Brits in Hollywood with a second interest with the Forest Lawn cemetery, written by Evelyn Waugh. It was very true to life as I knew it in Hollywood and the film made from it in black and white in 1965 was fought over for roles by the Brits there and included several very talented American comedic actors, including Jonathon Winters, Rod Steiger, Milton Berle, Dana Andrews, and Robert Morley and several others. Incidentally, the screen play was written by Christopher Isherwood, a pal of Aldous Huxley. Anyone who was a somebody in Southern California was buried in Forest Lawn, including my generous aunt and uncle.

I joined an Explorer Scout group and we played redskin, making our own moccasins, hunting knives, and beadwork. Outings were into the mountains where we would dogtrot for ten or more miles into the interior and camp next to a mountain stream often filled with Golden trout. As my last year of high school drew near to a close and I was working on Saturdays at a drug-store, across the street I noticed a small office where shares were being sold to build a proposed commuter system suspended over the Los Angeles River from the

San Fernando Valley to downtown. What a splendid idea, I thought. Several months later, as the Korean War was getting out of hand in 1951, a notice went up stating that the project was terminated due to the lack of steel availability and money was refunded. Years later and after the proliferation of commuter highways and massive real estate development particularly in the San Fernando Valley, it was revealed that an oil billionaire from Pasadena had bought the company and provided the refund.

The San Fernando Valley was essentially a shrub desert with one gas station in Van Nuys at that time. Several of we teen aviation enthusiasts built motorized free-flight aeroplanes and launched them in the San Fernando Valley, chasing them across the scrub lands in Model A's when they were caught in thermals. The Los Angeles River, used to be a biological paradise where I spent much time exploring, full of crayfish, snakes, red-wing blackbirds, and turtles. After the second year of the Korean War, the river was engineered into a concrete flood channel used primarily for filming police car chases of drug dealers and other criminals, as if such filmed action was substitute entertainment for street reality.

The U. S. Congress began seriously debating how to re-activate a draft law which entailed withdrawing university students to reinforce male youth numbers devoid of such opportunity through financial hardship or low academic motivation. The initial plan was to extract 50% of the freshman class at the end of the academic year and successively lower percentages in future year classes. Hence, a student could end up facing a Chinese bayonet charge following a bad grade. A perceptible axe over one's head certainly cheapened the idea of an exploratory and intellectual academic experience for eighteen year-olds. Although not an American citizen, therefore not legally subject to the draft, and without sufficient financial support for university anyway, I felt obliged to enlist and get it over with as a future citizen. In the USAF I went on a four year enlistment followed by the G.I. Bill.

It was not until several years later that I discovered two ancestors who were in North America some three hundred years earlier. The first

John Mason (1536-1635) born before the reign of Henry Eighth in Kings Lynn, a short distance from Dersingham where Linda and I had spent six months with GA Mary. He was a navy officer who claimed the Hebrides for the Crown and governed Newfoundland for some time (1615-1621) and died at age 99. The next John Mason (1600-1672) was born in the reign of Elizabeth I in Dersingham. He became an army major and emigrated to New England in 1632 as a religionist. That was some twelve years after the Mayflower landed in Virginia. He headed the militia for the Massachusetts colony, became General, conducted the Pequod War and wrote a book about his exploits. Later he became Deputy Governor of the new state of Connecticut. There is a statue of him in Boston. So my bloodline was in North America several centuries before most Americans of European origin.

STRATEGIC AIR COMMAND BOMBER EXPERIENCES

Basic training was in Texas and included a battery of exams which I scored maximum on, including cooking, and learned to march, left foot on the downbeat. I was then selected for electronic communications school and sent to Mississippi to communication school, radio operations etc. We went to school six days a week, twelve hours a day for nearly a year. The classes were held ina large aircraft hangar also containing the largest and hungriest mosquitoes I have ever met. During intermissions, we vacated the hangar while jeeps drove through to fog the interior with dense DDT spray. The mosquitoes were back inside within 20 minutes, concentrating on their feeding.

I volunteered for aviation training in bombers and ended up on a B-29 air crew as a radio operator in San Antonio. From there we went to SAC survival training in the High Sierras. That was an interesting experience. It involved hiking through some 110 miles of high Sierra mountains with nothing to eat except "honey bars" which were compressed slabs cut up by band-saw which could only derive sustenance by sucking on them for some time. We also caught frogs and captured a porcupine in a hollow log which several of the air crew clubbed to death when it decided to make a run for it. I volunteered to cook it, boiling it in creek water with some six rinses but the creosote odor was still there so I watched the others wolf it down.

During that trek, we were hunted by enemy units who obviously delighted in their work. Of several air crews involved, two crew-members were captured, one a bombardier and the other a flight engineer. The latter had been recently married. Standing at attention before the bird colonel in charge, he became irate when the colonel took his wallet and looked through it, finding a snap of his wife. Who is this slut, he intoned as the young engineer leaped across the desk and gave the interrogator a healthy fist in the mouth. For that action he was stripped naked and staked outside all night as the Apaches did to their enemies. The nights were very cold at altitude. The bombardier gave a brilliant show during interrogation. He had a degree in psychology and was considered somewhat wacko by his peers. However, at graduation, the colonel, who was in charge of interrogation of German prisoners in Europe loquaciously described his efforts to loosen the lieutenants tongue, lauding his resistance as the most brilliant psychological defense he had ever come across. The rest of us sniggered.

We then went into Eagle Squadron training in Kansas, then back to Texas for target bombing practice before getting orders to ship out to Kadena AFB on Okinawa. From there, we flew a complete combat tour to Korea. Thirteen has always been an unlucky number in Western culture and has survived in modern times. My thirteenth bombing mission over North Korea in B-29's was no exception. Routine bombing raids on industrial and marshalling yards in the Sinanju area began with daylight raids. Raids were switched to hours of darkness due to effective attacks from Mig 15's which were later trounced by U.S. fighter coverage. F3D jet fighters from Marine Corps squadrons stationed on aircraft carriers provided great coverage for the B-29's as night fighting became more technically advanced and Mig pilots soon learned to scram from our bombing target areas or go down in flames.

In the Sinanju area once again, we released our ten ton bomb load on a rail marshalling area, the air full of flack and ground searchlights. We turned off the target and raced south preparing for home base when number three engine decided to malfunction. Routine attempts to feather the engine failed and the large blades flattened out causing the engine to wind up. An uncontrollable engine fire started as the engine began disintegrating and the navigator was pressed to supply potential landing sites in this emergency. Two possibilities were identified, proceed south either to ditch over the Southern Yalu Sea or possibly gain the thirty-eighth Parallel for an emergency landing. As it was February 27 and the Yalu Sea was near freezing with hostile coastal military forces, the aircraft commander opted for an emergency landing south of the 8th Parallel.

The engine fire had spread extensively with flames exceeding the tail of the aircraft. Soon electricity circuits failed and cabin lights went out. As radio operator, my position was on the right side of the upper forward turret with the navigator on the left side. As the winding propeller had the potential of disintegrating or burning off its axle and coming through the fuselage to my position I was advised to come forward. I sent off an emergency message in code to Tokyo before coming around the upper forward turret and sitting on the nose-wheel well door. I held my flashlight on the engineer's instrument panel and got the navigator to pass up my chest-pack parachute in case a bail-out was required. Miraculously, the 38th Parallel was reached and we attempted to land at K-13, an advanced fighter strip just south. The downwind leg was accomplished and base emergency services prepared to deal with potential explosion.

At some 2000 feet of altitude and turning onto the final approach, difficulty in controlling the plane led the pilot to call for bailout and he opened the bomb doors with the landing gear down. The bombardier leaped up from his nose position as I lifted the nose wheel door and he slid out ahead of me. Climbing down into the opening I turned to the engineer, shouting "let's get out" but he made no moves, calmly scanning his instruments from my flashlight beam….apparently mentally adrift. The co-pilot then shook him to no avail and followed me down the well with his feet on my shoulders. Falling into the darkness was followed by looking up as I pulled my ripcord. The black silhouette of the bomber passed above me at midnight. Looking down, nothing but blackness met my eyes, no lights or other reference. I hit the ground heavily, onto my back on a frozen rice paddy, unable to move. I had drifted ground-ward facing the wind with no visual orientation or any possibility of preparing for a landing.

Laying there on the frozen ground I soon heard sibilant whispering in Korean some distance away, were they hostiles? They didn't approach me but continued their muttering. As I had been instrumental in suggesting that we not bother to shoulder our Colt 45's during missions, I became rather chagrined at my successful suggestion. All the revolvers were placed in an ammo box next to the generator near the rear escape hatch. Wearing a parachute harness exerted much pressure on one's arm pit from the shouldered revolver.

After an unknown time period, probably some 15 or so minutes later, I spotted bouncing headlights coming across the frozen paddies towards me. A jeep pulled up next to me and the driver got out. Can you get up, son, he said in a gruff voice. I answered, "perhaps with some help, my legs feel numb." He reached down and picked me up like a doll and placed me on the jeep seat. "We must go to the crash site, then I'll take you to the hospital. What do you want to do with your parachute?" "Leave it here, those farmers can use it." I could see them now, illuminated by the headlights of the jeep and I wanted to reward them. Bumping across the frozen paddies, we arrived at the crash site. Only the tail was recognizable, the rest was ashes. There in the ashes was a headless form with both hands now folded over its chest. I recognized the red-stoned signet ring of our flight engineer and identified him then we proceeded to the hospital. My rescuer was a major, a catholic priest from the Notre Dame football team.

At the hospital I was re-united with the four gunners who, with the radar navigator had bailed out through the back hatch. Three men failed to survive, the pilot, engineer, and the navigator. The two former went down with the plane and the navigator left through the forward bomb bay but left too late, just before impact. Had I remained in my regular position which called for me to exit that way, perhaps I could have stimulated the navigator to follow me quickly. All three casualties were married, the engineer with two children and the navigator with three, his wife had her fourth child several weeks later. He was a faithful Catholic, a petroleum engineer clawed back into active service by his reserve status as were both pilots. No sleep for me that night despite a handful of tranquilizers.

Prior to this bailout event we had several memorable experiences. On Christmas Eve the Operations major wielded his baton, pointing at the map of Korea…..Sinanju again, part of a two wing strike that also included the dam on the Yalu River at the Chinese border. Groans followed. Crews started to pre-flight their personal aircraft while bomb-loading crews began filling both bomb bays with 10 tons of 500 pounders on the racks. A briefing recall was heard. We discovered that Pentagonic gnomes had made last minute changes in target priorities for us to the Uigi-Uigi Mig field near Manchuria. The heavily-laden bombers labored off the Kadena runway on Ryakus Island as dusk approached. I used to sit up in the forward tunnel looking out ahead through the astrodome. Low cloud cover was thick and leaden, like a metallic barrier which we slowly rose through. Above this cloud cover, one could mentally walk on it, prompting the tail-gunner, alone in the tail, to exclaim on the intercom that he could see Jesus in the clouds.

Darkness grew as the Korean shoreline came into view. Approaching the target area at the IP (Initial Point) for the bomb run, searchlights began to flick on….they knew our intentions. Climbing up into the tunnel and looking forward through the astrodome, a dense wall of flack appeared, punctuated with myriad searchlights. Bomb bay doors flew open as several search lights fixed on our plane and my position next to the front doors was lighted sufficiently enough to read a newspaper…….if one was so inclined! There, hanging in space like a transfixed moth and seemingly suspended in time, bombs were released. By door closure time, massive explosions erupted below.

Turning off target, we sped south assisted by the low jet stream which had held us at 91 mph groundspeed over the target.

The crew was reminded of Christmas Eve as the co-pilot from Sacramento sang Ave Maria over the intercom like a cherub-faced choir boy. Landing on Okinawa at Kadena AFB several hours later, the routine involved intelligence de-briefing and mugs of brandy-laced coffee. The Wing suffered no casualties and no Migs were encountered no doubt due to the heavy artillery fire between 20 and 25 thousand feet. Seven more missions and this crew could be rotated back to the States. Meanwhile, a hot shower and bed to ready for the next mission.

A severe cyclone was approaching Okinawa from the north east one day and we prepared to keep our B-29 from being blown away. This was accomplished by extra tie-downs and riding out the cyclone all night with all four engines approaching one-third throttle. For several hours we flew on the concrete with the main landing gear periodically raising on the struts. That late afternoon the sky in the east turned almost pea-green with yellow streaks, quite eerie and foreboding, probably reflecting huge sandstorms arising across Chinese desert areas.

Within a week of our aircraft loss from mechanical problem which were due also to unsuccessful feathering of number three engine, enlisted crew members were assigned to a new crew with new officers, obviously the bottom of the barrel. We never saw our old officers again perhaps due to some pseudo-psychological reasons emanating from higher up….like avoiding the already high level of comraderie and possibly further elevation. The new pilot, a captain, was a Georgia cracker and I named his co-pilot McCormick, the Grim Reaper. On two occasions when the Reaper was allowed to land the B-29, he severely scraped the tail skid. I was not amused. On our first orientation flight around the Kadena area of southern Okinawa, the number three engine failed …….I seriously thought of manually activating the forward bomb bay doors and diving out but that idea was interrupted by the Georgian drawling out "y'all stay calm" on the intercom as he successfully feathered that engine and we returned to base.

My flying confidence improved somewhat until on a combat mission the new flight engineer forgot to close the engine cowl flaps on take-off, leaving them open 15 degrees which greatly increased our drag coefficient. On take-off, I used to jump up into the tunnel which ran above the two bomb bays and connected the forward and rear compartments, and look view forward through the astrodome. In this instance, I could see that the large array of runway lights at strip end were steadily nearing although the loaded plane was not showing any main gear lift properties yet. Finally we staggered off the runway, the main gear missing the lights by a few feet as we fanned across an adjacent native village. Looking back I could see the roof materials whirling around in great clouds which must have ventilated those houses emphatically.

The new crew was given the opportunity to ferry a B-29 to Tokyo, one that needed weight and balance (CG) analysis. We stayed two days in Tokyo in stifling heat although in April. Walking down the Ginza, in full medaled uniform, I was stopped by an elderly man who bowed politely and I returned his bow. What plane you fly he said in poor English. I replied a B-29. His response struck me as rather peculiar, perhaps melodramatic, as his face became a horrible sight as he leaned backwards with his hands in the air. Later on, in remembrance of this encounter, I realised that he may have lost all of his family in the massive fire bombings of Tokyo, or in one of the two nuclear blasts that terminated WW2 in the Pacific Theatre, Nagasaki or Hiroshima. Eventually I came to a sombre conclusion about massive bombing of civilian populations, with or without nuclear weapons…..recalling my childhood experiences during the bombing of London.

We returned to the airfield, prepped the aircraft for return to Okinawa and had more than two hours before take-off time. It was blisteringly hot and my tail gunner and I decided to visit the PX for a chocolate malt. Ground crew told us to take the No. 9 bus which would take us to the PX in ten minutes. We caught the same bus back about 20 minutes before take-off time but a short distance down the road paralleling the flight line the negro driver turned off onto a side road, stopped further on and turned off the engine. Why have you stopped, I asked. It's my routine, he said. I must stop here for 20 minutes before going back to the main road. No amount of explanation detailing the importance of our take-off time would sway him. I wished for my Colt 45 to create an effective argument. Finally he started the bus and returned to the main road. As we trundled down it towards flight operations I noticed two Air Police jeeps, fully manned speeding in the other direction. At the Operations gate we hurriedly alit and jogged towards our plane with its engines ticking over. A figure in a summer flight uniform approached us from the plane. I saluted with no response and noticed his glazed eyes and sweat-drenched flight suit. He staggered on back to Flight Operations. At the plane, the Georgian pilot, also sweat-drenched, climbed down the nose-wheel ladder. "Where you boys bin?" I quickly described our predicament but to no avail. "Yo asses is grass" was his reply.

His comment seemed ambiguous and colloquial. The return trip to Kadina AFB was made in total silence. There we two were told to report to his quarters in Class A uniforms the next morning. When I undertook to quietly and logically explain the tardiness it totally escaped him and he threatened a court marshal but finally calmed down giving us the excuse that he was due for rotation back stateside within a month and that proceedings would take much longer. The abject colonel was the assistant Wing Commander who had planned a joyous trip to Tokyo and planned to ride back with us. I later enjoyed imagining that this colonel had steadily chewed our pilot's rump in the cockpit in sweltering heat, possibly while suffering from a roaring hangover.

From that narrow escape, I realised that my personal rejection to potential appointment to the Air Academy at Colorado Springs made on Okinawa by several flight officers had intuitive value. Logical thought processes in the military mind can be overwhelmed and compensated by protocol and rank power expression rather than by logic and justice considerations. Completing my combat tour I returned to California for two weeks leave and was assigned to a combat Wing of B-50's at Castle Field, Merced, California. There I joined a heavily-ranked air crew of majors and captains, technical and master sergeants……all spot promoted. None of them had seen any combat. My position which now included electronic defence was some five feet from an A-bomb which stared at me malevolently through the front bomb bay door. I was sent to Texas for in-flight electronics evaluation for three days of flights over radar sites and written testing.

Two weeks after returning to Castle Field I was summons into the office of the Wing Electronics officer, a major. Had I flunked? He congratulated me on my performance stating that my results were the highest ever recorded in the Wing. Relieved and chirping, I asked if that meant a promotion. Sadly no, the Wing Commander has given all the available promotions to the ground crews. The two master sergeants, his assistants, looked away with sheepish faces. So I stayed a three-striper although I had made that rank in eighteen months of service and was now half-way through my third year and had undergone rigorous electronics training when not actually flying. That Wing was eventually scheduled to transition into B-47's and that electronics major was unfortunately blown away in a fiery B-47 explosion at high altitude over Sacramento.

I was involved in a major defense operation of the West Coast while in B-50's. Concern emanating from SAC HQ at Offut, Nebraska that the Soviet TU-4's stationed in the Russian sub-Arctic could allow a massive assault and this possibility was encouraged in Sac by pyromanic fears. This aircraft was possibly copied after the B-29 but carried a bigger bomb load and had superior engines. Our Wing was instructed to fly seaward then to return to "nuclear bomb" the major cities on the West coast. Several jet fighter squadrons would intercept us and "shoot us down". Gun camera film from both bombers and fighters would be evaluated to decide interception performance.

The results came back several weeks later but were not reported in the media. Bomber gun crews "shot down" every F-86 and we remained unscathed. Because our flight speeds (about 250 knots) forced the jet fighters to slow down and employ dive flaps, so before sighting their gun cameras they were blown out of the sky. Had the Russians made a real attempt, all major cities on the West Coast would have been incinerated. Though I was not an American citizen until 1954 I had a Top Secret Security clearance while flying next to atom bombs.

After serving a year in B-50's, my Wing began phasing into B-47's and I volunteered assignment to a RB36H Wing at Travis AFB, half-way between San Francisco and Sacramento. On that squadron lead crew I remained a three-striper surrounded by majors, captains, technical and master sergeants for the rest of my enlistment. Our job was to snoop about electronically and photographically around national perimeters without getting caught. The field grade officers were particularly boring and full of self-importance. One of them , a major, had a M.A. from Harvard in literature. He would come to my position where I was usually reading but if not, he would pick up my book and peruse it without comment. He never made any comment on my reading interests, philosophy, politics, or history, despite my hope that he would say something. Obviously he was being very careful.....or intellectually disinclined. We did make an eventful trip to Europe via Green land and refueling, followed by electronic nuclear bombing of the major cities in Northern Europe. On the return trip, we flew below 500 feet to escape radar detection, giving me a well-remembered view of the Arctic pack ice in all its glory, including fearful-looking up-thrusted pinnacles capable of tearing any aircraft to pieces.

A short time before my four-year enlistment was up in April, 1955, amid the swirling cigar smoke in SAC HQ, the Chinese were interpreted as getting too uppity, so General LeMay decided to send our Wing on a ninety day TDY (Temporary Duty) assignment to Guam. Quickly checking the calendar I discovered that I was three days short so didn't have to go. Having been to Guam previously, an island rock covered with gooney birds and patrolled by tiger sharks, I was not interested but I waited. Some five weeks before departure, the Wing Operations officer called me on the phone (by my first name), would

I come into his office. Apparently, he had full intentions of shuffling my personnel papers to allow the three day extension which I would have to sign. I declined to do so much to the major's dismay and his attempts to describe the Rock as a Paradise. Have you ever been to Guam, Major, I asked him. His negative reply was bolstered by the fact that he had never been out of the U.S.A. It's only three days! Yes, major but I have more important plans of my own. I have served this Air Force to the best of my ability, performed with a superior record and intend to depart at the termination of my contract. He was rather non-plussed and mystified at my response. Had there been a war on I would not have hesitated even if the conditions of conflict were considered transparent and or due to political power play.

The military response came within a week. Taken off flight status and losing my meagre supplemental pay packet, I was sent to work loading planes for the upcoming trip. As I left the crew, the aircraft-commander, a major who before becoming re-activated worked in Miami as a drapery salesman, sneeringly told me that I would fail in civilian life and be back in the USAF. My response was to inform him that possibly I would return to military duty but as a full-colonel in psychiatry, we might meet again.

Reporting to my new job, the obliging loading sergeant smiled and gave me a small electric fork lift which was fun to drive. Meanwhile, there was a frantic search to find my replacement as the entire plane would be grounded otherwise. Several weeks later, a week before departure for Guam, a senior technical sergeant from Wright Patterson Field where much experimental work was done, volunteered to replace me, probably lured with an imminent promotion. A week following mass departure orders came down (up?) from Gen. LeMay to fly the few remaining RB36H's to General Dynamics at Fort Worth for stripping and refitting for high altitude work. A test-flight crew was gathered together, consisting of other short time enlisted and officered men and I was asked to join them in communication systems testing and evaluation.

These flights were inoperable without my skills and my inclination to refuse this opportunity was blunted by the goodies. Per diem expenses were all paid, including hotels, restaurant meals etc. and we spent much time in night clubs and bowling alleys waiting to accept back improved planes, resulting in a series of escapades. One evening, while doing the night clubs in Dallas, I met a gorgeous-looking blonde who enlightened me on the Fort Worth technique of the male clutching both female buttocks with both hands. Looking up in to my widening eyes, she cooed "ah'd rather dance than eat 'ceptin when ah'm hongry."

Our trips to General Dynamics were prolonged on several occasions due to incompetent corporation technicians. Their aviation electronic technicians provided me the opportunity to gleefully identify glitches, giving us more days before accepting the plane back. I noticed that these fellows were earning five times my pitiful pay check, so the modification contracts were very lucrative for General Dynamics. However, we were given royal flight lunches, including fresh pies when we had accepted a plane.

Once, while cranking over the engines, there was a massive release of aviation gas cascading on to the flight pad. We bailed out with alacrity. Our routine testing included ascending to 30 thousand feet, nose up into a power-on stall, the plane shaking convulsively, then recovering in a steep power dive to regain control. On return trips to California, the chief flight engineer would jockey the throttles over Bakersfield to alert his wife.....rattling all the windows in town. I left Travis AFB and my military adventures without looking back (until now). I headed back to Laguna Beach in Southern California for some quiet time, beaching and playing bongos before starting university.

UNDERGRADUATE SUMMER JOBS IN BIOLOGY

I began biological studies with general zoology although history and political science were my main interests initially. Our neighbors had two sons in the diplomatic service, one as Ambassador to Brazil and the other as Director of the Foreign Services School in Washington, D.C. Despite their assurance that I was welcome to enter into diplomatic service I realised that some 29 years of my 30 year service would be spent in foreign locations, surely not London, Paris, Stockholm, Berlin, or Naples. However, from California I went to a Model United Nations exercise held at Oregon State that year. I headed an undergraduate group to attend the Model United Nations convention held that year in Corvallis. My team was assigned Indonesia and the diplomatic scuffles ongoing relating to the fate of New Guinea. Transfixed by the greenery, coolness, impressive campus landscaping, and smaller, less factory-orientated teaching, I transferred up to Oregon State for my second year, to major in Zoology and Fisheries Science. I obtained two summer jobs with the U.S. Dept. of Interior (USDI) at the Hydraulics Laboratory at Bonneville Dam on the Columbia River as a designated student-trainee.

The hydraulics laboratory at Bonneville Dam was constructed to investigate the fish passage performance of engineered design applicable to sockeye salmon. This facility located adjacent to the fish ladder on the Washington side of the river was designed to allow collection of subject sockeye to be timed through a miniature fish ladder. Upon reaching the final pool, the individual fish either continued to return to the main fish ladder or was subjected to a hydraulic drop back to the initial elevation to start its climb again. Most fish bulked the last upstream pool, anticipating the hydraulic drop after a few cycles through the system. However, one individual sockeye gamely proceeded to cooperate for more than 24 hours, racking up an accumulated climb of several hundred feet.

I watched this fish closely, noting that a bacterial disease appeared on its scalp which gradually expanded during its altitude feat. This disease known scientifically as Columnaris effectively affects sockeye salmon migrating upstream at water temperatures exceeding 65 deg. Fahr. and may cause significant mortality. The team of fishery biologists at the laboratory were much elated by this performance and sent the results to Washington, D.C. where much hoopla was generated by senior fishery engineer bureaucrats who, undoubtedly, envisioned no vertical limitations to the height of future dams!

While at Bonneville Dam, I met the biologist working for the Bonneville Power Administration and the Pacific Gas and Electric Corporation. He was a canny Scot who played the bagpipes who shook hands with me and announced that I should learn to play the pipes as I "had bagpipe hands." He was an innovative biologist, having developed a method of aging sturgeon from cross-sections of their pectoral fins, counting the annular rings as in trees. Additionally and of more potential value, he cleverly developed a method for gauging the effects on sea-ward migrating salmon smolts captured in the power turbines. Putting individual smolts into small plastic bags injected with oxygen and supplemental capsules which when wetted dissolved to produce helium. These capsules were developed to drive moles out of their tunnels.

Dropping the encased smolt into the turbine intake, the inflated sac then floated out below the dam and was captured by assistants in the downstream flow. Recovery of these fish after transition through the turbine system with its wide range of water pressures allowed examination for ruptured airbladders, physical bruising, and loss of equilibrium which would invite easy predation from the population of large squawfish (Pteichochilus oregonensis) that resided below the outfall from the power dam located on the Oregon side of the river.

Needless to say, his results were very revealing, common rupture of the swim bladder and disorientation and the downstream presence of excited squawfish busily consuming the victims. This biologist should have received a conservation medal for his innovative and decisive work but was instructed from Portland to just send in the daily water temperatures to the office. When the State of Oregon planned to construct a power dam across the Deschutes River upstream from Bonneville Dam, his volunteering to apply his smolt mortality method was declined. The Deschutes River had a substantial run of summer steelhead and, some years earlier, a former Governor of Nevada caught the largest steelhead there on record, over 28 pounds, on a dry fly in

1946. The resulting PG&E dam there saw the steelhead balking at the fish ladder and resulted in their capture by dip net and transport by truck around the dam. To my knowledge, the potential genetic selection of survivors to spawn has not been investigated, nor has the dam impact on native steelhead been documented. A hatchery was constructed to solve any problems.

In my second summer job at Bonneville Dam I was employed in a sonic tracking project applied primarily to adult chinook salmon above the dam. The procedure was to tag captured chinook in the back with a cylindrical sonic tag then releasing them in the fore-bay above the dam. Sonic signals captured on a chase boat allowed construction of tracking patterns. I was taken out on the river below the spillway dam on my second day by the biologist in charge who eventually decided to study whales. Water volume over the spillway dam was most impressive. It was June with the onset of peaking flow from snow melt in the headwater mountains. From a small aluminum boat with maximum throttle I was quite impressed.

Suddenly I noticed a very large chinook passing close to the boat, its head severely bashed and with the left eye dangling from its socket. This giant chinook was obviously stunned from a powerful drive up to the spillway concrete apron and been pounded there in its effort to move upstream. Why didn't that fish use the fish ladder, I asked the biologist. His reply: consider the relative flows in the fish way with those here, he replied. Large chinook probably prefer the larger flows here and so may become mortalities. Doesn't this circumstance suggest an artificial selection process for large chinook which were called "June hogs" by biologists? Many such fish proceed as far upstream as the Snake River in Idaho. I began to doubt whether or not the salmon runs in the Columbia River would last much longer as more dams were being planned. That year was 1958.

Historically, efforts to compensate for the substantial decay and near destruction of salmon runs have involved proliferation of hatcheries throughout Oregon and Washington states. They have been of dubious success. My concern for adequate upstream and downstream passage of salmondid fishes consequently led to my recognition of such difficulties also applying to the Columbia River sturgeon (Acipenser transmontanus)……transmontanus no more. I recovered small dead sturgeon on the fish ladder racks at Bonneville which showed that they originated from reproduction in upstream areas. The largest sturgeon captured in the river (over 1503 pounds) was taken in Idaho waters in 1898. The question remains, if adult sturgeon cannot pass upstream in fishways designed for Detroit-sized salmon, and they remain isolated between the proliferated dams, sub-population isolation may be inducing undesirable genetic effects in this stock which once roamed freely from the sea to Idaho.

While working at Bonneville Dam, I also discovered the vast collection system located in the spill way dam to assist in the enumeration of downstream migration of juvenile salmon to the sea. Responsibility for its operation and data-collection was given to the most junior federal biologist. The senior biologists there were completely engrossed in getting adult fish passed the dam! Downstream counts of salmon smolts to sea are highly significant to concerns for stock management: exploitation rates in the various fisheries, magnitude of escapements, and other potentially negative factors affecting production such as rising water temperatures and introduction of alien predatory fishes. Seemingly, any doubts on the potential negative effects of dams is counteracted by a dogmatic belief in engineering solutions. I was asked to prepare a report on my experiences at Bonneville as a student–trainee. It was selected in Washington as a model for their student-trainee program.

In my last discussion with the Research Director of the Montlake facility I disemboweled the engineering dogmas about "multiple use" much to his consternation and surprise. He had a doctorate from Harvard on a jump-across alewife stream in Massachusetts. I must admit he had a sense of humor in that he gave a hacksaw tie pin to a physiology student at Bonneville collecting blood samples for lactic acid analysis at the Seattle medical school. This fellow found the gates to the laboratory locked on a Sunday, preventing him from collecting samples so he hacked open the gate and caused a furor with the on-site security officials who descended on him as a terrorist.

GRADUATE STUDIES

I began my research studies in the last months of my senior year at Corvallis, in the Department of Fisheries and Wildlife as a research assistant in 1959. A woodland stream had been selected for environmental manipulations on salmon fry but my interest was in the abundant freshwater crayfish population (Pacifastacus trowbridgii). I enjoyed nearly three years of research and began accumulating a number of publications ending up with a master`s thesis on their life history and production, ecological role in the community, and energy sources from the surrounding woodland.

While writing this tome I was offered a Ph. D program in biochemistry and one in microbiology at Oregon State. Soon after there came an offer from the College of Fisheries in Seattle. I turned these three offers down and what was lurking in my subconscious in the latter case were comments by a full professor at Stanford in the publication Copeia that the College faculty started the day by prayerfully kneeling on a Pacific halibut in reverence to their management messiah whose name presently escapes me.

Prior to accepting an NRC financed opportunity at Corvallis, I had decided to consider the University of Hawaii as the Zoology Department head was a shore crab specialist. He encouraged me to come but the bursaries for the coming year were all allotted. Then came the offer from Corvallis financed by the National Research Council (NRC). Now that impressed me! I began organizing research on a new experimental stream that had been designed and built by Don Chapman who was busy running the first effects of logging research program on salmon. He did this on three adjacent small coastal streams. His far-sightedness and hardworking ambition provided me with opportunity. After several months I was ready to publish my first paper from this experimental stream facility when the Dean of

Graduate School suggested that I take a year of academic residence elsewhere, perhaps to shake off any intellectual limitations growing among the beautiful campus landscapes?

I chose the University of British Columbia (UBC) in Vancouver, specifically the Institute of Fisheries in the Zoology department as the Director was an Oxonian and I was curious about the research at Witham Woods, being conducted by the University of Oxford, Bureau of Animal Population. I arrived in Vancouver in late summer, welcomed by the Institute director, Peter Larkin, who advised me to tour the facility, familiarize myself academically, starting with Prof. Willimovsky. I met him in his spacious office, buzz-headed, smoking a big cigar and comfortably expanded in his swivel chair. Intend on taking any of my courses, he asked? Well, what do you teach? Ichthyology, population dynamics, and theoretical fisheries management was his reply.

My answer: probably not, I've had enough of those subjects and of applied mathematics. Harrumph! I left his office with that walrus epistle echoing in my ears to investigate other faculty who seemed less formidable and more interesting. This American general's ex-aide de camp called me into his office several days later, explaining that the entire department needed a telephone book of graduate students, names, addresses, and telephone numbers, can you accomplish that? I jumped at the chance as it would give me the opportunity to meet everyone, I commented, guessing that that his real intent was punishment. The task became rather boring due to student disinterest until I put up on the bulletin board that data was difficult to obtain, forcing me to take scraps of information that may include serious errors. Response was almost instantaneous as social shock and concern for correct labelling was clearly evident. The completed report turned in to Willimovsky was received with a nod of approval. His approval of me increased when he discovered that I was a combat flyer with the Strategic Air Command.

I was told two amusing stories associated with Professor Willimovsky. He was involved with the U.S. nuclear tests on

Kamchatka, on the potential ichthyological effects. He took with him a visiting Swedish scientist on sabbatical leave from Drottningholm who had published an excellent paper on Atlantic salmon behavior. They tented together on site which must have produced some friction as the Swede painted his toe-nails red from tagging materials one night, leaving his feet prominently exposed from his sleeping bag the next morning. He secured his own tent promptly from the military procurement officer. Another faculty member was off in the wilds of Southeast Asia looking for new species of fishes. A few days later, Willimovsky announced his intention to apply for the director's position before it was awarded to Larkin. Shortly thereafter, a frantic telegram arrived at the institute asking if that news was true. If so, the sender will be making alternate arrangements upon his return to Canada. Jungle drums!

My relationship with Willimovsky improved with time as he invited me to dinner at the faculty club much to the envy and back talk of some other graduate students. At the club table sat a visiting chemist who had senior-authored an excellent text book on sea water analytic techniques. He had left UBC and eventually went to Scripps Institute to continue his work due to poor financing. He asked me for my academic plans, so between mouthfuls, I stated that my immediate interest was achieving a doctoral degree. He snorted: "the educational system should be revolutionized so that academic doctorates could be unearned following birth." I discovered that he had only a M.Sc. degree in chemistry from Cambridge although his accomplishments obviously ranked him for a doctorate.

I had decided to take a number of courses: oceanic chemistry, animal behavior, statistics, animal physiology, and zooplankton ecology, some eighteen credits. Willimovsky objected," you cannot take more than 12 credits in Graduate School here, it's too much." Perhaps I'll discover that, I replied. Actually, I had to drop ocean chemistry as it was reserved for students doing chemical theses. During that school year I published two papers from my previous work. The zooplankton course was rather boring and I took no notes but the two Oxford graduate students scribbled furiously sitting next to me. One of them joined the faculty years later. In an effort to relieve my boredom I began dissecting lectures in class as they emphasized species identification of water masses.

In early Spring the lecturer, who was quite patient with me, began assigning yearly papers. Of course, he assigned me his speciality which I accepted eagerly. My paper was rated First Class with the red-inked comment that he encountered difficulty with some of my concepts. He left UBC to become the director of a small marine laboratory in Ireland, over-looking the glorious Arran Islands.

I had met the author of The Horokiwi Stream (K.R.Allen) at Corvallis where he was checking faculty opportunities and took the opportunity of asking him to read my Master's thesis on crayfish. He liked it, perhaps because I had used his graphic method for estimating organic net production of New Zealand trout for stream crayfish. This method had never been used before on decapod crustacea or since, as far as I know. Allen arrived at UBC subsequently as W.E. Ricker was stepping down from his position as director of the Pacific Biological Station in Nanaimo to become Chief Scientist. While in a coffee chat with Larkin at my elbow, Allen mentioned that he was looking for someone to re-do the Horokiwi project. I asked him what he would change if that opportunity came to fruition. To my embarrassment and then to his, he was stumped, hummed and erred several times then admitted that he had no idea.

I inadvertently also embarrassed Peter Larkin at a drink session at UBC. He was discussing basic science with an eagerly-convinced doctorate student. I listened for several minutes then broke in as they were both indicating scoffingly that applied research was of little value. As their social status inclinations were clearly discernable, I pricked their bubble by giving several examples of world-renowned scientists who straddled both basic and applied science with great productivity. My best example was Louis Pasteur and with him several others which caused much umbrage at my hint that imagined social status had no significant role in science.

I shared an office at UBC with an Indian student from Kerala who was pursuing a thesis on the production of lemon sole in Hecate Strait, using the usual accumulating mathematical rates of growth and mortality interdependence……boring accounting procedure, supervised by Willimovsky. I explained that Allen's graphic method was far superior as it gave one the opportunity to identify time element shifts in production as the season progressed. I spent several hours on the subject but he couldn't visualise the three-dimensional interaction in time. A few days prior to his oral examination which he passed without difficulty, he became rather nervous. Out of the blue he asked me if I believed in phrenology, the Asian technique of using skull bumps to determine personality traits and abilities which he apparently had faith in. I advised him to avoid that subject while facing his examining committee.

He returned to India although I had suggested to Don Chapman, Director of Research for the Oregon Fish Commission, to hire this fellow to do an historical analysis of Columbia River salmon runs. Funds were found but the Indian was too home-sick to take on a two year position and he returned to India. Some months later, a letter arrived from Kerala. He was stationed at some fish ponds and requested that I send him scientific papers to read, obviously bored and out on a limb.

I had several other interesting interactions with faculty members at UBC. Making arrangements to meet a fellow student working on salt water tolerance of juvenile salmon, I met him after waiting in the basement where he had his aquaria. While waiting, in came an anatomy professor to use the local elevator. He asked in a clipped British accent what I was up to. I explained my mission in the basement. "My digs are upstairs on the third floor, not down here in the basement", he stated with some scorn and the emphatic use of his vertical-driven right index finger. "Upstairs, downstairs, heaven or hell…..depends on one's point of view, don't you think" was my reply. He escaped promptly into the elevator but I noticed that he began entering the building on the first floor, coincidentally passing my office. With my door ajar I could detect his approach from the physical clipping of his left foot and would issue a cheery good morning as he passed without reply.

A newly-appointed faculty member also came from the Oxford faculty. He was a fascinating fellow who had worked for several decades on population cycles of lemmings, owls, and foxes in the Arctic. He finally realised that their numerical connections were driven by more than simple predator-prey relations and I was drawn to his intellectual honesty. Given my crayfish thesis to read, he returned it a week later with the comment that had I been at Oxford that effort would have earned me a doctorate. We both enjoyed a laugh at my response which was to emphasize that I had earned a M.Sc. Degree at OSU. My attempt at acerbic wit impugning the commonly accepted superiority of academic institutions was fully appreciated by him. I commented that I was more interested in the quality of their libraries than their public relations identities.

Returning to Corvallis, I threw myself back into the questions of environmentally-induced physiological stresses, growth, and mortality, and behavior patterns in my experimental laboratory streams. My additional contributions to Chapman's work on the associations of food supply (organic drift), territoriality, aggressive behavior, and downstream migration of defeated animals are a source of great personal satisfaction although I remain unsure that these findings have been fully appreciated in fisheries research and management quarters. Particularly the potential competition for spawning sites selected by the female and the range of sensory stimuli that probably related to oxygen content and intra-gravel flow.

THE QUEST FOR EMPLOYMENT AND OUTCOMES

After finishing my research work in Corvallis and defending my doctoral thesis, I was exhausted. Leaving the campus and having my sheepskin mailed I drove back to Laguna Beach where my family lived. Laying on the beach, drumming bongos and following the Viet

Nam War, I soon became bored and began looking for a scientific position. One was at the Univ. Alaska but I hate mosquitoes, another at La Jolla just down the road, so I investigated that.

Arriving there I was disappointed as the scientist researching euphausiid predation on eggs and larvae of the California sardine was away for some time. Euphausiids interested me. The sardine stock had been smashed to near destruction by over-fishing and a horrendous argument had arisen between two bureaucracies: California Fish and Game and the USDI, the latter taking the position that subtle environmental changes not over-fishing were the cause of near-collapse. Incidentally, the latter option was also taken by Fisheries and Oceans, Canada to account for the collapse of the cod fishery on the East Coast that caused economic and familial suffering. Similarly, the mis-forecasting of salmon runs in Western Canada has seen climate change identified by some fisheries "experts" as the potential goat.

While at La Jolla I met the managing director (non-scientist) of the USDI staff working on site, a brother of a former premier of British Columbia. Ensconced in his fancy office, with his fancy Mercedes sedan just parked outside, we talked for some time. Having followed an outstanding set of publications from the Moss Landing Laboratory describing cancerous and ulcerative growths found commonly in striped bass in San Francisco Bay, I expressed concern that such work was now discontinued. I asked him why seeing that he was in authority there also. They must reserve their research activities to the outer coast was his reply. Limited opportunities there, I replied, and the sand dab stock is managed by Cal. F&G.

Driving home, my thoughts centered on possible coincidence between the ascension of Gov. Regan to the White House, his political connections to corporate play in California affecting environment, and his newly-appointed Secretary of the Interior. I lost interest in working at La Jolla, even in the Institution. San Francisco Bay is now so toxic that off-limit signs for eating fish caught there are posted everywhere. The Bay also contains massive amounts of mercury in its sediments reflecting the Gold Rush days and hydraulic mining.

Another interesting position was publicized on the East Coast as Director of the Chesapeake Laboratory, so I applied. I was invited for a fully-paid interview by Eugene Cronin, a highly repected ecologist. My interest was the large and economically important crab and clam fisheries. He escorted me around there and at the Univ. Maryland as the job included a faculty position. Much to my concern, all three surrounding states had their own management systems spelling bureaucratic entanglements down to the county level to threaten rational management of the stocks. What really crystallized my negative decision was that on my second day there the Potomac River caught on fire from a massive oil leak, the smoke and flames clearly visible from the White House. Cronin appeared crest-fallen at my decision.

Behind several potential employment encounters in the U.S.A. my steadily increasing angst about American culture was precipitated by the Viet Nam War. My experience in combat operations in Korea stood out starkly in my memory. The continued insanity rife in foreign policy, military operations, and commercial collusions, and the descending quality of political representation affecting them weighed heavily on my mind. I recalled an accusative comment vented at me during campus discussions on this war at Corvallis: if you don't like it here why don't you go somewhere else? That comment echoed persistently in my mind although it was an anti-intellectual, weak and vacuous comment on reality driven by government and media.

A position popped up in Canada at the Pacific Biological Station in Nanaimo, on Vancouver Island. From my academic year at UBC and travel to this island, I was interested and applied. A second factor was news that K.R. Allen was to become the Station Director in the near future. A third factor was the erosion of my confidence in the U.S.A electorate to effectively combat the politically-motivated machinations severely affecting their impressive natural environment. The much lesser degree of environmental destruction in Canada on the richness and diversity of natural resources seemed evident to me.

Invited to Nanaimo by Bill Ricker, I gave a lecture on my research findings and interests and Ricker eagerly offered me the position of Coho Scientist. I accepted with alacrity and arrived there (the "somewhere else") in the spring of 1967. At the international border, having explained my purpose of crossing, the customer officer smiled and wished me good luck.

I settled down at PBS and on the recommendation of a fellow scientist, Percy Wicket, I adopted a field study that he had abandoned on Lymn Creek, complete with a reliable fish weir and trap facilities. This stream contained a substantial stock of coho salmon, an escapement of some 500 adults, a significant stock of cutthroat trout, and a small stock of chum salmon that spawned in the lower reaches and inter-tidal zone. With an able technician and some funds, I was excited and happy to be researching once more on stream ecology. I remember that Wickett advised me to keep a daily diary as such a record could come in handy. I questioned that ……."are you suggesting that trust relations among the staff might be unhealthy", I asked. Several years later his suggestion was revealed as valid. During my first several months at PBS I was invited to a private dinner by Bill Ricker and his wife and there met F.R.Hayes. He was a full professor at the Univ. Toronto who headed The Fisheries Research Board of Canada. We had some illuminating discussion. I later realised that Bill Ricker had invited me so as to introduce me to him.

I met another member of the Canadian illuminati, Roderick Haig-Brown, in 1971 following an invitation to meet with him in Campbell River. We spent the best part of the day in March touring the river from the power dam to the estuary. I remarked on several backwater areas filled with newly-emerged chinook fry sheltering from the rapid current flows and suggested that with some innovative engineering such areas could be enlarged for fry benefit. He thanked me and said he would look into that possibility. We parted after some amiable coffee at his house and I invited him to visit my project on Deep Bay where I was researching on Lymn Creek.

He arrived some two weeks later and we spent most of the morning on Lymn Creek. I outlined my research interests on coho smolt production, food supply, feeding and territorial behaviors as major factors determining smolt production to sea. I also discussed my interest in the small population of chum salmon that spawned in the lower reaches below the weir and in the inter-tidal zone. My observations and further research showed that they stayed in the estuary for some time, exposed to successive changes in salinity, and exploited both stream invertebrates and estuarine copepods before leaving to the open ocean.

Rod was an enthusiastic listener, being intrigued with the behavioral aspects of stream bio-dynamics. We ate our bag lunches on an impressive giant log cast up on the fore-beach then proceeded to a small restaurant at Oyster Bay for pie and coffee. Our favorite pie (a further common interest) was rhubarb pie with ice cream. We departed in mid-afternoon after a discussion of the ecological value of the Cook property that included Lymn and Cook creeks and the possibility of securing it for its research and conservation significance.

Several weeks later I received a formal invitation in embossed, multi-colored print to meet with the B.C. Centennial Commission (Nature Trust) at Oyster Bay. Looking at the list of Commission members, I noted Rod's name. Later that day, my director at PBS, an American named Wally Johnson, originally from Wisconsin, telephoned me excitedly, exclaiming that he had been invited too. His excitement stemmed from his recognition of the name Alastair Maclean on the list of commissioners. The author by that name was also a well-known author of adventure stories whom he seemed to adulate. I cautioned him on the improbable connection with this commission, as MacLean lived in Europe. The local MacLean turned out to be a forest researcher in the Interior for the provincial government.

The potentially important meeting with the Nature Trust arrived and I drove with Johnson from Nanaimo. During the drive, Johnson expressed his excitement at the prospect of meeting his Literary hero despite my words of discouragement. The banquet room at the facility was decked out formally: linen table cloths, silverware, and glassware on a long table. We were met at the door by Bert Hoffmeister, Nature Trust chairman, former army general and CEO of MacMillan & Bloedel. His other commissioners lined up behind him. I entered first, shaking hands down the line as they identified themselves. The last commissioner was a short, pudding-faced Scot, the forester. Johnson, who was following me, practically leaped on MacLean, showering him with the ardor usually accorded to Elvis Presley by young girl fans. He volubly exclaimed that he had read all of his books and was he writing another? The forester was visibly disturbed by Johnson's behavior but recovered quickly to mutter about mistaken identity.

I walked quickly to an adjacent window to hide my facial expression, one of initial hilarity followed by disgust and embarrassment.

This fiasco was handled with aplomb by Hoffmeister as we settled down to lunch followed by my discussion of the potential research and conservation value of the mile of waterfront, backed up by a B.C. experimental forest. My talk was abetted several times by Rod Hague Brown who related his tour on site with me. The ensuing discussion by the Trust emphasized favorable consideration of property purchase in next year's budget as all present monies were fully dedicated. Sitting at the head of the table with me on his right side, Bert Hoffmeister regaled me over coffee with a story of his last six months as CEO of M&B. He fought all efforts by his board to clear log all the remaining magnificent old-growth Douglas firs under Mt. Arrow-Smith, that he wanted to see added to the 301 ha. plot now called Cathedral Grove. He was temporarily victorious but was defeated by the sale of M&B rights to Weyerhauser, an American company who set about decimating all the surrounding timber.

I then recounted another environmental defeat concerning the Fisheries Research Board involving Nile Creek where Percy Wickett had developed his streambed permeability apparatus to evaluate oxygen conditions in spawning beds. Wickett had requested that FRB purchase the lower section of Nile Creek supporting a pink salmon run but was informed by Ottawa "that we aren't in the real estate business." Not the last time that government bureaucracy would win over science and conservation. Hoffmeister enjoyed my story.

The drive back to Nanaimo was made in dead silence broken several times by my attempts to remind Johnson gently that I had expressed serious doubts about his MacLean fantasy. I returned to my busy research activities.

Several months later I was informed at PBS that the upcoming budgetary planning precluded the continued token rent of $1500 for Lymn Creek and full access to the Cook property. The "MacLean Gate" episode was now official. The Cook family were greatly disappointed as they had committed themselves for many years to maintain the property as a conservation area despite financial struggles as working people to meet the tax obligations and were thrilled that the Trust was seriously considering purchasing it. I was enraged at Johnson`s scientific perfidy and forced myself to burn the weir facilities so as to prevent poaching. I speculate that Johnson's cheap bureaucratic manoeuvre reached Rod Haig Brown although he never contacted me afterwards. I speculated that PBS financial disinterest discouraged the further interest of the Nature Trust. Since then part of the property has been sold for housing and some logging taken place so the Cook family was forced to sacrifice some of the real estate to pay tax bills.

My work was thus terminated at Lymn Creek due to Johnson`s vindictiveness over the "MacLean Gate" affair but I published several scientific papers from my work there, one with a visiting Japanese biologist. I seriously considered leaving the PBS for medical school at Univ. Miami which offered the MD after two years in the case of doctorates. To my chagrin I was a year over the 35 year maximum age.

Following the destruction of the FRB and its replacement with an American style central organization with engineering emphasis, K.R. Allen left as director at PBS and was replaced by W. E. Johnson and scientific decay became prevalent at PBS. The FRB had consisted of university professors, superior government scientists, and representatives from the fishing industry. The FRB had steered fishery research in Canada with great competence and trust from the scientific community. I met F.R. Hayes again, chairman of the FRB at a quiet dinner at Allen`s house, a meeting arranged by Allen. He left PBS to take up the prodigious director`s position at CSIRO in Sidney, Australia soon after the FRB was abolished. I had suggested at PBS that we should erect a tombstone for the FRB in our landscaping but little interest was shown to such a politically-incorrect suggestion by the staff.

Johnson had worked at PBS before becoming Director of the Winnipeg Laboratory. He worked on zooplankton in Babine Lake, an important rearing lake for sockeye salmon. The lake`s potential was recognized from earlier limnological surveys by Rolly Brett, a superb scientist from the Univ. Toronto laboratory of F.E.J. Fry (another intellectual superba) and a member of the Royal Society of Canada. Almost single-handedly, from his physiological performance work at Nanaimo based on swimming performance and related physiology of returning sockeye, Brett`s work put a stop at plans to dam the Fraser River. His work was well-documented in the Scientific American magazine which probably helped defeat the engineers and associated bureaucrats.

Not surprisingly, Johnson`s work on Babine Lake dutifully followed Brett's work recognizing that the several small inlet streams failed to provide much spawning area and the majority of sockeye originated from spawning in the outlet stream, the Skeena River, with emerging fry migrating upstream into the lake. Not surprisingly, Johnson`s findings showed that the zooplankton abundance in Babine Lake appeared to be under-utilized, hence the green light was given to engineers to design and produce spawning channels there and elsewhere later. The resulting expansion of Babine stock from enhancement paralleled increased catches which served to over-exploit sockeye stocks in the lower, minor lakes that lowered productivity there. Lowered salmon productivity in these lower lakes receiving relatively higher rainfall was then theorized by Ricker as resulting from insufficient spawner biomass, reducing lake nutrient cycling. In political parley that is called "blowback" resulting from poor or hazy decisions.

Riding on the limnological findings of Rolly Brett and solidly connected to rising engineering influence in fisheries management, Johnson dropped into the vacuum left by the loss of K.R Allen to Australia.

Johnson earned his Ph.D. in pond limnology at U. Wisconsin. I met a full professor from that university at a scientific meeting in France. Over cocktails, he asked me if Wally Johnson was still working in Canada. Yes, I said, he is my director now at Nanaimo. What followed after his chuckling was an account of Johnson's predicament while sampling farm ponds and the farmer's daughter when discovered by the irate father. Johnson was kicked off the property and was forced to sneak back for further sampling so as to complete his data base. That showed that he had determination to complete his thesis, didn't it, was my reply.

A further and more criminal outcome than "MacLean Gate" was the outcome of Johnson`s flamboyancy resulting in a series of official memoranda directed to the owners of the Arctic Harvestor, a recently purchased trawler, assuring them of fishing rights in the Strait of Georgia and in Hecate Strait. Perhaps his flamboyant and effing comments reflected his serious diabetic condition, abetted by other personal vices. The pre-Arctic Harvestor was built in Japan, a stern trawler of dubious quality and reflecting the reluctance of Japanese fishing companies to buy it. It was finally bought by several investors in Prince Rupert. Considerable funds (millions) were winkled from the federal government to create a factory processing ship perhaps related to the fact that one of the investors was the brother of Iona Campanola, MP for Prince Rupert and presidential sec'y of the Federal Liberal party.

Johnson had no authority to issue decisions on fishing rights although he later became West Coast director of Fisheries and Oceans, at least for a short time. The principals were given a one-shot license for hake in the Strait of Georgia and the fishing community in Prince Rupert went up in arms. They considered this factory vessel as anathema to responsible fisheries management and a possible source of industry destruction as did senior groundfish scientists at PBS. On one of my many ichthyological cruises in the Strait I observed the Arctic Harvestor proceeding down the Strait in mid-channel. Behind it were thousands of gulls on the water in an extensive swathe of ground fish remains. Unlike less-discriminating gulls, human feeders at Vancouver MacDonalds outlets were not impressed with hake fish and chips, hence the supply contract was terminated.

As no further licenses were granted, the owners got impatient with the Head of Licensing in Vancouver who was doing his job as a responsible professional. They finally secured a short-term contract for exploratory fishing in the South Seas. Upon return to Canada, probably hoping that their licensing difficulties were abrogated, they faced financial realities and decided to sue Fisheries and Oceans for two million dollars of lost projected income that had been assured by Johnson. The vessel had been put up for sale for three million dollars and Johnson had been removed from his position and sent to the IPFSC with an office at UBC.

Fred Withler, a long-time scientist at Nanaimo was made PBS Director for a short while. I had requested from Fred Withler to be temporally transferred to the Groundfish Group at PBS to re-develop my interest in biological oceanography as it related to spawning and biology of larval fish. Fred knew of the Maclean fiasco. I started an ichthyoplankton program concentrating on the eggs and larvae of marine fishes important in fisheries. I called the program ELFS (egg and larval fish surveys) and applied an elf icon to our developing gear.

Fred Withler became seriously ill with cancer and was replaced temporally by a new fellow parachuted in from Ottawa. I visited Fred abed at home before he died and he warned me to be very careful with Beamish, now head of Groundfish. He had followed Johnson from Winnipeg along with his brother-in-law, McFarlane, a technician who assisted in seining suckers. This was a nepotistic appointment by Johnson, (wet pond water behind Beamish ears) despite the presence of several senior and experienced scientists at PBS working on ground fish fisheries, one of whom came to Canada from his job in Oregon as Head Scientist who developed the rockfish fishery there. On the urging of Keith Ketchen and with a reduced salary, Jergen Westrheim came to PBS. The senior ground fish scientists were much disgusted with Beamish's appointment as head of Ground Fisheries at PBS.

A bright young biologist working on groundfish came to me on several occasions lamenting about the lack of creative thinking in that section. I advised him to go to medical school and he graduated several years later in Calgary and came back to see me. Fred Withler`s demise saw the temporary appointment of an Ottawa fellow in his place at PBS. The Ottawa fellow competed with Beamish for the Director`s job at PBS and several days before the announcement of Beamish's appointment, Beamish went and told this fellow "get out of my office."

In a meeting with Beamish, now director, despite yowls from several fellow scientists, I met him with a candid, open mind, indicating that I was ready to support him with reservations, assuming that his decisions wouldn`t damage morale or scientific objectivity during his sojourn. With sufficient evidence to the contrary, I would withdraw my active support.

Later, I accepted a task from Beamish to design a funding application for Ottawa as the aging G.B. Reed side trawler, a sea-kindly 180 foot vessel was scheduled for replacement. This was my vessel for extended coastal ocean research. By this time I had developed two major marine programs: egg and larvae assessment of hake and Pollock stocks in the Strait of Georgia and an ichthyoplankton program encompassing the West Coast of Canada to Alaska, including the inside waters of Queen Charlotte Sound and Hecate Strait where most of the commercial fisheries for ground fish operated. I named this plan VASP (vessel acquisition strategy plan) which resulted in HQ Ottawa allotting some 17 million dollars to financed my plans.

I found a Lloyds Class One Atlantic cod trawler (Maquita) tied up in the U.K. as one of several like vessels retired from the U.K. cod fleet as an outcome of the fishing tribulations with the Icelandic government. This had seen British warships entering the fishing zone and some artillery shots fired across bows and entangling lines to foul propellors. The Maquita had three-inch ice shields on the bow, was three years old, and had DC electric winches. She was the top earner in the U.K. cod fleet. Sale price was 2.5 million. I talked to the chief engineer by telephone, an early-thirties Scot who was there when the keel was laid, ready to emigrate to Canada with his family. I suggested that if Canada decided to purchase this vessel I could come over to bring it here through the Panama Canal. He said he could organize a delivery crew, some of whom he fished with and some of whom might like to emigrate also.

Going in to Beamish`s office in high elation, I explained this opportunity to him. Strangely he was quiet and subdued. Finally he spoke, stating that we were buying the Arctic Harvestor for five million. He seemed to be following orders and I was astounded and mystified. I stated unequivocally that this vessel was not a fit replacement for research. Its beam is too narrow and it will roll like a pig in heavy seas. The recovery chute is nearly 45 degrees, very dangerous in our seas, especially when deploying research equipment like my multi-net plankton system controlled from deck computer. He remained stony-faced and I left to prepare for another of my ten day West Coast cruises.

Returning from that cruise, I was told inadvertently by a minor office bureaucrat gophering for Beamish that a commercial vessel agent in Vancouver had phoned demanding to know why we were paying five million for that boat when he could get it for three million. The bells went off in my head, three for the vessel and two for the intended damage suit claimed by its principals, avoiding all the embarrassing publicity.

Additionally, Beamish returned five million of the VASP grant to Ottawa without informing me. Part of the VASP was to finance a second vessel, a herring seiner, to modify it to work safely in the productive shallow bank areas on Hecate Strait where most of the recruitment of commercial ground fish would be settling and growing prior to recruitment. I could visualize Johnson and his supporting cronies in Ottawa grinning like Cheshire cats from boughs in the federal bureaucratic tree. At my next meeting with Beamish (called Blemish by his asst. director) I resigned from several committees. What about your research on hake and pollock, he asked. I replied in an even tone, if you desire to continue having your name on my publications you will have to submit to actual work at sea to establish your intellectual responsibility during analysis leading to publication. You cannot expect to continue successfully to justify your strategy of manipulating research activity budgetarily and to coercively assume authorship of other's work.

I remained silent to his known exploitation of technicians reading scales and otoliths in his aging laboratory, especially aging of rock-fish. Perhaps you aren`t needed here was his reply. Certainly not to compensate for his weak scientific ability and crass ambitions. That meeting led to a series of budgetary and personnel assignment manipulations intending to punish me for refusing to submit to his scurrilous ambitions. Fred Withler was so right! My research crew had spent more than twice the sea time of the entire Groundfish Group which had four times as many personnel.

My two published papers on the fecundity of Pacific hake and Alaskan Pollock, included planetary comparisons with all other stocks, used a novel suspended volume technique derived from plankton sampling. Beamish sent down a summer student to my laboratory to duplicate (challenge?) my published data without an appropriate memo. My biologists and I showed him carefully how to proceed.... with a certain amount of amusement.

Next, Beamish decided to transfer my senior biologist to another project, resulting in the two of us making strenuous objections due to the backlog of samples from our cruises. One biologist was analyzing and quantifying coelenterates from our West Coast cruises with me and a paper was published from that work. The other two biologists were sorting and quantifying egg and larvae from our Georgia Strait cruises aimed at estimating hake and pollock stocks from their egg production. This approach had only been used once, on a herring stock in the U.K. No one had attempted this approach on deep spawning gadid stocks.

Next, Beamish sent for my official records from the personnel clerk. He raided the file, removing all laudatory memoranda, those by

Ricker, Allen, and those provided previously by himself. The personnel clerk was so aghast at his action that she promptly transferred back to Vancouver. Finally, in April, 1984 Beamish decided that my scientific position at PBS was redundant as my work on blackcod, hake and pollock in particular, and larval fishes in general, including aspects of herring timing of spawning were irrelevant to needs.

I was given several months to vacate the premises. In response I wrote to the Minister if Fisheries outlying the difficulties at PBS, comparing the situation to that involving the religious court at Constantinople during the Byzantine Empire. I received a reply: "to be investigated" but heard nothing more as he was soon embroiled in the "tuna-gate affair" from which he departed Ottawa. Several calls came to me from the Director of Personnel in Ottawa, not directed at specific administrative acts which were unlawful but he sounded regretful at my circumstances. More courtier-type behavior in Ottawa. I suspect that the departed personnel clerk had communicated with him.

My case of outrageous bullying was not alone. Beamish had bullied other senor scientists, two of the best on site, Brett and Alderdice. His activities were well recognized but the communal intellectual vigor, scientific professionalism, and courage were lacking and he operated on the divide and conquer strategy of typical bullying cowards.

I began writing furiously, preparing manuscripts for publication, some eight papers, and started looking for another position, realising that Beamish was a backstreet thug but a successful bureaucrat….. not that the two characteristics are necessarily independent of each other. Other scientists had approached me earlier for advice on dealing with Beamish on specific scientific issues. I had reminded them that there was a significant difference between experienced intelligence and peasant cunning and to discern between the two when dealing with Beamish.

Two parasitologists were on staff at PBS, Nanaimo. Both had done significant work distinguishing parasitic load differences, one primarily while in Scotland. He and I shared a spacious office together as we arrived in Nanaimo in the same year. Differences between Asian and Canadian sockeye they found led to the longitudinal administrative barrier that then protected our sockeye from over-exploitation in an intensive Japanese fishery on the high seas. Leo Margolis, originally from Montreal, was well-established at PBS when he invited Bob Kabata to join him here. My sharing an office amiably with Kabata for several months with occasional comments made there by this intensively Catholic Pole obviously reflected his anti-semitic inclinations. He was quite envious of Margolis who rode his sockeye connection as a parasitical bureaucratic potentate through to retirement. This subtle feud continued for several years, enhanced by the retirement of Bill Ricker as Chief Scientist and their clashing ambition for that position.

Margolis got that position as he volunteered to defend Beamish at the upcoming confrontation over my dismissal after nearly 18 years as a productive scientist for Canada. Kabata declined that hack job using the excuse "of otherwise unavoidable stress," perhaps signaling that he actually had some deeply buried signs of conscience. Margolis`s glory as Chief Scientist proved a flash in the pan for he died six months after retirement, soon after. Meanwhile Kabata was given the job of keeping tabs on me in my search for employment. He asked me for the list of possible publications and application for other employment which I interpreted at the time as signifying his professional concern for me in finding another position.

The first signs of his treachery was indicated from a personal visit from the Director of the International Halibut Commission, a Canadian formerly from PBS, who had travelled from Seattle specifically to talk with me. He assured me that attempts he had received from Beamish to discourage consideration of me for that position were dismissed but that I couldn`t be considered as the new Director after him had to be an American by established rotational tradition. Kabata had supplied Beamish with news of my application.

That situation was followed several weeks later by a letter addressed to me from Alan Longhurst, Editor of Plankton Ecology in the U.K. He returned my lengthy manuscript on estimating the stock sizes of hake and pollock in the Strait of Georgia from egg production stating that the return was "as you requested." I wondered how many attempts Beamish had made to falsify my signature but I could not wisely follow up with embroiling Longhurst in local politics at PBS.

There were other information leaks but these two were the most serious as regards important areas of concern. After my last meeting with Kabata I turned to look back down the corridor to see Kabata looking after me while talking with apparent humor with Beamish who had suddenly appeared from his office across the corridor.... no doubt to get any pertinent information that I had given Kabata. That was the last straw for me and I left the building with a strong feeling of nausea.

A week later I met the Assistant Director in the hallway, Keith Ketchen, who personally stated his opposition to my treatment. My reply: "why not go to Ottawa and express your concern, then. It is the scientific integrity of this laboratory that is being destroyed by Beamish." He had no answer.

On the positive side, Rolly Brett (Roy. Soc. Can.) apparently stood up in the coffee room, the Monday morning following my leaving PBS, banged his mug on the table for silence, and announced in a loud voice that this Biological Station has just lost one of the best scientists ever to work here. Coming from a long-term member of the Royal Society of Canada when election to that esteemed group was once based on scientific merit was a comfort to me.

Some interesting events took place at PBS following my departure. Within three weeks in April, 1985 a cruise using my sampling gear and attempting to duplicate my cruises on black cod eggs and larvae (published) was put to sea under technician McFarlane, Beamish`s brother-in-law. The cruise must have been planned by Beamish some time before my departure in order to schedule ship time. Most of my newly-developed marine sampling gear and my biologists were taken by other researchers.

I had realised previously that marine biological research relative to fisheries was stymied by insufficient sampling designs. To remedy this I had designed a dredge capable of surmounting obstacles like rocks on the marine benthos. In 1976 I discovered glass sponge communities on Halibut Bank using this improved dredge. Another sampling problem that of the surface waters, particularly at night when the surface waters are alive with zooplankton and predatory fishes feeding on them as traditional towing took place in the boat`s wake or bow wave jeopardizing accurate sampling. An obliquely towed sled sampler out from the side of the vessel by some 5 to 7 meters caught huge quantities of animals at night in Georgia Strait and on the West Coast. While documenting the vertical migration of euphausiids in Saanich Inlet, not far from the Oceanographic Institute, I discovered that they began their descent back down below 100 meters as early as three-thirty a.m. several hours before dawn.

I had also calculated euphausiid biomass and productivity in Georgia Strait, a food resource originally utilized by several hundred humpback whales before their slaughter was completed by the early 1900`s, destroying the last 90 or so. I had insufficient opportunity to prepare these data for publication before Beamish's strategy. My multi-net plankton sampler apparently remained in storage until my departure from PBS but was discovered somehow by scientists at Scripps Institution. Their formal request to borrow this gear was refused by Beamish. He probably had some weaseling response. He was finally dismissed from the directorship due to his administrative arrogance that led to his disobedience of chemical use laws and public health protection. However, he managed to vault into the vacant position of Chief Scientist, thus denying Kabata that opportunity. He knew how to use the bureaucratic system, sullying that vacant position, too.

Upon realising the Beamish-Kabata mafia-like tendencies, I concluded that the chances of obtaining another scientific position in North America were limited. Any queries associated with my curriculum vitae that were sent to the PBS would be intercepted and sabotaged by Beamish. Unknown to me unless former associates of mine now involved in staff recruitment would detect his treachery and dismiss it as done by the director of the Halibut Commission. With a house mortgage and three children I had to fight to avoid depression leading to possible suicide. Returning home one day I found Beamish parked outside my hillside home reading the For Sale sign and he drove off abruptly as I approached.

A biologist position arose in Vancouver in salmon enhancement (Fisheries and Oceans, HQ) and I secured it out of desperation. During that eight year experience ending in my retirement, I came to the conclusion that decline of salmon stocks in Canada was inevitable, based on historic management dogmas avoiding scientific food chain analysis, smolt mortalities and their agents, and now aggravated by an avalanche of hatchery production of questionable ecological quality, plus the expansion of commercial fish farms. Plans of the B.C. government to license fish farms had been announced several years before and I had sent a memo concerning the use of Atlantic salmon in such farms to them, outlining twelve reasons why that introduction would be an imminent danger to native stocks of salmon and trout. That letter remained unacknowledged, a sure sign of bureaucratic arrogance. Hybrid damage to steelhead trout stocks has since been well-documented as has the explosive rise of sea lice in the migrating pathways of pink fry now with adjacent fish farms. Massive die-offs of pre-spawning chum salmon have been documented as disease-related. The coastal and open seas remain an enigma, a black box, now supplemented by concerns of climate change leading to minor temperature elevation in all salmonid environments. Another excuse for poor management and anemic science as it is applied to fisheries.

At Headquarters in Vancouver, I was treated primarily as a pariah by management and enhancement bureaucrats, probably out of fear and feelings of scientific insecurity although appropriate discussion by me would have been given to assist them in their dilemmas rather than to exploit them to their disadvantage and established positions. My audacity in taking an advertised position there no doubt caused some bowel disturbances but attempts to disregard my application could have proved problematic for them. Johnson came sniffing around several times later probably curious about my strategy there, reflecting his personal insecurity.

My biological responsibilities there in enhancement involved supporting production facilities at spawning channels and hatcheries and I had much opportunity to gauge their effectiveness. Fishery engineers were always wary and nervous in my field presence.

I co-published a paper evaluating Babine sockeye production emanating from two spawning channels. Although egg-to-fry survival exceeded that in natural streams by a factor of three (30%), I wondered why that level couldn`t be increased considerably. Weakness in channel design resulting in siltation, ineffective gravel-scouring gadgets and cement-like buildups in the lower reaches of channels was evident. At a spawning channel for sockeye above Francois Lake I plotted the redd digs in the summer after the channel had been dried of flow. Assuming that equitable use indicated by the redd digs would be revealed by a fairly normal distribution pattern throughout the channel, I found a very unequitable distribution pattern with major concentration of digs in the upper third of the channel with maximum density in one section next to the adjacent inclined topography. This suggested to me that groundwater input in this area had some attractive and directive influence on site choice by the spawning sockeye.

Fishery engineers had attempted to improve the stream above Francois Lake by adding gravel upstream from elsewhere. The entire "improved" length of stream where alien streambed materials was introduced was never used by sockeye ever again.

Ecological changes in seasonal flow patterns in supplying rivers caused by water storage also included lowered natural stream flows and higher temperatures. Temperature elevation has enhanced the development of freshwater mussel beds and mussels release parasitic larvae from their brood pouches in the early summer and these larvae attached to the gills of fishes, sucking blood until they become sedentary several weeks later. At Babine, my research there on mussels abundance in conjunction with increased water temperature due to dam storage were the probable causes for coho fry in the river to leave for the lake littoral zone……more ecological blow-back evidence. Mysteriously, my activities were soon transferred to the Coast.

On Haida Gwai, in Cumshewa Inlet, I then developed a large-scale release program to detect suspected local predation of chum smolts by towing their rearing impoundment net system seaward in a suspended float array to allow release at the inlet mouth. I also mass-marked chum releases directly from the rearing site by spraying them with fluorescent particles detectable under black light, and recovering them in timed fashion as they moved seaward down the inlet with beach seines. That program gave me estimates of migration timing and mortality rates within the inlet of some 70% due to local fish predators. These data matched those derived from fin-clipped pink fry on the Central Coast by Bob Parker and chum fry released in Hood Canal, in Washington. They also dove-tailed with an experiment in the Columbia River on chinook smolts exposed to manipulated aerial predator images (birds) flown over their tanks that reduced their mortality after release to the river. Additional pen experiments of mine in Cumshewa Inlet determined a daily ration of chum fry by six inch brown rockfish of 3-5 fry per day.

Seeing the chance for an early retirement in 1993, I produced twelve manuscripts evaluating enhancement facilities under my jurisdiction. I left ten copies of each as they were produced on my desk and significant numbers of each were taken surreptitiously on a daily basis by fellow employees! Several months previously I had been given a management report on coho salmon stocks presented to the Sports Fishery Advisory Committee for my comments. It was atrociously unscientific, meagrely supported by reliable data, and riddled with assumptions and dogma. I red-inked the entire manuscript and returned it to the provider. Upon exposure of my critique at their following meeting, the management biologist authors were enraged.

Afterwards, they went to the Director General in an attempt to have me fired. I had sent him a memo suggesting that by faithfully following enhancement techniques (esp. hatcheries) developed in the USA, we could expect the same disappointing results on salmon stocks here but got no response. For potentially good reason he decided to ignore these enraged management biologists and soon escaped himself to the East Coast as Director General there, facing the collapse cod dilemma.

The main cod scientist there had come to PBS previously and I asked him what were his interests here. He answered in a swaggering tone that he intended to advise local scientists on how to manage the Pacific cod fishery. I asked him if he knew that, to date, it has proved impossible to distinguish ages of cod reliably, and that dilemma suggested that rationale management remained elusive. His reaction was a toss of the head and walking away. He was promoted to an assistant-deputy minister's position after the cod crash on the East Coast later.

Other significant events following my departure from the Biological Station at Nanaimo after nearly eighteen years of research included re-naming the Arctic Harvestor twice, first to the Callistratus, then to the Ricker, much to Bill Ricker's discomfort in his retirement. During a usual Pacific storm at sea, the Ricker shipped some seas over the bow resulting in a near-four inch drop in the fore-deck. The panicked crew of experienced sailors who had worked with me, some of them with British Merchant Marine background, walked off the ship at return to Nanaimo declaring the vessel unsafe. Lloyds of London, the insurers, sent out an inspector who concluded that there was no further danger. Was his methodology and data made available to local ship designers and builders? That remains unknown. More than an accumulated expenditure of 20 million has been spent on that vessel which can only manage twelve knots in a calm sea. Blow-back functions remain with us due to bribery, corruption and waste of tax-payers hard-earned money.

Even more important than millions of dollars spent unwisely to back up decisions made in Ottawa to avoid rightfully deserved scandal is the general politicization of federal agencies, including gutting the Fisheries Act. The effect on environmental science in Canada has proved stifling. No scientist working for the federal government can now release any findings without the express permission from the PMO and ministerial watchdogs have every top level resource manager by the throat. Truth is no longer an essential part of reality. Additionally, cut-backs in operating budgets have seen productive scientists being urged by local administrators to seek funding from non-governmental sources.

The stifling and damage done to my professional career, including publication of my research as inflicted by Beamish, based purely on vicious reactions to my productive research programs devoid of his name and seconded by Johnson, pale in significance to the present position of working scientific compatriots in federal resource agencies and the ultimate damage on Canada's renewable resources as a whole. Hopefully, this situation will now change due to recent choices of the electorate.

ILLUMINATIONS WHILE BIOLOGICAL SAMPLING

("Dans les champs de l'observation, le hazard
ne favorise que les esprits prepare")

(Trans: In the fields of observation, chance
favors only the prepared mind…Pasteur)

In Georgia Strait

I encountered the Queen of Britain one Sunday in the early afternoon while deeply engrossed in my research of quantitative plankton sampling of the eggs and larvae of hake and pollock in Georgia Strait, British Columbia. I had established a grid sampling system of some ninety stations from Texada Island south to the international border, sampled for several weeks. The spawning peaks for both species were imminent and I desired to use my new multi-net sampler to gauge the vertical distributions of both eggs and larvae by stage of embryonic development in the water column. I had selected an offshore area of the Strait using the 180 foot G. B. Reed. It was on a Sunday when we usually didn't go to sea. The sampling gear was carefully hoisted over the side and steadily lowered to 300 meters, just above the sea bed. Then the sampling began using the first of the ten nets with the vessel turning in a wide continuous circle at five knots. At each revolution of the vessel track I executed the computer command to change to the next net at the ascent to the next prescribed depth. This closed the previous net with its depth-specific catch.

Halfway through the sampling series I noticed several large vessels coming north from the region of Victoria, in line like a row of ducks, so called the captain for information. His answer: it must be the Queen for she is due for an official visit to Nanaimo today. Do you have the appropriate fishing pennant hoisted on the main mast, I asked. Yes sir, he replied, I hoisted that when we began sampling. As I turned to the computer I said in that case we are maritimely legal so will continue with our work. There is no danger of a collision, is there? No Sir, but if you wish to continue this armada is getting close! They can go around us as there is plenty of room, I replied. At some thousand meters, the lead vessel, a destroyer (destroyer-escort by U.S. Naval standards) made an abrupt 45 degree turn eastward to starboard for some three hundred meters then reversed his course to the original setting. This navy captain's manoeuvre was dutifully followed by the royal yacht and several more naval ships following. A smart line of vessels defending the Queen's rights in Canada. As this flotilla passed I looked up from my computer data on depth, temperature, and salinity. The fifth net was operating at depth and the operation was going smoothly. Intellectually and psychologically I was riding the sampling gear without suffering from deep compression! On the fore-deck stood several of my ship's crew, standing at attention as the Royal yacht passed. They were ex-merchant marine and ex-Brits as was I. There was no radio communication from the leading naval ship.

Incidentally, in my major vertical tow efforts in Georgia Strait using my twin Bongo samplers, I tossed an empty styrofoam coffee cup into the net as it was hoisted overboard to depth. Upon net recovery I discovered that the cup was now less than one third of its original size and the comments that I had inked on the cup were also miniaturized, depicting the effect of some 1000 feet of depth, or 70 atmospheres, or some 1100 psi. The first such cup I gave to my middle daughter who took it to grade school in Departure Bay where it caused much excitement as she explained the effects of pressure on her teachers and her classmates. Some three decades later after working as a surgical nurse in the U.S. she returned to Canada and returned this cup to me. Intact, it's on a bookshelf presently.

I gave a number of such cups out to visitors during a public science display at the PBS and allowed the public to change nets on the multi-net system as it was suspended from the ceiling, by using the computer. That resulted in a rave review in the Nanaimo Free Press. My coffee cup technique was copied later at the more recent Oceanographic Institute at Pat Bay, in Saanich, with good reception. Shortly after my encounter with the royal yacht I was alerted by an administrative bureaucrat at PBS that government halls in Ottawa were still echoing with resentment from my Sunday research activities. Of course, any resentment did not arise from work on a Sunday but from my apparent challenge and restriction of naval style on a momentous occasion of displayed military might. In response to such disturbance in Ottawa I drafted a letter explaining the importance of my sampling timing to the peak spawning efforts of fish stocks in the Strait of Georgia and suggested that should anyone find the authority to command excited spawning fish to refrain from sexual excitement on a Sunday I and my working crew would be most grateful, spending the day at home with our families. No further correspondence arrived on this matter.

An open mind can allow for some illuminating surprises as suggested by Louis Pasteur. I realised that fishery scientists, in particular, should take the trouble of talking to (not down to) commercial fishermen. Had that happened on the East Coast of Canada (with open scientific minds) there was a very good chance that the collapse of the cod fishery could have been avoided. As it happened, the chief cod scientist there was promoted to assistant Deputy Minister after the stock crash.

Some cohorts and I were sent up to Prince Rupert to enlighten local ground fishermen on our business at PBS. The fellow who talked from the stage before me was a statistician working on fishery data sets. I stepped up next and explained my work on eggs and larvae of marine fishes, especially species of commercial value, and their potential relationships to recruitment and environmental factors that might be dictating recruitment strength. I finished by saying that such research work was expensive due primarily to ship time and technical equipment needs. After finishing my talk, a middle-aged fisherman stood up asking how big was the budget of the previous speaker. I asked him why he asked that question. His answer which was followed by an enthusiastic round of applause was that he was in favor of turning that budget over to me. The previous speaker, listening off-stage, left the hall straight-away and went to a nearby tavern (they are abundant in Prince Rupert) and proceeded to get sufficiently drunk and obnoxious, even by local standards, that he was forcefully-ejected by the bartender and several assistants. He later transferred to Stats Canada.

The opportunity to go commercial trolling for salmon with a retired fisherman off Nanaimo on several occasions resulted in my recognition that he was an encyclopedia of information on historic catches of coho in Georgia Strait. He also connected me with an even more elderly fisherman living in Lantzville, just for chinook in the Strait. Upon my asking what size troller he had, he burst out laughing. He had a sixteen foot rowboat from which he cast a line and spoon as he rowed. You made a living doing this, I asked. Yes, he replied, I raised four children on my earnings. My curiosity was now fully aroused. How many did you catch in a day? It varied, he said, from one or two to half a dozen, usually from 20 to 40 pounds apiece. I jumped to the assumption that his fishing took place in the late summer and early Fall, asking what did you do for the rest of the year. That was all year, he replied, large chinook were present in the Strait all year and

collective abundance of minor stocks and presently major stocks result did the latter leaving the Strait in summer while the abundant minor stocks remained resident for their first year in the Strait, providing sufficient food opportunity for large resident chinook salmon? Has the routine herring fishery in the early Spring when the stocks are still mixed resulted in the over-exploitation of minor stocks and reduced spawning in their individual habitats?

My interest in eelgrass beds stuck in my mind. While walking my two cairn terriers along the lower reaches of the Nanaimo River I was impressed with the configuration of the streambed and the banks that reflected massive flooding and downstream transport of geological materials from the intensive logging and disturbed slopes on the watershed. At one time, the Nanaimo Estuary supported large over-wintering populations of ducks and geese, some 30-35 thousand ducks and about 5 thousand black brant, according to historic records, prompting the ecological question: what did they eat while there? At one time there was a commercial cannon site located on Jacks Point overlooking the estuary that fired salvos of shot, bent nails etc. on the birds below and the mortalities were taken to Victoria for sale. I found the remnants of that system on Jacks Point. The question of over-wintering food supply persisted in my head.

I went to the No. 2 native reserve shortly afterwards. Driving close to the estuary edge I spotted a small house and parked. Walking over to the house I spotted an old fellow sitting in a deckchair so introduced myself and asked him some questions. Have you lived here for a long time, I asked. He answered to the affirmative saying he was born in that house a long time ago. I`m interested in the estuary, I said. Do you remember what this estuary looked like when you were a boy? Close your eyes and look out across the estuary, what do you see. He raised both arms in an outward sweep, saying that he saw a meadow of sea grass. Well. I said, now it`s solid mud except for a small depression on the far side that has some grass on it. When I was a boy, he said, the bottom was pure sand in between large areas of grass. We boys used to walk among the grass clumps and spear starry flounders on the sand and bring them up to cook them here in this fire-pit next to where you are standing.

I thanked him profusely for his recollections and left elated. That`s what the ducks and geese must have been eating, eelgrass rhizomes and the animal community living in the eelgrass? I doubt that these bird populations refrained from eating during several months of wintering. If we did some initial core tests to see if rhizome remnants at expected depositional depths were still present we could do the entire estuary, establish the original bed profile and calculate the tonnage of depositional debris that has reduced the estuary to a large mudflat devoid of profuse eelgrass. The economics to regain the original productive state could then be estimated.

I conveyed my idea to a geologist on faculty at the Univ. Victoria and he became quite enthused. I said that I would develop the research program for funding and would get back to him later. My suggestion made at the PBS was discouraged so I dropped my interest, suspecting that political concerns outpointed science that could document environmental degradation, especially as two scientists at PBS were studying the food habits of chinook fry in the estuary, finding that the fry were relying in a minute epi-benthic copepod for their sustenance, one that lives on mud!

Eelgrass beds create a habitat for a complex invertebrate community and I was struck with this visually when I visited an area on the east side of Jacks Point. There was a long canal with a tidal falls of several feet at the seaward end allowing partial flushing on the tidal cycle. Possibly this channel resulted when the original profile of the upper estuary began changing, stimulating a drainage to the east side of the estuary, since closed. The complexity and diversity of organisms I observed there was astounding. In the bountiful eelgrass were shrimp, amphipods, smaller zooplankton species, coelenterates including jellyfish, and very abundant pink salmon fry that probably originated from the Fraser River and were transported across the Strait in the Fraser plume. That productive environment was destroyed during the development of a large lumber processing industrial area by filling in the area to create additional real estate. At least some of us scientists managed to keep the commercial people out of the estuary itself, much to the umbrage of the Mayor and a lawyer crony of his who had bought up some of the estuary foreshore in anticipation of impressive real estate profits.

While using my improved plankton dredge in the area between Lasqueti Island and Comox, south of the bell buoy, I capture a few recently spawned adhesive eggs of Pacific cod along with many wood chips and fine wood debris in the benthos. Seemingly, the entire sea bed in that area was affected by the collection of mills situated along the lower reaches of the Courtenay River. I mentioned my finding to Kieth Ketchen, the Asst. Director at PBS, and was told that there was a significant cod fishery there many years ago. So, straggling Pacific cod were still attempting to maintain a stock in that area.

At the West Vancouver Laboratory established in the riding of Jack Davis, one-time Minister of Fisheries we called ``boot-black Jack`` as he dyed his sparse hair, geneticists had progressed in the area of heritable growth rate, aiming to produce giant-sized fish for commercial use. As their rearing tanks were only 8 feet in diameter, I recalled the growth restriction of container size on goldfish and wrote an advisory report suggesting that maximum size for such genetically-manipulated products might be obtained efficiently by planting such fish in a sea-like environment. I locating a potentially useful environment, Seymour Inlet, which has a shallow sill of less than 100 feet, and with several inner reaches that could provide for experimental conditions. By engineering suspended electric fence designs to keep out potential competitors and predators, like dogfish, seals and porpoises, this large inlet could be turned into a major culture system.

Food supply could be secured by fishing the euphausiid stock from the Strait of Georgia during daylight hours when they are concentrated below 100 meters depth like raspberry jam, quick-freezing the catch on a towed freezer raft having a diesel generator for power. The planted potential giant chinook could be conditioned to come for food to ringing feeder buoys having a mechanical, timed delivery system. If 50-60 pound chinook of similar size to some of those originating in large, glacially-fed rivers on the Central Coast resulted, a goldmine sport fishery would result and a floating resort would attract much world-wide attention. Financially rich anglers would be spared mal de mer, too! No response was generated, duh! When I detailed that proposal to a visiting senior scientist who came to see me from Norway, he was fascinated with the idea, lamenting that he had no access to fiords with shallow sills and no toxic bottom waters in his country and encouraged me to proceed.

A student from UBC came to meet me for possible assistance in selecting streams for a doctoral study on sympatric behavior between cutthroat trout and coho juveniles in rearing habitats. One stream that we selected on Vancouver Island near the town of Ladysmith had a huge cedar log jammed just above tidewater. The hydraulics allowed passage of spawner cutthroat trout but few coho which are much larger in size. A few sculpins were also present, primarily Cottus aleuticus. From his two years of work he estimated the total fish biomass to comprise 80% cutthroat trout, 15% coho, and 5% sculpins. Sculpins interested me as I had just completed a year-long study of sculpins in Lymn Creek with a visiting biologist from Japan which we published together. In that paper I had discovered that upstream penetration of sculpins was stopped by hydraulic jumps exceeding eight inches of summer flow and hypothesized in that paper that a reverse-lip concrete dam of minor height could prevent sculpins from entering the salmonid stream from the inter-tidal zone, thus allowing less food competition for the young salmonids.

By sheer coincidence in the following year, provincial management biologists decided to remove that giant cedar log without notifying anyone outside their bureaucracy. When the student again computed fish biomass in that stream, 80% of the biomass was sculpins and minor coho fry which clearly showed the limited trout growth and survival, seriously damaging the salmonid rearing capacity of that stream.

While studying behavioral interactions between cutthroat trout and coho salmon juveniles in Lymn Creek, I installed several small observation chambers side by side just beneath a riffle area. I placed a chair in the stream of some 35 cm deep and sat there quietly taking notes of behavioral interactions in separate species and combined species cases. An adult mink swam between my legs, passing upstream to continue its foraging.

I had used the chair technique in the intertidal area to observe pre-migrant chum fry feeding behavior. As the tide turned to flood I had to vacate my seat as the chums proceeded upstream a short distance to stay ahead of the salinity wedge. By sacrificing some marked fry for feeding analysis on both phases of the tide I found by careful analysis of their intestinal tracts that they ate freshwater insect larvae (midge) during low tide but ate estuarine copepods on the high tide and did this for several days prior to migrating seaward. I torpedoed the dogma that chum fry went straight to sea upon exposure to higher salinity, dogma well-expressed in a UBC doctoral thesis done in the UBC basement that allowed the author to become Director of the Zoology Department at Univ. Victoria.

My sampling intensity in the Strait of Georgia gave me the opportunity to estimate the stock size and productivity of the euphausiid population there. As their production was prodigious, some 30 thousand tons per year by my calculations, I related this potential productivity to its possible predators. Nowadays, Pacific hake and Alaska pollock were obvious candidates at least during daylight hours as they are distributed in deep waters. In the last few decades before they were wiped out by 1903 by commercial whaling there were at least 95 humpback whales feeding in the Strait of Georgia. They may have been semi-permanent residents with the pregnant females leaving for warmer Mexican bays to give birth, or all leaving for warmer waters.

I surmise that they were opportunistically feeding on the euphausiid stock and forage fishes, including herring. The scope and thoroughness of whaling in offshore waters was followed by whaling stations in Georgia Strait, the last one located in Pipers Lagoon, with slaughter some 6 thousand in outside waters. If these primarily Humpback whales in Georgia Strait made large inroads into the euphausiid stock, at least during their summer stays they may have greatly thinned that stock. Using an average humpback weight of 32 tons (25-40), daily ration of 4.5%, or 1440 pounds/day, for either 90 days or 180 days of feeding in Georgia Strait (June-August summer feeding, or April to September feeding), for 95 whales, results in them consuming 12,312 tons/yr or 24,624 tons/yr.

This intensity of feeding would require major inroads on my estimated euphausiid stock in April of 30,000 tons of 41-82% of the euphausiid stock. Higher euphausiid exploitation would have occurred in Georgia Strait when the humpback whale population was considerably higher prior to decimation.

The present pollock stock on the outer coast originates in concentration in Alaska with some southern feeding. The historic hake migrate northward from California in their Spring to summer feeding migration. Both stocks of gadids in Georgia Strait (minor sub-stocks) may have found the unutilized and abundant euphausiid stock after the early 1900's, following decimation of the whales, very attractive, and set up expanded resident populations in both Puget Sound and Georgia Strait, separated from their forbears when sub-stock separation may have occurred a long time ago. One possible clue that would support entry of the hake sub-stock in the Strait of Georgia many ages ago can be identified.

This original and ancient introduction came from the offshore stock. Georgia Strait hake contain two myxosporidian parasites also found in offshore hake but in different relativities of infection, supporting the idea of an ancient separation from the offshore stock. These enzymes are activated in the dying hake, rendering the flesh too soft for human use unless pH manipulations are applied on the prepared fillets . I suspect that genetic differences are involved but no scientific research has been done to better evaluate the possible commercial use of hake in the Strait of Georgia other than manipulate the pH of their fillets.

Using my results estimating the present hake and Pollock stocks from their egg production, published in 1984 there were about 160 tons of Hake and nearly 60 tons of Pollock in the Strait of Georgia and these populations remain hardly fished commercially hence probably fairly stable in size. Using a 5% of body weight as an average daily ration for some 300 days a year would see their inroads into the euphausiid stock as no more than 12%, by adult hake and pollock, although the rate of feeding of younger stocks remains unknown. That euphausiid productivity is also shared by younger age-classes of hake and pollock with that of other sight-feeding fish species to some minor degree as the krill stay below 100 meters depth during daylight and ascend at night to feed.

This is obviously an anti-predation behavior which I also found in a small bathypelagic fish species (Leuroglossus schmidti) in Georgia Strait which I also published (1985). This species is probably the most abundant fish species in Georgia Strait and has a low fecundity.

The dramatic reversal of species biomass relations in a local trout stream on Vancouver Island had similar outcomes in the sea for important species of marine fishes. Georges Bank is located medially on the international line between Eastern U.S.A. and Canada, most of this Bank is now in American hands while the eastern tip stayed in Canada. The Bank has been actively harvested since the 1600`s, accelerated by development of steam-driven, then diesel-driven trawls and mostly in American hands since they invoked a 200 mile limit. At one time, the relative biomasses of marine fishes there (80%) were dominated by gadoid (cod-like) fishes of commercial value. Foreign fleets were excluded by the Americans yet over-exploitation continued by the American fleet and the biomass flipped over in 1974 from about 80% gadids like halibut, hakes and cod to ``trash`` species like grenadiers, skates, and slime eels. This situation seemed to be irreversible and a grand effort began by scientists at Woods Hole Institute to commence ecological scrutiny. I met them at an international meeting.

Starting with water chemistry, then phytoplankton, then zooplankton they found no abnormalities in the food chain links. The hypothesis then emerged that the meagre recruitment of gadids (recovery) was due to minimum spawning resulted in an effective predatory function from the ``trash`` species on the sparse gadid settled larvae and juveniles. Urging the adjoining States to subsidize the fishing of these abundant predators they assumed that the system could be re-balanced. Politicians were not interested in diverting tax funds to such a politically frivolous and therefore dangerous strategy, hence the stock has not changed. Interestingly, the stock on the Canadian side remains healthy although of minor size suggesting that the oceanographic features discouraged the Canadian fish to mitigate for the sorry state of affairs on the American side. The general area is served by the Labrador Current which mingles with the Gulf Stream Current coming north.

There has been little recent interest in managing dogfish stocks in Georgia Strait since WW2 when liver oil was in demand, at least from an ecological point of view. Dogfish are abundant and a nuisance to salmon fishermen as they attack their spoon lures. Ergo, they are predators! They are also prey. Only minor efforts have been made to examine gut contents and those efforts suggest that dogfish only eat jellyfish!

My observations suggest otherwise. Firstly, once while sailing my racing multi-hull sailboat in mid-strait an enormous male Stellar sea lion errupted close to my boat, seemingly almost out of breath as he came more than half his body length out of the water, while in his jaws, like a dog bone, was clamped a dogfish nearly four feet in length. Secondly, while beach seining on the lower tidal mudflat of Lymn Creek one sunny day in late May on an abating tide I was looking for chum fry that I had marked up stream. Some fry became moribund in the net probably due to high mud temperatures. Most were saved and returned to deeper water. Within a few minutes several dogfish appeared, up to nearly two feet in length, busy capturing slow fry. One dogfish I stepped on with my hip boots, grinding it into the mud.

These dogfish had arrived from the adjacent Deep Bay possibly after detecting stress odors from the chum fry. That experience left me with a heightened concern for their predator abilities, especially as Deep Bay was an assembly zone for coho smolts coming out of local streams and preparing to migrate seaward. Dogfish are also found in deep water in Georgia Strait and may well be exploiting the euphausiid stock when not interested in feeding on juvenile salmon before the latter species migrate seaward.

One of my concerns in enhancement biology was the possible negative effects of artificial rearing strategies on the behavior of young salmonids due to be released to the marine environment. The environmental transition to salt water involves both physiological and behavioral adjustments where transitional difficulties are surely related to increased mortality, especially from predation, although passage through dams should not be forgotten. There was an amusing event at the College of Fisheries, Seattle. One day a chief scientist there was busy feeding his hatchery salmon. A lady walking her dog stopped to watch him and the fish swimming around in circles. She asked him, if that is all they can do, swim around in your circular cement ponds, they must be insane! The terse Scot replied in the affirmative.

Studies of animal behavior have revealed that young animals have heritable features that are triggered by what behaviorists like Konrad Lorenz, Carl von Frisch, and Peter Klopfer call ziet-gebers, or time-related stimuli which may dramatically modify behavior for valuable ecological reasons during critical periods of development. For fish, a classical study by a Swedish scientist I met at the Drottningholm Laboratory north of the city studied European pike and showed that a series of environmental steering mechanisms put the pike in their upstream spawning habitat. Other than pink salmon fry which go to sea very soon after emerging from the spawning gravel, other species of anadromous salmonids may spend considerable time in freshwater up to two or more years where they learn to feed on the organic insect drift or forage for zooplankton in lakes, and also to learn to recognize and avoid predator fish, birds and reptiles. This includes chum fry in spawning streams of the Kamchatka Peninsular, some of which are several hundred miles long from spawning areas to the sea, so fry here may spend several weeks feeding in freshwater.

Ziet-geber documentation has been most dramatically illustrated in birds, particularly in ducks and geese, involving parental sensory attachment clues within the coinage of the "critical period," also documented in penguins, gulls, and other animal species many of whom pair for life. Ziet-gebers are probably active also in fishes which also must learn to forage, instantly recognize rapid passage of invertebrates in flowing water and to learn how to catch hovering insects above water. Such learning and discriminatory needs may be linked to the critical period concept and its ecological reality. In artificial culture environments like hatchery ponds and raceways, devoid of natural levels of dynamic and turbulent flow, opportunity to recognize and defend habitats of forage value are replaced by bombardment with synthetic food pellets in timed periods of mass consumption, an application of agricultural technique applied to domestic animals. The ability to develop sophisticated and discriminating behavior of survival value is discouraged for reasons of production efficiency. Are such environments similar to consumptive behavior of humans in gigantic sales events in malls?

As hatchery situations, including their lights (for human convenience) attract congregating insects, feeding attempts can be commonly observed, particularly in raceways. They suggest that insect attraction by light, capture and venting onto the water surface is there to exploit by designing units suspended above the water surface. Insects contain considerable vitamin and lipid stores and industrial food pellets are a poor substitute for natural foods. Salmonid enhancement strategies are routinely designed and driven by fishery engineers with concrete, pipes and valves dominating their concept of enhancement. Their biological expertise is limited to their job label. I suggest that for stream salmonids locked into enhancement facilities until time of release into Nature, opportunity to experience turbulent flow with its attendant exercise, and behavioral experience like avoiding aerial predation with models, would more closely parallel the natural rearing expectations that have been selected in their genes for hundreds of thousands of years.

I visualize an enhancement facility designed to allow "work-out" exercise routines by shunting sub-populations of juvenile salmon for periodic periods of exercise in turbulent flow and stream bed rugosity designs. The high, documented mortality rates following release of several species of salmon are depressible by intelligent biological input, if it was accepted in the accumulated operatic dogmas in fisheries. The perfection of discriminatory feeding behavior in stream salmonids particularly in Atlantic and Pacific salmon has gained little attention of ichthyologists and fishery biologists.

Anglers dedicated to fly-fishing, especially dry-fly fishing, like my former acquaintance, Rod Haig Brown, fully recognize the "pickiness" of summer steelhead and brown trout. Awareness of insect hatching cycles and careful attempts to mimic natural forms are associated with productive fly fishing. German brown trout in English chalk streams have developed rather sophisticated discriminatory feeding behavior through genetic selection and favored reproduction of wily individuals. This theme is duly reflected in the classic book on fly-fishing written by Isaac Walton in The Compleat Angler, published in 1653.

My concern here doesn't rule out plankton-feeding salmonid juveniles in lakes, either. Evidence exists from study of juvenile sockeye in mountain lakes in B.C. that they actively select certain species of copepods and may over-graze them. Discriminatory behavior associated with aerial predation, predation from larger fish species, and responses to light, shadow, cover, turbulence, and streambed materials could improve the awareness, hence survival, of hatchery products. Robotic technology has recently developed aquatic robots capable of simulating predation in controlled, monotonous rearing environments.

There is a distinct possibility that discriminatory behavior research could reduce effective enhancement economics to thirty percent or less of their present operational costs and such advances might continue to serve in the marine environment, especially in the estuarine and near-shore coastal environments. To be sure, the traditional "black box" mentality of most fishery biologists towards the marine environment is ludicrous and should be corrected, perhaps from the advice of marine biologists and oceanographers.

By observing the behavior of chum salmon fry in nature, especially following mass release from enhancement facilities, I detected major behavioral differences in estuarine waters. On Haida Gwai, in Cumshewa Inlet, mass release of pen-reared chum fry found them scattering across he bay, showing no orienting aggregations although most moved towards the northern shore initially, possibly reflecting a magnetic effect. Those naturally-reared fry from the adjacent stream, Pallant Creek, entered the mixing waters in a highly-coordinated ribbon of fry some 6 to 10 fish wide, producing a long, serpentine ribbon possibly from surface salinity dynamics and possibly as a predator-defense mechanism. My study of immediate post-release mortality of enhancement chum fry there documented a 70% mortality before the survivors reached the outer reaches of Cumshewa Inlet.

To further depict my concern for natural, adapted behavior, while seining in Departure Bay in late June, I captured yearling coho that had been recently released from PBS in Rolly Brett's artificial rearing experiments. These coho yearlings were some 150 mm. in length, and emaciated. What were they feeding on after release? Checking their stomach contents revealed that the only organic particles there were the floats of Jap weed which match the size of the pellets on which they had been raised. Did they tear them off the floating weeds in desperate hunger, reflecting their complete ignorance of natural foods available in Departure Bay?

This lack of interest and understanding of the behavioral ecology, including anti-predation conditioning rampart in both the driving engineering influence and that of agriculturally-fixed aquaculturists in both designing and running hatcheries, supplemented by bureaucratic control of government purse-strings has generated much rationalization to account for hatchery failures to meet enhancement goals both in the Western United States (California, Oregon, and Washington), and in British Columbia. For example, lack of enhancement success in all four regions has been identified as the bogeyman result of very minor temperature increases in coastal waters.

This is despite considerable research evidence in both freshwater and coastal environments that indicates major mortality of release enhancement products within a short time after release prior to more recent times detecting minor changes in temperature. Mortalities exceeding 70% of numbers released in adjacent waters to points of release. From an ecological point of view, and one supported by ornithological and entomological research in Europe, temperature increases can have both negative and positive outcomes, not just negative effects as posed by salmonid fishery biologists, or by plankton specialists pursuing minor sampling in Georgia Strait showing the same biased and non-evidential leanings.

I suspect that such massive mortality in juvenile enhancement salmonids reflects the application of simple agricultural techniques to produce numbers (Detroit production fixation) while completely ignoring behavioral qualities that include food recognition and awareness of predators. Thus, the release of large outputs of naïve, unfit juvenile salmon have no doubt encouraged greatly improved predation, probably leading to the enhancement of coastal predator populations. Nature is unforgiving of attempts to manipulate her when such activity is based on ignorance and technological arrogance of Man. The dynamics or enhancement of predator populations in coastal waters, including Georgia Strait remain undocumented and the "before, after" opportunities don't exist.

Recounting my marine coastal work In Georgia Strait, I remind you that I had concluded that biological research in coastal waters was hampered by lack of concerted effort to develop more adequate sampling gear in order to capture biological realities. A ten-net sampling system controlled by deck computer was designed and built for plankton sampling of eggs and larvae of marine fishes. With the assistance of an engineer that I had met in Nova Scotia and local electronic technicians, the sampling system flew like a kite in underwater tows. Eagerly, I also wanted to document the vertical feeding ascent of euphausiids and performed successful tests in Saanich Bay, adjacent to the Oceanographyic Institute at Pat Bay, north of Victoria, from where I borrowed a new, unused sophisticated winch and a towing cable with gold connections which insured strong electronic commands from the computer down to depths of 300 or more meters.

My light sled capable of climbing over otherwise-blocking boulders on the substrate rewarded me with the discovered presence of a fragile glass sponge community on Halibut Bank in the Strait of Georgia from collection of their fragments and spicules in 1977. There is so much to discover! Net avoidance in surface waters by forage fishes caused by the wake of the towing boat was at least subdued in my surface sampler, a floated sled system towed laterally from the side of the 180 foot boat that sampled the upper 15 cm. of surface water. As plankton typically ascends to the upper euphotic zone to surface waters at night, I speculated that predator-prey activities involving fish and zooplankton, including euphausiids, would be accurately sampled by a fast, ruddered surface sled held some five to ten meters out from the side of the towing ship. Tests showed that very large catches of planktivorous fish up to 20 cm. in length were available during hours of darkness using this system.

OUTER COAST SAMPLING

Sampling the Outer Coast system from the Juan de Fuca Trench northward to Alaska, including Queen Charlotte Sound and Hecate Strait for ichthyoplankton in my ELFS program, also involved taking temperature profiles along with my twin Bongo samplers. Failing to successfully borrow one of their latest salinity instruments from Pat Bay and discouraged there by oceanographers who insisted that salinity measurements with less than 5-6 decimal place accuracy would be of dubious value, I left that institution thankful for the loan of a salinity instrument that they no longer used. It worked fine and we secured enough data to derive temperature, salinity, and sigma-t (density) profiles for the entire outer West Coast of Canada from a series of 20 latitudinal-derived sampling tracks spaced some 50 km. apart leading each track seaward for 100 km. and with sampling stations at 20 km. intervals from the coast (if my memory serves me correctly). That supplied some 100 samples for five ten day cruises made between March and April when the Spring productivity cycles were most active.

The inside waters of Queen Charlotte Sound and Hecate Strait were similarly sampled, adding another 25 samples which gave us some 625 samples to process in the laboratory. Regrettably, I failed to obtain an oxygen meter but we found a tongue of warm, dense (highly saline) water off the northern coast of Vancouver Island that seemed to be flowing northward. In retrospect, had that tongue originated from the sub-tropics, was of relatively low oxygen concentration and flowed across the southern outer banks coincident with the benthic settlement of crab and pink shrimp larval stages, it could generate massive mortality and possibly affect the recruitment of herring.

We also discovered two possible major gyres in the inner waters, one in the center of Queen Charlotte Sound and the other off McIntire Bay west of Prince Rupert in northern Hecate Strait, possibly driven by tidal dynamics. McIntire Bay east of Masset on Graham Island supports a significant crab fishery, suggesting that either or both gyres could be enhancing local conservation of plankton and larval stages. Many ground fish species of commercial value spawn in the vicinity of Queen Charlotte Sound and northern transport by tide may see their offspring deposited on the extensive and shallow sand banks along the east coast of Haida Gwai.

I have also noted from fly-overs that the area lying between the north east end of Vancouver Island and the opposite coastline of Haida Gwai is fairly shallow on ebbing tides. There is good visual sightings there of definite ploughing lines from the heavy, sagging tow cables of barge traffic. Such ploughing causes disruption and destruction of benthos communities that feed ground fish and are well-recognized in European waters as caused by the heavy steel deflectors attached to bottom seines.

Due to the shallows off southern Haida Gwai, during storm conditions, extremely large incoming waves can be generated. A wave measuring device positioned off Cape St. James on Haida Gwai recorded a maximum wave height of 105 feet some years ago. As some of the suggested effects of climate change include increased wind velocities during storms, 105 feet or more wave heights may be routinely generated in the future.

My research work on Haida Gwai enabled me to employ a competent sailing acquaintance to assist me in elector-shocking streams to document their standing crops of salmonid fishes during the summer. He had sailed to Haida Gwai in his multi-hull sailboat and anchored it locally in Cumshewa Inlet. I decided to return south to Vancouver Island with him as a sailing adventure when research was completed by initiating some of my well-earned holiday back-log. Sailing down the Outer Coast onward from Cape Saint James we ran into a ferocious summer storm some 60 miles west of the northern tip of Vancouver Island with winds exceeding 70 mph.

Notification of this storm by radio was sent a few hours prior to its arrival at our position. After employing a large parachute drogue which failed after several hours our vessel turned over and partially-filled with water. We were upside down for eighteen days and finally detected some 70 miles west of the Brooks Peninsular when rescued. Details are recorded elsewhere.

RECAP REFLECTIONS

Looking back on my conservation and research activities there are some looming trends affecting our natural environments. My experience has been personal but other resource scientists involved with biology have had comparable experiences, at least those in government organizations. When in Graduate School, I decided to aim for a faculty position to teach future resource-related biological students how to maintain their creativity and motivation in a bureaucracy. Having had experience in both military and governmental bureaucracies, I had come to the conclusion that course-work could be developed that would tackle deadening bureaucratic influences. I further concluded that I should broaden my bureaucratic experiences to include scientific positions at the doctoral level, hence, to work for five years at least before seeking a faculty position somewhere that recognized my concerns.

After earning a doctorate, I studiously avoided position opportunities in resource management that showed rampant bureaucratic inclinations, often driven by politics. I carefully avoided them. The position offered me in Canada at the PBS in Nanaimo was offered by a world-renowned scientist of wide biological and mathematical performance, W. E. Ricker, and I accepted without hesitation. The scientific reputation of the PBS at that time was impressive throughout North America and reflected shepherding by the Fisheries Research Board which also looked after the Biological station in New Brunswick which had a comparable record to that in Nanaimo.

After five years of intensive research work and an accumulating publication record, I was ready to seek a faculty position. Communications with other faculty scientists that I had associated with in Graduate School advised me to stay put, citing many negative factors in their work habitat, and commenting that they were envious of my position, so I stayed, busy also raising a family.

I have traditionally held a distance from government-sponsored or approved professional organizations, especially those involved with fisheries, as concern for real science there is anemic. I never accepted membership in the American Fisheries Society or published there, and, anyway, suggested that the name should be changed to NAFS. Neither did I pursue participating in the Pacific Biologists Society or the FRS, although I edited a major workshop meeting on Pink salmon for PBS and snuck in some poetry. The last PBS meeting that I attended through invitation from a member was arrogantly questioned by a buzz-headed, intellectual dwarf president representing the Washington State Department of Fisheries.

In a previous PFB meeting, during discussion of the possible impending doom of all wild salmon, I stood up and stated that if such prophesies were indeed scientifically acceptable, I would resign from my position as a research scientist in fisheries and elect to sell neckties on the street corner. George Eicher, PG&E, giggled then laughed uproariously. At that meeting, I also suggested that rather than concentrate on cutting off the neckties of individuals attending, that the PBS should make wearing hip boots to their meetings mandatory, to emphasize the need to "get into the water that salmonids swim in."

In a publication on the ecological role of sculpins in salmonid rearing streams in coastal BC, I suggested that these food competitors with limited jump capacity could be prevented from stream entry by erecting a reversed lipped concrete dam in the lower reaches, and suggested an experiment to evaluate this strategy. This suggestion was emphatically supported by a Ph.D. student of mine (UBC) who documented a biomass turnover in a Vancouver Island stream from 80% cutthrout trout juveniles, 10 % coho juveniles, and 10% sculpins to 80% sculpins in the following production year after the Provincial fish biologist had a large cedar stump removed from the stream just above tide-water. In a fit of self-righteous ire, a tennis-shoed junior professor at UC Davis published a critique of that suggestion in the AFS defending the rights of non-salmonid fish species in streams. As he studied low-flow, tepid Californian streams, I understood his tennis-shoe vituperation and ignored it.

In a discussion with Bill Ricker who was busy chastising me for biological interests somewhat displaced from direct, fisheries concerns (accepted fisheries dogma), although he had a keen interest in stone-flies, I commented that his original paper on stock-recruitment and the "Ricker curve" that resulted from it, accepted by fishery biologists and their managers as dogma, was highly dangerous, considering the scattering of plots in a time sequence sense that described his curve for Fraser River sockeye was indicative of significant ecological functions lurking in the background. Of course, the latter functions remain anathema in fisheries management dogma, manifested by the "marine black box."

Human organization in general has trended to constantly growing size, no doubt reflecting the increasingly complex Western culture driven by population growth and the obsessive fixation on growth driven by capitalism and this trend has resulted in exploitation of renewable resource assets approaching the breaking point. The outcome is now aptly described by the imminence of massive climate change threatening the very existence of humans, certainly the conservation of our present level of civilization in many areas on the planet. We have arrived at this state of affairs carrying with us levels of aggression, material greed, and xenophobic inclinations that are now threatening our survival and atomic science has given us nuclear energy solutions that can put us in autoclave. A major difficulty remaining is insufficiency in organizational processes, suggesting that we have not yet overcome the small, tribal organizational behavior that we developed while living in caves.

Ever-increasing bureaucracy size has gone hand-in hand with the centralization of power and authority which has made the selection of authoritative figures a critical concern, and selective failures have given us persistent dictators and similar psychopathic personalities in authoritative positions that have led to much human suffering and death. Less drastic outcomes have included worker slavery, economic slavery, misuse and abuse of creative personnel and the generation of courtier roles and their slavish obedience to autocratic figure-heads, reminiscent of regal courts in the Middle Ages, and they are driven by both fear and cowardice, often personally shrouded in modernity by rationalization.

This situation has been well-reflected in Fisheries and Oceanography, particularly at the Pacific Biological Station in Nanaimo from two recent so-called figure-heads that I am well-aware of. Narcissism combined with psycho-pathology has led to routine punishment for opposition defending science. Intellectual opposition although well-grounded has been interpreted there as an insult to personal narcissism, resulting in punishment. The intent on producing personal legend, using exploitation of bureaucratic subservient staff, including plagiarism, and without personal conscience or scientific professionalism is ludicrous, dangerous and pathetic. Perhaps an older sibling's academic success as a faculty member back east lurks behind such behavior in one of these two cases.

Bureaucracies exist throughout human organization, in government, corporation, religion, and the military. In fact, now we have government corporations! The common concerns for power and authority, richly rewarded financially, are dove-tailed between these four types of organization. A good example lies in the United Nations which has failed miserably since its formation in preventing or solving aggressive relations between states despite enormous budgetary outlays from states creating major problems. Thus, when the imperfect and often lax selection mechanics awarding power at governmental, political, and commercial levels nationally all effect Science and Majority Good, results are magnified further at the international level so mayhem often results. Projecting this picture downward in bureaucracy by reducing its complexity and size does little to change the outcome as the power and authority cables connecting the various grades of bureaucracy within centralization remain secure and selection failures causing negative outcome slide down these cables with ease. In my experience selection failures in our federal fisheries organization began with the destruction of the Fisheries Research Board of Canada.

At PBS this precipitated Director K.R. Allen to opt out and to accept the directorship of CSIRO in Australia. He was followed to Australia shortly by a senior scientist at PBS, Bob Parker, who's innovative work on pink salmon migration and mortality followed that by Ferris Neave's work on density-dependent recruitment dynamics. Allen's intellectual and administrative hand at PBS left a vacuum that has never been filled and has led to a steady decay of directive stature and ethics, scientific morale and productivity abetted by federal government policy in recent years. Thus the maladies in bureaucratic operation that I had recognized in my twenties and studiously avoided through my mid-thirties finally reared its ugly head at PBS in my mid-fifties. All I can feel is concern for those coming behind me and others like me who finally succumbed to this organizational Black Plague and the psycho-pathology behind it.

Having retired from active biological research in 1995 at the age of 63 after some 28 years of employment with Fisheries and Oceans, Canada, an international presidency, and publications in five countries, I have remained thankful that my curiosity and passion for research has sustained my productivity and creativity. I turned my attention to increased sailing in the Salish Sea and prepared my 34 foot cruising-racing trimaran for distant sub-tropical shores, settling on the Sea of Cortez. Despite eligibility, my wife was reluctant to leave her students, wanting to carry them through their third grade. This led me to accept the challenge of a single-handed sailing down the Pacific Coast to Baja California at the age of 65. I left for Mexico in 1998 where I anchored all winter in the Bay of La Paz, adjacent to the city of La Paz which is the capital of Southern Baja. Dalia flew down at Christmas time and we enjoyed local sailing, sun-bathing, and eating at interesting restaurants. As her linguistic talents (five) included Spanish she accelerated my social connections in La Paz after she flew back to Canada. I overwintered in Mexico for two winters, leaving my trimaran in dry storage for the first summer, returning to Victoria again single-handling my sailboat in 2000.

Dalia retired and was diagnosed with blood cancer some two years later and went through all the intense treatment effects. She survived well for over a year before succumbing to the lethal form in 2003. Death stops one in their tracks, not only personal death but that of emotionally-close others and is accompanied by intense mourning and suffering. Dalia was a very gentle and tolerant soul, a God-botherer, who burnt candles in many places. Although not an established member of the Anglican church she was given a High Mass service by a local bishop whom she had known for many years although she was raised in a strict Catholic family. The bishop read my full memoriam for her verbatim in his church. My mother died not long after Dalia, three weeks before her 100th birthday. The family cat, Pushkin, and I mourned Dalia together and in our individual ways over the next year, then I decided to move to a condominium. Pushkin died at age eighteen shortly afterwards.

While unpacking my movables at my new abode, I found a box of watercolor paints and brushes that I had kept unused for nearly three decades. Findings the pigments still useable, I set about rediscovering my interest in art, reminded by two paintings of mine stored in the attic. I had begun painting when the children were still quite small, after putting them to bed, followed later by my first wife. I was getting less than five hours sleep before rising for work which proved too exhausting, hence I put things away. Upon rediscovering these materials I began painting furiously, sometimes several paintings in a week's time, finding myself concentrating on local coastal landscapes.

I began composing poetry again and then went on to historical novels. Now I have two such novels, several plays, a collection of short stories, and a collection of a hundred poems, two of which have been published. I must return to publishing my non-scientific works. I had a very successful showing for a month of nearly forty of my paintings, some with related poetry which was either the stimulus or outcome of paintings on Salt Spring Island, near Victoria in the Southern Coastal Islands. My creativity has been retained despite attempts to manipulate or exploit it although it remains now unassociated with formal biology. I have written this autobiography primarily stimulated by a saying attributed to Socrates: THE UNEXAMINED LIFE IS NOT WORTH LIVING. For me, life is definitely worth living and, hopefully, my personal examination can be useful to other scientists, particularly those involved in environmental biology and in fisheries related biology in avoiding situations to which I have been exposed or, in similar situations, for I'm sure those situations will continue, and I encourage active scientists to rise above them in joyous expression of their creativity and ethics.

CPSIA information can be obtained
at www.ICGtesting.com
Printed in the USA
LVOW03s2139110517
534075LV00012B/66/P